Simulated Annealing Theory with Applications

Edited by Rui Chibante

Republished by InTech

Janeza Trdine 9, 51000 Rijeka, Croatia

Publishing Process Manager Ana Nikolic

Technical Editor Goran Bajac

Cover Designer Martina Sirotic

Additional hard copies can be obtained from orders@intechopen.com

Simulated Annealing Theory with Applications, Edited by Rui Chibante
p. cm.
ISBN 978-953-307-134-3

Simulated Annealing Theory with Applications

edited by
Rui Chibante

For EU product safety concerns:
IN TECH d.o.o., Prolaz Marije Krucifikse Kozulić 3, 51000 Rijeka, Croatia,
info@intechopen.com or visit our website at intechopen.com.

Meet the editor

Rui Chibante is currently a lecturer in the Department of Electrical Engineering and Computers, at School of Engineering, Polytechnic of Porto (ISEP/IPP). He received in 1999 the M.Sc. degree in Electrical and Computers Engineering from the Faculty of Engineering of Porto University (FEUP). In 2006 received the Ph.D degree in Science Engineering from FEUP. He is member of LEMA group. He is member of the following IEEE Societies: IEEE Power Electronics Society IEEE Industrial Electronics Society IEEE Education Society IEEE Computational Intelligence Society His research interests are: modelling of power electronic devices simulation of power electronic systems heuristic optimization techniques (Particle Swarm Optimization, Simulated Annealing) modelling of fuel cells.

Contents

Preface

This book presents recent contributions of top researchers working with Simulated Annealing (SA). Although it represents a small sample of the research activity on SA, the book will certainly serve as a valuable tool for researchers interested in getting involved in this multidisciplinary field. In fact, one of the salient features is that the book is highly multidisciplinary in terms of application areas since it assembles experts from the fields of Biology, Telecommunications, Geology, Electronics and Medicine.

The book contains 15 research papers. Chapters 1 to 3 address inverse problems or parameter identification problems. These problems arise from the necessity of obtaining parameters of theoretical models in such a way that the models can be used to simulate the behaviour of the system for different operating conditions. Chapter 1 presents the parameter identification problem for power semiconductor models and chapter 2 for heat and mass transfer problems. Chapter 3 discusses the use of SA in radiotherapy treatment planning and presents recent work to apply SA in interstitial light therapies. The usefulness of solving an inverse problem is clear in this application: instead of manually specifying the treatment parameters and repeatedly evaluating the resulting radiation dose distribution, a desired dose distribution is prescribed by the physician and the task of finding the appropriate treatment parameters is automated with an optimisation algorithm.

Chapters 4 and 5 present two applications in Telecommunications field. Chapter 4 discusses the optimal design and formation of micromobility domains for extending location privacy protection capabilities of micromobility protocols. In chapter 5 SA is used for large-scale IP traffic matrix estimation, which is used by network operators to conduct network management, network planning and traffic detecting.

Chapter 6 and 7 present two SA applications in Geology and Molecular Biology fields, particularly the optimisation problem of land sampling schemes for land characterisation and primer design for PCR processes, respectively.

Some Electrical Engineering applications are analysed in chapters 8 to 11. Chapter 8 deals with network reconfiguration for reliability worth enhancement in electrical distribution systems. The optimal design of an interior permanent magnet motor for power steering applications is discussed in chapter 9. In chapter 10 SA is used for optimal control systems design and in chapter 11 for feature selection and dimensionality reduction for image classification tasks. Chapters 12 to 15 provide some depth to SA theory and comparative studies with other optimisation algorithms. There are several parameters in the process of annealing whose values affect the overall performance. Chapter 12 focuses on the initial temperature and proposes a new approach to set this control parameter. Chapter 13 presents improved approaches on the multilevel hierarchical floorplan/placement for large-scale circuits. An improved format of !-neighborhood and !-exchange algorithm in SA is used. In chapter 14 SA performance is compared with Steepest Ascent and Ant Colony Optimization as well as an hybridisation version. Control of adaptive optics system that compensates variations in the speed of light propagation is presented in last chapter. Here SA is also compared with Genetic Algorithm, Stochastic Parallel Gradient Descent and Algorithm of Pattern extraction.

Special thanks to all authors for their invaluable contributions.

Editor

Rui Chibante
Department of Electrical Engineering,
Institute of Engineering of Porto,
Portugal

1

Parameter identification of power semiconductor device models using metaheuristics

Rui Chibante[1], Armando Araújo[2] and Adriano Carvalho[2]
[1] *Department of Electrical Engineering, Institute of Engineering of Porto*
[2] *Department of Electrical Engineering and Computers, Engineering Faculty of Oporto University*
Portugal

1. Introduction

Parameter extraction procedures for power semiconductor models are a need for researchers working with development of power circuits. It is nowadays recognized that an identification procedure is crucial in order to design power circuits easily through simulation (Allard et al., 2003; Claudio et al., 2002; Kang et al., 2003c; Lauritzen et al., 2001). Complex or inaccurate parameterization often discourages design engineers from attempting to use physics-based semiconductor models in their circuit designs. This issue is particularly relevant for IGBTs because they are characterized by a large number of parameters. Since IGBT models developed in recent years lack an identification procedure, different recent papers in literature address this issue (Allard et al., 2003; Claudio et al., 2002; Hefner & Bouche, 2000; Kang et al., 2003c; Lauritzen et al., 2001).
Different approaches have been taken, most of them cumbersome to be solved since they are very complex and require so precise measurements that are not useful for usual needs of simulation. Manual parameter identification is still a hard task and some effort is necessary to match experimental and simulated results. A promising approach is to combine standard extraction methods to get an initial satisfying guess and then use numerical parameter optimization to extract the optimum parameter set (Allard et al., 2003; Bryant et al., 2006; Chibante et al., 2009b). Optimization is carried out by comparing simulated and experimental results from which an error value results. A new parameter set is then generated and iterative process continues until the parameter set converges to the global minimum error.
The approach presented in this chapter is based in (Chibante et al., 2009b) and uses an optimization algorithm to perform the parameter extraction: the Simulated Annealing (SA) algorithm. The NPT-IGBT is used as case study (Chibante et al., 2008; Chibante et al., 2009b). In order to make clear what parameters need to be identified the NPT-IGBT model and the related ADE solution will be briefly present in following sections.

2. Simulated Annealing

Annealing is the metallurgical process of heating up a solid and then cooling slowly until it crystallizes. Atoms of this material have high energies at very high temperatures. This gives the atoms a great deal of freedom in their ability to restructure themselves. As the temperature is reduced the energy of these atoms decreases, until a state of minimum energy is achieved. In an optimization context SA seeks to emulate this process. SA begins at a very high temperature where the input values are allowed to assume a great range of variation. As algorithm progresses temperature is allowed to fall. This restricts the degree to which inputs are allowed to vary. This often leads the algorithm to a better solution, just as a metal achieves a better crystal structure through the actual annealing process. So, as long as temperature is being decreased, changes are produced at the inputs, originating successive better solutions given rise to an optimum set of input values when temperature is close to zero. SA can be used to find the minimum of an objective function and it is expected that the algorithm will find the inputs that will produce a minimum value of the objective function. In this chapter's context the goal is to get the optimum set of parameters that produce realistic and precise simulation results. So, the objective function is an expression that measures the error between experimental and simulated data.

The main feature of SA algorithm is the ability to avoid being trapped in local minimum. This is done letting the algorithm to accept not only better solutions but also worse solutions with a given probability. The main disadvantage, that is common in stochastic local search algorithms, is that definition of some control parameters (initial temperature, cooling rate, etc) is somewhat subjective and must be defined from an empirical basis. This means that the algorithm must be tuned in order to maximize its performance.

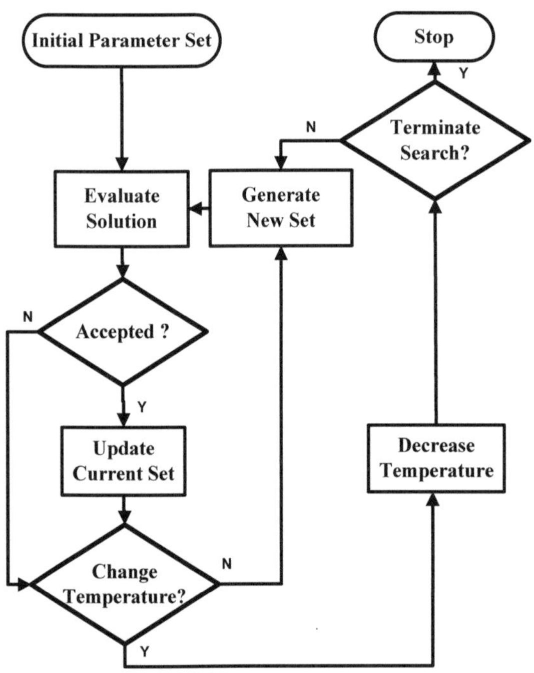

Fig. 1. Flowchart of the SA algorithm

The SA algorithm is represented by the flowchart of Fig. 1. The main feature of SA is its ability to escape from local optimum based on the acceptance rule of a candidate solution. If the current solution (f_{new}) has an objective function value smaller (supposing minimization) than that of the old solution (f_{old}), then the current solution is accepted. Otherwise, the current solution can also be accepted if the value given by the Boltzmann distribution:

$$e^{-\frac{f_{new}-f_{old}}{T}} \quad (1)$$

is greater than a uniform random number in [0,1], where T is the 'temperature' control parameter. However, many implementation details are left open to the application designer and are briefly discussed on the following.

2.1 Initial population

Every iterative technique requires definition of an initial guess for parameters' values. Some algorithms require the use of several initial solutions but it is not the case of SA. Another approach is to randomly select the initial parameters' values given a set of appropriated boundaries. Of course that as closer the initial estimate is from the global optimum the faster will be the optimization process.

2.2 Initial temperature

The control parameter 'temperature' must be carefully defined since it controls the acceptance rule defined by (1). T must be large enough to enable the algorithm to move off a local minimum but small enough not to move off a global minimum. The value of T must be defined in an application based approach since it is related with the magnitude of the objective function values. It can be found in literature (Pham & Karaboga, 2000) some empirical approaches that can be helpful not to choose the 'optimum' value of T but at least a good initial estimate that can be tuned.

2.3 Perturbation mechanism

The perturbation mechanism is the method to create new solutions from the current solution. In other words it is a method to explore the neighborhood of the current solution creating small changes in the current solution. SA is commonly used in combinatorial problems where the parameters being optimized are integer numbers. In an application where the parameters vary continuously, which is the case of the application presented in this chapter, the exploration of neighborhood solutions can be made as presented next.
A solution $\mathbf{s}$ is defined as a vector $\mathbf{s} = (x_1,..., x_n)$ representing a point in the search space. A new solution is generated using a vector $\boldsymbol{\sigma} = (\sigma_1,..., \sigma_n)$ of standard deviations to create a perturbation from the current solution. A neighbor solution is then produced from the present solution by:

$$x_{i+1} = x_i + N(0,\sigma_i) \quad (2)$$

where $N(0, \sigma_i)$ is a random Gaussian number with zero mean and σ_i standard deviation.

2.4 Objective function

The cost or objective function is an expression that, in some applications, relates the parameters with some property (distance, cost, etc.) that is desired to minimize or maximize. In other applications, such as the one presented in this chapter, it is not possible to construct an objective function that directly relates the model parameters. The approach consists in defining an objective function that compares simulation results with experimental results. So, the algorithm will try to find the set of parameters that minimizes the error between simulated and experimental. Using the normalized sum of the squared errors, the objective function is expressed by:

$$f_{obj} = \sqrt{\sum_{c} \sum_{i} \left(\frac{g_s(x_i) - g_e(x_i)}{g_e(x_i)} \right)^2} \tag{3}$$

where $g_s(x_i)$ is the simulated data, $g_e(x_i)$ is the experimental data and c is the number of curves being optimized.

2.5 Cooling schedule

The most common cooling schedule is the geometric rule for temperature variation:

$$T_{i+1} = sT_i \tag{4}$$

whit $s < 1$. Good results have been report in literature when s is in the range [0.8 , 0.99]. However many other schedules have been proposed in literature. An interesting review is made in (Fouskakis & Draper, 2002).

Another parameter is the number of iterations at each temperature, which is often related with the size of the search space or with the size of the neighborhood. This number of iterations can even be constant or alternatively being function of the temperature or based on feedback from the process.

2.6 Terminating criterion

There are several methods to control termination of the algorithm. Some criterion examples are:

a) maximum number of iterations;
b) minimum temperature value;
c) minimum value of objective function;
d) minimum value of acceptance rate.

3. Modeling power semiconductor devices

Modeling charge carrier distribution in low-doped zones of bipolar power semiconductor devices is known as one of the most important issues for accurate description of the dynamic behavior of these devices. The charge carrier distribution can be obtained solving the Ambipolar Diffusion Equation (ADE). Knowledge of hole/electron concentration in that region is crucial but it is still a challenge for model designers. The last decade has been very productive since several important SPICE models have been reported in literature with an interesting trade-off between accuracy and computation time. By solving the ADE, these models have a strong physics basis which guarantees an interesting accuracy and have also the advantage that can be implemented in a standard and widely used circuit simulator (SPICE) that motivates the industrial community to use device simulations for their circuit designs.

Two main approaches have been developed in order to solve the ADE. The first was proposed by Leturcq *et al.* (Leturcq et al., 1997) using a series expansion of ADE based on Fourier transform where carrier distribution is implemented using a circuit with resistors and capacitors (RC network). This technique has been further developed and applied to several semiconductor devices in (Kang et al., 2002; Kang et al., 2003a; Kang et al., 2003b; Palmer et al., 2001; Santi et al., 2001; Wang et al., 2004). The second approach proposed by Araújo *et al.* (Araújo et al., 1997) is based on the ADE solution through a variational formulation and simplex finite elements. One important advantage of this modeling approach is its easy implementation into general circuit simulators by means of an electrical analogy with the resulting system of ordinary differential equations (ODEs). ADE implementation is made with a set of current controlled RC nets which solution is analogue to the system of ordinary differential equations that results from ADE formulation. This approach has been applied to several devices in (Chibante et al., 2008; Chibante et al., 2009a; Chibante et al., 2009b).

In both approaches, a complete device model is obtained adding a few sub-circuits modeling other regions of the device: emitter, junctions, space-charge and MOS regions. According to this hybrid approach it is possible to model the charge carrier distribution with high accuracy maintaining low execution times.

3.1 ADE solution

This section describes the methodology proposed in (Chibante et al., 2008; Chibante et al., 2009a; Chibante et al., 2009b) to solve ADE. ADE solution is generally obtained considering that the charge carrier distribution is approximately one-dimensional along the n^- region. Assuming also high-level injection condition ($p \approx n$) in device's low-doped zone the charge carrier distribution is given by the well-known ADE:

$$\frac{\partial p(x,t)}{\partial t} = D\frac{\partial^2 p(x,t)}{\partial x^2} - \frac{p(x,t)}{\tau} \tag{5}$$

with boundary conditions:

$$\frac{\partial p(x,t)}{\partial x} = \frac{1}{2qA}\left(\frac{I_n}{D_n} - \frac{I_p}{D_p}\right) \tag{6}$$

In (5)-(6) D, D_n and D_p are diffusion constants, I_n and I_p are electron and hole currents and A the device's area. It is shown that ADE can be solved by a variational formulation with posterior solution using the Finite Element Method (FEM) (Zienkiewicz & Morgan, 1983).

$$[M]\left[\frac{\partial p(t)}{\partial t}\right]+[G][p(t)]+[F]=[0] \tag{7}$$

with:

$$[M]=\frac{A_e L_{Ee}}{6D}\begin{bmatrix} 2 & 1 & & & \\ 1 & 4 & 1 & & \\ & \ddots & \ddots & \ddots & \\ & & 1 & 4 & 1 \\ & & & 1 & 2 \end{bmatrix} \tag{8}$$

$$[G]=\frac{A_e}{2L_{Ee}}\begin{bmatrix} 2 & -2 & & & \\ -2 & 4 & -2 & & \\ & \ddots & \ddots & \ddots & \\ & & -2 & 4 & -2 \\ & & & -2 & 2 \end{bmatrix}+\frac{A_e L_{Ee}}{6D\tau}\begin{bmatrix} 2 & 1 & & & \\ 1 & 4 & 1 & & \\ & \ddots & \ddots & \ddots & \\ & & 1 & 4 & 1 \\ & & & 1 & 2 \end{bmatrix} \tag{9}$$

$$[F]=\begin{bmatrix} -f(t)A_1 & 0 & \cdots & 0 & -g(t)A_{n+1} \end{bmatrix} \tag{10}$$

The symmetry of these matrices enables to solve the system (7) making an analogy with a system of equations of a RC network:

$$[C]\left[\frac{\partial v(t)}{\partial t}\right]+[G][v(t)]+[I]=[0] \tag{11}$$

where voltages in each node represent carrier concentration along the n^- zone of the device. A normalization constant (10^{17}) is used in order to limit the voltages in IsSpice simulator to acceptable values. Resistors values are defined by [G] and capacitors by [C]. Current sources defined by [I] in first and last nodes implement boundary conditions accordingly to (6) and are defined specifically to the type of device being modeled. Corresponding RC nets for the presented formulation are illustrated in Fig. 2 where A_e and L_{Ee} are, respectively, area and width of each finite element.

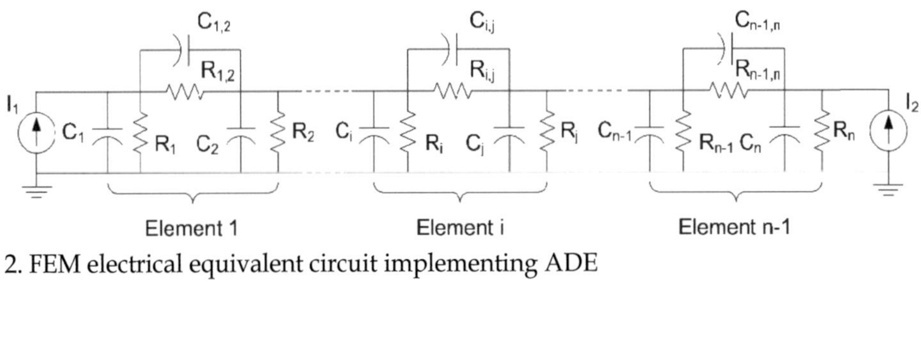

Fig. 2. FEM electrical equivalent circuit implementing ADE

Related values of resistors and capacitors are:

$$C_{ij} = -\frac{A_e L_{Ee}}{6D}; \quad C_i = C_j = \frac{A_e L_{Ee}}{2D}$$
$$R_{ij} = \frac{6D\tau L_{Ee}}{6D\tau A_e - A_e L_{Ee}^2}; \quad R_i = R_j = \frac{2D\tau}{A_e L_{Ee}} \tag{12}$$

3.2 IGBT model

This section briefly presents a complete IGBT model (Chibante et al., 2008; Chibante et al., 2009b) with a non-punch-through structure (NPT-IGBT) in order to illustrate the relationship between the ADE formulation and remaining device sub-models, as well as making clear the model parameters that will be identified using the SA algorithm. Fig. 3 illustrates the structure of an NPT-IGBT.

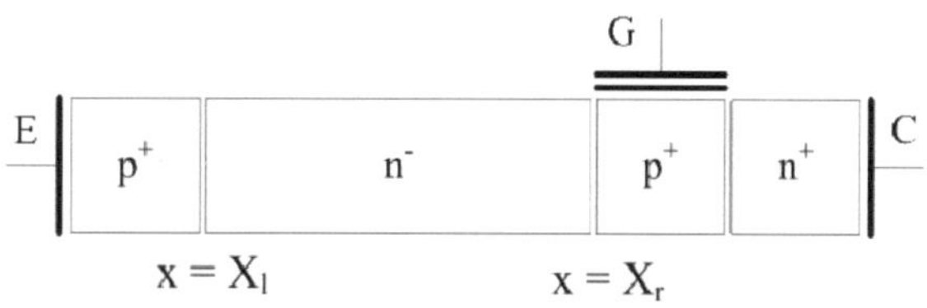

Fig. 3. Structure of a NPT-IGBT

3.2.1 ADE boundary conditions

In order to complete the ADE formulation appropriate boundary conditions must be defined, accordingly to the device being modeled. Current I_{p_l} is a recombination term modeled with the "h" parameter theory, I_{n_r} is the channel current from MOS part of the device and I_T is the total current. So, boundary conditions (6) are defined considering:

$$\begin{aligned} I_{p|x=Xl} &= I_{p_l} \\ I_{n|x=Xl} &= I_T - I_{p_l} \\ I_{n|x=Xr} &= I_{n_r} \\ I_{p|x=Xr} &= I_T - I_{n_r} \end{aligned} \tag{13}$$

3.2.2 Emitter model

The contribution of the carrier concentration for the total current is well described by the theory of "h" parameters for high doped emitters, assuming a high injection level in the carrier storage region:

$$I_{n_l} = q h_p A p_0^2 \tag{14}$$

That relates electron current I_{n_l} to carrier concentration at left border of the n^- region (p_0). Emitter zone is seen as a recombination surface that models the recombination process of electrons that penetrate p^+ region due to limited emitter injection efficiency.

3.2.3 MOSFET model

The MOS part of the device is well represented with standard MOS models, where the channel current is given by:

$$I_{mos} = K_p K_f \left[\left(V_{gs} - V_{th}\right) V_{ds} - \frac{K_f V_{ds}^2}{2} \right] \times \frac{M}{1 + \theta\left(V_{gs} - V_{th}\right)} \tag{15}$$

for triode region and:

$$I_{mos} = \frac{K_p \left(V_{gs} - V_{th}\right)^2}{2} \times \frac{M}{1 + \theta\left(V_{gs} - V_{th}\right)} \tag{16}$$

for saturation region.

Transient · behaviour is ruled by capacitances between device terminals. Well-known nonlinear Miller capacitance is the most important one in order to describe switching behaviour of MOS part. It is comprehended of a series combination of gate-drain oxide capacitance (C_{ox}) and gate-drain depletion capacitance (C_{gdj}) resulting in the following expression:

$$C_{gd} = \frac{C_{ox}}{1 + \frac{W_{sc}^{'} C_{ox}}{\varepsilon_{si} A_{gd}}} \tag{17}$$

Drain-source capacitance (C_{ds}) is defined as:

$$C_{ds} = \frac{\varepsilon_{si} A_{ds}}{W_{sc}} \tag{18}$$

Gate-source capacitance is normally extracted from capacitance curves and a constant value may be used.

3.2.4 Voltage drops

As the global model behaves like a current controlled voltage source it is necessary to evaluate voltage drops over the several regions of the IGBT. Thus, neglecting the contribution of the high- doped zones (emitter and collector) the total voltage drop (forward bias) across the device is composed by the following terms:

$$V_{IGBT} = V_{p^+ n^-} + V_{\Omega} + V_{sc} \tag{19}$$

The p^+n^- junction voltage drop can be calculated according to Boltzmann approximation:

$$V_{p^+n^-} = V_T \ln\left(\frac{p_0^2}{n_i^2}\right) \tag{20}$$

Voltage drop across the lightly doped storage region is described integrating electrical field. Assuming a uniform doping level and quasi-neutrality ($n = p + N_D$) over the n^- zone, and neglecting diffusion current, we have:

$$V_\Omega \cong \frac{1}{q}\int_{x_l}^{x_r} \frac{J}{p(\mu_n + \mu_p) + \mu_n N_D} dx \tag{21}$$

Equation (21) can be seen as a voltage drop across conductivity modulated resistance. Applying the FEM formulation and using the mean value of p in each finite element results:

$$V_\Omega = I_T \times \sum_{e=1}^{r} \frac{l_e}{qA_e\left[\frac{p_e + p_{e+1}}{2}(\mu_n + \mu_p) + \mu_n N_D\right]} \tag{22}$$

Voltage drop over the space charge region is calculated by integrating Poisson equation. For a uniformly doped base the classical expression is:

$$V_{sc} = \frac{qN_D}{2\varepsilon_{si}} W_{sc}\left(W_{sc} + 2\sqrt{\frac{2\varepsilon_{si}V_{bi}}{qN_D}}\right) \tag{23}$$

3.3 Parameter identification procedure

Identification of semiconductor model parameters will be presented using the NPT-IGBT as case study. The NPT-IGBT model has been presented in previous section. The model is characterized by a set of well known physical constants and a set of parameters listed in Table 1 (Chibante et al., 2009b). This is the set of parameters that must be accurately identified in order to get precise simulation results. As proposed in this chapter, the parameters will be identified using the SA optimization algorithm. If the optimum parameter set produces simulation results that differ from experimental results by an acceptable error, and in a wide range of operating conditions, then one can conclude that obtained parameters' values correspond to the real ones.

It is proposed in (Chibante et al., 2004; Chibante et al., 2009b) to use as experimental data results from DC analysis and transient analysis. Given the large number of parameters, it was also suggested to decompose the optimization process in two stages. To accomplish that the set of parameters is divided in two groups and optimized separately: a first set of parameters is extracted using the DC characteristic while the second set is extracted using transient switching waveforms with the optimum parameters from DC extraction. Table 1 presents also the proposed parameter division where the parameters that strongly influences DC characteristics were selected in order to run the DC optimization. In the following sections the first optimization stage will be referred as DC optimization and the second as transient optimization.

Optimization	Symbol	Unit	Description
Transient	A_{gd}	cm^2	Gate-drain overlap area
	W_B	cm	Metallurgical base width
	N_B	cm^{-3}	Base doping concentration
	V_{bi}	V	Junction in-built voltage
	C_{gs}	F	Gate-source capacitance
	C_{oxd}	F	Gate-drain overlap oxide capacitance
DC	A	cm^2	Device active area
	h_p	$cm^4.s^{-1}$	Recombination parameter
	K_f	-	Triode region MOSFET transconductance factor
	K_p	A/V^2	Saturation region MOSFET transconductance
	V_{th}	V	MOSFET channel threshold voltage
	τ	s	Base lifetime
	θ	V^{-1}	Transverse field transconductance factor

Table 1. List of NPT-IGBT model parameters

4. Simulated Annealing implementation

As described in section two of this chapter, application of the SA algorithm requires definition of:

a) Initial population;
b) Initial temperature;
c) Perturbation mechanism;
d) Objective function;
e) Cooling schedule;
f) Terminating criterion.

SA algorithm has a disadvantage that is common to most metaheuristics in the sense that many implementation aspects are left open to the designer and many algorithm controls are defined in an ad-hoc basis or are the result of a tuning stage. In the following it is presented the approach suggested in (Chibante et al., 2009b).

4.1 Initial population

Every iterative technique requires definition of an initial guess for parameters' values. Some algorithms require the use of several initial parameter sets but it is not the case of SA. Another approach is to randomly select the initial parameters' values given a set of appropriated boundaries. Of course that as closer the initial estimate is from the global optimum the faster will be the optimization process. The approach proposed in (Chibante et al., 2009b) is to use some well know techniques (Chibante et al., 2004; Kang et al., 2003c; Leturcq et al., 1997) to find an interesting initial solution for some of the parameters. These simple techniques are mainly based in datasheet information or known relations between parameters. Since this family of optimization techniques requires a tuning process, in the sense that algorithm control variables must be refined to maximize algorithm performance, the initial solution can also be tuned if some of parameter if clearly far way from expected global optimum.

4.2 Initial temperature

As stated before, the temperature must be large enough to enable the algorithm to move off a local minimum but small enough not to move off a global minimum. This is related to the acceptance probability of a worst solution that depends on temperature and magnitude of objective function. In this context, the algorithm was tuned and the initial temperature was set to 1.

4.3 Perturbation mechanism

A solution x is defined as a vector $x = (x_1,\ldots, x_n)$ representing a point in the search space. A new solution is generated using a vector $\boldsymbol{\sigma} = (\sigma_1,\ldots, \sigma_n)$ of standard deviations to create a perturbation from the current solution. A neighbor solution is then produced from the present solution by:

$$x_{i+1} = x_i + N(0,\sigma_i) \tag{24}$$

where $N(0, \sigma_i)$ is a random Gaussian number with zero mean and σ_i standard deviation. The construction of the vector $\boldsymbol{\sigma}$ requires definition of a value σ_i related to each parameter x_i. That depends on the confidence used to construct the initial solution, in sense that if there is a high confidence that a certain parameter is close to a certain value, then the corresponding standard deviation can be set smaller. In a more advanced scheme the vector $\boldsymbol{\sigma}$ can be made variable by a constant rate as a function of the number of iterations or based in acceptance rates (Pham & Karaboga, 2000). No constrains were imposed to the parameter variation, which means that there is no lower or upper bounds.

4.4 Objective function

The cost or objective function is defined by comparing the relative error between simulated and experimental data using the normalized sum of the squared errors. The general expression is:

$$f_{obj} = \sqrt{\sum_{c}\sum_{i}\left(\frac{g_s(x_i)-g_e(x_i)}{g_e(x_i)}\right)^2} \tag{25}$$

where $g_s(x_i)$ is the simulated data, $g_e(x_i)$ is the experimental data and c is the number of curves being optimized. The IGBT's DC characteristic is used as optimization variable for the DC optimization. This characteristic relates collector current to collector-emitter voltage for several gate-emitter voltages. Three experimental points for three gate-emitter values were measured to construct the objective function:

$$f_{obj} = \sqrt{\sum_{c=1}^{3}\sum_{i=1}^{3}\left(\frac{g_s(x_i) - g_e(x_i)}{g_e(x_i)}\right)^2} \tag{26}$$

So, a total of 9 data points were used from the experimental DC characteristic $g_e(x_i)$ and compared with the simulated DC characteristic $g_e(x_i)$ using (26).

The transient optimization is a more difficult task since it is required that a good simulated behaviour should be observed either for turn-on and turn-off, considering the three main variables: collector-emitter voltage (V_{CE}), gate-emitter voltage (V_{GE}) and collector current (I_C). Although optimization using the three main variables (V_{CE}, V_{GE}, I_C) could probably lead to a robust optimization process, it has been observed that optimizing just for V_{CE} produces also good results for remaining variables, as long as the typical current tail phenomenon is not significant. Collector current by itself is not an adequate optimization variable since the effects of some phenomenon (namely capacitances) is not readily visible in shape waveform. Optimization using switching parameters values instead of transient switching waveforms is also a possible approach (Allard et al., 2003). In the present work collector-emitter voltage was used as optimization variable in the objective function:

$$f_{obj} = \sqrt{\sum_{i=1}^{n}\left(\frac{V_{CE\_s}(t_i) - V_{CE\_e}(t_i)}{V_{CE\_e}(t_i)}\right)^2} \tag{27}$$

using n data points of experimental (V_{CE_e}) and simulated (V_{CE_s}) waveforms. It is interesting to note from the realized experiments that although collector-emitter voltage is optimized only at turn-off a good agreement is obtained for the whole switching cycle.

4.5 Cooling schedule

The cooling schedule was implemented using a geometric rule for temperature variation:

$$T_{i+1} = sT_i \tag{28}$$

A value of $s = 0.4$ was found to give good results.

4.6 Terminating criterion

For a given iteration of the SA algorithm, IsSpice circuit simulator is called in order to run a simulation with the current trial set of parameters. Implementation of the interaction between optimization algorithm and IsSpice requires some effort because each parameter set must be inserted into the IsSpice's netlist file and output data must be read. The simulation time is about 1 second for a DC simulation and 15 seconds for a transient simulation. Objective function is then evaluated with simulated and experimental data accordingly to (26) and (27). This means that each evaluation of the objective function takes about 15 seconds in the worst case. This is a disadvantage of the present application since evaluation of a common objective function usually requires computation of an equation that is made almost instantaneously. This imposes some limits in the number of algorithm iterations to avoid extremely long optimization times. So, it was decided to use a maximum of 100 iterations as terminating criterion for transient optimization and a minimum value of 0.5 for the objective function in the DC optimization.

4.7 Optimization results

Fig. 4 presents the results for the DC optimization. It is clear that simulated DC characteristic agrees well with the experimental DC characteristic defined by the 9 experimental data points. The experimental data is taken from a BUP203 device (1000V/23A). Table 2 presents the initial solution and corresponding **σ** vector for DC optimization and the optimum parameter set. Results for the transient optimization are presented (Fig. 5) concerning the optimization process but also further model validation results in order to assess the robustness of the extraction optimization process. Experimental results are from a BUP203 device (1000V/23A) using a test circuit in a hard-switching configuration with resistive load. Operating conditions are: V_{CC} = 150V, R_L = 20Ω and gate resistances R_{G1} = 1.34kΩ, R_{G2} = 2.65kΩ and R_{G3} = 7.92kΩ. Note that the objective function is evaluated using only the collector-emitter variable with R_{G1} = 1.34kΩ. Although collector-emitter voltage is optimized only at turn-off it is interesting to note that a good agreement is obtained for the whole switching cycle. Table 3 presents the initial solution and corresponding **σ** vector for transient optimization and the optimum parameter set.

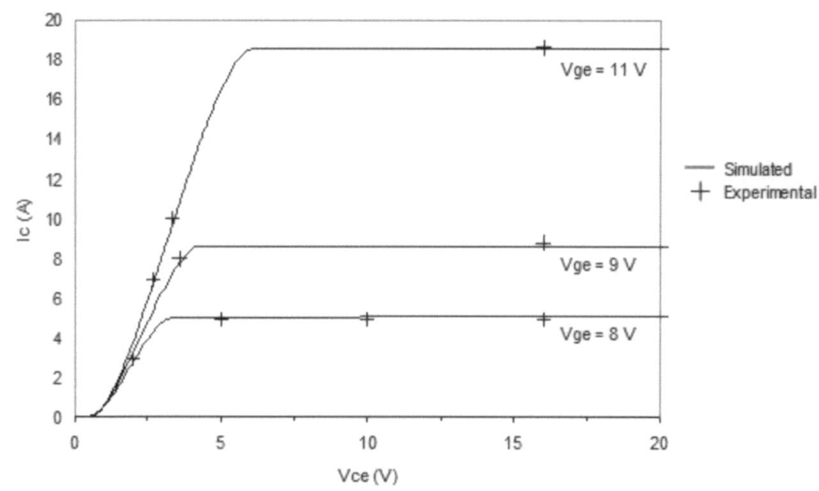

Fig. 4. Experimental and simulated DC characteristics

Parameter	A (cm²)	h_p (cm⁴.s⁻¹)	K_f	K_p (A/V²)	V_{th} (V)	τ (μs)	θ (V⁻¹)
Initial value	0.200	500×10^{-14}	3.10	0.90×10^{-5}	4.73	50	12.0×10^{-5}
Optimum value	0.239	319×10^{-14}	2.17	0.72×10^{-5}	4.76	54	8.8×10^{-5}

Table 2. Initial conditions and final result (DC optimization)

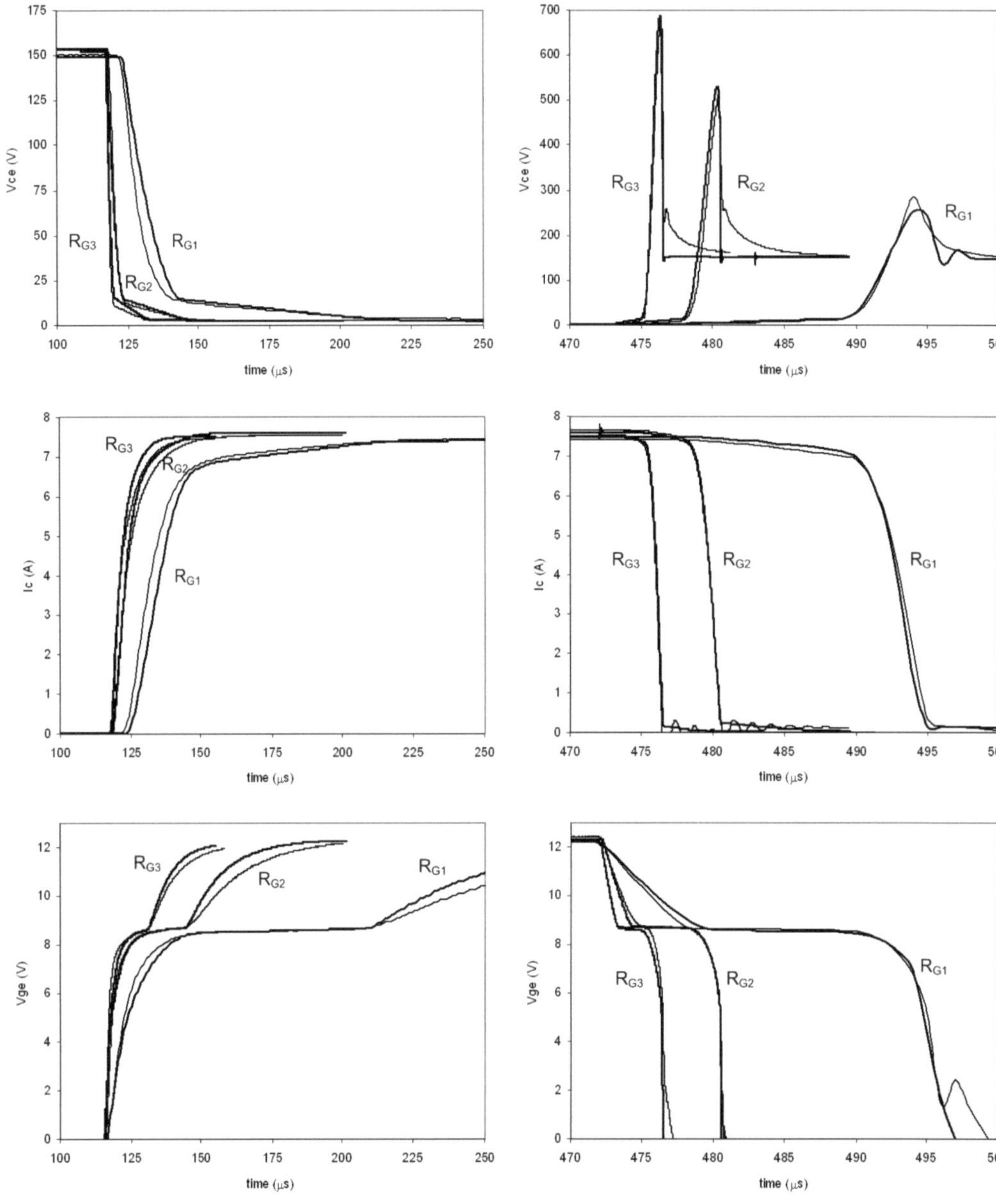

Fig. 5. Experimental and simulated (bold) transient curves at turn-on (left) and turn-off

Parameter	A_{gd} (cm^2)	C_{gs} (nF)	C_{oxd} (nF)	N_B (cm^{-3})	V_{bi} (V)	W_B (cm)
Initial value	0.090	1.80	3.10	0.40×10^{14}	0.70	18.0×10^{-3}
Optimum value	0.137	2.46	2.58	0.41×10^{14}	0.54	20.2×10^{-3}

Table 3. Initial conditions and final result (transient optimization)

5. Conclusion

An optimization-based methodology is presented to support the parameter identification of a NPT-IGBT physical model. The SA algorithm is described and applied successfully. The main features of SA are presented as well as the algorithm design. Using a simple turn-off test the model performance is maximized corresponding to a set of parameters that accurately characterizes the device behavior in DC and transient conditions. Accurate power semiconductor modeling and parameter extraction with reduced CPU time is possible with proposed approach.

6. References

Allard, B. et al. (2003). Systematic procedure to map the validity range of insulated-gate device models, *Proceedings of 10th European Conference on Power Electronics and Applications (EPE'03)*, Toulouse, France, 2003

Araújo, A. et al. (1997). A new approach for analogue simulation of bipolar semiconductors, *Proceedings of the 2nd Brazilian Conference Power Electronics (COBEP'97)*, pp. 761-765, Belo-Horizonte, Brasil, 1997

Bryant, A.T. et al. (2006). Two-Step Parameter Extraction Procedure With Formal Optimization for Physics-Based Circuit Simulator IGBT and p-i-n Diode Models, *IEEE Transactions on Power Electronics*, Vol. 21, No. 2, pp. 295-309

Chibante, R. et al. (2004). A simple and efficient parameter extraction procedure for physics based IGBT models, *Proceedings of 11th International Power Electronics and Motion Control Conference (EPE-PEMC'04)*, Riga, Latvia, 2004

Chibante, R. et al. (2008). A new approach for physical-based modelling of bipolar power semiconductor devices, *Solid-State Electronics*, Vol. 52, No. 11, pp. 1766-1772

Chibante, R. et al. (2009a). Finite element power diode model optimized through experiment based parameter extraction, *International Journal of Numerical Modeling: Electronic Networks, Devices and Fields*, Vol. 22, No. 5, pp. 351-367

Chibante, R. et al. (2009b). Finite-Element Modeling and Optimization-Based Parameter Extraction Algorithm for NPT-IGBTs, *IEEE Transactions on Power Electronics*, Vol. 24, No. 5, pp. 1417-1427

Claudio, A. et al. (2002). Parameter extraction for physics-based IGBT models by electrical measurements, *Proceedings of 33rd Annual IEEE Power Electronics Specialists Conference (PESC'02)*, Vol. 3, pp. 1295-1300, Cairns, Australia, 2002

Fouskakis, D. & Draper, D. (2002). Stochastic optimization: a review, *International Statistical Review*, Vol. 70, No. 3, pp. 315-349

Hefner, A.R. & Bouche, S. (2000). Automated parameter extraction software for advanced IGBT modeling, *7th Workshop on Computers in Power Electronics (COMPEL'00)* pp. 10-18, 2000

Kang, X. et al. (2002). Low temperature characterization and modeling of IGBTs, *Proceedings of 33rd Annual IEEE Power Electronics Specialists Conference (PESC'02)*, Vol. 3, pp. 1277-1282, Cairns, Australia, 2002

Kang, X. et al. (2003a). Characterization and modeling of high-voltage field-stop IGBTs, *IEEE Transactions on Industry Applications*, Vol. 39, No. 4, pp. 922-928

Kang, X. et al. (2003b). Characterization and modeling of the LPT CSTBT - the 5th generation IGBT, *Conference Record of the 38th IAS Annual Meeting*, Vol. 2, pp. 982-987, UT, United States, 2003b

Kang, X. et al. (2003c). Parameter extraction for a physics-based circuit simulator IGBT model, *Proceedings of the 18th Annual IEEE Applied Power Electronics Conference and Exposition (APEC'03)*, Vol. 2, pp. 946-952, Miami Beach, FL, United States, 2003c

Lauritzen, P.O. et al. (2001). A basic IGBT model with easy parameter extraction, *Proceedings of 32nd Annual IEEE Power Electronics Specialists Conference (PESC'01)*, Vol. 4, pp. 2160-2165, Vancouver, BC, Canada, 2001

Leturcq, P. et al. (1997). A distributed model of IGBTs for circuit simulation, *Proceedings of 7th European Conference on Power Electronics and Applications (EPE'97)*, pp. 494-501, 1997

Palmer, P.R. et al. (2001). Circuit simulator models for the diode and IGBT with full temperature dependent features, *Proceedings of 32nd Annual IEEE Power Electronics Specialists Conference (PESC'01)*, Vol. 4, pp. 2171-2177, 2001

Pham, D.T. & Karaboga, D. (2000). Intelligent optimisation techniques: genetic algorithms, tabu search, simulated annealing and neural networks, Springer, New York

Santi, E. et al. (2001). Temperature effects on trench-gate IGBTs, *Conference Record of the 36th IEEE Industry Applications Conference (IAS'01)*, Vol. 3, pp. 1931-1937, 2001

Wang, X. et al. (2004). Implementation and validation of a physics-based circuit model for IGCT with full temperature dependencies, *Proceedings of 35th Annual IEEE Power Electronics Specialists Conference (PESC'04)*, Vol. 1, pp. 597-603, 2004

Zienkiewicz, O.C. & Morgan, K. (1983). Finite elements and aproximations, John Wiley & Sons, New York

2

Application of simulated annealing and hybrid methods in the solution of inverse heat and mass transfer problems

Antônio José da Silva Neto[1], Jader Lugon Junior[2,5], Francisco José da Cunha Pires Soeiro[1], Luiz Biondi Neto[1], Cesar Costapinto Santana[3], Fran Sérgio Lobato[4] and Valder Steffen Junior[4]

Universidade do Estado do Rio de Janeiro[1],
Instituto Federal de Educação, Ciência e Tecnologia Fluminense[2],
Universidade Estadual de Campinas[3],
Universidade Federal de Uberlândia[4],
Centro de Tecnologia SENAI-RJ Ambiental[5]
Brazil

1. Introduction

The problem of parameter identification characterizes a typical inverse problem in engineering. It arises from the difficulty in building theoretical models that are able to represent satisfactorily physical phenomena under real operating conditions. Considering the possibility of using more complex models along with the information provided by experimental data, the parameters obtained through an inverse problem approach may then be used to simulate the behavior of the system for different operation conditions. Traditionally, this kind of problem has been treated by using either classical or deterministic optimization techniques (Baltes et al., 1994; Cazzador and Lubenova, 1995; Su and Silva Neto, 2001; Silva Neto and Özişik 1993ab, 1994; Yan et al., 2008; Yang et al., 2009). In the recent years however, the use of non-deterministic techniques or the coupling of these techniques with classical approaches thus forming a hybrid methodology became very popular due to the simplicity and robustness of evolutionary techniques (Wang et al., 2001; Silva Neto and Soeiro, 2002, 2003; Silva Neto and Silva Neto, 2003; Lobato and Steffen Jr., 2007; Lobato et al., 2008, 2009, 2010).

The solution of inverse problems has several relevant applications in engineering and medicine. A lot of attention has been devoted to the estimation of boundary and initial conditions in heat conduction problems (Alifanov, 1974, Beck *et al.*, 1985, Denisov and Solov'yera, 1993, Muniz et al., 1999) as well as thermal properties (Artyukhin, 1982, Carvalho and Silva Neto, 1999, Soeiro et al., 2000; Su and Silva Neto, 2001; Lobato et al., 2009) and heat source intensities (Borukhov and Kolesnikov, 1988, Silva Neto and Özisik, 1993ab, 1994, Orlande and Özisik, 1993, Moura Neto and Silva Neto, 2000, Wang *et al.*, 2000) in such diffusive processes. On the other hand, despite its relevance in chemical engineering, there is not a sufficient number of published results on inverse mass transfer or heat convection problems. Denisov (2000) has considered the estimation of an isotherm of absorption and Lugon et al. (2009) have investigated the determination of adsorption isotherms with applications in the food and pharmaceutical industry, and Su et al., (2000) have considered the estimation of the spatial dependence of an externally imposed heat flux from temperature measurements taken in a thermally developing turbulent flow inside a circular pipe. Recently, Lobato et al. (2008) have considered the estimation of the parameters of Page's equation and heat loss coefficient by using experimental data from a realistic rotary dryer.

Another class of inverse problems in which the concurrence of specialists from different areas has yielded a large number of new methods and techniques for non-destructive testing in industry, and diagnosis and therapy in medicine, is the one involving radiative transfer in participating media. Most of the work in this area is related to radiative properties or source estimation (Ho and Özisik, 1989, McCormick, 1986, 1992, Silva Neto and Özisik, 1995, Kauati et al., 1999). Two strong motivations for the solution of such inverse problems in recent years have been the biomedical and oceanographic applications (McCormick, 1993, Sundman et al., 1998, Kauati et al., 1999, Carita Montero et al., 1999, 2000).

The increasing interest on inverse problems (IP) is due to the large number of practical applications in scientific and technological areas such as tomography (Kim and Charette, 2007), environmental sciences (Hanan, 2001) and parameter estimation (Souza et al., 2007; Lobato et al., 2008, 2009, 2010), to mention only a few.

In the radiative problems context, the inverse problem consists in the determination of radiative parameters through the use of experimental data for minimizing the residual between experimental and calculated values. The solution of inverse radiative transfer problems has been obtained by using different methodologies, namely deterministic, stochastic and hybrid methods. As examples of techniques developed for dealing with inverse radiative transfer problems, the following methods can be cited: Levenberg-Marquardt method (Silva Neto and Moura Neto, 2005); Simulated Annealing (Silva Neto and Soeiro, 2002; Souza et al., 2007); Genetic Algorithms (Silva Neto and Soeiro, 2002; Souza et al., 2007); Artificial Neural Networks (Soeiro et al., 2004); Simulated Annealing and Levenberg-Marquard (Silva Neto and Soeiro, 2006); Ant Colony Optimization (Souto et al., 2005); Particle Swarm Optimization (Becceneri et al, 2006); Generalized Extremal Optimization (Souza et al., 2007); Interior Points Method (Silva Neto and Silva Neto, 2003); Particle Collision Algorithm (Knupp et al., 2007); Artificial Neural Networks and Monte Carlo Method (Chalhoub et al., 2007b); Epidemic Genetic Algorithm and the Generalized Extremal Optimization Algorithm (Cuco et al., 2009); Generalized Extremal Optimization and Simulated Annealing Algorithm (Galski et al., 2009); Hybrid Approach with Artificial Neural Networks, Levenberg-Marquardt and Simulated Annealing Methods (Lugon, Silva Neto and Santana, 2009; Lugon and Silva Neto, 2010), Differential Evolution (Lobato et al., 2008; Lobato et al., 2009), Differential Evolution and Simulated Annealing Methods (Lobato et al., 2010).

In this chapter we first describe three problems of heat and mass transfer, followed by the formulation of the inverse problems, the description of the solution of the inverse problems with Simulated Annealing and its hybridization with other methods, and some test case results.

2. Formulation of the Direct Heat and Mass Transfer Problems

2.1 Radiative Transfer

Consider the problem of radiative transfer in an absorbing, emitting, isotropically scattering, plane-parallel, and gray medium of optical thickness τ_0, between two diffusely reflecting boundary surfaces as illustrated in Fig.1. The mathematical formulation of the direct radiation problem is given by (Özişik, 1973)

$$\mu\frac{\partial I(\tau,\mu)}{\partial\tau}+I(\tau,\mu)=\frac{\omega}{2}\int_{-1}^{1}I(\tau,\mu')d\mu', \quad 0<\tau<\tau_0, \quad -1\leq\mu\leq1 \tag{1}$$

$$I(0,\mu)=A_1+2\rho_1\int_0^1 I(0,-\mu')\mu' d\mu', \quad \mu>0 \tag{2}$$

$$I(\tau_0,\mu)=A_2+2\rho_2\int_0^1 I(\tau_0,\mu')\mu' d\mu', \quad \mu<0 \tag{3}$$

where $I(\tau,\mu)$ is the dimensionless radiation intensity, τ is the optical variable, μ is the direction cosine of the radiation beam with the positive τ axis, ω is the single scattering albedo, and ρ_1 and ρ_2 are the diffuse reflectivities. The illumination from the outside is supplied by external isotropic sources with intensities A_1 and A_2.

No internal source was considered in Eq. (1). In radiative heat transfer applications it means that the emission of radiation by the medium due to its temperature is negligible in comparison to the strength of the external isotropic radiation sources incident at the boundaries $\tau=0$ and/or $\tau=\tau_0$.

In the direct problem defined by Eqs. (1-3) the radiative properties and the boundary conditions are known. Therefore, the values of the radiation intensity can be calculated for every point in the spatial and angular domains. In the inverse problem considered here the radiative properties of the medium are unknown, but we still need to solve problem (1-3) using estimates for the unknowns.

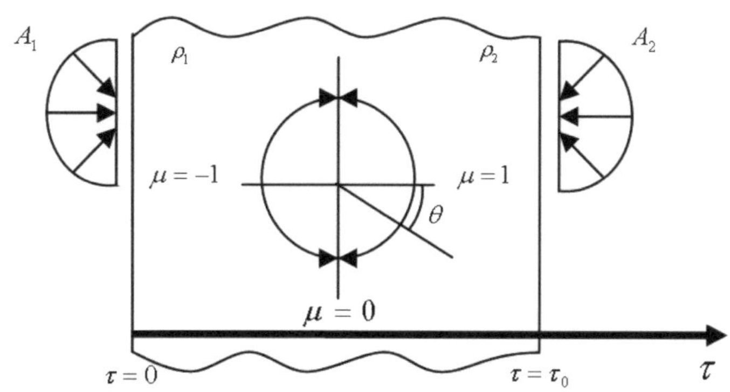

Fig. 1. The geometry and coordinates.

2.2 Drying (Simultaneous Heat and Mass Transfer)

In Fig. 2, adapted from Mwithiga and Olwal (2005), it is represented the drying experiment setup considered in this section. In it was introduced the possibility of using a scale to weight the samples, sensors to measure temperature in the sample, and also inside the drying chamber.

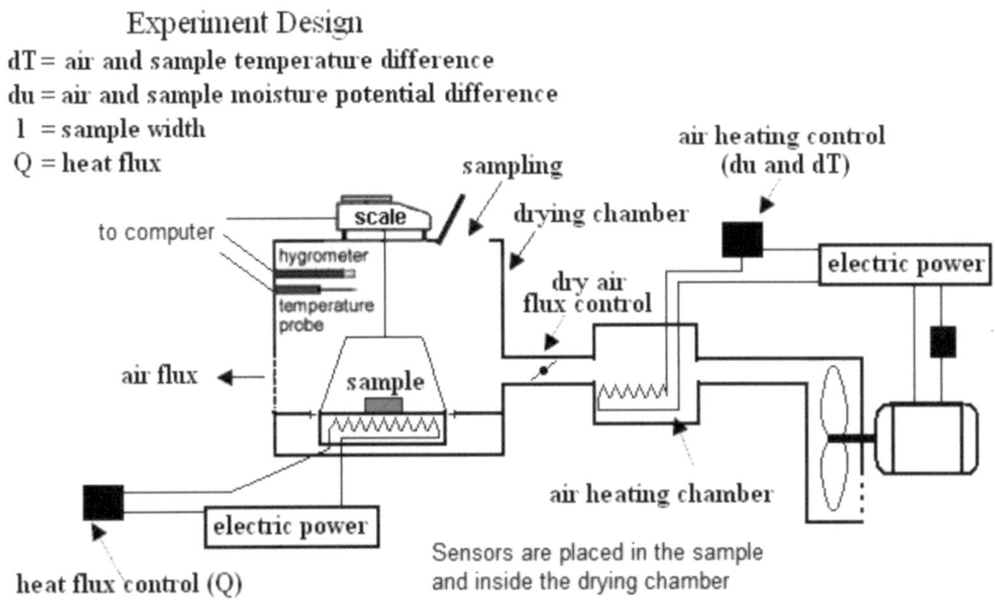

Fig. 2. Drying experiment setup (Adapted from Mwithiga and Olwal, 2005).

In accordance with the schematic representation shown in Fig. 3, consider the problem of simultaneous heat and mass transfer in a one-dimensional porous media in which heat is supplied to the left surface of the porous media, at the same time that dry air flows over the right boundary surface.

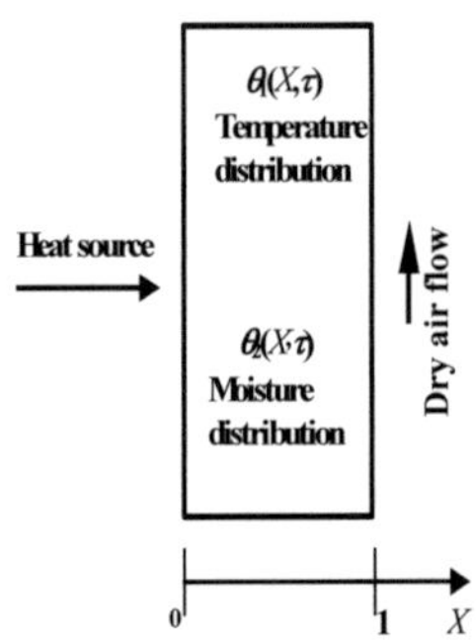

Fig. 3. Drying process schematic representation.

The mathematical formulation used in this work for the direct heat and mass transfer problem considered a constant properties model, and in dimensionless form it is given by (Luikov and Mikhailov, 1965; Mikhailov and Özisik, 1994),

$$\frac{\partial\theta_1(X,\tau)}{\partial\tau}=\alpha\frac{\partial^2\theta_1}{\partial X^2}-\beta\frac{\partial^2\theta_2}{\partial X^2},\quad 0<X<1,\quad \tau>0 \tag{4}$$

$$\frac{\partial\theta_2(X,\tau)}{\partial\tau}=Lu\frac{\partial^2\theta_2}{\partial X^2}-Lu\,Pn\frac{\partial^2\theta_1}{\partial X^2},\quad 0<X<1,\quad \tau>0 \tag{5}$$

subject to the following initial conditions, for $0\le X\le 1$

$$\theta_1(X,0)=0 \tag{6}$$

$$\theta_2(X,0)=0 \tag{7}$$

and to the boundary conditions, for $\tau>0$

$$\frac{\partial\theta_1(0,\tau)}{\partial X}=-Q \tag{8}$$

$$\frac{\partial\theta_2(0,\tau)}{\partial X}=-Pn\,Q \tag{9}$$

$$\frac{\partial\theta_1(1,\tau)}{\partial X}+Bi_q\theta_1(1,\tau)=Bi_q-(1-\varepsilon)KoLuBi_m\left[1-\theta_2(1,\tau)\right]=0 \tag{10}$$

$$\frac{\partial\theta_2(1,\tau)}{\partial X}+Bi_m^*\theta_2(1,\tau)==Bi_m^*-Pn\,Bi_q\left[\theta_1(1,\tau)-1\right] \tag{11}$$

where

$$\alpha=1+\varepsilon\,Ko\,Lu\,Pn \tag{12}$$

$$\beta=\varepsilon\,Ko\,Lu \tag{13}$$

$$Bi_m^*=Bi_m\left[1-(1-\varepsilon)Pn\,Ko\,Lu\right] \tag{14}$$

and the dimensionless variables are defined as

$$\theta_1(X,\tau)=\frac{T(x,t)-T_0}{T_s-T_0},\ \text{temperature} \tag{15}$$

$$\theta_2(X,\tau)=\frac{u_0-u(x,t)}{u_0-u^*},\ \text{moisture potential} \tag{16}$$

$$X=\frac{x}{l},\ \text{spatial coordinate} \tag{17}$$

$$\tau=\frac{at}{l^2},\ \text{time} \tag{18}$$

$$Lu=\frac{a_m}{a},\ \text{Luikov number} \tag{19}$$

$$Pn=\delta\frac{T_s-T_0}{u_0-u^*},\ \text{Possnov number} \tag{20}$$

$$Ko = \frac{r\, u_0 - u^*}{c\, T_s - T_0}, \text{ Kossovitch number} \quad (21)$$

$$Bi_q = \frac{hl}{k}, \text{ heat Biot} \quad (22)$$

$$Bi_m = \frac{h_m l}{k_m}, \text{ mass Biot} \quad (23)$$

$$Q = \frac{ql}{k(T_s - T_0)}, \text{ heat flux} \quad (24)$$

When the geometry, the initial and boundary conditions, and the medium properties are known, the system of equations (4-11) can be solved, yielding the temperature and moisture distribution in the media. The finite difference method was used to solve the system (4-11).
Many previous works have studied the drying inverse problem using measurements of temperature and moisture-transfer potential at specific locations of the medium. But to measure the moisture-transfer potential in a certain position is not an easy task, so in this work it is used the average quantity

$$\bar{u}(t) = \frac{1}{l} \int_{x=0}^{x=l} u(x,t)dx \quad (25)$$

or

$$\bar{\theta}_2(\tau) = \int_{X=0}^{X=1} \theta_2(X,\tau)dX \quad (26)$$

Therefore, in order to obtain the average moisture measurements, $\bar{u}(t)$, one have just to weight the sample at each time (Lugon and Silva Neto, 2010).

2.3 Gas-liquid Adsorption

The mechanism of proteins adsorption at gas-liquid interfaces has been the subject of intensive theoretical and experimental research, because of the potential use of bubble and foam fractionation columns as an economically viable means for surface active compounds recovery from diluted solutions, (Özturk et al., 1987; Deckwer and Schumpe, 1993; Graham and Phillips, 1979; Santana and Carbonell, 1993ab; Santana, 1994; Krishna and van Baten, 2003; Haut and Cartage, 2005; Mouza et al., 2005; Lugon, 2005).
The direct problem related to the gas-liquid interface adsorption of bio-molecules in bubble columns consists essentially in the calculation of the depletion, that is, the reduction of solute concentration with time, when the physico-chemical properties and process parameters are known.
The solute depletion is modeled by

$$\frac{dC_b}{dt} = -\frac{6v_g}{\left(1-\varepsilon_g\right)Hd_b}\Gamma \quad (27)$$

where C_b is the liquid solute concentration (bulk), d_b is the bubble diameter, H is the bubble column height, v_g is the superficial velocity (gas volumetric flow rate divided by the area of the transversal section of the column A), and Γ is the surface excess concentration of the adsorbed solute.

The symbol ε_g represents the gas volumetric fraction, which can be calculated from the dimensionless correlation of Kumar (Özturk et al., 1987),

$$\varepsilon_g = 0.728U - 0.485U^2 + 0.095U^3 \tag{28}$$

where

$$U = v_g \left[\frac{\rho_l^2}{\gamma(\rho_l - \rho_g)g} \right]^{\frac{1}{4}} \tag{29}$$

ρ_l is the liquid density, γ is the surface tension, g is the gravity acceleration, and ρ_g is the gas density.

The quantities Γ and C are related through adsorption isotherms such as:

(i) Linear isotherm

$$\Gamma = B + KC \tag{30}$$

(ii) Langmuir isotherm

$$\Gamma_1 = \frac{1}{\hat{a}} \left[\frac{K_1(T)C}{1 + K_1(T)C} \right] \tag{31}$$

(iii) Two-layers isotherm

$$\Gamma_t = \Gamma_1 + \Gamma_2 = \frac{K_1(T)\exp(-\lambda\Gamma_1)C\left[1 + K_2(T)\hat{a}C\right]}{\hat{a}\left[1 + K_1\exp(-\lambda\,\Gamma_1)C\right]} \tag{32}$$

where Γ_1 and Γ_2 are the excess superficial concentration in the first and second adsorption layers respectively (see Fig. 4).

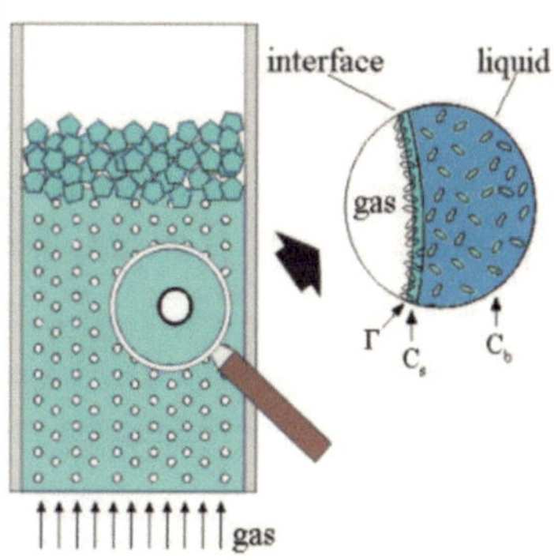

Fig. 4. Schematic representation of the gas-liquid adsorption process in a bubble and foam column.

Considering that the superficial velocity, bubble diameter and column cross section are constant along the column,

$$\frac{\partial \Gamma(z,t)}{\partial z} = \frac{(k_l a) d_b \left[C_b(t) - C_s(z,t) \right]}{6 v_g} \tag{33}$$

where z represents the spatial coordinate along the column, C_s is the solute concentration next to the bubbles and $(k_l a)$ is the volumetric mass transfer coefficient.

There are several correlations available for the determination of $(k_l a)$ but following the recommendation of Deckwer and Schumpe (1993) we have adopted the correlation of Öztürk et al. (1987) in the solution of the direct problem:

$$Sh = 0{,}62\, Sc^{0,5}\, Bo^{0,33}\, Ga^{0,29} \left(\frac{v_g}{\sqrt{g d_b}} \right)^{0,68} \left(\frac{\rho_g}{\rho_l} \right)^{0,04} \tag{34}$$

where

$$Sc = \left(\frac{\nu_l}{D_i} \right), \text{ Schmidt number} \tag{35}$$

$$Sh = \frac{(k_l a) d_b^2}{D_i}, \text{ Sherwood number} \tag{36}$$

$$Bo = \frac{\nu_l}{D_i}, \text{ Bond number} \tag{37}$$

$$Ga = \frac{g d_b^3}{\nu_l^2}, \text{ Galilei Number} \tag{38}$$

D_i is the tensoactive diffusion coefficient and ν_l is the liquid dynamic viscosity.

Combining Eqs. (27) and (33) and using an initial condition, such as $C_b = C_{b0}$ when $t = 0$, and a boundary condition, like $\Gamma = 0$ at $z = 0$, the solute concentration can be calculated as a function of time, $C_b(t)$. Santana and Carbonell (1993ab) developed an analytical solution for the direct problem in the case of a linear adsorption isotherm and the results presented a good agreement with experimental data for BSA (Bovine Serum Albumin).

In order to solve Eq. (27) a second order Runge Kutta method was used, known as the mid point method. Given the physico-chemical and process parameters, as well as the boundary and initial conditions, the solute concentration can be calculated for any time t (Lugon et al., 2009).

3. Formulation of Inverse Heat and Mass Transfer Problems

The inverse problem is implicitly formulated as a finite dimensional optimization problem (Silva Neto and Soeiro, 2003; Silva Neto and Moura Neto, 2005), where one seeks to minimize the cost functional of squared residues between the calculated and experimental values for the observable variable,

$$S(\mathbf{P}) = [\mathbf{G}_{calc}(\mathbf{P}) - \mathbf{G}_{meas}(\mathbf{P})]^T \mathbf{W} [\mathbf{G}_{calc}(\mathbf{P}) - \mathbf{G}_{meas}(\mathbf{P})] = \mathbf{F}^T \mathbf{F} \tag{39a}$$

where $\mathbf{G}_{meas}$ is the vector of measurements, $\mathbf{G}_{calc}$ is the vector of calculated values, $\mathbf{P}$ is the vector of unknowns, $\mathbf{W}$ is the diagonal matrix whose elements are the inverse of the measurement variances, and the vector of residues $\mathbf{F}$ is given by

$$\mathbf{F} = \mathbf{G}_{calc}(\mathbf{P}) - \mathbf{G}_{calc}(\mathbf{P}) \tag{39b}$$

The inverse problem solution is the vector $\vec{P}^*$ which minimizes the norm given by Eq. (39a), that is

$$S(\mathbf{P}^*) = \min_{\mathbf{P}} S(\mathbf{P}) \tag{40}$$

Depending on the direct problem, different measurements are to be taken, that is:

a) Radiative problem

Using calculated values given by Eq. (1) and experimental radiation intensities at the boundaries $\tau = 0$ and $\tau = \tau_0$, as well as at points that belong to the set Ω (points inside the domain τ - internal detectors) we try to estimated the vector of unknowns $\mathbf{P}$ considered. Two different vectors of unknowns $\vec{P}$ are possibly considered for the minimization of the difference between the experimental and calculated values: (i) τ_0, ω, ρ_1 and ρ_2; (ii) τ_0, ω, A_1 and A_2.

b) Drying problem

Using temperature measurements, T, taken by sensors located inside the medium, and the average of the moisture-transfer potential, $\bar{u}$, during the experiment, we try to estimate the vector of unknowns $\mathbf{P}$, for which a combination of variables was used: Lu (Luikov number), δ (thermogradient coefficient), r/c (relation between latent heat of evaporation and specific heat of the medium), h/k (relation between heat transfer coefficient and thermal conductivity), and h_m/k_m (relation between mass transfer coefficient and mass conductivity).

c) Gas-liquid adsorption problem

Different vectors of unknowns $\mathbf{P}$ are possibly considered, which are associated with different adsorption isotherms: (i) K and B (Linear isotherm); (ii) $K_1(T)$ and $\hat{a}$ (Langmuir isotherm); (iii) $K_1(T)$, $K_2(T)$, λ and $\hat{a}$ (two-layers isotherm). Here the BSA (Bovine Serum Albumin) adsorption was modeled using a two-layer isotherm.

4. Solution of the Inverse Problems with Simulated Annealing and Hybrid Methods

4.1 Design of Experiments

The sensitivity analysis plays a major role in several aspects related to the formulation and solution of an inverse problem (Dowding et al., 1999; Beck, 1988). Such analysis may be performed with the study of the sensitivity coefficients. Here we use the modified, or scaled, sensitivity coefficients

$$SC_{P_jV(t)} = P_j \frac{\partial V(t)}{\partial P_j}, \quad j = 1,2,...,N_p \tag{41}$$

where V is the observable state variable (which can be measured), P_j is a particular unknown of the problem, and N_p is the total number of unknowns considered.

As a general guideline, the sensitivity of the state variable to the parameter we want to determine must be high enough to allow an estimate within reasonable confidence bounds. Moreover, when two or more parameters are simultaneously estimated, their effects on the state variable must be independent (uncorrelated). Therefore, when represented graphically, the sensitivity coefficients should not have the same shape. If they do it means that two or more different parameters affect the observable variable in the same way, being difficult to distinguish their influences separately, which yields to poor estimations.

Another important tool used in the design of experiments is the study of the matrix

$$\mathbf{SC} = \begin{bmatrix} SC_{P_1V_1} & SC_{P_2V_2} & \cdots & SC_{P_{Np}V_1} \\ SC_{P_1V_2} & SC_{P_2V_2} & \cdots & SC_{P_{Np}V_2} \\ \cdots & \cdots & \cdots & \cdots \\ SC_{P_1V_m} & SC_{P_2V_m} & \cdots & SC_{P_{Np}V_m} \end{bmatrix} \tag{42}$$

where V_i is a particular measurement of temperature or moisture potential and m is the total number of measurements.

Maximizing the determinant of the matrix $\mathbf{SC}^T\mathbf{SC}$ results in higher sensitivity and uncorrelation (Beck, 1988).

4.2 Simulated Annealing Method (SA)

Based on statistical mechanics reasoning, applied to a solidification problem, Metropolis et al. (1953) introduced a simple algorithm that can be used to accomplish an efficient simulation of a system of atoms in equilibrium at a given temperature. In each step of the algorithm a small random displacement of an atom is performed and the variation of the energy ΔE is calculated. If $\Delta E<0$ the displacement is accepted, and the configuration with the displaced atom is used as the starting point for the next step. In the case of $\Delta E>0$, the new configuration can be accepted according to Boltzmann probability

$$P(\Delta E) = \exp(-\Delta E / k_B T) \tag{43}$$

A uniformly distributed random number p in the interval [0,1] is calculated and compared with $P(\Delta E)$. Metropolis criterion establishes that the new configuration is accepted if $p<P(\Delta E)$, otherwise it is rejected and the previous configuration is used again as a starting point.

Using the objective function $S(\mathbf{P})$, given by Eq. (39a), in place of energy and defining configurations by a set of variables $\{P_i\}, i = 1,2,.N_p$, where N_p represents the number of unknowns we want to estimate, the Metropolis procedure generates a collection of

configurations of a given optimization problem at some temperature T (Kirkpatric et al., 1983). This temperature is simply a control parameter. The simulated annealing process consists of first "melting" the system being optimized at a high "temperature", then lowering the "temperature" until the system "freezes" and no further change occurs.
The main control parameters of the algorithm implemented ("cooling procedure") are the initial "temperature", T_0, the cooling rate, r_t, number of steps performed through all elements of vector $\mathbf{P}$, N_s, number of times the procedure is repeated before the "temperature" is reduced, N_t, and the number of points of minimum (one for each temperature) that are compared and used as stopping criterion if they all agree within a tolerance ε, N_ε.

4.3 Levenberg-Marquardt Method (LM)

The Levenberg-Marquardt is a deterministic local optimizer method based on the gradient (Marquardt, 1963). In order to minimize the functional $S(\mathbf{P})$ we first write

$$\frac{dS}{d\mathbf{P}} = \frac{d}{d\mathbf{P}}\left(\mathbf{F}^T\mathbf{F}\right) = 0 \rightarrow \mathbf{J}^T\mathbf{J} = 0 \quad (44)$$

where J is the Jacobian matrix, with the elements $J_{ps} = \partial C_{bp}/\partial P_s$ being $p = 1, 2, ..., M$, and $s = 1, 2, ..., N_p$, where M is the total number of measurements and N_p is the number of unknowns. It is observed that the elements of the Jacobian matrix are related to the scaled sensitivity coefficients presented before.
Using a Taylor's expansion and keeping only the terms up to the first order,

$$\mathbf{F}(\mathbf{P}+\Delta\mathbf{P}) \cong \mathbf{F}(\mathbf{P}) + \mathbf{J}\Delta\mathbf{P} \quad (45)$$

Introducing the above expansion in Eq. (44) results

$$J^T J \Delta\vec{P} = -J^T \vec{F}\left(\vec{P}\right) \quad (46)$$

In the Levenberg-Marquardt method a damping factor γ^n is added to the diagonal of matrix $\mathbf{J}^T\mathbf{J}$ in order to help to achieve convergence.
Equation (46) is written in a more convenient form to be used in the iterative procedure,

$$\Delta\mathbf{P}^n = -\left[(\mathbf{J}^n)^T\mathbf{J}^n + \gamma^n\mathbf{I}\right]^{-1}(\mathbf{J}^n)^T\mathbf{F}(\mathbf{P}^n) \quad (47)$$

where $\mathbf{I}$ is the identity matrix and n is the iteration index.
The iterative procedure starts with an estimate for the unknown parameters, $\mathbf{P}^0$, being new estimates obtained with $\mathbf{P}^{n+1} = \mathbf{P}^n + \Delta\mathbf{P}^n$, while the corrections $\Delta\mathbf{P}^n$ are calculated with Eq. (46). This iterative procedure is continued until a convergence criterion such as

$$\left|\Delta P_k^n / P_k^n\right| < \varepsilon, \qquad n = 1,\ 2,\ \cdots,\ N_p \quad (48)$$

is satisfied, where ε is a small number, e.g. 10^{-5}.
The elements of the Jacobian matrix, as well as the right side term of Eq. (47), are calculated at each iteration, using the solution of the problem with the estimates for the unknowns obtained in the previous iteration.

4.4 Artificial Neural Network (ANN)

The multi-layer perceptron (MLP) is a collection of connected processing elements called nodes or neurons, arranged in layers (Haykin, 1999). Signals pass into the input layer nodes, progress forward through the network hidden layers and finally emerge from the output layer (see Fig. 5). Each node i is connected to each node j in its preceding layer through a connection of weight, w_{ij}, and similarly to nodes in the following layer.

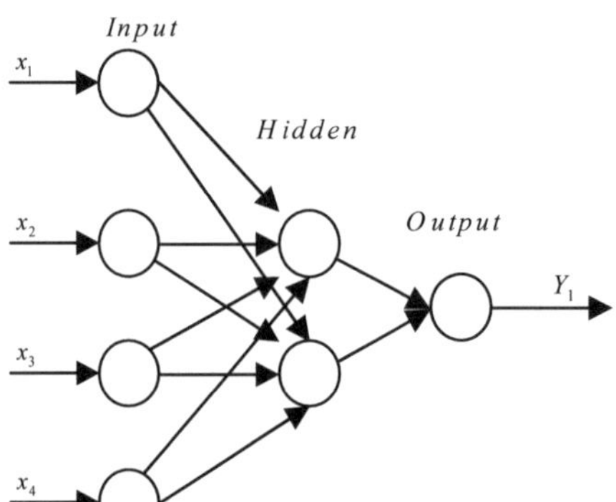

Fig. 5. Multi-layer perceptron network.

A weighted sum is performed at i of all the signals x_j from the preceding layer, yielding the excitation of the node; this is then passed through a nonlinear activation function, f, to emerge as the output of the node x_i to the next layer, as shown by the equation

$$y_i = f\left(\sum_j w_{ij}x_j\right) \tag{49}$$

Various choices for the function f are possible. Here the hyperbolic tangent function $f(x) = \tanh(x)$ is used.
The first stage of using an ANN to model an input-output system is to establish the appropriate values for the connection weights w_{ij}. This is the "training" or learning phase. Training is accomplished using a set of network inputs for which the desired outputs are known. These are the so called patterns, which are used in the training stage of the ANN. At each training step, a set of inputs are passed forward through the network yielding trial outputs which are then compared to the desired outputs. If the comparison error is considered small enough, the weights are not adjusted. Otherwise the error is passed backwards through the net and a training algorithm uses the error to adjust the connection weights. This is the back-propagation algorithm.

Once the comparison error is reduced to an acceptable level over the whole training set, the training phase ends and the network is established. The parameters of a model (output) may be determined using the real experimental data, which are inputs of the established neural network. This is the generalization stage in the use of the ANN. More details can be found in (Soeiro et al., 2004).

4.5 Differential Evolution

The Differential Evolution (DE) is a structural algorithm proposed by Storn and Price (1995) for optimization problems. This approach is an improved version of the Goldberg's Genetic Algorithm (GA) (Goldberg, 1989) for faster optimization and presented the following advantages: simple structure, easiness of use, speed and robustness (Storn and Price, 1995).
Basically, DE generates trial parameter vectors by adding the weighted difference between two population vectors to a third vector. The key parameters of control in DE are the following: *N*, the population size, *CR*, the crossover constant and, *D*, the weight applied to random differential (scaling factor). Storn and Price (1995) have given some simple rules for choosing key parameters of DE for any given application. Normally, *N* should be about 5 to 10 times the dimension (number of parameters in a vector) of the problem. As for *D*, it lies in the range 0.4 to 1.0. Initially, $D = 0.5$ can be tried, and then *D* and/or *N* is increased if the population converges prematurely.
DE has been successfully applied to various fields such as digital filter design (Storn, 1995), batch fermentation process (Chiou and Wang, 1999), estimation of heat transfer parameters in a bed reactor (Babu and Sastry, 1999), synthesis and optimization of heat integrated distillation system (Babu and Singh, 2000), optimization of an alkylation reaction (Babu and Gaurav, 2000), parameter estimation in fed-batch fermentation process (Wang et al., 2001), optimization of thermal cracker operation (Babu and Angira, 2001), engineering system design (Lobato and Steffen, 2007), economic dispatch optimization (Coelho and Mariani, 2007), identification of experimental data (Maciejewski et al., 2007), apparent thermal diffusivity estimation during the drying of fruits (Mariani et al., 2008), estimation of the parameters of Page's equation and heat loss coefficient by using experimental data from a realistic rotary dryer (Lobato et al., 2008), solution of inverse radiative transfer problems (Lobato et al., 2009, 2010), and other applications (Storn et al., 2005).

4.6 Combination of ANN, LM and SA Optimizers

Due to the complexity of the design space, if convergence is achieved with a gradient based method it may in fact lead to a local minimum. Therefore, global optimization methods are required in order to reach better approximations for the global minimum. The main disadvantage of these methods is that the number of function evaluations is high, becoming sometimes prohibitive from the computational point of view (Soeiro et al., 2004).
In this chapter, different combinations of methods are used for the solution of inverse heat and mass transfer problems, involving in all cases Simulated Annealing as the global optimizer:

a) when solving radiative inverse problems, it was used a combination of the LM and SA;
b) when solving adsorption and drying inverse problems, it was used a combination of ANN, LM and SA.

Therefore, in all cases it was run the LM, reaching within a few iterations a point of minimum. After that we run the SA. If the same solution is reached, it is likely that a global

minimum was reached, and the iterative procedure is interrupted. If a different solution is obtained it means that the previous one was a local minimum, otherwise we could run again the LM and SA until the global minimum is reached.
When using the ANN method, after the training stage one is able to quickly obtain an inverse problem solution. This solution may be used as an initial guess for the LM. Trying to keep the best features of each method, we have combined the ANN, LM and SA methods.

5. Test Case Results

5.1 Radiative Transfer

5.1.1 Estimation of $\{\tau_0, \omega, \rho_1, \rho_2\}$ using LM-SA combination

The combined LM-SA approach was applied to several test problems. Since there were no real experimental data available, they were simulated by solving the direct problem and considering the output as experimental data. These results may be corrupted by random multipliers representing a white noise in the measuring equipment. In this effort, since we are developing the approach and trying to compare the performance of the optimization techniques involved, the output was considered as experimental result without any change.
The direct problem is solved with a known vector $\{\tau_0, \omega, \rho_1, \rho_2\}$, which will be considered as the exact solution for the inverse problem. The correspondent output is recorded as experimental data. Now we begin the inverse problem with an initial estimate for the above quantities, obviously away from the exact solution. The described approach is, then, used to find the exact solution.
In a first example the exact solution vector was assumed as {1.0,0.5,0.95,0.5} and the initial estimate as {0.1,0.1,0.1,0.1}. Using both methods the exact solution was obtained. The difference was the computational effort required as shown in Table 1.

Method	Iterations/Cycles	Number of function evaluations	Final value of the objective function
LM	8 iterations	40	2.265E-13
SA	90 cycles	36000	2.828E-13

Table 1. Comparison LM – SA for the first example.

In a second example the exact solution was assumed as {1.0,0.5,0.1,0.95} and the starting point was {5.0,0.95,0.95,0.1}. In this case the LM did not converge to the right answer. The results are presented in Table 2.

Iteration	τ_0	ω	ρ_1	ρ_2	Obj. Function
0	5.0	0.95	0.95	0.1	10.0369
1	5.7856	9.63E-1	6.60E-2	1.00E-4	1.7664
:	:	:	:	:	:
20	9.2521	1.0064	1.00E-4	1.00E-4	2.4646
Exact Solution	1.0	0.5	0.1	0.95	0.0

Table 2. Results for Z_{exact} = {1.0,0.5,0.1,0.95} and Z_o = {5.0,0.95,0.95,0.1} using LM.

The difficulty encountered by LM in converging to the right solution was due to a large plateau that exists in the design space for values of τ_o between 6.0 and 10.0. In this interval the objective function has a very small variation. The SA solved the problem with the same performance as in the first example. The combination of both methods was then applied.
SA was let running for only one cycle (400 function evaluations). At this point, the current optimum was {0.94,0.43,0.61,0.87}, far from the plateau mentioned above. With this initial estimate, LM converged to the right solution very quickly in four iterations, as shown in Table 3.

Iteration	τ_o	ω	ρ_1	ρ_2	Obj. Function [Eq. (39a)]
0	0.94	0.43	0.61	0.87	1.365E-2
1	1.002	0.483	0.284	0.945	5.535E-5
:	:	:	:	:	:
4	0.999	0.500	0.100	0.9500	9.23E-13
Exact Sol.	1.0	0.5	0.1	0.95	0.0

Table 3. Results for Z_{exact} = {1.0,0.5,0.1,0.95} and Z_o = {5.0,0.95,0.95,0.1} using LM after one cycle of SA.

5.1.2 Estimation of { ω , τ_0 , A_1 , A_2 } using SA and DE

In order to evaluate the performance of the methods of Simulated Annealing and Differential Evolution for the simultaneous estimation of both the single scattering albedo, ω, and the optical thickness, τ_0, of the medium, and also the intensities A_1 and A_2 of the external sources at $\tau = 0$ and $\tau = \tau_0$, respectively, of a given one-dimensional plane-parallel participating medium, the four test cases listed in Table 4 have been performed (Lobato et al., 2010).

Parameter	Meaning	Problem			
		1	2	3	4
ω	Single scattering albedo	0.1	0.1	0.9	0.9
τ_0	Optical thickness of the layer	0.5	5.0	0.5	5.0
A_1	Intensity of external source at $\tau = 0$	1.0	1.0	1.0	1.0
A_2	Intensity of external source at $\tau = \tau_0$	0.0	0.0	0.0	0.0
n	Number of experimental data points	20	20	20	20

Table 4. Parameters used to define the illustrative examples.

It should be emphasized that 20 points were used for the approximation of the variable μ, and 10 collocation points were taken into account to solve the direct problem. All test cases were solved by using a microcomputer PENTIUM IV with 3.2 GHz and 2 GB of RAM. Both the algorithms were executed 10 times for obtaining the values presented in the Tables (6-9).

The parameters used in the two algorithms are presented in Table 5.

Parameter		SA	DE	
Iteration number	N_{gen}	100	100	
Population size	N	-	10	
Crossover probability	CR	-	0.8	
Perturbation rate	D	-	0.8	
Strategy	-	-	DE/rand/1/bin	
Temperature number for each temperature	N_{temp}	50	-	
Temp. initial/final	T_i/T_f	0.5/0.01	-	
Initial Estimate	Case 1	[0.25 0.25 0.5 0.5]	Randomly generated	$0 \leq w, \tau_0 \leq 1$; $1 \leq A_1 \leq 1.5$; $0 \leq A_2 \leq 1$
	Case 2	[0.25 0.45 0.5 0.5]		$0 \leq w, A_2 \leq 1$; $3 \leq \tau_0 \leq 5$; $1 \leq A_1 \leq 1.5$
	Case 3	[0.75 0.25 0.5 0.5]		$0 \leq w \leq 1.0$; $0 \leq \tau_0, A_2 \leq 1$; $1 \leq A_1 \leq 1.5$
	Case 4	[0.75 0.45 0.5 0.5]		$0 \leq w \leq 1.0$; $3 \leq \tau_0 \leq 5$; $1 \leq A_1 \leq 1.5$; $0 \leq A_2 \leq 1$

Table 5. Parameters used to define the illustrative examples.

			ω	τ_0	A_1	A_2	Objective Function [Eq. (39a)]
Exact	*Error in experimental data*		0.1	0.5	1.0	0.0	-
DE*	0.0	*Worst*	0.1003	0.5002	1.0000	0.0001	1.5578×10^{-6}
		Average	0.0998	0.4999	0.9999	0.0000	5.7702×10^{-7}
		Best	**0.1000**	**0.4999**	**0.9999**	**0.0000**	**4.4564×10^{-9}**
	0.5%	*Worst*	0.1015	0.4991	0.9980	0.0012	8.4403×10^{-4}
		Average	0.1007	0.4985	0.9976	0.0010	8.4244×10^{-4}
		Best	**0.1006**	**0.4983**	**0.9974**	**0.0011**	**8.4144×10^{-4}**
	5.0%	*Worst*	0.0876	0.5018	0.9992	0.0058	0.0842
		Average	0.0876	0.5018	0.9992	0.0058	0.0842
		Best	**0.0870**	**0.5017**	**0.9990**	**0.0057**	**0.0842**
SA**	0.0	*Worst*	0.0994	0.4999	1.0001	0.0000	5.3920×10^{-7}
		Average	0.0996	0.4998	0.9999	0.0000	3.4741×10^{-7}
		Best	**0.0999**	**0.4999**	**0.9999**	**0.0000**	**2.1496×10^{-7}**
	0.5%	*Worst*	0.0944	0.4917	0.9922	0.0001	9.6060×10^{-4}
		Average	0.0962	0.4959	0.9970	0.0000	8.5299×10^{-4}
		Best	**0.0984**	**0.4976**	**0.9974**	**0.0000**	**8.4058×10^{-4}**
	5.0%	*Worst*	0.0885	0.5012	0.9991	0.0059	0.0849
		Average	0.0880	0.5010	0.9990	0.0059	0.0844
		Best	**0.0879**	**0.5010**	**0.9989**	**0.0056**	**0.0842**

* *NF*=1010, *cputime*=4.1815 min and ** *NF*=7015, *cputime*=30.2145 min.

Table 6. Results obtained for case 1.

			ω	τ_0	A_1	A_2	Objective Function [Eq. (39a)]
Exact	*Error in experimental data*		0.1	5.0	1.0	0.0	-
DE*	0.0	*Worst*	0.1024	4.9982	0.9988	0.0013	6.3559x10^{-6}
		Average	0.1004	4.9976	0.9992	0.0000	2.6107x10^{-6}
		Best	**0.0998**	**5.0036**	**1.0008**	**0.0000**	**1.1856x10^{-7}**
	0.5%	*Worst*	0.0978	4.9438	0.9844	0.0007	8.0356x10^{-4}
		Average	0.0984	4.9470	0.9847	0.0008	8.0333x10^{-4}
		Best	**0.0983**	**4.9494**	**0.9850**	**0.0010**	**8.0310x10^{-4}**
	5.0%	*Worst*	0.0453	4.9678	0.9683	0.0000	0.0878
		Average	0.0454	4.9675	0.9682	0.0000	0.0878
		Best	**0.0455**	**4.9674**	**0.9680**	**0.0000**	**0.0878**
SA**	0.0	*Worst*	0.0997	5.0097	1.0026	0.0004	8.6468x10^{-7}
		Average	0.0998	4.9981	0.9995	0.0003	7.7231x10^{-7}
		Best	**0.0994**	**4.9956**	**0.9988**	**0.0005**	**7.1664x10^{-7}**
	0.5%	*Worst*	0.0929	4.9487	0.9789	0.0009	9.4786x10^{-3}
		Average	0.0971	4.9256	0.9848	0.0005	8.0999x10^{-3}
		Best	**0.0987**	**4.9390**	**0.9841**	**0.0004**	**8.0645x10^{-4}**
	5.0%	*Worst*	0.0483	4.9578	0.9689	0.0001	0.0892
		Average	0.0484	4.9575	0.9685	0.0001	0.0890
		Best	**0.0485**	**4.9554**	**0.9680**	**0.0001**	**0.0888**

* *NF*=1010, *cputime*=21.4578 min and ** *NF*=8478, *cputime*=62.1478 min.
Table 7. Results obtained for case 2.

			ω	τ_0	A_1	A_2	Objective Function [Eq. (39a)]
Exact	*Error in experimental data*		0.9	0.5	1.0	0.0	-
DE*	0.0	*Worst*	0.8998	0.5001	1.0000	0.0000	4.0332x10^{-9}
		Average	0.8999	0.5000	1.0000	0.0000	2.1772x10^{-9}
		Best	**0.9000**	**0.5000**	**1.0000**	**0.0000**	**2.0152x10^{-9}**
	0.5%	*Worst*	0.9028	0.4978	0.9979	0.0001	8.9999x10^{-3}
		Average	0.9020	0.4980	0.9984	0.0000	8.8788x10^{-4}
		Best	**0.9018**	**0.4988**	**0.9994**	**0.0000**	**8.6296x10^{-4}**
	5.0%	*Worst*	0.9020	0.4700	0.9864	0.0000	0.0776
		Average	0.9022	0.4790	0.9870	0.0000	0.0746
		Best	**0.9032**	**0.4807**	**0.9871**	**0.0000**	**0.0736**
SA**	0.0	*Worst*	0.8998	0.5000	1.0000	0.0001	8.3002x10^{-8}
		Average	0.8998	0.5000	1.0000	0.0000	4.7782x10^{-8}
		Best	**0.8999**	**0.5000**	**1.0000**	**0.0000**	**2.0152x10^{-8}**
	0.5%	*Worst*	0.9039	0.4981	0.9981	0.0000	8.7988x10^{-4}
		Average	0.9025	0.4980	0.9986	0.0000	8.7744x10^{-4}
		Best	**0.9021**	**0.4990**	**0.9994**	**0.0000**	**8.7014x10^{-4}**
	5.0%	*Worst*	0.9049	0.4790	0.9859	0.0000	0.0760
		Average	0.9024	0.4792	0.9860	0.0000	0.0756
		Best	**0.9030**	**0.4800**	**0.9864**	**0.0000**	**0.0738**

* *NF*=1010, *cputime*=3.8788 min and ** *NF*=8758, *cputime*=27.9884 min.
Table 8. Results obtained for case 3.

			ω	τ_0	A_1	A_2	Objective Function [Eq.(39)]
Exact	*Error in experimental data*		0.9	5.0	1.0	0.0	-
DE*	0.0	*Worst*	0.9000	5.0002	0.9996	0.0000	2.8555×10^{-8}
		Average	0.9000	5.0001	0.9999	0.0000	2.6683×10^{-8}
		Best	**0.9000**	**5.0000**	**0.9999**	**0.0000**	**2.6203×10^{-8}**
	0.5%	*Worst*	0.8985	5.0043	1.0040	0.0008	7.8547×10^{-4}
		Average	0.8990	5.0030	1.0038	0.0009	7.5553×10^{-4}
		Best	**0.8993**	**5.0023**	**1.0028**	**0.0009**	**7.4263×10^{-4}**
	5.0%	*Worst*	0.8999	5.0599	1.0118	0.0001	0.0844
		Average	0.8992	5.0592	1.0117	0.0000	0.0824
		Best	**0.8979**	**5.0562**	**1.0107**	**0.0000**	**0.0804**
SA**	0.0	*Worst*	0.9001	5.0003	0.9998	0.0000	3.7788×10^{-8}
		Average	0.9000	5.0002	0.9999	0.0000	$2.9988. \times 10^{-8}$
		Best	**0.9000**	**5.0000**	**0.9999**	**0.0000**	**2.7245×10^{-8}**
	0.5%	*Worst*	0.8988	5.0034	1.0040	0.0009	7.9877×10^{-4}
		Average	0.8989	5.0033	1.0040	0.0009	7.7747×10^{-4}
		Best	**0.8990**	**5.0033**	**1.0041**	**0.0009**	**7.5245×10^{-4}**
	5.0%	*Worst*	0.8999	5.0692	1.0090	0.0001	0.0855
		Average	0.8994	5.0691	1.0189	0.0001	0.0834
		Best	**0.8981**	**5.0566**	**1.0179**	**0.0001**	**0.0811**

* *NF*=1010, *cputime*= 16.3987 min and ** *NF*=8588, *cputime*= 58.9858 min.

Table 9. Results obtained for case 4.

The comparisons between the two algorithms are done according to the perspective of both the number of function evaluations (*NF*) and the running time (*cputime*) given in minutes.

The present case studies used synthetic experimental data considering 20 control elements to discretize μ and 20 control elements for τ, resulting in 400 synthetic experimental points, that is, 40 (2 x 20) representing points along the boundaries and 360 (18 x 20) inside the domain.

In Table 6 the results obtained for case 1 are presented. It can be observed that when using noiseless data both algorithms presented good estimates for the unknown parameters. However, if noise is increased, it can be observed that the optimal values of the parameters demonstrate that the estimates are poorer. The same behavior was observed for test cases 2-4 whose results are presented in Tables 7-9, respectively. However, the results obtained can be considered satisfactory.

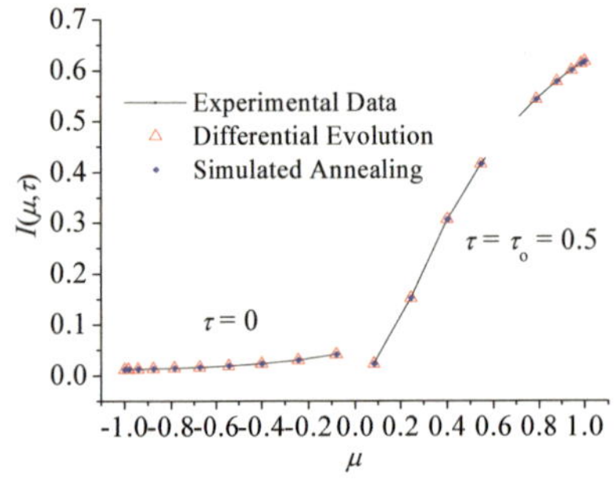

(a)

Case 1: ω=0.1, τ_o=0.5, A_1=1 and A_2=0.

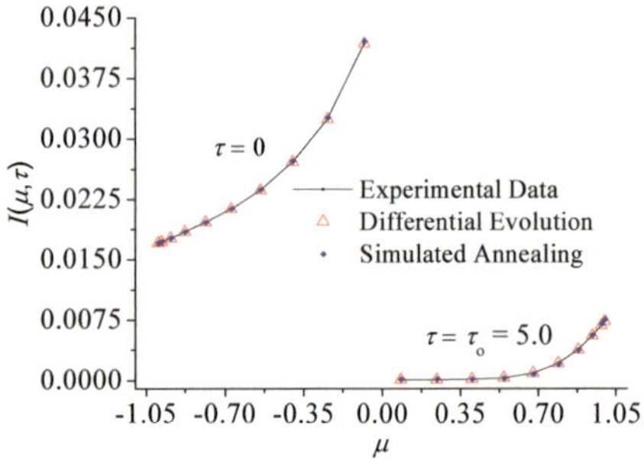

(b)

Case 2: ω=0.1, τ_o=5.0, A_1=1 and A_2=0.

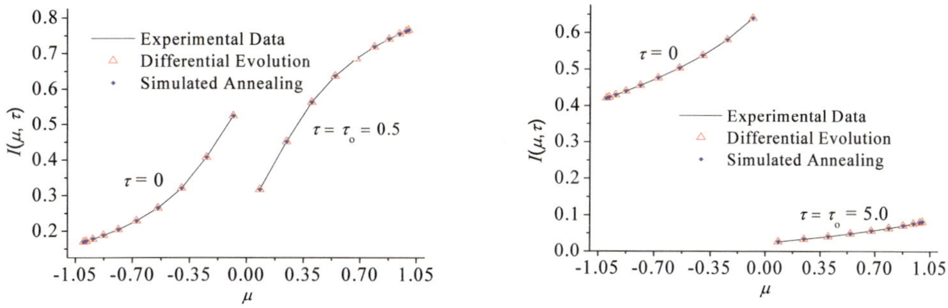

(c) Case 3: ω=0.9, τ_o=0.5, A_1=1 and A_2=0. (d) Case 4: ω=0.9, τ_o=5.0, A_1=1 and A_2=0.

Fig. 6. Radiance generated by using DE and SA - without noise.

Figure 6 illustrates the results presented in Tables 6 to 9 obtained for the radiation intensities using the estimates for the radiative properties, which are now shown on a graphical form for the case without noise in the experimental data.

5.2 Drying (Simultaneous Heat and Mass Transfer)

Much research effort has already been made in order to estimate the Possnov, Kossovitch, heat Biot and mass Biot numbers (Dantas et al., 2003; Huang and Yeh, 2002; Lugon and Silva Neto, 2004), but it was only considered the possibility of optimizing the number and location of temperature sensors, experiment duration, etc. In this work instead, δ, r/c, h/k and h_m/k_m are estimated using an "optimum" experiment (Dowding et al., 1999 and Beck, 1988) for wood drying, and doing so, it was considered also the following process control parameters: heat flux, Q, the medium width, l, the difference between the medium and the air temperatures, $dT = T_s - T_0$, and the difference between the moisture potential between the medium and the air, $du = u_0 - u^*$.

There is no difference between the sensitivity coefficients for the two sets of variable, that is, the scaled sensitivity coefficients are exactly the same for both vectors $\{Lu, Pn, Ko, Bi_q, Bi_m, \varepsilon\}^T$ and $\{Lu, \delta, r/c, h/k, h_m/k_m, \varepsilon\}^T$,

$$SC_{\delta}(X,\tau) = \delta \frac{\partial V(X,\tau)}{\partial \delta} = Pn \frac{\partial V(X,\tau)}{\partial Pn} = SC_{Pn}(X,\tau) \tag{50}$$

$$SC_{r/c}(X,\tau) = r/c \frac{\partial V(X,\tau)}{\partial r/c} = Ko \frac{\partial V(X,\tau)}{\partial Ko} = SC_{Ko}(X,\tau) \tag{51}$$

$$SC_{h/k}(X,\tau) = h/k \frac{\partial V(X,\tau)}{\partial h/k} = Bi_q \frac{\partial V(X,\tau)}{\partial Bi_q} = SC_{Bi_q}(X,\tau) \tag{52}$$

$$SC_{h_m/k_m}(X,\tau) = h_m/k_m \frac{\partial V(X,\tau)}{\partial h_m/k_m} = Bi_m \frac{\partial V(X,\tau)}{\partial Bi_m} = SC_{Bi_m}(X,\tau) \tag{53}$$

The reasons for changing the estimated variables are the use of the design of experiment tools and interpretation. Consider the heat and mass Biot numbers for example. If one changes the media width, l, both heat and mass Biot numbers changes. The mathematical problem would be different, even though the material is still the same, because one is estimating two different heat and mass Biot numbers. In order to solve this problem, it was decided to estimate the relation between heat transfer coefficient and thermal conductivity, h/k, and the relation between mass transfer coefficient and mass conductivity, h_m/k_m, so that we could change the media width and continue with the same value for both variables to be estimated.

The same idea was used, choosing to estimate the thermogradient coefficient (δ) and the relation between latent heat of evaporation and specific heat of the medium (r/c), instead of the Possnov (Pn) and Kossovitch (Ko) numbers. Doing so, one is able to optimize the experiment considering the difference between the medium and the air temperatures, $dT = T_s - T_0$, and the difference between the moisture-transfer potential between the media and the air, $du = u_0 - u^*$, without affecting the estimated parameters values.

In Fig. 7 it is represented the variation of the value of the matrix $\mathbf{SC}^T\mathbf{SC}$ determinant as a function of the temperature differences and moisture potential differences between the medium and the air flowing over it. It is not difficult to understand that one could not build such a graph using a vector of unknown parameters containing Possnov (Pn) and Kossovitch (Ko) numbers. In order to achieve greater sensitivities, while the temperature difference has to be the lowest, the moisture potential difference has to be the highest possible. The solid square represents the chosen designed experiment, considering the existence of practical difficulties that may limit our freedom of choice.

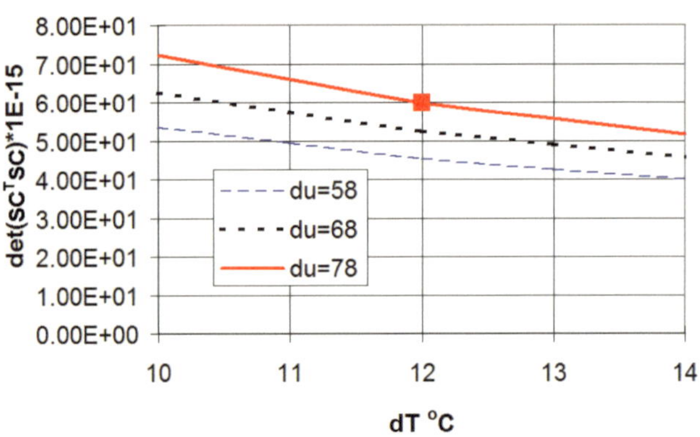

Fig. 7. Determinant of matrix Y^TY as a function of temperature (dT) and moisture potential ($d\bar{u}$) differences.

In Fig. 8 it is represented the values of the determinant of matrix $\mathbf{SC}^T\mathbf{SC}$ for different values of the heat flux Q and media thickness l. It is also easy to understand that one could not build such a graph using a vector of unknown parameters containing heat and mass Biot numbers. For practical reasons it was chosen to limit the sample temperature to 130° C. In Fig. 8 the same curve has a continuous-line part and a dashed-line one, when the sample temperature exceeds the limit of 130° C. The solid square shows the chosen designed experiment.

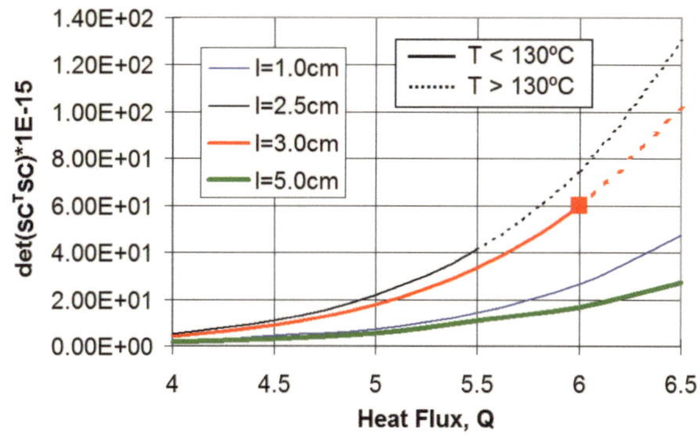

Fig. 8. Determinant of $\mathbf{SC}^T\mathbf{SC}$ matrix for different values of the heat flux Q and medium thickness l.

Considering the previous analysis of the sensitivity graphs and matrix $\mathbf{SC}^T\mathbf{SC}$ determinant, it was designed the experiment whose geometric and process parameters are shown in Table 10. Since the average moisture potential, $\bar{u}$, is more difficult to measure than temperature, θ_1, the measurement interval for the average moisture potential, $\Delta\tau_{\bar{u}}$, was considered larger than the interval for the temperature $\Delta\tau_{\theta_1}$.

Geometric or process parameter	Values	Geometric or process parameter	Values
$dT = T_s - T_0$	12 ºC	Q	6.0
T_0	24 ºC	l	0.03 m
T_s	36 ºC	τ_0	0
$du = u_0 - u^*$	78 ºM	τ_f	20
u_0	86 ºM	$\Delta\tau_{\theta_1}$	0.2
u^*	8 ºM	$\Delta\tau_{\bar{u}}$	1
ε	0.2		

τ_0 and τ_f represent the initial and sampling times, respectively.

Table 10. Reference values for the designed experiment.

An experiment was designed to perform the simultaneous estimation of Lu, δ, r/c, h/k and h_m/k_m. In order to study the proposed method, since real experiment data were not available, we generated synthetic data using

$$\theta_{1meas_i} = \theta_{1calc_i}(\mathbf{P}_{exact}) + \sigma_{\theta_1} r_i, \quad i = 1, 2, ..., M_{\theta_1} \tag{54a}$$

$$\bar{u}_{meas_i} = \bar{u}_{meas_i}(\mathbf{P}_{exact}) + \sigma_{\bar{u}} r_i, \quad i = 1, 2, ..., M_{\bar{u}} \tag{54b}$$

where r_i are random numbers in the range [-1,1], M_{θ_1} and $M_{\bar{u}}$ represent the total number of temperature and moisture-transfer potential experimental data, and σ_{θ_1} and $\sigma_{\bar{u}}$ emulates the standard deviation of measurement errors. It was established a standard deviation of

$\sigma_{\theta_1} = 0.03$ considering 100 temperature measurements ($\Delta\tau = 0.2$), resulting in a maximum error of 2%, and $\sigma_{\bar{u}} = 0.001$ considering 20 moisture measurements ($\Delta\tau = 1.0$), resulting in a maximum error of 4%.

In Fig. 9 the graphics of temperature (θ_1) and moisture potential ($\bar{\theta}_2$) measurements are presented. The continuous line represents the direct problem solution and the squares represent noisy data. In order to show a better representation, only 20 temperature (θ_1) measurements were represented.

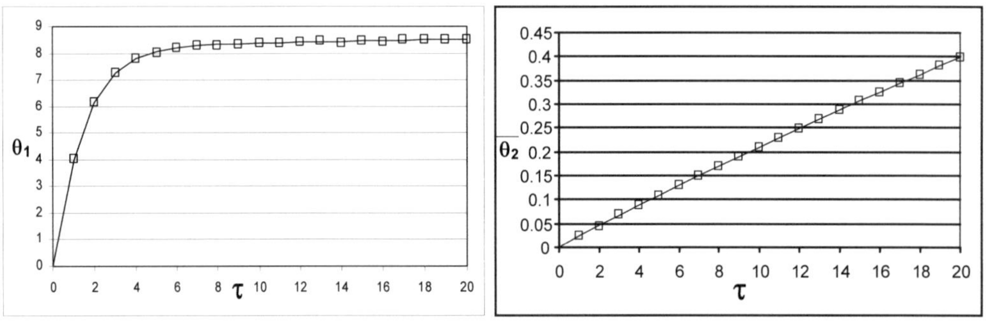

Fig. 9. Temperature (θ_1) and moisture potential ($\bar{\theta}_2$) artificially simulated data.

The results obtained using the methods LM 1 (gradient approximated by FDM - Finite Difference Method), LM 2 (gradient approximated by ANN - Artificial Neural Network), ANN, SA and hybrid combinations, for different levels of noise represented by different values of the standard deviation of measurements errors in temperature and average moisture potential, σ_T and $\sigma_{\bar{u}}$, respectively in Eqs. (54a,b) are shown in Table 11.

Case	Method	σ_{θ_1}	$\sigma_{\bar{u}}$	Information	Lu	δ	r/c	h/k	h_m/k_m	Time (s)	S Eq. (39a)
-	-	-	-	Exact values	0.0080	2.0	10.83	34.0	114.0	-	-
1	LM 1 (grad. FDM)	0	0	Initial guess	0.0040	1.50	8.00	20.0	80.0	15	0
				Result $\vec{Z}_{LM^{FDM}}$	0.0080	2.00	10.83	34.0	114.0		
2	LM 2 (grad. ANN)	0	0	Initial guess	0.0040	1.50	8.00	25.0	80.0	10	0
				Result $\vec{Z}_{LM^{ANN}}$	0.0080	2.00	10.83	34.0	114.0		
3	LM 1 (grad. FDM)	0.03	0.001	Initial guess	0.0040	1.50	8.00	20.0	80.0	15	977
				Result $\vec{Z}_{LM^{FDM}}$	0.0076	2.09	10.76	34.1	121.2		
4	LM 2 (grad. ANN)	0.03	0.001	Initial guess	0.0040	1.50	8.00	20.0	80.0	11	897
				Result $\vec{Z}_{LM^{ANN}}$	0.0093	1.71	10.73	34.1	95.7		

5	ANN (without initial guess)	0.03	0.001	Result $\vec{Z}_{ANN}$	0.0083	2.10	10.04	35.0	117.1	1	3190
6	LM 1 (grad. FDM)	0.03	0.001	Initial guess $\vec{Z}_{ANN}$	0.0083	2.10	10.04	35.0	117.1	16	974
				Result $\vec{Z}_{LM^{FDM}}$	0.0083	1.92	10.75	34.1	110.0		
7	LM 2 (grad. ANN)	0.03	0.001	Initial guess $\vec{Z}_{ANN}$	0.0083	2.10	10.04	35.0	117.1	11	903
				Result $\vec{Z}_{LM^{ANN}}$	0.0082	1.79	9.89	35.1	114.5		
8	SA (SA 20,000 evaluations)	0.03	0.001	Initial guess	0.0040	1.50	8.00	25.0	80.0	300	856
				Result $\vec{Z}_{SA}$	0.0094	1.58	9.96	35.0	98.2		
9	ANN-LM 2-SA (SA 2,000 evaluations)	0.03	0.001	Initial guess $\vec{Z}_{ANN}$	0.0083	2.10	10.04	35.0	117.1	47	760
				Result $\vec{Z}_{LM^{ANN}}$	0.0082	1.79	9.89	35.1	114.5		
				Result $\vec{Z}_{SA}$	0.0079	2.01	11.00	33.9	113.8		
				Result $\vec{Z}_{LM^{ANN}}$	0.0080	2.05	10.93	33.8	113.9		

Table 11. Results obtained using LM 1, LM 2, ANN, and hybrid combinations.

One observes that when there is no noise, that is, the standard deviation of measurements errors are zero, the LM method was able to estimate all variables very quickly (see test cases 1 and 2). When noise is introduced, the LM is retained by local minima (test cases 3 and 4); the ANN did not reach a good solution, but quickly got close to it (test case 5). The ANN solution was then used as a first guess for the LM method with good performance in test cases 6 and 7. The SA reached a good solution but required the largest CPU time, and finally the combination of all methods was able to reach a good solution, without being retained by local minima without taking too much time, i.e. one sixth of the SA time. The time shown in the eleventh column of Table 11 corresponds to the CPU time on a Pentium IV 2.8 GHz processor.

5.3 Gas-liquid Adsorption

Recently, the inverse problem of interface adsorption has attracted the attention of an increasing number of researchers (Lugon, 2005; Forssén et al., 2006; Garnier et al., 2007; Voelkel and Strzemiecka, 2007; Ahmad and Guiochon, 2007).

In order to solve the inverse problem of gas-liquid adsorption considering the two-layer isotherm given by Eq. (32), it was necessary to design two different experiments. One to estimate $K_2(T)$ and $\hat{a}$, called experiment 1, and another one to estimate λ, called experiment 2. In all cases studied the sensitivity to $K_1(T)$ is low and therefore this parameter was not estimated with the inverse problem solution.

In Fig. 10 are shown the sensitivity coefficients related to the parameters $K_1(T)$, $K_2(T)$, λ and $\hat{a}$ in experiment 1. It is observed that the sensitivity to $K_2(T)$ and $\hat{a}$ for BSA (Bovine Serum Albumin) are higher than the sensitivity to the other parameters and their shapes are different.

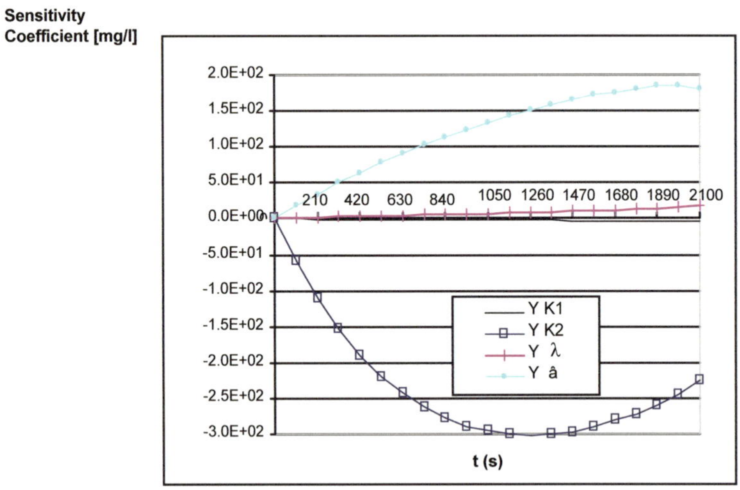

Fig. 10. Scaled sensitivity coefficients for BSA - Experiment 1.

In Fig. 11 are shown the sensitivity coefficients related to the parameters $K_1(T)$, $K_2(T)$, λ and $\hat{a}$ for BSA in experiment 2. It is observed that the sensitivity to λ is higher than the sensitivity to the other parameters.

Another important tool used in the design of experiments is the study of the matrix $\mathbf{SC}^T\mathbf{SC}$, that is, maximizing the determinant of the matrix $\mathbf{SC}^T\mathbf{SC}$ results in higher sensitivity and uncorrelation (Dowding et al., 1999).

The difference between the two experiments is related to the BSA concentration, being larger in the first experiment (see Table 12).

In Fig. 12 are shown the values of the determinant of the matrix $\mathbf{SC}^T\mathbf{SC}$ for BSA in experiment 1. The designed experiment is marked with a full square. Its choice is justified by the small gain in sensitivity considering the operational difficulties in using a longer column or a higher superficial velocity.

Considering the analysis of the sensitivity graphs and the determinant of the matrix $\mathbf{SC}^T\mathbf{SC}$, two experiments were designed, one to estimate $K_2(T)$ and $\hat{a}$, and another to estimate λ, as shown in Table 12.

The results achieved using the ANN, LM 1 (gradient approximated by FDM), LM 2 (gradient approximated by ANN), SA and hybrid combinations, for different standard deviations for the measurements errors, σ, are shown in Tables 13 and 14.

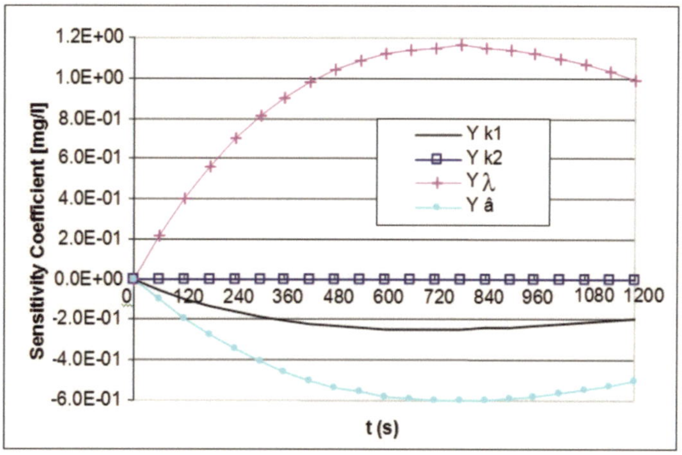

Fig. 11. Scaled sensitivity coefficients for BSA - Experiment 2.

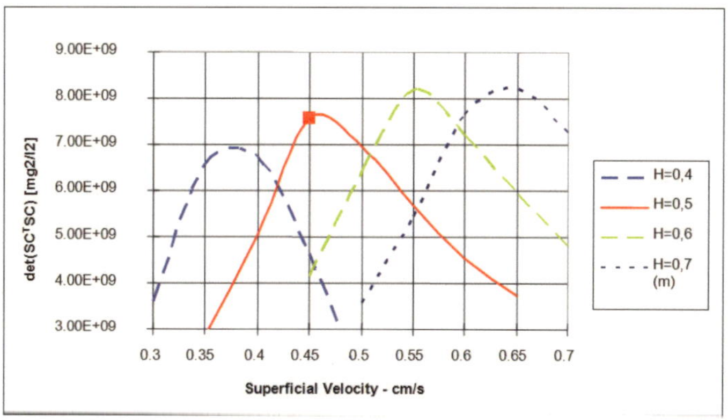

Fig. 12. Matrix $Y^T Y$ determinant for BSA - Experiment 1.

	Units	Experiment 1	Experiment 2
Estimated parameters	-	K_2, $\hat{a}$	λ
Initial solute concentration, C_{b0}	g/m³	1,000	10
Bubble column height, H	m	0.50	0.80
Superficial velocity, v_g	m/s	4.50E-3	1.00E-3
First measurement	s	210	120
time measurement steps	s	210	120
Last measurement	s	2100	1200

Table 12. Reference values for the designed experiment (Lugon 2005, Lugon et al., 2009).

In Table 13 are presented the results obtained for the estimation of $K_2(T)$ and $\hat{a}$, using the designed experiment number 1. Test cases 3-9 used simulated artificial data generated with the direct problem solution corrupted with white gaussian noise with standard deviation $\sigma = 10 mg/l$, which corresponds to measurement errors of the order of 4%. While in test cases numbers 1, 2, 3, 4 and 8 the initial guesses are $K_2 = 0{,}0080\,mg/(m^2\,wt\%)$ and $\hat{a} = 0{,}100\,m^2/mg$, in test cases numbers 6, 7 and 9 the initial guesses are the estimates obtained with the ANN.

Case	Method	σ	Information	k_2	$\hat{a}$	Time (s)	S [mg²/l²] Eq. (39a)
1	LM 1 (grad. FDM)	0	Result $\vec{Z}_{LM^{FDM}}$	0.01040	0.322	169	0
2	LM 2 (grad. ANN)	0	Result $\vec{Z}_{LM^{ANN}}$	0.01040	0.322	80	0
3	LM 1 (grad. FDM)	10	Result $\vec{Z}_{LM^{FDM}}$	0.00790	0.158	170	8.39
4	LM 2 (grad. ANN)	10	Result $\vec{Z}_{LM^{ANN}}$	0.00805	0.157	78	8.64
5	RNA	10	Result $\vec{Z}_{ANN}$	0.01101	0.377	1	6.81
6	LM 1 (grad. FDM)	10	Result $\vec{Z}_{LM^{FDM}}$	0.01080	0.335	172	6.27
7	LM 2 (grad. ANN)	10	Result $\vec{Z}_{LM^{ANN}}$	0.01058	0.314	79	5.68
8	SA (2.000 evaluations)	10	Result $\vec{Z}_{SA}$	0.01050	0.312	6034	4.22
9	ANN-LM-SA SA (200 evaluations)	10	Result $\vec{Z}_{LM^{ANN}}$	0.01101	0.377	682	4.16
			Result $\vec{Z}_{LM^{ANN}}$	0.01058	0.335		
			Result $\vec{Z}_{SA}$	0.01054	0.314		

Table 13. Results obtained using ANN, LM 1, LM 2, SA and hybrid combinations for experiment 1.

In Table 14 are presented the results obtained for the estimation of λ, using the designed experiment number 2.
The exact values used are: $k_2 = 0.0104 mg/(m^2 wt\%)$ and $\hat{a} = 0.322\,m^2/mg$.

Case	Method	σ	Information	λ	Time (s)	S [mg²/l²] Eq. (39a)
1	LM 1 (grad. FDM)	0	Result $\vec{Z}_{LM^{FDM}}$	1.117	40	0
2	LM 2 (grad. ANN)	0	Result $\vec{Z}_{LM^{ANN}}$	1.117	29	0
3	LM 1 (grad. FDM)	0.1	Result $\vec{Z}_{LM^{FDM}}$	1.159	45	7.96
4	LM 2 (grad. ANN)	0.1	Result $\vec{Z}_{LM^{ANN}}$	1.159	30	7.96
5	RNA	0.1	Result $\vec{Z}_{ANN}$	1.432	1	202.9
6	LM 1 (grad. FDM)	0.1	Result $\vec{Z}_{LM^{FDM}}$	1.159	6	7.96
7	LM 2 (grad. ANN)	0.1	Result $\vec{Z}_{LM^{ANN}}$	1.159	4	7.96
8	SA (2.000 evaluations)	0.1	Result $\vec{Z}_{SA}$	1.099	5937	10.12
9	ANN-LM-SA SA (200 evaluations)	0.1	Result $\vec{Z}_{ANN}$	1.432	601	7.92
			Result $\vec{Z}_{LM^{ANN}}$	1.159		
			Result $\vec{Z}_{SA}$	1.156		

The exact value used is: $\lambda = 1.117\,m^2/mg$.

Table 14. Results obtained using ANN, LM 1, LM 2, SA and hybrid combinations for experiment 2.

Test cases 3-9 used simulated artificial data generated with the direct problem solution corrupted with white gaussian noise with standard deviation $\sigma = 0.10 mg/l$, which corresponds to measurement errors of the order of 3%. While in test cases numbers 1, 2, 3, 4 and 8 the initial guess is $\lambda = 0,700 m^2/mg$, in test cases numbers 6, 7 and 9 the initial guesses are the estimates obtained with the ANN.

6. Conclusions

6.1 Radiative Transfer

6.1.1 Estimation of {τ_0, ω, ρ_1, ρ_2} using LM-SA combination

A combination of SA (global optimization method) and LM (local optimization method) was used to solve the inverse radiative transfer problem. It was demonstrated its effectiveness in the solution of this type of problems since one can guarantee the convergence to a good approximation of the global optimum with higher accuracy and less computational effort if it is compared with the application of any global optimization method alone.

6.1.2 Estimation of {ω, τ_0, A_1, A_2} using SA and DE

In the present work, the effectiveness of using Differential Evolution and Simulated Annealing for the estimation of radiative properties through an inverse problem approach was analyzed. In this sense, four benchmark cases were studied and it was possible to conclude that both algorithms led to good results for an acceptable number of generations. It should be pointed out that the Differential Evolution Algorithm led to optimal values that are very similar to those obtained by Simulated Annealing, requiring however a smaller number of objective function evaluations. This result was expected, since for the Simulated Annealing Algorithm, for a given iteration, every "temperature" is submitted to a proper number of internal iterations for refinement purposes making the evolutionary process longer, thus increasing the total processing time. On the other hand, as previously mentioned in the works of Storn and Price (1995), Storn (1999) and Angira and Babu (2005), the number of evaluations of the objective function resulting from the Differential Evolution Algorithm is smaller because the evolution scheme is much simpler.

Another interesting aspect is that by adding noise to the synthetic experimental points result an increase in the objective function values, as observed in Tables 6 to 9. Such a behavior was previously expected since noise does not permit the convergence of the optimization algorithm to the exact values of the parameters. Consequently, the user should be aware of this behavior when using real experimental data, which is always affected by noise.

6.2 Drying (Simultaneous Heat and Mass Transfer)

The direct problem of simultaneous heat and mass transfer in porous media modeled with Luikov equations can be solved using the finite difference method, yielding the temperature and moisture distribution in the media, when the geometry, the initial and boundary conditions, and the medium properties are known.

Inverse problem techniques can be useful to estimate the medium properties when they are not known. After the use of an experiment design technique, the hybrid combination ANN-LM-SA resulted in good estimates for the drying inverse problem using artificially generated data.
The design of experiments technique is of great importance for the success of the estimation efforts, while previous works studied the estimation of Lu, Pn, Ko, Bi_q and Bi_m, in this work it was considered Lu, δ, r/c, h/k and h_m/k_m. The main advantage of such approach is to be able to design an "optimum" experiment using different medium width, l, porous medium and air temperature difference, $T_s - T_0$, and porous medium and air moisture potential difference, $u_0 - u^*$.
The combination of deterministic (LM) and stochastic (ANN and SA) methods achieved good results, reducing the time needed and not being retained by local minima. The use of ANN to obtain the derivatives in the first steps of the LM method reduced the time required for the solution of the inverse problem.

6.3 Gas-liquid Adsorption

After the use of an experiment design technique, the hybrid combination ANN-LM-SA resulted in good solutions for the gas-liquid adsorption isotherm inverse problem.
The use of the ANN to obtain the derivatives in the first step of the LM method reduced the time necessary to solve the inverse problem.

7. References

Ahmad, T. and Guiochon, G, 2007, Numerical determination of the adsorption isotherms of tryptophan at different temperatures and mobile phase composition, J. of Chromatography A, v. 1142, pp. 148-163.

Alifanov, O. M., 1974, Solution of an Inverse Problem of Heat Conduction by Iteration Methods, J. of Engineering Physics, Vol.26, pp.471-476.

Angira, R. and Babu, B. V., 2005, Non-dominated Sorting Differential Evolution (NSDE): An Extension of Differential Evolution for Multi-objective Optimization, In Proceedings of the 2nd Indian International Conference on Artificial Intelligence (IICAI-05).

Artyukhin, E. A, 1982, Recovery of the Temperature Dependence of the Thermal Conductivity Coefficient from the Solution of the Inverse Problem, High Temperature, Vol.19, No.5, pp.698-702.

Babu, B. V. and Angira, R., 2001, Optimization of Thermal Cracker Operation using Differential Evolution, in Proceedings of International Symposium and 54th Annual Session of IIChE (CHEMCON-2001).

Babu, B. V. and Sastry, K. K. N., 1999, Estimation of Heat-transfer Parameters in a Trickle-bed Reactor using Differential Evolution and Orthogonal Collocation, Computers & Chemical Engineering, Vol. 23, pp. 327-339.

Babu, B. V. and Singh, R. P., 2000, Synthesis and Optimization of Heat Integrated Distillation Systems Using Differential Evolution, in Proceedings of All-India seminar on Chemical Engineering Progress on Resource Development: A Vision 2010 and Beyond, IE (I).

Babu, B. V. and Gaurav, C., 2000, Evolutionary Computation Strategy for Optimization of an Alkylation Reaction, in Proceedings of International Symposium and 53rd Annual Session of IIChE (CHEMCON-2000).

Baltes, M., Schneider, R., Sturm, C., and Reuss, M., 1994, Optimal Experimental Design for Parameter Estimation in Unstructured Growth Models, Biotechnology Programming, vol. 10, pp. 480-491.

Becceneri, J. C., Stephany, S., Campos Velho, H. F. and Silva Neto, A. J., 2006, "Solution of the Inverse Problem of Radiative Properties Estimation with the Particle Swarm Optimization Technique", 14th Inverse Problems in Engineering Seminar, Ames, USA.

Beck, J. V., Blackwell, B. and St. Clair Jr., C. R., 1985, Inverse Heat Conduction, Wiley, New York.

Beck, J. V., 1988, Combined Parameter and Function Estimation in Heat Transfer with Application to Contact Conductance, J. Heat Transfer, v. 110, pp. 1046-1058.

Borukhov, V. T. and Kolesnikov, P. M., 1988, Method of Inverse Dynamic Systems and Its Application for Recovering Internal Heat Sources, Int. J. Heat Mass Transfer, Vol.31, No.8, pp.1549-1556.

Carita Montero, R. F., Roberty, N. C. and Silva Neto, A J., 2000, Absorption Coefficient Estimation in Two-Dimensional Participating Media Using a Base Constructed with Divergent Beams, Proc. 34th National Heat Transfer Conference, Pittsburgh, USA.

Carvalho, G. and Silva Neto, A J., 1999, An Inverse Analysis for Polymers Thermal Properties Estimation, Proc. 3rd International Conference on Inverse Problems in Engineering: Theory and practice, Port Ludlow, USA.

Cazzador, L. and Lubenova, V., 1995, Nonlinear Estimation of Specific Growth Rate for Aerobic Fermentation Processes, Biotechnology and Bioengineering, vol. 47, pp. 626-634.

Chalhoub, E. S., Campos Velho, H. F., and Silva Neto, A. J., 2007a, A Comparison of the Onedimensional Radiative Transfer Problem Solutions obtained with the Monte Carlo Method and Three Variations of the Discrete Ordinates Method, Proc. 19th International Congress of Mechanical Engineering - COBEM.

Chalhoub, E. S., Silva Neto, A. J. and Soeiro, F. J. C. P., 2007b, Estimation of Optical Thickness and Single Scattering Albedo with Artificial Neural Networks and a Monte Carlo Method, Inverse Problems, Design and Optimization Symposium, vol. 2, pp. 576-583, Miami.

Chiou, J. P. and Wang, F. S., 1999, Hybrid Method of Evolutionary Algorithms for Static and Dynamic Optimization Problems with Application to a Fed-batch Fermentation Process, Computers & Chemical Engineering, vol. 23, pp. 1277-1291.

Coelho L. S. and Mariani V. C., 2007, Improved Differential Evolution Algorithms for Handling Economic Dispatch Optimization with Generator Constraints, Energy Conversion and Management, 48, 2007, 1631-1639.

Cuco, A. P. C., Silva Neto, A. J., Campos Velho, H. F. and de Sousa, F. L., 2009 Solution of an Inverse Adsorption Problem with an Epidemic Genetic Algorithm and the Generalized Extremal Optimization Algorithm, Inverse Problems in Science and Engineering. Vol. 17, No. 3, pp. 289-302

Dantas, L. B., Orlande, H.R.B. and Cotta, R. M., 2003, An Inverse Problem of Parameter Estimation for Heat and Mass Transfer in Capillary Porous Media, Int. J. Heat Mass Transfer, v. 46, pp. 1587-1598.

Deckwer, W. R. and Schumpe, A., 1993, Improved Tools for Bubble Columns Reactor Design and Scale-up, Chem. Eng. Sc., v.48, No., pp. 889-911.

Denisov, A M. and Solo'Yera, S. I., 1993, The Problem of Determining the Coefficient in the Non-Linear Stationary Heat-Conduction Equation, Comp. Math. Phys., Vol.33, No. 9, pp.1145-1153.

Denisov, A M., 2000, Inverse Problems of Absorption Dynamics, Minisymposium on Inverse Problems In Medicine, Engineering and Geophysics, XXIII Brazilian Congress on Applied and Computational Mathematics Invited Lecture, Santos Brasil.

Dowding, K. J., Blackwell, B. F. and Cochran, R. J., 1999, Applications of Sensitivity Coefficients for Heat Conduction Problems, Numerical Heat Transfer, Part B, v. 36, pp. 33-55.

Forssén, P., Arnell, R. and Fornstedt, T., 2006, An improved algorithm for solving inverse problems in liquid chromatography, Computers and Chemical Engineering, v.30, pp.1381-1391.

Galski, R. L., de Sousa, F. L., Ramos, F. M. and Silva Neto, A. J., 2009. Application of a GEO+SA Hybrid Optimization Algorithm to the Solution of an Inverse Radiative Transfer Problem, Inverse Problems in Science and Engineering. Vol. 17, No. 3, pp. 321-334.

Goldberg, D. E. 1989, "Genetic Algorithms in Search, Optimization, and Machine Learning", MA:Addison-Wesley.

Garnier, C., Görner, T., Villiéras, F., De Donato, Ph., Polakovic, M., Bersillon, J. L. and Michot, L. J., 2007, Activated carbon surface heterogeneity seen by parallel probing by inverse liquid chromatography at the solid/liquid interface and by gas adsorption analysis at the solid/gas interface, Carbon, v. 45, pp. 240-247.

Graham, D. E. and Phillips, M. C., 1979, Proteins at Liquid Interfaces, II. Adsorption Isotherms, J. Colloid and Interface Science, v. 70, No. 3, pp. 415-426.

Hanan, N. P., 2001, "Enhanced Two-layer Radiative Transfer Scheme for a Land Surface Model with a Discontinuous Upper Canopy". Agricultural and Forest Meteorology, vol. 109, pp. 265-281.

Haut, B. and Cartage, T., 2005, Mathematical Modeling of Gas–liquid Mass Transfer Rate in Bubble Columns Operated in the Heterogeneous Regime, Chem. Eng. Science, v. 60, n. 22, pp. 5937-5944.

Haykin, S., 1999, Neural Networks - A Comprehensive Foundation, Prentice Hall.

Ho, C.-H. and Özisik, M. N., 1989, An Inverse Radiation Problem, Int. J. Heat Mass Transfer, Vol.32, No.2, pp.335-341.

Huang, C. H. and Yeh, C. Y., 2002, An Inverse Problem in Simultaneous Estimating the Biot Number of Heat and Moisture Transfer for a Porous Material, Int. J. Heat Mass Transfer, v. 45, pp. 4643-4653.

Kauati, A. T., Silva Neto, A. J. and Roberty, N. C., 1999, A Source-Detector Methodology for the Construction and Solution of the One-Dimensional Inverse Transport Equation, Proc. 3rd International Conference on Inverse Problems in Engineering: Theory and Practice, Port Ludlow, USA.

Kirkpatrick, S., Gellat, Jr., C. D. and Vecchi, M. P., 1983 Optimization by Simulated Annealing, Science, v. 220, pp. 671-680.

Knupp, D. C., Silva Neto, A. J. and Sacco, W. F., 2007, Estimation of Radiative Properties with the Particle Collision Algorithm, Inverse Problems, Design an Optimization Symposium, Miami, Florida, USA, April, 16-18.

Krishna, R. and van Baten, J. M., 2003, Mass Transfer in Bubble Columns, Catalysis Today, v. 79-80, pp. 67-75.

Lobato, F. S. and Steffen Jr., V., 2007, Engineering System Design with Multi-Objective Differential Evolution, In Proceedings in 19th International Congress of Mechanical Engineering - COBEM.

Lobato, F. S., Steffen Jr., V., Arruda, E. B. and Barrozo, M. A. S., 2008, Estimation of Drying Parameters in Rotary Dryers using Differential Evolution, Journal of Physics: Conference Series, Vol. 135, doi:10.1088/1742-6596/135/1/012063.

Lobato, F. S., Steffen Jr. V. and Silva Neto, A. J, 2009, Solution of Inverse Radiative Transfer Problems in Two-Layer Participating Media with Differential Evolution, Inverse Problems in Science and Engineering, Vol.115, p. 1054-1064, 2009, doi: 10.1080/17415970903062054.

Lobato, F. S., Steffen Jr., V. and Silva Neto, A. J., 2010, A Comparative Study of the Application of Differential Evolution and Simulated Annealing in Inverse Radiative Transfer Problems, Journal of the Brazilian Society of Mechanical Sciences and Engineering, Accepted for publication.

Lugon Jr., J. and Silva Neto, A. J., 2004, Deterministic, Stochastic and Hybrid Solutions for Inverse Problems in Simultaneous Heat and Mass Transfer in Porous Media, Proc. 13th Inverse Problems in Engineering Seminar, pp. 99-106, Cincinatti, USA.

Lugon Jr., J., 2005, Gas-liquid Interface Adsorption and One-dimensional Porous Media Drying Inverse Problems Solution, D.Sc Thesis, Universidade do Estado do Rio de Janeiro (in Portuguese).

Lugon Jr., J, Silva Neto, A. J. and Santana, C. C., 2009, A Hybrid Approach with Artificial Neural Networks, Levenberg-Marquardt and Simulated Annealing Methods for the Solution of Gas-Liquid Adsorption Inverse Problems, Inverse Problems in Science and Engineering, Vol. 17, No. 1, pp.85-96.

Lugon Jr., J and Silva Neto, A. J., 2010, Solution of Porous Media Inverse Drying Problems Using a Combination of Stochastic and Deterministic Methods, Journal of the Brazilian Society of Mechanical Sciences and Engineering, Accepted for publication.

Luikov, A. V. and Mikhailov, Y. A., 1965, Theory of Energy and Mass Transfer, Pergamon Press, Oxford, England.

Maciejewski L., Myszka W. and Zietek G., 2007, Application of Differential Evolution Algorithm for Identification of Experimental Data, The Arquive of Mechanical Engineering, 4, 327-337.

Mariani V. C., Lima A. G. B. and Coelho L. S., 2008, Apparent Thermal Diffusivity Estimation of the Banana during Drying using Inverse Method, Journal of Food Engineering, 85, 569-579.

Marquardt, D. W., 1963, An Algorithm for Least-Squares Estimation of Nonlinear Parameters, J. Soc. Industr. Appl. Math., v. 11, pp. 431-441.

McCormick, N. J., 1986, Methods for Solving Inverse Problems for Radiation Transport-an Update, Transp. Theory Statist. Phys., Vol.15, pp.759-772.

McCormick, N. J., 1992, Inverse Radiative Transfer Problems: A Review, Nuclear Science and Engineering, Vol.112, pp.185-198.

McCormick, N. J., 1993, Inverse Photon Transport Methods for Biomedical Applications, Proc. 1st International Conference on Inverse Problems in Engineering: Theory and Practice, Florida, USA., pp.253-258.

Metropolis, N., Rosenbluth, A. W., Teller, A. H. and Teller, E., 1953, Equation of State Calculations by Fast Computing Machines, J. Chem. Physics, v.21, pp.1087-1092.

Mikhailov, M. D. and Özisik, M. N., 1994, Unified Analysis and Solutions of Heat and Mass Diffusion, Dover Publications, Inc.

Mouza, A. A., Dalakoglou, G. K. and Paras, S. V., 2005, Effect of Liquid Properties on the Performance of Bubble Column Reactors with Fine Pore Spargers, Chem. Eng. Science, v. 60, n. 5, pp. 1465-1475.

Moura Neto, F. D. and Silva Neto, A. J., 2000, Two Equivalent Approaches to Obtain the Gradient in Algorithms for Function Estimation in Heat Conduction Problems, Proc. 34th National Heat Transfer Conference, Pittsburgh, USA.

Muniz, W. B., Campos Velho, H. F. and Ramos, F. M., 1999, A Comparison of Some Inverse Methods for Estimating the Initial Condition of the Heat Equation, Journal of Computational and Applied Mathematics, Vol.103, pp.145-163.

Mwithiga, G., and Olwal, J. O., 2005, The drying kinetics of kale (Brassica oleracea) in a convective hot air dryer, J. of Food Engineering, v. 71, No. 4, pp. 373-378.

Orlande, H. R. B. and Özisik, M. N., 1993, Determination of the Reaction Function in a Reaction-Diffusion Parabolic Problem, Proc. 1st International Conference on Inverse Problems in Engineering: Theory and Practice, Florida, USA, pp.117-124.

Özişik, M. N., 1973, Radiation Transfer and Iterations with Conduction and Convection, John Wiley.

Özturk, S. S., Schumpe, A. and Deckwer, W.D., 1987, Organic Liquids in a Bubble Column: Holdups and Mass Transfer Coefficients, AIChE Journal, v. 33, No. 9, pp. 1473-1480.

Santana, C. C. and Carbonell, R. G., 1993a, Waste Minimization by Flotation: Recovery of Proteins and Other Surface-Active Compounds, 3rd Int. Conf. Waste Management, Bahia, Brazil.

Santana, C. C. and Carbonell, R. G., 1993b, Adsorptive Bubble Separation as a Means of Reducing Surface-Active Contaminants in Industrial Wastewaters, Proc. Int. Symp. on Heat and Mass Transfer, Cancun, Mexico, pp. 1-11.

Santana, C. C., 1994, Adsorptive Bubble Separation Process as a Means of Reducing Surface-Active Contaminants in Industrial Wastewaters, Brazilian J. Engineering- Chemistry, v. 5.

Silva Neto, A. J. and Özişik, M. N., 1993a, Inverse Problem of Simultaneously Estimating the Timewise-varying Strength of Two Plane Heat Sources, J. Applied Physics, Vol. 73, no 5, pp. 2132-2137.

Silva Neto, A. J. and Özişik, M. N., 1993b, Simultaneous Estimation of Location and Timewise-varying Strength of a Plane Heat Source, Numerical Heat Transfer, Vol. 24, pp. 467-477.

Silva Neto, A. J. and Özişik, M. N., 1994, The Estimation of Space and Time Dependent Strength of a Volumetric Heat Source in a One-Dimensional Plate, Int. J. Heat Mass Transfer, Vol. 37, no 6, pp. 909-915.

Silva Neto, A. J. and Özisik, M. N., 1995, An Inverse Problem of Simultaneous Estimation of Radiation Phase Function, Albedo and Optical Thickness, J. Quant. Spectrosc. Radiat. Transfer, Vol.53, No.4, pp.397-409.

Silva Neto, A. J. and Moura Neto, F. D., 2005, Inverse Problems: Fundamental Concepts and Applications, EdUERJ, Rio de Janeiro. (in Portuguese).

Silva Neto, A. J. and Soeiro, F. J. C. P., 2003, Solution of Implicitly Formulated Inverse Heat Transfer Problems with Hybrid Methods, Mini-Symposium Inverse Problems from Thermal/Fluids and Solid Mechanics Applications - 2nd MIT Conference on Computational Fluid and Solid Mechanics, Cambridge, USA.

Silva Neto, A. J. and Soeiro, F. J. C. P., 2002, "Estimation of the Phase Function of Anisotropic Scattering with a Combination of Gradient Based and Stochastic Global Optimization Methods. In Proceedings of 5th World Congress on Computational Mechanics, Vienna, Austria, July, 7-12.

Silva Neto, C. A. and Silva Neto, A. J., 2003, Estimation of Optical Thickness, Single Scattering Albedo and Diffuse Reflectivities with a Minimization Algorithm Based on an Interior Points Method. In Proceedings of 17th International Congress of Mechanical Engineering, ABCM, São Paulo, Brazil.

Silva Neto, A. J. and Soeiro, F. J. C. P., 2006, The Solution of an Inverse Radiative Transfer Problem with the Simulated Annealing and Levenberg-Marquardt Methods, Boletim da SBMAC, Vol. VII, No. 1, pp. 17-30.

Soeiro, F. J. C. P., Carvalho, G. and Silva Neto, A. J., 2000, Thermal Properties Estimation of Polymeric Materials with the Simulated Annealing Method, Proc. 8th Brazilian Congress of Engineering and Thermal Sciences, Porto Alegre, Brazil (in Portuguese).

Soeiro, F.J.C.P., Soares, P.O. and Silva Neto, A.J., 2004, Solution of Inverse Radiative Transfer Problems with Artificial Neural Networks and Hybrid Methods, Proc. 13th Inverse Problems in Engineering Seminar, pp. 163-169, Cincinnati, USA.

Souza, F. L., Soeiro, F. J. C. P., Silva Neto, A. J., and Ramos, F. M., 2007, Application of the Generalized External Optimization Algorithm to an Inverse Radiative Transfer Problem, Inverse Problems in Science and Engineering, 15, 7, 699-714.

Souto, R. P., Stephany, S., Becceneri, J. C., Campos Velho, H. F. and Silva Neto, A. J., 2005, Reconstruction of Spatial Dependent Scattering Albedo in a Radiative Transfer Problem using a Hybrid Ant Colony System Implementation Scheme, 6th World Congress on Structural and Multidisciplinary Optimization, Rio de Janeiro, Brazil.

Storn, R., 1995, "Differential Evolution Design of an IIR-Filter with Requirements for Magnitude and Group Delay," International Computer Science Institute, TR-95-026.

Storn, R., 1999, System Design by Constraint Adaptation and Differential Evolution, IEEE Transactions on Evolutionary Computation, vol. 3, pp. 22-34.

Storn, R. and Price, K., 1995, Differential Evolution: A Simple and Efficient Adaptive Scheme for Global Optimization over Continuous Spaces, International Computer Science Institute, vol. 12, pp. 1-16.

Storn, R., Price, K. and Lampinen, J. A., 2005, Differential Evolution - A Practical Approach to Global Optimization, Springer - Natural Computing Series.

Su, J. and Silva Neto, A. J., 2001, Two-dimensional Inverse Heat Conduction Problem of Source Strength Estimation in Cylindrical Rods. Applied Mathematical Modelling, Vol. 25, pp. 861-872.

Su, J., Silva Neto, A. J. and Lopes, A. B., 2000, Estimation of Unknown Wall Heat Flux in Turbulent Circular Pipe Flow, Proc. 8th Brazilian Congress of Engineering and Thermal Sciences, Porto Alegre, Brazil (in Portuguese).

Sundman, L. K., Sanchez, R. and McCormick, N. J., 1998, Ocean Optical Source Estimation with Widely Spaced Irradiance Measurements, Applied Optics, Vol.37, No.18, pp.3793-3803.

Voelkel, A. and Strzemiecka, B., 2007, Characterization of fillers used in abrasive articles by means of inverse gas chromatography and principal components analysis, Int. J. of Adhesion and Adhesives, v. 27, pp. 188-194.

Wang, F. S., Su, T. L. and Jang, H. J., 2001, Hybrid Differential Evolution for Problems of Kinetic Parameter Estimation and Dynamic Optimization of an Ethanol Fermentation Process, Industry Engineering Chemical Research, vol. 40, pp. 2876-2885.

Wang, J.-Z., Su, J. and Silva Neto, A. J., 2000, Source Term Estimation in Non-Linear Heat Conduction Problems with Alifanov's Iterative Regularization Method, Proc. 8th Brazilian Congress of Engineering and Thermal Sciences, Porto Alegre, Brazil (in Portuguese).

Yan, L., Fu, C. L. and Yang, F. L., 2008, The Method of Fundamental Solutions for the Inverse Heat Source Problem, Engineering Analysis with Boundary Elements, Vol. 32, pp. 216-222.

Yang, F. L., Yan, L. and Wei, T., 2009, Reconstruction of Part of a Boundary for the Laplace Equation by using a Regularized Method of Fundamental Solutions, Inverse Problems in Science and Engineering, vol. 17, pp. 1113-1128.

Acknowledgements

The authors acknowledge the financial support provided by CNPq, Conselho Nacional de Desenvolvimento Científico e Tecnológico, FAPERJ, Fundação Carlos Chagas Filho de Amparo à Pesquisa do Estado do Rio de Janeiro, FAPESP, Fundação de Amparo à Pesquisa do Estado de São Paulo, and FAPEMIG, Fundação de Amparo à Pesquisa do Estado de Minas Gerais.

3

Towards conformal interstitial light therapies: Modelling parameters, dose definitions and computational implementation

Emma Henderson, William C. Y. Lo and Lothar Lilge
Department of Medical Biophysics, University of Toronto
Canada

1. Introduction

External beam radiation therapy and high dose-rate brachytherapy were among the first tested medical applications for simulated annealing as an inverse planning optimization algorithm. The choice of these two applications is justified, as the tissue response to a given radiation dose is well established across different tissue types, leading to standardized clinical dosimetry concepts. A brief overview of the current state of simulated annealing in radiotherapy treatment planning is provided in Section 2. By contrast, the use of this popular optimization technique for interstitial light therapies, such as interstitial photodynamic therapy (IPDT), interstitial laser hyperthermia (ILH) and interstitial laser photocoagulation (ILP), requires an appreciation of the unique dosimetry challenges and the resulting development of new computational tools adapted to the requirements of light transport in tissue. Light transport is governed by interaction coefficients varying as a function of wavelength and differs between tissue types and between individuals.

This chapter introduces the clinical motivation behind conformal interstitial light therapies, the concept of using light dosimetry as a basic approach to clinical dosimetry, as well as our ongoing work on creating a computational framework for real-time light and clinical dosimetry (***http://code.google.com/p/gpu3d/***), in order to extend the benefit of simulated annealing. This presents a very timely application for simulated annealing, as these light-based therapies carry the possibility of low-cost general treatments in oncology and an alternative to surgical intervention. Presently, the efficacy of light-based therapies is, to a certain extent, limited by currently used heuristic treatment plans to illuminate the clinical target volume with sufficient energy or power density. Individualized treatment plans, tailored to a specific patient's anatomy and preferably also the local light-tissue interaction coefficients, can overcome the shortcomings of the heuristic treatment plans, and thus maximize the benefits and impact of light-based treatments.

2. Treatment planning using simulated annealing

To help readers understand how simulated annealing can be applied clinically for treatment planning, this section reviews the progress made in the well-established field of radiotherapy treatment planning. This provides the basis for the discussion of emerging interstitial light therapies and the clinical utility of simulated annealing in planning for these novel treatment options.

2.1 Simulated annealing in radiotherapy

Simulated annealing has been used as an optimization technique for radiation treatment planning in the clinical setting, with successes reported in both external beam radiation therapy (EBRT) (Aubry et al., 2006; Beaulieu et al., 2004; Morrill et al., 1995) and high dose-rate (HDR) brachytherapy (Lessard & Pouliot, 2001; Martin et al., 2007). For EBRT, the basic optimization problem is the determination of the appropriate temporal and spatial arrangements of multiple external radiation beams, which can be tailored in highly sophisticated and precise ways in modern 3-D conformal radiation therapy. For HDR-brachytherapy (which delivers a high radiation dose directly by implanting intense radioactive sources within the tumour for a short time), the optimization involves adjusting the duration (or *dwell time*) that a source pauses or *dwells* at each position (called *dwell position*) along the implanted catheter. Treatment delivery is accomplished using a computer-controlled robotic unit called a *stepping source device* or an *afterloader*, which moves the radioactive sources (commonly ^{192}Ir) along the catheters according to the optimized dwell time distribution in order to deliver the desired radiation dose distribution.

There is now a shift in paradigm as we strive to achieve the century-old objective of delivering a curative radiation dose to the tumour while sparing sensitive structures and surrounding normal tissues. That is, instead of manually specifying the treatment parameters and repeatedly evaluating the resulting radiation dose distribution (*forward planning*), a desired dose distribution is prescribed by the physician and the task of finding the appropriate treatment parameters is automated with an optimization algorithm (*inverse planning*). The latter approach, or inverse planning, is much more goal-oriented and efficient.

The concept of inverse planning, using simulated annealing as the optimization engine, can be briefly summarized as follows. Note that the following description focuses on HDR-brachytherapy and is greatly simplified, although the steps are quite similar for EBRT.

1. **3-D imaging of anatomical structures:** The first step typically involves the definition and contouring of the anatomical structures of interest using 3-D imaging modalities such as ultrasound, computed tomography (CT) and magnetic resonance imaging (MRI). Functional imaging techniques such as magnetic resonance spectroscopy (MRS) and positron emission tomography (PET) are also investigated for better localization and targeting of the tumour, thus permitting the administration of an escalated dose to the target (Scheidler et al., 1999). The anatomical structures of interest include the entire tumour and an estimated margin for the microscopic tumour spread, together referred to as the *clinical target volume* (CTV), as well as surrounding normal tissue and *organs at risk* (OAR). For convenience, all these structures are considered the *treatment planning volume* (TPV) in this chapter.

2. **Specification of desired dose distribution:** For each anatomical structure or organ, the desired 3-D dose distribution is prescribed by the physician through a set of dose constraints. Using the prostate as an example, a physician may define a minimum acceptable radiation dose D^{min} to the prostate (CTV) to ensure complete coverage and a maximum permissible dose D^{max} to the surrounding structures such as the rectum or urethra (OAR) to avoid complications. Each structure can be assigned a different set of dose constraints (D^{min} and D^{max}). A weighting factor w is also used to specify the relative importance of meeting a specific set of dose constraints or clinical objectives. A

penalty value p_i, computed using Equation 1 (Lessard & Pouliot, 2001), can be assigned to each dose point i (usually chosen to be either on the surface or inside the volume of the CTV or OAR) after calculating the dose distribution D_i resulting from a proposed set of treatment parameters. For details on brachytherapy dose calculations, see the American Association of Physicists in Medicine (AAPM) Task Group No. 43 Report (Rivard et al., 2004).

$$p_i = \begin{cases} w^{min}(D_i - D^{min}) & \text{if } D_i < D^{min} \\ w^{max}(D_i - D^{max}) & \text{if } D_i > D^{max} \\ 0 & \text{if } D^{min} <= D_i <= D^{max} \end{cases} \quad (1)$$

To evaluate a treatment plan, a global penalty function called a *cost function* or *objective function*, denoted E here, can be defined by summing the penalty values over all dose points for every anatomical structure. Note that variations of the cost function defined above exist, but the basic idea is similar in most cases. That is, the closer the calculated dose distribution is to the prescribed distribution, the lower the value of the cost function becomes.

3. **Optimization of treatment parameters:** The objective becomes minimizing the cost function, E, by solving for the appropriate combination of treatment parameters required to meet the clinical objectives. For example, in HDR-brachytherapy, one of the treatment parameters that needs to be optimized is the dwell time values (or dwell time distribution) for the different source positions or radioactive seed positions (also known as dwell positions) to achieve the desired dose coverage (Lessard & Pouliot, 2001). To illustrate how simulated annealing can be applied to treatment planning in HDR-brachytherapy, a generic pseudo code is shown in Algorithm 1 as a simplified example. (Note that the exact implementation details, such as the choice of the terminating condition, the definition of the cost function, or the selection of the cooling schedule, can differ depending on the clinical scenario and computational resources available.) First, the initial dwell time values are set and the corresponding cost function E_0 for this initial distribution is computed. Then, the dwell time value for a randomly chosen dwell position is randomly incremented or decremented. This change leads to a new dwell time distribution, from which a new dose distribution D_i and its associated penalty p_i can be computed. Next, the global penalty value or cost function E_k is compared against the previous one E_{k-1}. If the new dwell time distribution leads to a lower cost function ($\Delta E < 0$), then the change is accepted. Otherwise, the new treatment parameter is accepted with a probability of $P(\Delta E) = exp[-\Delta E/T(k)]$. For shorter computation time, a faster cooling schedule (fast simulated annealing) can be used by defining $T(k) = T_0/k^{\alpha}$ where T_0 is the initial temperature and α is the speed parameter. The entire process can be repeated until the cost function has reached a threshold as defined by clinical requirements or when further iterations do not produce a clinically significant difference.

The end result of this inverse planning process is an optimized set of treatment parameters forming the individualized treatment plan - in this case, a dwell time distribution delivered by an afterloader that produces a clinically acceptable radiation dose distribution tailored to an individual patient's anatomy. The notion of precisely shaping the dose distribution to match one's anatomy forms the basis of conformal radiation therapy.

Algorithm 1 Example of using simulated annealing for treatment planning

Initialize
while $E > threshold$ **do**
  Modify treatment parameters
  Compute new dose distribution D_i //**NOTE: Dose definition and dose calculation for radiotherapy and light-based therapies are fundamentally different.**
  Assign penalty p_i (Eq. 1)
  Compute cost function $E_k \leftarrow \sum p_i$
  $\Delta E = E_k - E_{k-1}$
  $P(\Delta E) = exp[-\Delta E / T(k)]$
  if $\Delta E < 0$ **then**
    Accept new treatment parameters
  else
    Accept new treatment parameters with a probability of $P(\Delta E)$
  end if
  $k \leftarrow k + 1$
end while

2.2 Fundamental differences between radiation therapy and light-based therapies

As the mass attenuation coefficient of ionizing radiation is on the order of < 0.3 cm^2/g for clinical applications and scattering of high-energy photons is weak, conformality in radiation therapy - that is, achieving high dose within the CTV combined with a steep dose gradient at its boundary and resulting low dose in surrounding tissue and OAR - can be achieved by superimposing radiation fields emanating from implanted sources, as described above, or from external beams so that they overlap at the CTV. For external beams, further conformality can be achieved by spatially modifying the exposure over each beam's cross section, as in intensity-modulated radiation therapy (IMRT) (Bortfeld, 2006). However, in light-based therapies, the very high attenuation coefficient and scattering coefficient necessitate different means to achieve conformality. For interstitial PDT in particular, the parameter space is given by the number and emission properties of implantable optical fibres and the length over which they emit. While for ionizing radiation the tissue interaction coefficients of the CTV and the OAR do not vary appreciably, light can encounter rather large differences in its interaction coefficients with tissue, ranging from, for example, < 2 cm^{-1} to 30 cm^{-1} in pig muscle and rabbit liver, respectively. Achieving conformality is further complicated if the other efficacy-determining parameters are not homogeneously distributed across the TPV, as discussed next. Despite these fundamental differences between radiation therapy and light-based therapies, the optimization algorithm based on simulated annealing (shown in Algorithm 1) can be similarly applied for planning light-based therapies, although the dose computation step would differ significantly as new definitions of dose are required for these novel therapies.

3. Dosimetry concepts for light-based therapies

This section provides the clinical background for interstitial light therapies as well as their unique treatment planning problem.

3.1 Dose definitions

For any medical therapy, the preferred definition of "dose" is a measurable quantity directly correlated with the desired biological or clinical outcome. In radiotherapy, this quantity is the energy absorbed by the tissue, shown to correlate with the tissue's response, and is possibly modulated by various external and internal factors such as tissue hypoxia. While the sensitivity of different tissues varies somewhat, the threshold to induce cell death varies by less than a factor of 2. Because the attenuation of ionizing radiation in soft tissues is low and is a function of its quantum energy, the energy density to be delivered can be directly calculated. The dose definition is less clear for ILH and ILP due to the biological response to temperature increase and heat transfer: active, convection through the vascular system, or passive, by diffusion. These two parameters depend on the extent of the vascular system, tissue density, and other structural tissue properties. For photodynamic therapy (PDT), owing to its complex mechanism requiring a drug and molecular oxygen, different efficacy-determining parameters apply. The dose definitions for these three therapies are further discussed below.

3.1.1 Interstitial Laser Photocoagulation (ILP) and Interstitial Laser Hyperthermia (ILH)

When describing photothermal applications such as ILP and ILH, the Bioheat Equation (Pennes, 1948) needs to be considered:

$$\rho_t c_t \frac{\partial T(\vec{r},t)}{\partial t} = \nabla(k_t \nabla T(\vec{r},t)) - \omega_b c_b \rho_b (T_{art}(\vec{r},t) - T(\vec{r},t)) + S(\vec{r},t) \tag{2}$$

In Equation 2, $S(\vec{r},t)$ describes the heat source distribution as a function of space and time. The resulting thermal energy distribution in the tissue, $\partial T(\vec{r},t)/\partial t$, is affected by the heat capacity of the vascular system c_b and tissue c_t, the thermal conductivity of the tissue k_t, as well as the general heat diffusion or blood perfusion rate ω_b throughout the tissue. Other important quantities include the density ρ and the temperature of the arterial blood $T_{art}(\vec{r},t)$. Note that additional terms can be added to Equation 2 to account for other effects such as metabolic heat generation and evaporation of water from the tissue. Equation 2 is sufficient for long light exposure when a steady state of the heat distribution is achieved. For short exposure time, and when using a pulsed light source, the actual damage for a given temperature is better described by the Arrhenius Integral (Henriques Jr & Moritz, 1947), given in Equation 3, which also considers the tissue's activation energy E_α, and tissue specific factors, A, temperature, T, and universal gas constant, R. The thermal damage parameter, denoted $\Omega(\vec{r},t)$ [dimensionless], is a measure of the degree of thermal injury and is computed as follows:

$$\Omega(\vec{r},t) = \int_0^t A e^{\frac{-E_\alpha}{RT(\vec{r},t)}} dt \tag{3}$$

Hence, accurate dosimetry for laser thermal therapies requires the knowledge of both the optical properties (absorption coefficient μ_a and scattering coefficient μ_s) and thermal properties (E_α) of tissue. Another significant complication is the temporal variation of these optical and thermal parameters, such as through the thermal transition from normal to, for example, coagulated tissue. Hence, simulated annealing based optimizations would need to be executed in a temporally resolved manner to account for such temporal variations in these thermal therapies.

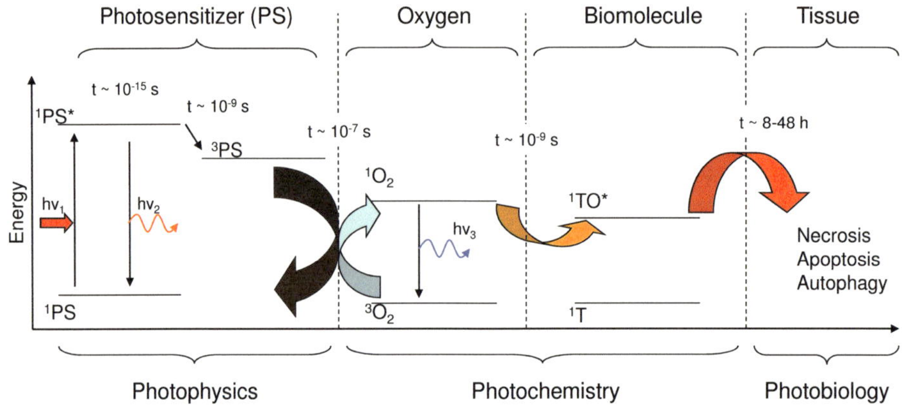

Fig. 1. The photophysics, photochemistry, and photobiology of PDT. The symbol $h\nu_1$ represents the incoming light, $h\nu_2$ represents the fluorescence by the photosensitizer (PS), and $h\nu_3$ is represents the singlet oxygen phosphorescence.

3.1.2 Interstitial Photodynamic Therapy (IPDT)

Before settling on a definition of dose for IPDT, one must understand the mechanism of its therapeutic effect. Figure 1 shows the photophysical, photochemical, and photobiological steps leading from the initial light absorption to cell apoptosis or tissue necrosis. The quantum energy of a photon is absorbed by the photosensitizer (PS), lifting it into an electronic excited singlet state. Photosensitizers have a high intersystem quantum yield, trapping them for microseconds in the triplet state. Collisional exchange of spin and energy with ground state molecular oxygen ($^3O_2$), which is a triplet, can result in highly reactive singlet oxygen ($^1O_2$) and ground state PS. Singlet oxygen has a lifetime in the low nanoseconds in biological systems and oxidizes lipids and proteins within its range indiscriminately ($^1T \rightarrow {}^1TO^*$). Accumulation of oxidative damage disrupts normal cell function and triggers apoptosis or necrosis. From this description, it should be clear that

1. Singlet oxygen is the main cytotoxic mediator of PDT-induced damage (Weishaupt et al., 1976);
2. There are three main parameters that govern $^1O_2$ production: light energy density, concentration and molar extinction coefficient of PS, and concentration of $^3O_2$. Note that all three parameters must be spatially and temporally co-localized.

Although $^1O_2$ fulfills the requirement for an ideal dose metric by virtue of directly correlating with the biological outcome, its quantification *in vivo* is very difficult and not currently feasible for the desired interstitial applications. Its characteristic phosphorescence at 1270 nm has a low quantum yield and there are few detectors with sufficient sensitivity at this wavelength. The strategy, then, is to deduce $^1O_2$ deposition based on the other PDT efficacy determining parameters (i.e., light, PS, and oxygen). This approach is called *explicit* or *extrinsic* since $[^1O_2]$ is directly calculated based on the interactions of its precursors (Niedre et al., 2003). By contrast, the *implicit* or *intrinsic* approach quantifies an interim photoproduct, the dynamics of which is directly related to $[^1O_2]$ and thus serves as a surrogate which *implies* the production of $^1O_2$. A possible interim photoproduct is the excited singlet state of the PS, quantified through its fluorescence intensity (Pogue, 1994).

Among the explicit approaches to PDT dosimetry, one will find both empirical and analytical models which aim to quantify the tissue response for a set of conditions. Empirical models include the critical fluence model (Jankun et al., 2004) and the threshold model (Farrell et al., 1998).

The critical fluence model defines the dose in terms of the light parameter alone; the quantity of interest is the total fluence (in units of joules per unit area) delivered to the target. Details on how this calculation is carried out will be explained in Section 3.2. When employing this approach, one must assume that PS and $^3O_2$ are present in unlimited quantities throughout the target for the duration of irradiation.
In the threshold model, the dose definition is the number of photons absorbed by the photosensitizer per unit mass of tissue. Here, only ubiquitous molecular oxygen availability is assumed. Information about the light distribution within and surrounding the target is combined with information about the PS distribution, considering tissue specific responsivity.
Two analytical approaches include the $^1O_2$ production (Zhu et al., 2007) and oxygen consumption models (Wang et al., 2007), which solve a set of differential equations representing the photophysical and photochemical reactions in PDT, assuming constant interaction coefficients.
Each of the models discussed above employs different definitions of dose and makes different assumptions about the efficacy-determining parameters. The utility of each will depend on the particular clinical problem. For clinical targets that are well-vascularized and confined to surfaces (some examples include the skin, oesophagus, or bladder), one may confidently apply the critical fluence or threshold model as the assumptions are likely justified. When the target is a solid tumour in an enclosed site, such as the prostate (Aniola et al., 2003), or a large, advanced tumour, these models are likely to fail. Solid tumours are known to have hypoxic regions, and drug distribution within them is often heterogeneous (Di Paolo & Bocci, 2007). Furthermore, these deep-seated tumours require an interstitial approach to light delivery which will render treatment planning even more difficult. In spite of these known issues, the prescribed dose used in the clinic remains the light energy density alone, due to limitations in the current technical ability to collect all required data in a spatially resolved manner. Typically, light energy density is calculated by applying the diffusion approximation to the transport equation along with finite-element based methods and using population-averaged tissue optical properties. These techniques are further detailed in Section 3.2. Optimizing conformal IPDT thus becomes an iterative process to attain the required minimum "dose" across, preferably, the entire CTV without exceeding the maximum permissible dose for the OAR. Minimization is executed in an N-dimensional parameter space comprising nominal (number of optical fibres) and interval (length, orientation, emission profile, and total power delivered for each fibre) data.

3.2 Light dosimetry models

With the exception of the oxygen consumption model in PDT, all other dose metrics require knowledge of the light distribution or, more precisely, its propagation in tissue. Unlike ionizing radiation, two interaction coefficients - light scattering and absorption - need to be considered and their values are large (Cheong et al., 1990), leading to rather steep gradients of light energy density. Additionally, there is a large difference in tissue optical properties between organs and individuals, as is evident from the visible appearance of these organs. For most wavelengths of interest in IPDT, ILH, and ILP, the light scattering coefficient is larger than the absorption coefficient and light transport follows the Boltzmann Transport equation. When distal to boundaries and light sources, light transport can be well approximated by diffusion theory.

3.2.1 Transport theory

Light has both wave-like and particle-like behaviours, and both treatments of it are widely accepted among physical scientists. In tissue optics, it is often more useful to consider light in terms of its particle-like properties owing to the heterogeneity in the coefficients of permittivity and permeability (ϵ_r, μ_r) within tissue. The quantities of interest, then, include

1. **Photon distribution**, $N(\vec{r}, \hat{s}, t)$ with units $[\frac{1}{m^3 sr}]$, representing the number of photons per unit volume propagating in the direction denoted $\hat{s}$ within solid angle $d\omega$ at position $\vec{r}$ at time t.
2. **Radiance**, $L(\vec{r}, \hat{s}, t) = h\nu c N(\vec{r}, \hat{s}, t)$ with units $[\frac{W}{m^2 sr}]$, where h is Planck's constant, ν is the frequency of light, and c is the speed of light. Note that the unit of radiance is the power per unit area per steradian.
3. **Fluence rate**, $\phi(\vec{r}, t) = \int_{4\pi} L(\vec{r}, \hat{s}, t) d\omega$ with units $[\frac{W}{m^2}]$, which is commonly used in tissue optics as it can be readily measured.

There are two quantities used to describe scattering: the scattering coefficient, μ_s, and the anisotropy, $g \equiv < cos\theta >$, where θ is the scattering angle (or deflection angle). μ_s is the probability of a scattering event per unit length, while g describes the average cosine of the scattering direction. Most tissues are forward-scattering and have g values of 0.9. These two terms are often combined into the reduced scattering coefficient, $\mu_s' \equiv (1-g)\mu_s$.
Absorption occurs when there is a match in energy between the incoming light and two electronic states of the chromophore upon which the light is incident. The absorption coefficient, μ_a, is the probability of an absorption event per unit length. It is spectrally dependent for a given chromophore, and for a given tissue may be represented as $\mu_a(\lambda) = \sum \epsilon_i(\lambda_i) C_i$, where ϵ_i and C_i are the extinction coefficient and concentration, respectively, for chromophore i in the tissue.
The radiative transport equation (RTE) (Ishimaru, 1977) is a description of photon transport through a medium, derived from conservation of energy:

$$\int_V \frac{\partial N}{\partial t} dV = \int_V q\, dV + \int_V v\mu_s \int_{4\pi} p(\hat{s}', \hat{s}) N\, d\omega' dV - \oint_S vN\hat{s}\hat{n}\, dS - \int_V v\mu_s N\, dV - \int_V v\mu_a N\, dV \quad (4)$$

The left-hand side of the equation represents the net change of photon distribution integrated over a small volume V. The first two terms on the right-hand side of Equation 4 include a source term (q = the number of photons emitted per unit volume, time, and steradian) and another term describing any photons that are scattered from direction $\hat{s}'$ into the direction of interest $\hat{s}$ (where $p(\hat{s}', \hat{s})$ is the scattering phase function and v is the speed of light in the medium), respectively. The three loss terms are, from left to right, those photons lost to boundary crossing (where S denotes the surface of the boundary and $\hat{n}$ is the unit normal pointing outwards), scattering out of the direction of interest, and absorption.

The above equation can be re-written, in terms of the radiance, and without integrating over volume:

$$\frac{1}{v}\frac{\partial L}{\partial t} = h\nu q + \mu_s \int_{4\pi} p(\hat{s}',\hat{s})L\,d\omega' - \hat{s}\cdot\nabla L - \mu_s L - \mu_a L \tag{5}$$

There are only a few conditions for which an exact solution of Equation 5 is possible; therefore, simplification of the RTE is necessary. The first-order diffusion approximation, developed hereafter, is one such approach.
In this approach, the radiance, source term, and scattering function are expanded into a series of spherical harmonics; the first-order diffusion approximation truncates the series at the first-degree term. The radiance then becomes:

$$L(\vec{r},\hat{s},t) \approx \frac{1}{4\pi}\phi(\vec{r},t) + \frac{3}{4\pi}\vec{F}(\vec{r},t)\cdot\hat{s} \tag{6}$$

where $\phi(\vec{r},t) = \int_{4\pi} L(\vec{r},\hat{s},t)d\omega$ is the fluence rate in units of $[W/m^2]$, while $\vec{F}(r,t)=\int_{4\pi} L(\vec{r},\hat{s},t)\hat{s}d\omega$ is the photon flux in units of $[\mathrm{W}/m^2]$. The first term on the right hand side is isotropic, and the second is linearly anisotropic. Inserting Equation 6 into the RTE results in two coupled equations:

$$(\frac{1}{v}\frac{\partial}{\partial t} + \mu_a)\,\phi + \nabla\vec{F} = q_0 \tag{7}$$

$$(\frac{1}{v}\frac{\partial}{\partial t} + \mu_a + \mu_s')\,\vec{F} + \frac{1}{3}\nabla\phi = \vec{q_1} \tag{8}$$

Two assumptions are made at this point:

1. Sources are isotropic, i.e., the linearly anisotropic source term $\vec{q_1} = 0$.
2. Photon flux is in steady-state, i.e., $\frac{\partial\vec{F}}{\partial t} = 0$

We are left with Fick's Law:

$$\vec{F} = -\frac{1}{3(\mu_a + \mu_s')}\nabla\phi \tag{9}$$

with diffusion coefficient $D \equiv \frac{1}{3(\mu_a+\mu_s')}$. This is substituted into Equation 7 to obtain the Diffusion Equation:

$$\frac{1}{v}\frac{\partial\phi(\vec{r},t)}{\partial t} - \nabla D(\vec{r})\nabla\phi(\vec{r},t) + \mu_a(\vec{r})\phi(\vec{r},t) = q_0(\vec{r},t) \tag{10}$$

Since the assumption was made that sources are isotropic, diffusion theory may only be used when $\mu_s{}'$ is much larger than μ_a(a good rule of thumb is that $\mu_s{}' > 10\mu_a$) or when the point of interest is far (at least 1 mean free path, defined as $1/(\mu_a + \mu_s')$ (Jacques & Pogue, 2008)) from sources or boundaries. Small geometries are, therefore, excluded.

3.2.2 Finite-element method (FEM) based models

The finite-element method operates by first breaking the volume of interest into a mesh of discrete elements. The diffusion equation is then solved over these discrete elements, assuming a linear solution over the interpolation between nodes. FEM can handle heterogeneous tissue optical properties and complex geometries, depending on the size of discretization. The trade-off is the large amount of memory required, which will limit the mesh size, or number of nodes (Davidson et al., 2009).

3.2.3 Monte Carlo Method

The Monte Carlo (MC) method is a statistical sampling technique that has been widely applied to a number of important problems in medical biophysics and many other fields, ranging from photon beam modelling in radiation therapy treatment planning (Ma et al., 1999) to protein evolution simulations in biology (Pang et al., 2005). The name *Monte Carlo* is derived from the resort city in Monaco which is known for its casinos, among other attractions. As its name implies, one of the key features of the MC method is the exploitation of random chance or the generation of random numbers with a particular probability distribution to model the physical process in question (Metropolis & Ulam, 1949). Since the MC method inherently relies on repeated sampling to compute the quantity of interest, the development of the MC method has parallelled the evolution of modern electronic computers. In fact, initial interests in MC-based computations stemmed from von Neumann's vision of using the first electronic computer - the ENIAC (Goldstine & Goldstine, 1996) - for the modelling of neutron transport (Metropolis, 1989), which was later adopted for the development of the atomic bomb in World War II.

Despite the increased variety and sophistication of MC-based simulations today, most MC-based models still retain the same essential elements, including the extensive use of random numbers and repeated sampling. For example, in the case of photon transport, random numbers are used to determine the distance of photon propagation and the direction of scattering, among other interactions. Each photon is tracked for hundreds of iterations and typically thousands to millions of photons are required to accurately compute the quantity of interest, such as the light dose distribution. Due to the large number of iterations required, different variance reduction techniques (Kahn & Marshall, 1953) have been introduced to reduce the number of samples required to achieve a similar level of statistical uncertainty or variance in MC-based computations. Conversely, variation reduction schemes allow more equivalent samples to be computed within the same amount of time. Unfortunately, the simulation time remains high for solving complex optimization problems such as those for treatment planning, which require many of these MC simulations (as shown earlier in Algorithm 1). To circumvent this obstacle, we propose a novel computational framework to make the MC method a practical approach for light dosimetry in the next section.

4. Computational framework for light dosimetry

In biomedical optics, the MC method is considered the gold standard approach for modeling light transport in biological tissue due to its accuracy and flexibility in handling realistic 3-D geometry with heterogeneities in the light-tissue interaction coefficients. However, the use of MC simulations in iterative optimization problems, such as treatment planning for photodynamic therapy and other light-based therapies, has been hindered by its long computation time (Luu, J. et al., 2009; Lo, W.C.Y. and Redmond, K. et al., 2009; Lo, W.C.Y. et al., 2009). Hence, it is often replaced by diffusion theory, when homogeneous light-tissue interaction coefficients are assumed (Altschuler et al., 2005; Rendon, 2008), or diffusion theory in combination with the finite element method (Davidson et al., 2009; Johansson et al., 2007). Unfortunately, neither approach provides the flexibility desired for treatment planning. On the other hand, the iterative nature of treatment planning within an N-dimensional parameter space makes it infeasible for MC-based computation to become the core dose calculation method in simulated annealing. Overcoming this computational burden is essential for the clinical application of MC simulations and simulated annealing for treatment planning. Instead of using the traditional networked computer cluster approach, this section explores the

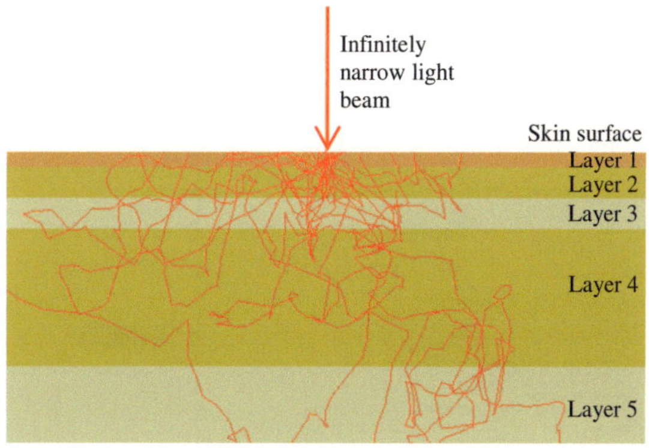

Fig. 2. MC simulation of photon propagation in a skin model (λ=633 nm).

use of modern computer graphics processing units (GPUs) for acceleration. To demonstrate the practicality of the GPU-based approach, a gold standard MC code package for modelling light propagation in multi-layered biological media (called MCML) was implemented on multiple NVIDIA GPUs. The final implementation was validated using an optical skin model to show the close correspondence between simulated isodose contours generated by the different computational platforms.

4.1 The MCML Algorithm

The MCML algorithm (Wang et al., 1995) models steady-state light transport in multi-layered turbid media using the MC method. The MCML implementation assumes infinitely wide layers, each of which is described by its thickness and its optical properties, comprising the absorption coefficient, scattering coefficient, anisotropy factor, and refractive index. A diagram illustrating the propagation of photon packets in a multi-layered skin geometry (Tuchin, 1997) is shown in Figure 2, using ASAP (Breault Research Organization, Tucson, AZ) as the MC simulation tool to trace the paths of photons (*ASAP - Getting Started Guide*, 2009).

In the MCML code, three physical quantities – absorption, reflectance, and transmittance – are calculated in a spatially-resolved manner. Absorption is recorded in a 2-D absorption array called $A[r][z]$, which represents the photon absorption probability density [cm^{-3}] as a function of radius r and depth z for a point source impinging on the tissue. Absorption probability density can be converted into more commonly used quantities in treatment planning such as photon fluence (measured in cm^{-2} for the impulse response of a point source). Fluence can be obtained by dividing the absorption probability density by the local absorption coefficient. To model finite-sized sources, the photon distribution obtained for the impulse response can be convolved with tools such as the CONV program (Wang et al., 1997).

The simulation of each photon packet consists of a repetitive sequence of computational steps and can be made independent of other photon packets by creating separate absorption arrays and decoupling random number generation for each group using different seeds. Therefore, a conventional software-based acceleration approach involves processing multiple photon packets simultaneously on multiple processors. Figure 3 shows a flow chart of the key steps in an MCML simulation, which includes photon initialization, position update, direction update, fluence update, and photon termination. Further details on each computational step may be found in the original papers by Wang et al.

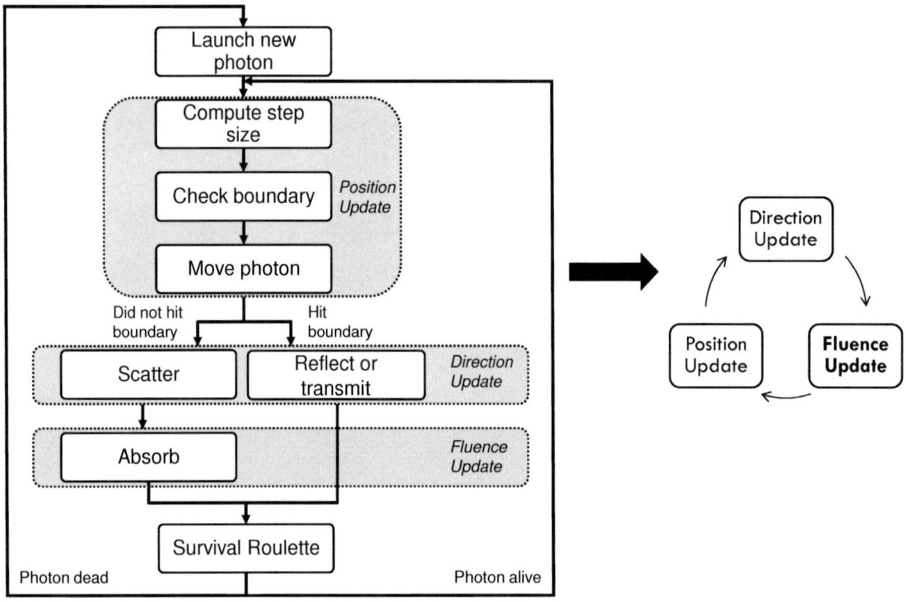

Fig. 3. Left: Flow-chart of the MCML algorithm. Right: Simplified representation used in subsequent sections.

4.2 Programming Graphics Processing Units with CUDA

The rapid evolution of GPUs and recent advances in general-purpose GPU computing have prompted the use of GPUs for accelerating scientific applications, including time-consuming MC simulations. This section introduces the key terminology for understanding graphics processing hardware, which was instrumental to the successful acceleration of the MCML code. Similarly, for other related applications, this learning curve is required to fully utilize this emerging scientific computing platform.

GPU-accelerated scientific computing is becoming increasingly popular with the release of an easier-to-use programming model and environment from NVIDIA (Santa Clara, CA), called CUDA, short for Compute Unified Device Architecture (*CUDA Programming Guide 2.3*, 2009). CUDA provides a C-like programming interface for NVIDIA GPUs and it suits general-purpose applications much better than traditional GPU programming languages. While some acceleration compared to the CPU is usually easily attainable, full performance optimization of a CUDA program requires careful consideration of the GPU architecture.

4.2.1 NVIDIA GPU Architecture

The underlying hardware architecture of a NVIDIA GPU is illustrated in Figure 4 (*CUDA Programming Guide 2.3*, 2009), showing both a unique processor layout and memory hierarchy. Using the NVIDIA GeForce GTX 280 GPU as an example, there are 30 *multiprocessors*, each with 8 *scalar processors* (SPs). Note that the 240 SPs (total) do not represent 240 independent processors; instead, they are 30 independent processors that can perform 8 similar computations at a time. From the programmer's perspective, computations are performed in parallel by launching multiple *threads*, each containing a parallel unit of work. For example, a thread can simulate a group of photon packets in the MCML algorithm.

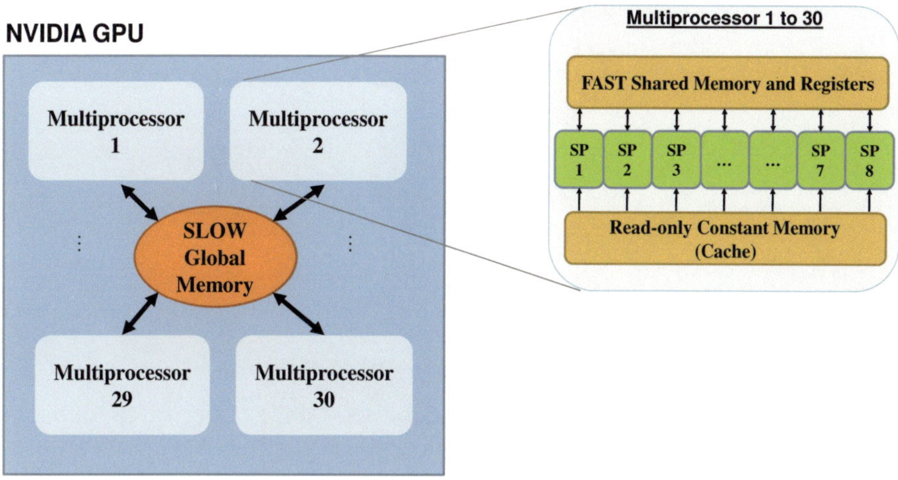

Fig. 4. Simplified representation of the NVIDIA GPU architecture for GTX 280

Second, the programmer must understand the different layers or types of memory on the GPU, due to the significant differences in memory access time. The outermost layer, which is also the largest and slowest (with a latency of up to 600 clock cycles), is the off-chip *device memory* (also known as *global memory*). Closer to the GPU are various kinds of fast, on-chip memories, including *registers* with typically a single clock cycle of access time, *shared memory* at close to register speed, and a similarly fast cache for *constant memory*. On-chip memories are roughly a hundred times faster than the off-chip memory; however, their storage space is limited. Finally, there is a region in device memory called *local memory* for storing large data structures, such as arrays, which cannot be mapped into registers by the compiler. As a result, it is important to map the computation efficiently to the different types of memories (e.g., depending on the frequency of memory accesses for different variables) to attain high performance.

4.2.2 Atomic Instructions

CUDA also provides a mechanism to synchronize the execution of threads using *atomic instructions*, which coordinate sequential access to a shared variable (such as the absorption array in the MCML code). Atomic instructions guarantee data consistency by allowing only one thread to update the shared variable at any time; however, in doing so, it stalls other threads that require access to the same variable. As a result, atomic instructions can give rise to performance bottlenecks. The cconcept of atomicity is illustrated in Figure 5.

4.2.3 Related Work

Previous attempts to use GPUs for MC-based photon simulations include the work by Alerstam et al., who reported ~1000x speedup on the NVIDIA GeForce 8800GT graphics card compared to an Intel Pentium 4 processor. Their implementation simulates time-resolved photon migration (for photon time-of-flight spectroscopy) in a homogeneous, semi-infinite geometry (Alerstam et al., 2008). Fang et al. recently reported a GPU implementation of the tMCimg

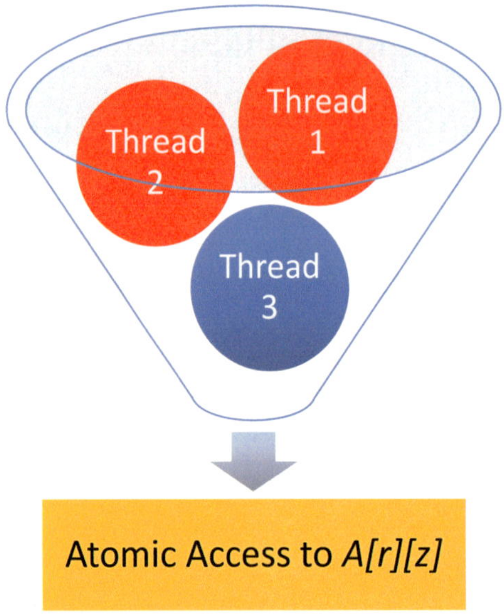

Fig. 5. Concept of an atomic access represented by a funnel: as thread 3 is accessing the absorption array, threads 1 and 2 must wait. Atomic instructions can cause bottlenecks in a computation, especially with thousands of threads common in GPU programming.

code for modelling 3-D voxelized geometry, with a speedup of 300x (without using atomic instructions to ensure data consistency) on the 8800GT graphics card compared to a 1.86GHz Xeon processor (Fang & Boas, 2009). However, the speedup dropped to 75x, or 4 times slower, when atomic instructions were used to guarantee data consistency. Note that one difference between the implementations from these two groups is that Alerstam et al. only used a 1-D vector output (for a time-of-flight histogram with 201 bins), while Fang et al. required a much larger 3-D matrix that needs to be accessed atomically. One could argue that inconsistencies or errors due to non-atomic memory access will only significantly affect the high-fluence region close to the light sources and hence are of little consequence in the critical fluence and threshold models. However, when considering the high photodynamic consumption of oxygen in the high-fluence region, and the resulting PDT-induced hypoxia, a "low dose" region would paradoxically be formed. As a result, for expanded PDT dose distributions, the assumption may not hold true and errors due to non-atomic data accesses can have severe consequences for treatment planning.

This work proposes a different approach to handle the inefficiency in the use of atomic instructions for large 2-D and 3-D result matrices, and addresses the question of how various optimizations can dramatically affect the performance of MC-based simulations for photon migration on NVIDIA GPUs. The final, optimized implementation was also extended to support multiple GPUs to show the possibility of using a cluster of GPUs for complex inverse problems which may require additional computational resources.

4.3 GPU-accelerated MCML Code

In this section, the implementation details of the GPU-accelerated MCML program (named GPU-MCML) are presented, showing how a high level of parallelism is achieved, while avoiding memory bottlenecks caused by atomic instructions and global memory accesses. The optimization process is described to summarize the challenges encountered before arriving at the final solution. This may assist other investigators in related efforts since the MC method is widely applied in computational biophysics and most MC simulations share a set of common features.

4.3.1 Implementation Overview

One difference between writing CUDA code and writing a traditional C program (for sequential execution on a CPU) is the need to devise an efficient parallelization scheme for the case of CUDA programming. Although the syntax used by CUDA is in theory very similar to C, the programming approach differs significantly. Figure 6 shows an overview of the parallelization scheme used to accelerate the MCML code on the NVIDIA GPU. Compared to serial execution on a single CPU where only one photon packet is simulated at a time, the GPU-accelerated version can simulate many photon packets in parallel using multiple threads executed across many scalar processors. Note that the total number of photon packets to be simulated are split equally among all created threads.

The GPU program or kernel contains the computationally intensive part or the key loop in the MCML simulation (represented by the position update, direction update, and fluence update loop in the figure). Other miscellaneous tasks, such as reading the simulation input file, are performed on the host CPU. Each thread executes a similar sequence of instructions, except for different photon packets simulated based on a different random number sequence.

In the current implementation, the kernel configuration is specified as 30 thread blocks (Q=30), each containing 256 threads (P=256). As shown in Figure 6, each thread block is physically mapped onto one of the 30 multiprocessors and the 256 threads interleave their execution on the 8 scalar processors within each multiprocessor. Increasing the number of threads helps to hide the global memory access latency. However, this also increases competition for atomic access to the common $A[r][z]$ array. Therefore, the maximum number of threads, which is 512 threads per thread block on the graphics cards used in this work, was not chosen. A lower number would not be desirable since more than 192 threads are required to avoid delays in accessing a register (due to potential register read-after-write dependencies and register memory bank conflicts (*CUDA Programming Guide 2.3*, 2009)). A similar reasoning applies to the number of thread blocks chosen. A lower number than 30 thread blocks would underutilize the GPU computing resources since there are 30 multiprocessors available. A larger number, such as 60 thread blocks, would decrease the amount of shared memory available for caching and also increase competition for access to the $A[r][z]$ array. The need to alleviate the competition for atomic access is discussed in detail next.

4.3.2 Key Performance Bottleneck

To understand further why atomic accesses to the $A[r][z]$ array could become a key performance bottleneck, notice that all threads add to the same absorption array in the global memory during the fluence update step. In CUDA, atomic addition is performed using the `atomicAdd` instruction. However, using `atomicAdd` instructions to access the global memory is particularly slow, both because global memory access is a few orders of magnitude slower than that of on-chip memories and because atomicity prevents parallel execution of

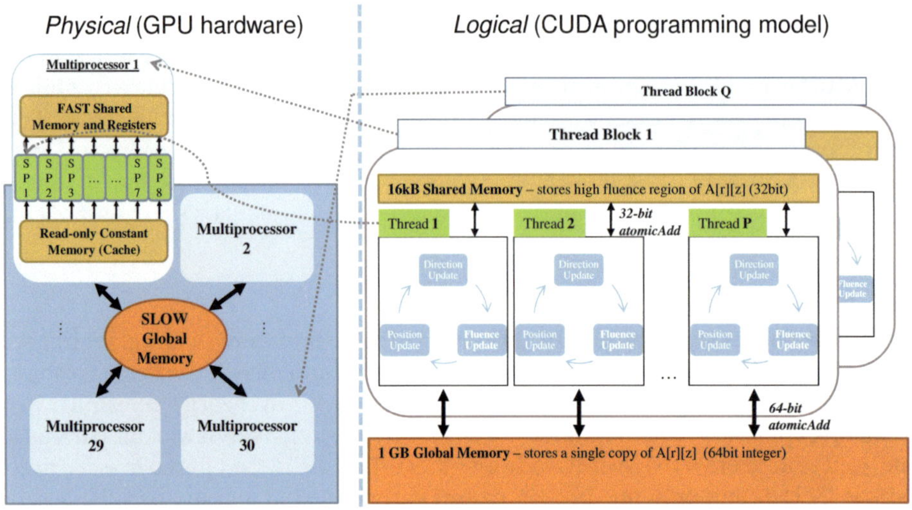

Fig. 6. Parallelization scheme of the GPU-accelerated MCML code (Q=30 and P=256 for each GPU). Note the mapping of the threads to the GPU hardware. In general, this is a many-to-one mapping.

the code (by stalling other threads in the code segment where atomic instructions are located). This worsens with increasing number of threads due to the higher probability of simultaneous access to an element, also known as contention.

Note that although the $A[r][z]$ array could, in theory, be replicated per thread to completely avoid atomic instructions, this approach is limited by the size of the device memory and would not be feasible in the general 3-D case with much larger absorption arrays. Therefore, a more general approach was explored to solve this performance problem.

4.3.3 Solution to Performance Issue

To reduce contention and access time to the $A[r][z]$ array, two memory optimizations, caching in registers and shared memory, were applied.

The first optimization is based on the idea of storing the recent write history, representing past absorption events, in temporary registers to reduce the number of atomic accesses to the global memory. It was observed that consecutive absorption events can happen at nearby, or sometimes the same, locations in the $A[r][z]$ array, depending on the absorption grid geometry and optical properties of the layers. Since the number of registers is limited, in the final solution, only the most recent write history is stored in 2 registers – one for the last memory location and one for the total accumulated weight. In each thread, consecutive writes to the same location of the $A[r][z]$ array are accumulated in these registers until a different memory location is computed. Once a different location is detected, the total accumulated weight in the temporary register is flushed into the global memory using an `atomicAdd` operation and the whole process is repeated.

The second optimization, illustrated in Figure 6, is based on the high event rate, and hence memory access rate, for the $A[r][z]$ elements near the photon source (or at the origin in the MCML model), causing significant contention when atomic instructions are used. Therefore, the region of the $A[r][z]$ array near the source is cached in the shared memory. This optimization has two significant implications. First of all, contention in the most competitive region of the $A[r][z]$ array is reduced by up to 30-fold since the shared memory copy of the array is updated atomically by only 256 threads within each thread block instead of 7680 threads across 30 blocks. Second of all, accesses to the shared memory are ~100-fold faster than those to the global memory. Together, these two factors explain the significant improvement in performance (~2x) observed after this optimization. (Note that the 3000-fold improvement suggested earlier is an optimistic upper bound estimate and is not likely attainable due to the small size of the shared memory and other technical limitations such as shared memory bank conflicts.)

To store as many elements near the photon source as possible in the shared memory, the size of each element in the $A[r][z]$ array was reduced to 32 bits (as opposed to 64 bits for the master copy in the global memory). Given the size of the shared memory is 16 kB, 3584 32-bit elements can be cached compared to only 1792 elements if 64-bit elements were used (3584 x 32 bits or 4 bytes = 14 kB, with the remaining shared memory space allocated elsewhere). However, this reduction also causes a greater risk of computational overflow, which occurs when the accumulated value exceeds $\sim 2^{32}$ (instead of $\sim 2^{64}$ in the 64-bit case). To prevent overflow, the old value is always checked before adding a new value. If overflow is imminent, the value is flushed to the absorption array in global memory, which still uses a 64-bit integer representation. From this calculation, it also becomes evident that 32-bit shared memory entries may not be optimal for 3D applications and 16 bits may be preferable to better cover the larger high access volume.

As an additional optimization technique to avoid atomic access, in the GPU version, photon packets at locations beyond the coverage of the absorption grid no longer accumulate their weights at the perimeter of the grid, unlike in the original MCML code. Note that these boundary elements were known to give invalid values in the original MCML code (Wang et al., 1995). This optimization does not change the correctness of the simulation, yet it ensures that performance is not degraded if the size of the detection grid is decreased, which forces photon packets to be absorbed at boundary elements (significantly increasing contention and access latency to these elements in the $A[r][z]$ array).

4.3.4 Other Key Optimizations

Another major problem with the original MCML code for GPU-based implementation is its abundance of branches (e.g., `if` statements), leading to significant code divergence. In the CUDA implementation, the function for computing the internal reflectance and determining whether a photon packet is transmitted or reflected at a tissue interface was significantly restructured to remove or to reduce the size of a large number of branches.

Finally, this implementation also includes a number of other optimizations, such as using GPU-intrinsic math functions (namely __sincosf(x) and __logf(x)), reducing local memory usage by expanding arrays into individual elements, and storing read-only tissue layer specifications in constant memory.

4.3.5 Scaling to Multiple GPUs

To scale the single-GPU implementation to multiple GPUs, multiple host threads were created on the CPU side to simultaneously launch multiple kernels, to coordinate data transfer to and from each GPU, and to sum up the partial results generated by the GPUs for final output. The same kernel and associated kernel configuration were replicated N times where N is the number of GPUs, except that each GPU initializes a different set of seeds for the random number generator and declares a separate absorption array. This allows the independent simulation of photon packets on multiple GPUs, similar to the approach taken in CPU-based cluster computing.

4.4 Performance

The execution time of the GPU-accelerated MCML program (named GPU-MCML) was first measured on a single GPU — the NVIDIA GTX 280 graphics card — with 30 multiprocessors. The code was migrated to a Quad-GPU system consisting of two NVIDIA GTX 280 graphics cards and a NVIDIA GTX 295 graphics card with 2 GPUs. This Quad-GPU system contains a total of 120 multiprocessors. The final GPU-MCML was compiled using the CUDA Toolkit and was tested in both a Linux and Windows environment. The number of GPUs used can be varied at run-time and the simulation is split equally among the specified number of GPUs. For baseline performance comparison, a high-performance Intel Xeon processor (Xeon 5160) was selected. The original, CPU-based MCML program (named here CPU-MCML) was compiled with the highest optimization level (gcc -O3 flag) and its execution time was measured on one of the two available cores on the Intel processor.

4.4.1 Skin Model

For performance comparison, a seven-layer skin model at λ=600 nm (shown in Table 1) (Meglinsky & Matcher, 2001) was used. Table 2 shows the execution time of the GPU-MCML program as the number of GPUs was increased. In all cases, the kernel configuration for each GPU was fixed at 30 thread blocks, each with 256 threads. Using one GTX 280 graphics card or 1 GPU with 30 multiprocessors (which contain a total of 240 scalar processors), the speedup was 309x when absorption, reflectance, and transmittance were recorded. The speedup increased to 483 x when absorption was not recorded. Using all 4 GPUs or equivalently 960 scalar processors, the simulation time for 50 million photon packets in the skin model was reduced from approximately 3 h on an Intel processor to only 9.7 s on 4 GPUs. This represents an overall speedup of 1101x ! When only reflectance and transmittance were recorded, the simulation took 5.9 s (1810x) ! Note that the overhead of synchronization between the GPUs and the summation of the partial simulation results would not be noticeable with larger simulation runs.

Layer	n	μ_a (cm^{-1})	μ_s (cm^{-1})	g	Thickness (cm)
1. stratum corneum	1.53	0.2	1000	0.9	0.002
2. living epidermis	1.34	0.15	400	0.85	0.008
3. papillary dermis	1.4	0.7	300	0.8	0.01
4. upper blood net dermis	1.39	1	350	0.9	0.008
5. dermis	1.4	0.7	200	0.76	0.162
6. deep blood net dermis	1.39	1	350	0.95	0.02
7. subcutaneous fat	1.44	0.3	150	0.8	0.59

Table 1. Tissue optical properties of a seven-layer skin model (λ=600 nm).

4.5 Validation

Figure 7 shows the simulated fluence distribution after launching 10^7 photon packets in the skin model shown in Table 1. The outputs produced by the GPU-MCML and CPU-MCML programs match very well. To further quantify any potential error introduced in the imple-

Number of GPUs	Platform Configuration	Time (s)	Speedup
1	GTX 280	34.6 (22.1)	309x (483x)
2	2 x GTX 280	17.5 (11.3)	610x (945x)
3	1 x GTX 280 + GTX 295 (2 GPUs)	12.7 (7.6)	841x (1405x)
4	2 x GTX 280 + GTX 295 (2 GPUs)	9.7 (5.9)	1101x (1810x)

Table 2. Speedup as a function of the number of GPUs for simulating 5×10^7 photon packets in a skin model (λ=600 nm). Baseline (1x) execution time on the Intel Xeon CPU was 10680 s or ~3 h. Values in brackets were generated without tracking absorption; only reflectance and transmittance were recorded.

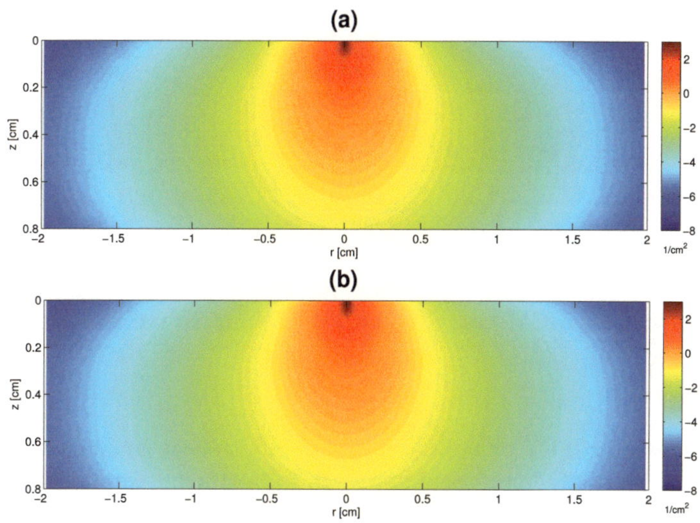

Fig. 7. Logarithm of simulated fluence distribution in the skin model (10^7 photon packets) for the impulse response: (a) generated by GPU-MCML, (b) generated by CPU-MCML.

mentation, the relative error $E[i_r][i_z]$ is computed for each voxel using Equation 11.

$$E[i_r][i_z] = \frac{|A_{gpu}[i_r][i_z] - A_{cpu}[i_r][i_z]|}{A_{cpu}[i_r][i_z]} \tag{11}$$

where A_{cpu} is the gold standard absorption array produced by the CPU-MCML software while A_{gpu} contains the corresponding elements produced by the GPU-MCML program. Figure 8 plots the relative error as a function of position, showing that the differences observed are within the statistical uncertainties between two simulation runs of the gold standard CPU-MCML program using the same number of photon packets.

5. Current challenges

The current challenges in this field mainly arise from the complexity of light-tissue interaction and that of the implementation of full 3D models in hardware. The complicated interactions among light treatment parameters - namely the light fluence rate, photosensitizer, and

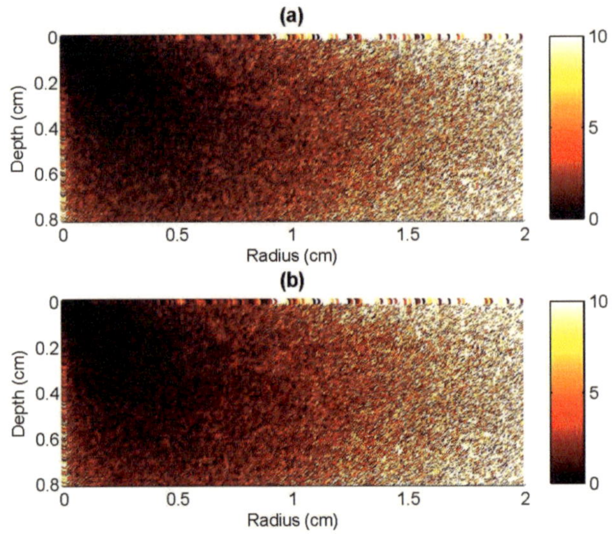

Fig. 8. Distribution of relative error for the skin model (10^7 photon packets): (a) GPU-MCML vs. CPU-MCML, (b) CPU-MCML vs. CPU-MCML. Colour bar represents percent error from 0% to 10%.

ground-state oxygen for IPDT or light absorption and bioheat equation for ILH and ILP - clearly indicate that a solely light-based approach to treatment planning and monitoring of delivered dose will be insufficient in attaining the best achievable clinical outcome, particularly in cases of tissue hypoxia, heterogeneity in photosensitizer concentration, heterogeneity in tissue optical properties, or presence of major vessels. In ILP and ILH, major vessels will result in significant local heat convection. Conversely, the characteristic leakiness of the tumour blood vessels plays a part in the preferential accumulation of PS in the tumour, and their characteristic tortuosity leads to hypoxic or anoxic regions, resulting in poor PDT efficacy. Additionally, over the course of an IPDT treatment, there will be events such as photosensitizer photobleaching, vascular shutdown, oxygen depletion, or inflammation, which will affect PDT efficacy. These complications are driving technical advances in monitoring one or more of the three efficacy-determining parameters: fluence rate, concentration of photosensitizer, and tissue pO_2. Ideally, treatment monitoring devices would capture the dynamics of the photochemical reactions and the spatial heterogeneities as dictated by the anatomy and physiology of the target. The desired spatial sampling of the light fluence rate will be on the order of μ_{eff}, approximately 4 cm^{-1}. For PDT, temporally, a relatively low sampling rate, around 0.03 Hz, is sufficient to capture the changes in tissue optical properties due to vascular events such as inflammation or thrombus formation which occur on the order of minutes. For ILP in particular, a sampling rate closer to 1 Hz may be required. The spatial distribution of the photosensitizer will depend on its delivery via the vasculature; for an intercapillary distance of 100 μm, one would want at least 2 samples per 100 μm, or 0.02 μm^{-1}. Photobleaching will affect the temporal variation in [PS]; thus, sampling at 0.05 Hz is desired, based on reported rates of photobleaching in vitro (Kruijt et al., 2009). No such monitoring is required for ILP and ILH. As for the photosensitizer, availability of molecular oxygen is dependent on

the vasculature - spatially 0.02 μm^{-1} is the approximate sampling resolution goal. For a PDT consumption rate of 30 μMs^{-1}, a temporal sampling rate of 0.08 Hz is required.
While it is possible to monitor these quantities at selected points using implanted optical sensors, there is a limit on the number of fibres which can be inserted and thus a limit on the spatial resolution of treatment monitoring; the volume will be under-sampled, and means to extrapolate the desired quantity to the entire volume are required. These dynamic changes in the CTV and the OAR need to be considered and the treatment plan should be re-adjusted in real time, as discussed further in Section 6. In terms of the hardware implementation of the complete computational framework, memory access time is currently an important consideration for real-time treatment planning. This problem is exacerbated in 3D treatment planning, and it needs to be addressed.

6. Future direction: Real-time, adaptive treatment planning

With the rapid improvement of GPU hardware and the release of the next-generation Fermi GPU architecture for general-purpose computing, GPU-based, real-time treatment planning may soon become a reality. In particular, the new Fermi GPU architecture from NVIDIA features a new memory/cache architecture that offers better memory access time, including faster atomic accesses which are especially important for 3D treatment planning. The dramatic reduction in treatment planning time potentially accomplished by a GPU cluster may, in the future, enable real-time adaptive treatment planning based on the most recent dose parameters obtained from the treatment volume. Currently, pretreatment models assume constant values for tissue optical properties based on population-averaged historical data and ignore the dynamic nature of tissues over the course of the therapy, which directly affects treatment outcomes in interstitial light therapies, especially for ILH and ILP. The implications of real-time dosimetry on the parameter space for optimization are also important. For example, the post-implantation constraints in the optical fibre positions would result in a more confined search space, making simulated annealing an even more attractive approach. From the original N-dimensional search space, only the total power per optical source fibre would remain. However, time-dependent changes in light-tissue interaction parameters and treatment efficacy determining coefficients require frequent execution of the algorithm. Considering a typical PDT treatment lasts 10 to 60 minutes, a temporal resolution of $\sim$5 seconds can be set for real-time computation as an initial research goal. Finally, to realize the full potential of real-time treatment planning, there is a need for more comprehensive dosimetry models that take into account not only physical parameters, but also biological parameters, possibly through real-time treatment monitoring. As we move towards conformal interstitial light therapies with the development of a real-time computational framework for treatment planning, (Lo, W.C.Y. et al., 2010) simulated annealing will likely become an indispensable tool for exploring the increasingly sophisticated landscape of optimization.

7. Acknowledgements

The authors wish to acknowledge the funding support from NSERC and CIHR as well as the contributions of David Han and Erik Alerstam to code development. Research infrastructure support was provided by the Ontario Ministry of Health and Long Term Care (OMHLTC). The views expressed do not necessarily reflect those of OMHLTC.

The GPU implementation described in this chapter has been integrated with the CUDAMCML software (Alerstam et al.). The most updated source code and documentation can be downloaded from **`http://code.google.com/p/gpumcml/`**

8. References

Alerstam, E., Svensson, T. & Andersson-Engels, S. (2008). Parallel computing with graphics processing units for high-speed Monte Carlo simulation of photon migration, *Journal of Biomedical Optics* **13**: 060504.

Altschuler, M., Zhu, T., Li, J. & Hahn, S. (2005). Optimized interstitial PDT prostate treatment planning with the Cimmino feasibility algorithm, *Medical Physics* **32**: 3524.

Aniola, J., Selman, S., Lilge, L., Keck, R. & Jankun, J. (2003). Spatial distribution of liposome encapsulated tin etiopurpurin dichloride (SnET2) in the canine prostate: Implications for computer simulation of photodynamic therapy, *International Journal of Molecular Medicine* **11**: 287–292.

ASAP - Getting Started Guide (2009). *Breault Research Organization* . `http://www.breault.com/resources/kbasePDF/broman0108_getstart.pdf`.

Aubry, J., Beaulieu, F., Sévigny, C., Beaulieu, L. & Tremblay, D. (2006). Multiobjective optimization with a modified simulated annealing algorithm for external beam radiotherapy treatment planning, *Medical Physics* **33**: 4718.

Beaulieu, F., Beaulieu, L., Tremblay, D. & Roy, R. (2004). Simultaneous optimization of beam orientations, wedge filters and field weights for inverse planning with anatomy-based MLC fields, *Medical Physics* **31**: 1546.

Bortfeld, T. (2006). IMRT: a review and preview, *Physics in medicine and biology* **51**: R363.

Cheong, W., Prahl, S. & Welch, A. (1990). A review of the optical properties of biological tissues, *IEEE Journal of Quantum Electronics* **26**(12): 2166–2185.

CUDA Programming Guide 2.3 (2009). *NVIDIA Corporation* . `http://developer.download.nvidia.com/compute/cuda/2_3/toolkit/docs/NVIDIA_CUDA_Programming_Guide_2.3.pdf`.

Davidson, S., Weersink, R., Haider, M., Gertner, M., Bogaards, A., Giewercer, D., Scherz, A., Sherar, M., Elhilali, M., Chin, J. et al. (2009). Treatment planning and dose analysis for interstitial photodynamic therapy of prostate cancer, *Physics in Medicine and Biology* **54**(8): 2293–2313.

Di Paolo, A. & Bocci, G. (2007). Drug distribution in tumors: mechanisms, role in drug resistance, and methods for modification, *Current Oncology Reports* **9**(2): 109–114.

Fang, Q. & Boas, D. A. (2009). Monte carlo simulation of photon migration in 3d turbid media accelerated by graphics processing units, *Opt. Express* **17**(22): 20178–20190.

Farrell, T., Hawkes, R., Patterson, M. & Wilson, B. (1998). Modeling of photosensitizer fluorescence emission and photobleaching for photodynamic therapy dosimetry, *Applied Optics* **37**: 7168–7183.

Goldstine, H. & Goldstine, A. (1996). The electronic numerical integrator and computer (ENIAC), *IEEE Annals of the History of Computing* pp. 10–16.

Henriques Jr, F. & Moritz, A. (1947). Studies of Thermal Injury: I. The Conduction of Heat to and through Skin and the Temperatures Attained Therein. A Theoretical and an Experimental Investigation*, *The American Journal of Pathology* **23**(4): 530.

Ishimaru, A. (1977). Theory and application of wave propagation and scattering in random media, *Proceedings of the IEEE* **65**(7): 1030–1061.

Jacques, S. & Pogue, B. (2008). Tutorial on diffuse light transport, *Journal of Biomedical Optics* **13**: 041302.

Jankun, J., Lilge, L., Douplik, A., Keck, R., Pestka, M., Szkudlarek, M., Stevens, P., Lee, R. & Selman, S. (2004). Optical characteristics of the canine prostate at 665 nm sensitized with tin etiopurpurin dichloride: need for real-time monitoring of photodynamic therapy, *The Journal of urology* **172**(2): 739–743.

Johansson, A., Axelsson, J., Andersson-Engels, S. & Swartling, J. (2007). Realtime light dosimetry software tools for interstitial photodynamic therapy of the human prostate, *Medical Physics* **34**: 4309.

Kahn, H. & Marshall, A. (1953). Methods of reducing sample size in Monte Carlo computations, *Journal of the Operations Research Society of America* pp. 263–278.

Kruijt, B. et al. (2009). Monitoring interstitial m-THPC-PDT in vivo using fluorescence and reflectance spectroscopy, *Lasers in Surgery and Medicine* **41**(9): 653–664.

Lessard, E. & Pouliot, J. (2001). Inverse planning anatomy-based dose optimization for HDR-brachytherapy of the prostate using fast simulated annealing algorithm and dedicated objective function, *Medical Physics* **28**: 773.

Ma, C., Mok, E., Kapur, A., Pawlicki, T., Findley, D., Brain, S., Forster, K. & Boyer, A. (1999). Clinical implementation of a Monte Carlo treatment planning system, *Medical Physics* **26**: 2133.

Martin, A., Roy, J., Beaulieu, L., Pouliot, J., Harel, F. & Vigneault, E. (2007). Permanent prostate implant using high activity seeds and inverse planning with fast simulated annealing algorithm: A 12-year Canadian experience, *International Journal of Radiation Oncology Biology Physics* **67**(2): 334–341.

Meglinsky, I. & Matcher, S. (2001). Modelling the sampling volume for skin blood oxygenation measurements, *Medical and Biological Engineering and Computing* **39**(1): 44–50.

Metropolis, N. (1989). The beginning of the Monte Carlo method, *From Cardinals to Chaos: Reflections on the Life and Legacy of Stanislaw Ulam* p. 125.

Metropolis, N. & Ulam, S. (1949). The monte carlo method, *Journal of the American Statistical Association* pp. 335–341.

Morrill, S., Lam, K., Lane, R., Langer, M. & Rosen, I. (1995). Very fast simulated reannealing in radiation therapy treatment plan optimization, *International Journal of Radiation Oncology Biology Physics* **31**: 179–179.

Niedre, M., Secord, A., Patterson, M. & Wilson, B. (2003). In vitro tests of the validity of singlet oxygen luminescence measurements as a dose metric in photodynamic therapy, *Cancer Research* **63**(22): 7986.

Pang, A., Smith, A., Nuin, P. & Tillier, E. (2005). SIMPROT: using an empirically determined indel distribution in simulations of protein evolution, *BMC bioinformatics* **6**(1): 236.

Pennes, H. (1948). Analysis of tissue and arterial blood temperatures in the resting human forearm, *Journal of Applied Physiology* **1**(2): 93.

Pogue, M. (1994). Mathematical model for time-resolved and frequency-domain fluorescence spectroscopy in biological tissues, *Appl. Opt* **33**: 1963–1974.

Rendon, A. (2008). *Biological and Physical Strategies to Improve the Therapeutic Index of Photodynamic Therapy*, PhD thesis, University of Toronto.

Rivard, M., Coursey, B., DeWerd, L., Hanson, W., Huq, M., Ibbott, G., Mitch, M., Nath, R. & Williamson, J. (2004). Update of AAPM Task Group No. 43 Report: A revised AAPM protocol for brachytherapy dose calculations, *Medical Physics* **31**: 633.

Scheidler, J., Hricak, H., Vigneron, D., Yu, K., Sokolov, D., Huang, L., Zaloudek, C., Nelson, S., Carroll, P. & Kurhanewicz, J. (1999). Prostate cancer: localization with three-dimensional proton MR spectroscopic imaging-clinicopathologic study, *Radiology* **213**(2): 473.

Tuchin, V. (1997). Light scattering study of tissues, *Physics-Uspekhi* **40**(5): 495–515.

Wang, K., Mitra, S. & Foster, T. (2007). A comprehensive mathematical model of microscopic dose deposition in photodynamic therapy, *Medical Physics* **34**: 282.

Wang, L., Jacques, S. & Zheng, L. (1995). MCML - Monte Carlo modeling of light transport in multi-layered tissues, *Computer Methods and Programs in Biomedicine* **47**(2): 131–146.

Wang, L., Jacques, S. & Zheng, L. (1997). CONV - convolution for responses to a finite diameter photon beam incident on multi-layered tissues, *Computer Methods and Programs in Biomedicine* **54**(3): 141–150.

Weishaupt, K., Gomer, C. & Dougherty, T. (1976). Identification of singlet oxygen as the cytotoxic agent in photo-inactivation of a murine tumor, *Cancer Research* **36**(7 Part 1): 2326.

Zhu, T., Finlay, J., Zhou, X. & Li, J. (2007). Macroscopic modeling of the singlet oxygen production during PDT, *Proceedings of SPIE*, Vol. 6427, p. 642708.

FPGA-based Monte Carlo computation of light absorption for photodynamic cancer therapy,2009 17th IEEE Symposium on Field Programmable Custom Computing Machines, 157–164, IEEE.

Hardware acceleration of a Monte Carlo simulation for photodynamic therapy treatment planning,Journal of Biomedical Optics, Vol. 14, p. 014019.

GPU-accelerated Monte Carlo simulation for photodynamic therapy treatment planning,Proceedings of SPIE, Vol. 7373, p. 737313.

Computational Acceleration for Medical Treatment Planning: Monte Carlo Simulation of Light Therapies Accelerated using GPUs and FPGAs,VDM Verlag Dr. Muller, ISBN: 978-3639250381.

4

A Location Privacy Aware Network Planning Algorithm for Micromobility Protocols

László Bokor, Vilmos Simon, Sándor Imre
Budapest University of Technology and Economics, Department of Telecommunications, Mobile Communication and Computing Laboratory – Mobile Innovation Centre Magyar Tudosok krt. 2, H-1117, Budapest Hungary
{goodzi | svilmos | imre}@mcl.hu

1. Introduction

Telecommunication systems both are converging into a complex and synergistic union of wired and wireless technologies, where protocols and terminals will provide integrated services on a universal IP-based infrastructure (Huber, 2004). The Internet itself is evolving towards a more pervasive and ubiquitous architecture in which users are expected to be able to apply different technologies enabling accessibility anytime and anywhere. Not only wireless networks are evolving toward heterogeneous, convergent, broadband, all-IP mobile communication architectures but also end terminals are becoming more and more versatile and powerful devices. Contemporary mobile phones are implementing extremely large scale of functions from making voice and video calls through sharing multimedia and providing Internet connection till exploiting the advantages of geographic positioning solutions – e.g., Global Positioning System (El-Rabbany, 2006) or IP address-based methods (Connolly, Sachenko, & Markowsky, 2003) – in order to use navigational applications and Location Based Services. However mobile terminals' location data possess important service-enabler potentials, in the wrong hands it can be used to build up private and intimate profile of the mobile user. Such a profile can be set up from accurate location information of a user in real time using GPS, network and cell based tracking or even exploiting knowledge of actual IP addresses. There is a strong motivation for creating and maintaining such profiles but the access of this sensitive data must be supervised, controlled and regulated by authorities or even by the operators themselves to ensure privacy protection of mobile users. As mobility becomes one of the most unique characteristics of future's convergent architectures, more attention to the above privacy issues must be given. A whole bunch of new challenges are emerging, but not only solutions to efficiently manage mobile users in the widest range of different application scenarios are needed. More care has to be taken on the privacy issues, even at the earliest phases of design: at the network planning level.

When discussing network planning in next generation, IP based wireless networks, at least two main types of mobility should be considered. On one hand the case when a mobile terminal moves across different administrative domains or geographical regions and thus changes its actual IP address has to be taken into account (i.e. macromobility). On the other hand, roaming across multiple subnets within a single domain resulting in more frequent address changes also need to be managed (i.e. micromobility). The aim of the latter case is to provide fast, seamless, and local handoff control in areas where mobile nodes change their point of attachment to the network so often that the general macromobility scheme originates significant overhead in terms of packet delay, packet loss, and excrescent signalling (Reinbold & Bonaventure, 2003). Next generation micro-cell based heterogeneous wireless networks are quite sensitive to the above Quality of Service (QoS) factors which implies the spreading of micromobility protocols – e.g., (Valko, 1999), (Bokor, Nováczki, & Imre, A Complete HIP based Framework for Secure Micromobility, 2007), (Soliman, Castelluccia, Malki, & Bellier, 2005) – and the need of advanced network planning algorithms to support real-life deployment issues.

One of the issues of deploying micromobility protocols in next generation mobile environments is the optimal design of micromobility domains. Inside a domain the given micromobility protocol deals with mobility management but at each domain boundary crossing, mobile nodes must register their new locations through signalling messages of the used macromobility protocol in order to update the global address management database for their global reachability. In this way the system is able to maintain the current domain of each user, but this will produce a registration cost in the network. Therefore the question arises, what size (in means of consisting subnets) the micromobility domain should be for reducing the cost of paging, maintaining routing tables and registration signalling. Existing network planning algorithms are focusing on minimizing the signalling costs (Bhattacharjee, Saha, & Mukherjee, 1999), (Pack, Nam, & Choi, 2004), (Loa, Kuo, Lam, & Lic, 2004). In our earlier works we also gave solutions for optimized domain forming, which are capable of reducing the signalling overhead caused by the subnet boundary crossing (Simon & Imre, A Simulated Annealing Based Location Area Optimization in Next Generation Mobile Networks, 2007), (Simon, Bokor, & Imre, A Hierarchical Network Design Solution for Mobile IPv6, 2009). In these studies two main factors were considered. On one hand if we join more and more subnets (i.e., wireless points of attachment with their relevant coverage area) into one micromobility domain, then the number of inter-domain movements will be smaller, so the number of macromobility location update messages sent to the upper levels will decrease. But in the case of big number of subnets belonging to a domain, more possible mobile nodes can join into one micromobility domain (increasing the possibility of routing table explosion), and an incoming call will cause lot of paging messages. On the other hand if we decrease the number of subnets, then we do not need to send so much paging messages (hereby we will load less links and the processing time will decrease too) and the scalability problem can be solved as well, but then the number of domain changes will increase. Therefore the overall problem in micromobility domain planning comes from the trade-off between the paging cost and the registration cost, considering the scalability issues as well.

However, an important factor is left out from all the existing algorithms: the potential of micromobility protocols to efficiently support location privacy has never taken into consideration in any domain planning algorithms available in the literature. The privacy supporting potential of micromobility management lies in the fact that subnet border crossings inside a micromobility domain will remain hidden from the outside world, thus reducing signalling overhead and hiding location information easily exposable by IP address changes of handovers. Only in cases of inter-domain handovers, the location is updated and revealed to outside of the domain; not on each subnet handover.

This chapter will guide the reader through the evolution steps of network planning algorithms designed to optimally form domain structures for (micro)mobility protocols by introducing all the important methods and schemes. The chapter will also discuss the main privacy issues of next generation mobile and wireless telecommunication systems, focusing on the protection of location information of mobile users in an all-IP world. The importance of location privacy protection in future mobile networks will be emphasized by proposing a novel, uniquely developed and evaluated, simulated annealing based micromobility domain optimization approach, which introduces privacy awareness in network planning methodologies.

The remainder of the chapter is organized as follows. Section 2 presents the background and the related work; Section 3 introduces our novel, simulated annealing-based and location privacy aware network planning algorithm, while in Section 4 the evaluation of the described scheme is detailed. Finally, we conclude the chapter in Section 5 and sketch the scope of future research.

2. Background

As communication architectures evolve, the complex set of user requirements will also align to the changing environmental characteristics. The concept of global reachability fuelled with the advanced mobility schemes and the "anytime, anywhere" paradigm has already started entering the everyday life of people, as real-time multimedia-driven services gain more and more popularity. This is the reason that the requirements for security and privacy in the global Internet era differs a lot from the ones of a decade ago. Despite the fact that the problem space of trust, security and privacy addresses the whole spectrum of computer and communication sciences, this chapter focuses only on a subset of these issues, namely the location privacy questions defined by locators (i.e., IP addresses) in the network layer.

2.1 Location privacy in nutshell

Generally speaking, privacy is procreated as an appropriate combination of anonymity, pseudonymity and unlinkability. Anonymity means that an individual communicating on the network can not be identified by third party entities belonging to a definite group or without some a priori knowledge. The concept of pseudonymity is more permissive compared to anonymity in the means of that it provides protection on the individual's identity but not on linking the actions to the used pseudonym identifier (i.e., supplies no linkability protection). Emanated from this, unlinkability is the feature which prevents traceable bonds between actions of individuals and their identity or pseudonym identifiers. Location privacy is a bit more specific privacy case and its significant influence on the evolution of communication systems in the pervasive computing era was firstly described by (Beresford & Stajano, 2003). Here the authors defined location privacy as the ability to prevent others from learning one's actual or past location. Assuming an all-IP world and global mobility, location privacy concerns the relation between the identifier of a communicating node and its actual or past topological location (Haddad W. , Nordmark, Dupont, Bagnulo, & Patil, 2006), (Koodli, 2007). In the current Internet architecture (which also plays as the basis for all-IP mobile and wireless communication systems), an IP address not only identifies a node (or an interface) on the network but also serves as the essential element for routing packets through the Internet topology. Accordingly, when an IP packet is sent from one Internet node to another, both sender and receiver entities reveal their topological location (i.e., their IP addresses) in the network, which can then easily be translated to a quite accurate estimation of the peers' current geographical location (Lakhina, Byers, Crovella, & Matta, 2003), (Freedman, Vutukuru, Feamster, & Balakrishnan, 2005), (Gueye, Ziviani, Crovella, & Fdida, 2006), (Baden, 2008) (Eriksson, Barford, Sommersy, & Nowak, 2010), and thus making third parties able to track mobiles' real-life movements or posing other threats to users (Haddad W. , et al., 2006).

In order to protect location privacy in next generation networks, several ideas, schemes and protocols have already been proposed in the literature. These location privacy preserving methods apply various approaches – like policy negotiation and control (Snekkenes, 2001), (Langheinrich, 2002), path confusion (Hoh & Gruteser, 2005), anonymization (Cornelius, Kapadia, Kotz, Peebles, Shin, & Triandopoulos, 2008), change of pseudonyms and mix-zones (Beresford & Stajano, 2003) – which could be deployed either centrally on trusted third-party entities or on end-user terminals to prevent bogus nodes from easily learning past or current locations of communicating hosts. Also various protocol extensions are available implementing protective measures for mobile users' location privacy by advancing existing mobility management protocols and mechanisms. RFC 5726 (Qiu, Zhao, & Koodli, 2010) introduces efficient and secure techniques for Mobile IPv6 nodes (Johnson, Perkins, & Arkko, 2004) to protect their location privacy. For the promising Host Identity Protocol (Moskowitz, Nikander, Jokela, & Henderson, 2008) the HIP Location Privacy Framework was proposed (Matos, Santos, Sargento, Aguiar, Girao, & Liebsch, 2006) where authors cover only part of the location privacy problem space, as some exceptions are allowed on correspondents or trustworthy nodes. A complete HIP location privacy solution was proposed by (Maekawa & Okabe, 2009) where authors decouple identifiers for mobility from identifiers for end-to-end communications and construct an extensional mobility management protocol of BLIND (Ylitalo & Nikander, BLIND: A Complete Identity Protection Framework for End-Points, 2006). Similarly, Stealth-LIN6 (Ichikawa, Banno, & Teraoka, 2006) was proposed for LIN6 (Kunishi, Ishiyama, Uehara, Esaki, & Teraoka, 2000) in order to achieve anonymity of node's identity in the IP layer by dynamic generation of addresses for every single transmission and also to provide anonymity of users' location by introducing special proxy entities in the network.

A further and special kind of protocol extensions providing location privacy in mobile environments is formed by the micromobility solutions which are developed to complement the base macromobility protocols with localized mobility management.

2.2 Micromobility protocols: providers of simple location privacy

Over the past decade a number of micromobility protocols have been proposed, designed and implemented in order to extend the base macromobility protocols like Mobile IPv6 (Johnson, Perkins, & Arkko, 2004) or Host Identity Protocol (Moskowitz, Nikander, Jokela, & Henderson, 2008). The research on such solutions has generated significant interest in industry and academia, aiming to improve global mobility management mechanisms.

One of the most known micromobility solutions is the Cellular IP protocol (Valko, 1999) that introduces a Gateway Router dealing with local mobility management while also supporting a number of handoff techniques and paging. To minimize control messaging, regular data packets transmitted by mobile hosts are also used to refresh host location information inside the domain. A similar approach is the handoff-aware wireless access Internet infrastructure or HAWAII (Ramjee, Porta, Thuel, Varadhan, & Wang, 1999), which is a separate routing protocol to handle micro-mobility. In TeleMIP (Das, Misra, Agrawal, & Das, 2000) a mobility agent is used to reduce the location update traffic, leading to a new architecture. Terminal Independent Mobility for IP (Grilo, Estrela, & Nunes, 2001) combines some advantages from Cellular IP and HAWAII, where terminals with legacy IP stacks have the same degree of mobility as terminals with mobility-aware IP stacks. Nevertheless, it still uses Mobile IP for macro-mobility scenarios. Auto-Update Micromobility (Sharma & Ananda, 2004) exploits the hierarchical nature of IPv6 addressing and uses specialized mechanisms for handover control, while μHIP (Bokor, Nováczki, & Imre, A Complete HIP based Framework for Secure Micromobility, 2007) integrates micro-mobility management functionalities into the Host Identity layer by introducing a local rendezvous server into the architecture and uses macromobility capabilities of HIP for global mobility. Multicast-based Micromobility (Helmy, Jaseemuddin, & Bhaskara, 2004) is a local mobility management method where a visiting node gets multicast address to use while moving inside a domain, and intra-domain handover is realised using multicast join/prune mechanisms. Anycast-based Micromobility (Bokor, Dudás, Szabó, & Imre, 2005) is similar to M&M: a mobile node obtains a unique anycast care-of address, forms a virtual anycast group, and lets the underlying anycast routing protocol to handle the intra-domain movements. Hierarchical Mobile IPv6 (Soliman, Castelluccia, Malki, & Bellier, 2005) is also a well-known and significant micromobility solution to reduce the number of signalling messages to the home network and to reduce the handover latency. The basic idea of this approach is to use domains organized in a hierarchical architecture with a mobility agent on the top of the domain hierarchy. The deployment of such agents will reduce the signalling load over the air interface produced by Mobile IPv6, by limiting the amount of Mobile IPv6 signalling outside the locally managed domain. A novel, network-based paradigm for micromobility management is called Proxy Mobile IPv6 (Gundavelli, Leung, Devarapalli, Chowdhury, & Patil, 2008), that is based on the concept that the network provides always the same home prefix to the MN independently of its point of attachment to the domain. Special anchor and gateway entities are responsible in the network for tracking the movements of the mobiles and initiating the required mobility signalling on behalf of them.

As the above examples show and (Reinbold & Bonaventure, 2003) express, micromobility protocols denote mobility signalling between the mobile node and an intermediate node (real or virtual) that is located in the local operator network, and at the same time hide inside locators from the outside world. The routing path that goes via the intermediate node offers location privacy for end hosts because it obliterates the actual location of the host while it roams within a micromobility domain: mobiles can benefit from local mobility, which hides the regional movement from the peer nodes, optimizes the signalling between end terminals, therefore reduces the handoff related latency and increases location privacy (Ylitalo, Melen, Nikander, & Torvinen, 2004). This behaviour is similar to the operation of privacy proxies (Reed, Syverson, & Goldschlag, 1998). Note, that such usage necessitates that the intermediate node/proxy is trusted to keep the mobile's real locator (i.e., inside domain address) secret.

In this article we focus on these micromobility proposals, more precisely on how to design and form micromobility domains for extending location privacy protection capabilities of micromobility protocols.

2.3 Optimization of micromobility domains

The problem is that none of the existing micromobility protocols addresses the realization of the domain structure in detail; none provides clear guidance or instructions for network design. It is not clear and usually hard to determine the size of a micromobility area (i.e., locally administrated domain). Several important questions arise: how to group wireless points of attachments with their relevant coverage (like cells in cellular networks) into different micromobility domains, what kind of principles must be used to configure the hierarchical levels if the protocol makes them able to be applied (like in case of HMIPv6), and in which hierarchical level is advisable to implement special functions like mobility anchors or gateways. The traffic load and mobility of mobile nodes may vary, therefore a fixed structure lacks of flexibility.

The key issues here are on which level of hierarchy to deploy the anchor/gateway functionalities, and how to group wireless point of access nodes (access routers) and the coverage areas they implement, actually how many cells should be beneath an anchor or gateway node within a single domain. An obvious solution is to group those cells and access nodes into one domain, which has a high rate of handovers among each others. In that way the number of cell and access router changes for the mobile hosts will be decreased. But joining too much cell and access router into one domain would degrade the overall performance since it will generate a high traffic load on anchor/gateway nodes, which results in a high cost of packet delivery (Casteluccia, 2000). Contrarily a small number of cells inside a micromobility domain will lead to a huge amount of location updates to the home network. Based on these assumptions, (He, Funato, & Kawahara, 2003) proposed a dynamic micromobility domain construction scheme which is able to dynamically compose each micromobility domain according to the aggregated traffic information of the network. The related questions are very similar to the Location Area (LA) planning problem where cells must be grouped into location areas in an optimal way (Markoulidakis, Lyberopoulos, Tsirkas, & Sykas, 1995), (Tabbane, 1997), (Rubin & Choi, 1997), as in micromobility domain planning we also need to search for a trade-off compromise between the location update and the packet delivery cost.

One of the most known LA planning schemes is the solution called Traffic-Based Static Location Area Design - TB-LAD (Cayirci & Akyildiz, 2003), that groups cell pairs with higher inter-cell mobile traffic into the same LA. In this algorithm a list of neighbours is created for each cell, in a decreasing order by the inter-cell traffic. The neighbour with the highest inter-cell traffic will be selected from the list and included in the same LA with this cell. In the next step the algorithm finds neighbours with the highest traffic from the neighbour lists of the cells that are included for the current LA and includes them into the current LA. This is terminated, when there are no more neighbours that can be included or the maximum number of cells is reached for the current LA. After this loop the algorithm starts the forming of the next LA in the same way. However, in case of the Location Area Forming Algorithm - LAFA (Simon & Imre, 2009), LAs are not formed one after the other, but simultaneously, always including the actual cell-pair to an already existing LA or creating a new one, enabling to build the LA structure in a distributed way. Based on the experiments of LAFA, the duet of the Greedy LA Forming Algorithm (GREAL) and the Simulated Annealing Based Location Area Forming Algorithm (SABLAF) was proposed by (Simon & Imre, A Simulated Annealing Based Location Area Optimization in Next Generation Mobile Networks, 2007). In this scheme GREAL is adopted to form a basic partition of cells into LAs in a greedy way without any additional assumptions for cell contraction, and then SABLAF is applied for getting the final partition. Authors of (Prajapati, Agravat, & Hasan, 2010) also proposed a similar simulated annealing based LA planning method giving a heuristic and near-optimal solution for LA planning in tolerable run-times. There is also a specific Location Area planning algorithm for GEO Mobile Satellite Systems: by the way of extensive comparison of the cost of location management using different types of location area designs, an appropriate scheme was separated by the authors satisfying the special requirements of GEO satellite systems (Qian, Guang-xia, Jing, Yi-qun, & Ming, 2010).

A dominant part of current Location Area and micromobility domain planning algorithms is not able to handle network structures with hierarchical levels. Despite the fact that there are existing proposals for that deficiency (Simon, Bokor, & Imre, A Hierarchical Network Design Solution for Mobile IPv6, 2009), (Pack, Choi, & Nam, 2006), in this work we still stick to the "flat nature" of the original idea. However this study does not consider hierarchical structures, our contribution is still applicable in those cases.

It is important to emphasise that while there exists quite a broad literature on location area and micromobility domain forming, it leaves a substantial and a-priori question unexplored: how to integrate location privacy requirements into the algorithms. To the best of our knowledge, at the time of the writing this is the first study about location privacy aware micromobility domain planning.

3. A location privacy aware network planning algorithm

3.1 Motivation

As we introduced above, an open question of any micromobility proposal and domain/LA forming algorithm is the optimal design of the domains, aiming to minimize the signalling costs while to maximize the domains' location privacy protection capabilities at the same time. At each domain boundary crossing, mobile hosts reveal and register their new locations through signalling mechanisms of the applied macromobility protocol (e.g., Mobile IPv6) in order to update the global location management database (i.e., the Home Agent in case of MIPv6) and their actual peer nodes. In this way the network is able to maintain the current location of each user, but this will produce a registration cost in the network and will go hand in hand with the disclosure of the actual location to potential bogus nodes. Therefore the question arises: what size the micromobility domain should be for reducing the cost of paging and registration signalling, and increasing built-in location privacy. On one hand if we join more and more cells into one domain, then the number of inter-domain handovers will be smaller, so the number of macromobility location update messages sent to the upper levels will decrease. Also the domain's potential to hide inside movements of mobile terminals from the outside network will become more powerful and effective. But in the case when big number of cells belong to a single domain, more possible mobile nodes can join into one micromobility area (such increasing also the possibility of routing table explosion), and an incoming call will cause tremendous paging overhead. On

the other hand if we decrease the number of cells, then we do not need to send so much paging messages (hereby we will load less links and the processing time will decrease, too) and the scalability problem can be solved as well, but then the number of subnet changes will increase and the location privacy of mobile nodes moving between different domains gets more vulnerable. Therefore the overall problem in location privacy aware micromobility domain planning comes from the trade-off between the paging cost and the registration cost, considering the location privacy issues as well.
In order to deal with this, we qualify the paging cost as a constraint; therefore the registration cost is left alone in the objective function. Hence we define and formulate a problem in which the final goal is the determination of optimum number of cells per a domain for which the registration cost is minimum, with the paging cost limitation as an inequality constraint function. Based on this cost structure we propose a domain optimization algorithm that contains two phases: first a greedy grouping is adopted which forms a basic partition of cells or any kind of point of access nodes into micromobility domains by also using a rate weighting technique to cover location privacy issues of micromobility, and then a simulated annealing based algorithm is applied for getting the final and near-optimal partition within tolerable run time. This novel network planning solution is a natural extension of our former, simulated annealing based domain optimization methods (Bokor, Simon, Dudás, & Imre, 2007), (Simon & Imre, A Simulated Annealing Based Location Area Optimization in Next Generation Mobile Networks, 2007). We designed and implemented a realistic mobile environment simulator in order to generate the algorithm input metrics (cell boundaries crossing and incoming session statistics, location privacy model parameters, etc.,), and to execute and study the algorithms with and without location privacy awareness for extensive comparison and performance analysis.

3.2 Cost structures

The goal of employing micromobility is to keep the boundary crossing between different coverage areas (e.g., cells) inside a well defined local domain (i.e., hidden from the upper levels), therefore an administrative message for the global registration of the new location of the mobile host will not be generated during intra-domain handovers, and also location privacy is provided for hosts moving inside the domain. Hence for the purpose to make calculations about the movement of mobile nodes among the domains and such temporarily loosing their location privacy protection, a simple and well known choice is the fluid flow model. The fluid flow model characterizes the aggregate mobility of the mobile nodes in a given region (for example micromobility domain) as a flow of liquid. The model assumes that hosts are moving with an average speed v, and their direction of movement is uniformly distributed in the region. Hence the rate of outflow from that region can be described by (Kumar, Umesh, & Jha, 2000)

$$R_{out} = \frac{v \cdot \rho \cdot P}{\pi} \tag{1}$$

where v is the average speed of the mobile nodes (MN), ρ is the density of mobiles in the region and P is the perimeter of the given region. This model is very simple and convenient to analyze and to use for the definition of the registration cost function. We can define easily the density of the mobile nodes in a domain:

$$\rho = \frac{K}{N_k \cdot S} \tag{2}$$

where K is the number of mobile hosts in the k th domain, N_k is the number of cells in the k th domain, and S is the area of a cell.

Every time when a mobile node crosses a cell boundary which is micromobility domain boundary also, a global registration process is initiated, and a special update message is sent to the upper level. This signalling cause the registration cost and that the location information of the mobile node can be revealed to third parties and communication peers. From this point of view the intra-domain boundary crossing is negligible, and this handoff cost should be not considered in the registration cost. Similarly to (Bokor, Simon, Dudás, & Imre, 2007), we need to determine the number of cells located on the boundary of the k th micromobility domain, like a subset of N_k, and the proportion of the cell perimeter which contributes to the k th domain perimeter. Using this, the perimeter of the k th domain:

$$P_k = N_p \cdot \nu_p(N_k) \tag{3}$$

where N_p is the number of boundary cells in the k th domain, and ν_p is the average proportion of the boundary cell perimeter in the k th domain perimeter in the function of N_k. The number of the boundary cells can be approximated according to (Simon & Imre, A Domain Forming Algorithm for Next Generation, IP Based Mobile Networks, 2004):

$$N_p = \kappa \cdot \sqrt{N_k} \tag{4}$$

The average proportion of the cell perimeter which will be the part of the domain perimeter too can be expressed with an empirical relation (Bhattacharjee, Saha, & Mukherjee, 1999):

$$\nu_p(N_k) \approx \nu \cdot \left(a + b \cdot N_k^{\eta-1}\right) \tag{5}$$

where ν is the perimeter of a cell and $a = 0.3333$, $b = 0.309$, $\eta = 0.574965$. Substituting the values of N_p and $\nu_p(N_k)$ in (3), the expression for the perimeter of the k th domain becomes:

$$P_k = \kappa \cdot \sqrt{N_k} \cdot \nu \cdot \left(a + b \cdot N_k^{\eta-1}\right) \tag{6}$$

Therefore the number of crossing the k th micromobility domain boundary can be given by substituting the values of ρ and P_k in the outflow rate of the fluid flow model:

$$R_{out} = \left(\frac{v \cdot \frac{K}{N_k \cdot S} \cdot \kappa \cdot \sqrt{N_k} \cdot v \cdot \left(0.333 + 0.309 \cdot N_k^{-0.425}\right)}{\pi} \right) \quad (7)$$

As we mentioned earlier a registration process is initiated when the mobile node crosses a cell boundary which is also a domain boundary, hence the total registration cost will be:

$$C_{\mathrm{Re}g_k} = B_{LU} \cdot R_{out} \quad (8)$$

$$C_{\mathrm{Re}g_k} = B_{LU \cdot} \cdot v \cdot K \cdot \kappa \cdot v \cdot \left(\frac{0.333 \cdot N_k^{-0.5} + 0.309 \cdot N_k^{-0.925}}{\pi \cdot S} \right) \quad (9)$$

where B_{LU} is the cost required for transmitting a global location update message. The final goal is the determination of optimum number of cells per a micromobility domain for which the registration cost is minimum and the domains' location privacy protection potential is maximum, with the paging cost as an inequality constraint function.

To have a feasible micromobility support, the network capacities assigned for paging should not be exceeded; therefore we need to define a paging constraint per micromobility domains. The limited network capabilities of locating the exact location of a stand-by mobile node in case of an incoming session will cause a limit on the peak session arrival rate; therefore we need to define an upper paging cost constraint for every domain. The paging cost for the k th domain should not exceed the paging cost constraint (the paging cost for the k th micromobility domain will be the sum of C_{P_i} over the N_k cells):

$$C_{P_k} = \sum_{i=1}^{N_k} C_{P_i} = \sum_{i=1}^{N_k} B_P \cdot N_k \cdot \lambda_i < C_k \quad (10)$$

$$C_{P_k} = B_P \cdot N_k \cdot \sum_{i=1}^{N_k} \lambda_i < C_k \quad (11)$$

where B_P is the cost required for transmitting a paging message and λ is the number of incoming sessions terminated to a mobile node. If we assume that the mobile hosts have the same average number of terminated sessions for all cells in the k th domain ($\lambda_i = \lambda$), the paging cost reduces to

$$C_{P_k} = B_P \cdot N_k \cdot K \cdot \lambda < C_k \quad (12)$$

3.3 Cost optimization

The problem is to find the optimum number of cells per a micromobility domain for which the registration cost is minimum and the paging constraint (C_k must not be exceeded) is satisfied. If we know that the session arrivals (λ) follow a Poisson process and the function of the registration cost (9) is a monotonically decreasing function, the paging constraint can be expressed in the following way:

$$P(C_{P_k} < C_k) < 1 - e^{-\gamma} \tag{13}$$

where $\gamma = (10,100)$, depending on the accuracy of the paging constraint. The monotonically decreasing attribute of the registration cost function and the nature and modality of location privacy provision inside micromobility domains will mean, that we need to find the highest value of the N_k for which the (13) will be still satisfied.
Substituting the expression of the paging cost in (13):

$$P(B_P \cdot N_k \cdot K \cdot \lambda < C_k) < 1 - e^{-\gamma} \tag{14}$$

Furthermore if we know that the λ probability variable follows a Poisson process, then the maximum value of N_k can be easily calculated ($N_{\max}$):

$$P(\lambda < \frac{C_k}{B_P \cdot N_k \cdot K}) = 1 - e^{-\gamma} \tag{15}$$

Substituting the calculated value of N_k in (9) will give us the minimum of the registration cost. We will use this calculated N_k as an input for our location privacy aware micromobility domain forming algorithm.

3.3 The algorithm

The optimal partitioning of cells into micromobility domains is proofed to be an NP-complete problem (Cayirci & Akyildiz, 2003). Since the time required solving this problem increases exponentially with the size of the problem space, no algorithm exists that provides the optimal result within acceptable run times. Therefore, special techniques offering near-optimal solutions in reasonable amount of time are needed. A suitable approach is the use of heuristic approximation that runs in polynomial-time for finding the optimum or near-optimum cell configuration.
Simulated annealing is considered as an effective approximation scheme fitting to this specific application and also to various problems in general. Simulated annealing is a random-search method that exploits the analogy between the way in which metals cool and freeze into their minimum-energy crystal structure (the so called annealing process) and the search for a minimum in a general space (Laarhoven & Aarts, 1987). By this analogy, each step of a simulated annealing-based heuristic algorithm replaces the current solution by a "neighbouring" solution from the solution space, randomly chosen with a probability depending on the difference between the corresponding function values and on a global parameter called the Temperature, which is gradually decreased during the run. The technique grants the basis of a whole family of optimization schemes for combinatorial and

other mathematical challenges and also for dealing with highly nonlinear problems. This motivated us to use simulated annealing in order to find a near-optimal solution in our cell partitioning problem without searching the entire solution space.

As we described, the registration cost is proportional to the number of handovers among different domains (q), therefore the registration cost can be minimized by designing the domains such that the cells belonging to one domain have the lowest boundary crossing rates among each other. However, if location privacy is to be taken into consideration, the crossing rates also must contain location privacy specific information from both user and the network side. This is achieved by introducing a simple location privacy policy model and a special rate weighting technique.

In the location privacy policy model we applied, a combination of cells' static location privacy significance and mobile nodes' location privacy profile creating dynamic demands in the network is used to provide boundary conditions for location privacy aware domain planning.

From the mobile network operators' perspective we can separate coverage areas considered to be more sensitive to location privacy than others. In order to capture the difference in this sensitivity, we introduce the *static location privacy significance level of the cells*. This attribute defines what level (in scale of 1-5) of location privacy protection is required at a given cell in the design phase, such allowing for network designers to take maximally into consideration the operator's location privacy requirements and needs.

Mobile node's location privacy profile for different location types is defined to describe what level (in scale of 1-5) of location privacy protection is required for a mobile user at a given type of location. We specified four types of location for cells (micro-cell at home, workplace, hospital or hotel), and mobile nodes -when entering a certain type of cell- can announce their required level of location privacy protection for that cell type. These dynamic demands are cumulated during the cell operation. The average of the cumulated demands will be compared with the static location privacy significance level of the issued cell at every announcement, and the bigger value - named as the cell's *overall location privacy factor* - will take over the role of the cell's static significance level. In this simple way not only operators' requirements, but also the dynamic demands of mobile users can be respected during the location privacy aware network design.

Our special *rate weighting technique* is used to integrate the effects of the cells' static location privacy significance and mobile nodes dynamic demands into the boundary crossing rates between neighbouring cells. According to the mathematical representation we use (where the cells are the nodes of a graph, and the cell border crossing directions are represented by the graph edges) weights can be defined to the edges of this graph based on the cell border crossing (i.e., handover) rates of every direction (i.e., rates of entering or leaving a cell are summarized and assigned to the corresponding edge as its weight). These rates are weighted with the overall location privacy factor of the destination cell, as the *weighted rate* is generated by the sum of product of every incoming and outgoing rate and their appropriate destination cell's overall location privacy factor, respectively:

$$WRate_{[k][l]} = Rate_{[k][l]} \cdot OverallLocPFact_{[l]} + Rate_{[l][k]} \cdot OverallLocPFact_{[k]} \tag{16}$$

where $WRate_{[k][l]}$ is the weighted rate of edge between cells (graph nodes) k and l, the notation of $Rate_{[k][l]}$ stands for the cell border crossing rate from cell k to l, and the $OverallLocPFact_{[l]}$ is the overall location privacy factor of cell l.

Based on the above, our location privacy aware micromobility domain planning algorithm will start with a greedy phase that will provide the basic domain partition as an input (i.e., initial solution) of the simulated annealing. In the beginning of this greedy phase, we choose the cell pair with the biggest weighted rate in our cell structure ($q_{\max}$). If there is more than one biggest rate, then we choose one of them randomly and include the two cells belonging to that handover rate into the $Domain_1$ set of cells. In the next step, we search for the second biggest weighted rate (if there are more than one, we choose it in the same way as in the first step) among the cell pairs for which is true, that one of them belongs to the $Domain_1$ set of cells. We must check if inequality

$$N_k < N_{\max} \tag{17}$$

satisfied, where $N_{\max}$ is the maximum value of N_k calculated from (15), namely the maximum possible number of cells in a single micromobility domain which will give us the minimum of the registration cost and the maximum size of the location privacy protective micromobility domain. If the inequality is satisfied, the cell can be included into the $Domain_1$ set of cells. If the inequality is not satisfied, the cell can not be included into this set in order to prevent exceeding the paging cost constraint (12). In this way we can join the most important cells according to the location privacy policy model which are also in the same dominant moving directions (highways, footpaths, etc.,). Therefore the number of handovers among domains can be decreased while the location privacy is also considered in the created structure.

After the processing of all cell pairs in the above sequential and greedy way, a system of domains will be created, which is likely not the optimal solution. However, this will be only a basic domain partition which will serve as an input to the simulated annealing based domain forming scheme.

The simulated annealing procedure starts with this basic partition or initial solution s_0. A neighbour to this solution s_1 is then generated as the next solution, and the change in the registration cost $\Delta C_{\mathrm{Reg}}(s_0, s_1)$ is evaluated. If a reduction in the cost is found, the current solution is replaced by the generated neighbour, otherwise we decide with a certain probability set to $e^{\left(-\frac{\Delta C_{\mathrm{Reg}}}{T}\right)}$ (usually called the acceptance function) whether remains or becomes the current solution, where T is the control parameter (i.e., the temperature in the simulation annealing terminology). The algorithm is started with a relatively high value of T, to have a better chance to avoid being prematurely trapped in a local minimum. The cooling schedule consists of three parameters, used like an input to the algorithm: the initial temperature (T), step of decrement ($decr$), and the stopping rule of the algorithm. The stopping rule is the maximal iteration step number or maximum number of steps when ΔC_{Reg} do not changes. Another important input parameter is the calculated maximum number of cells in a micromobility domain ($N_{\max}$). The performance of our algorithm depends heavily on the cooling schedule and the initial partition, which should be carefully investigated and optimized to have the best results. The detailed flowchart of the whole algorithm is depicted on Fig. 1.

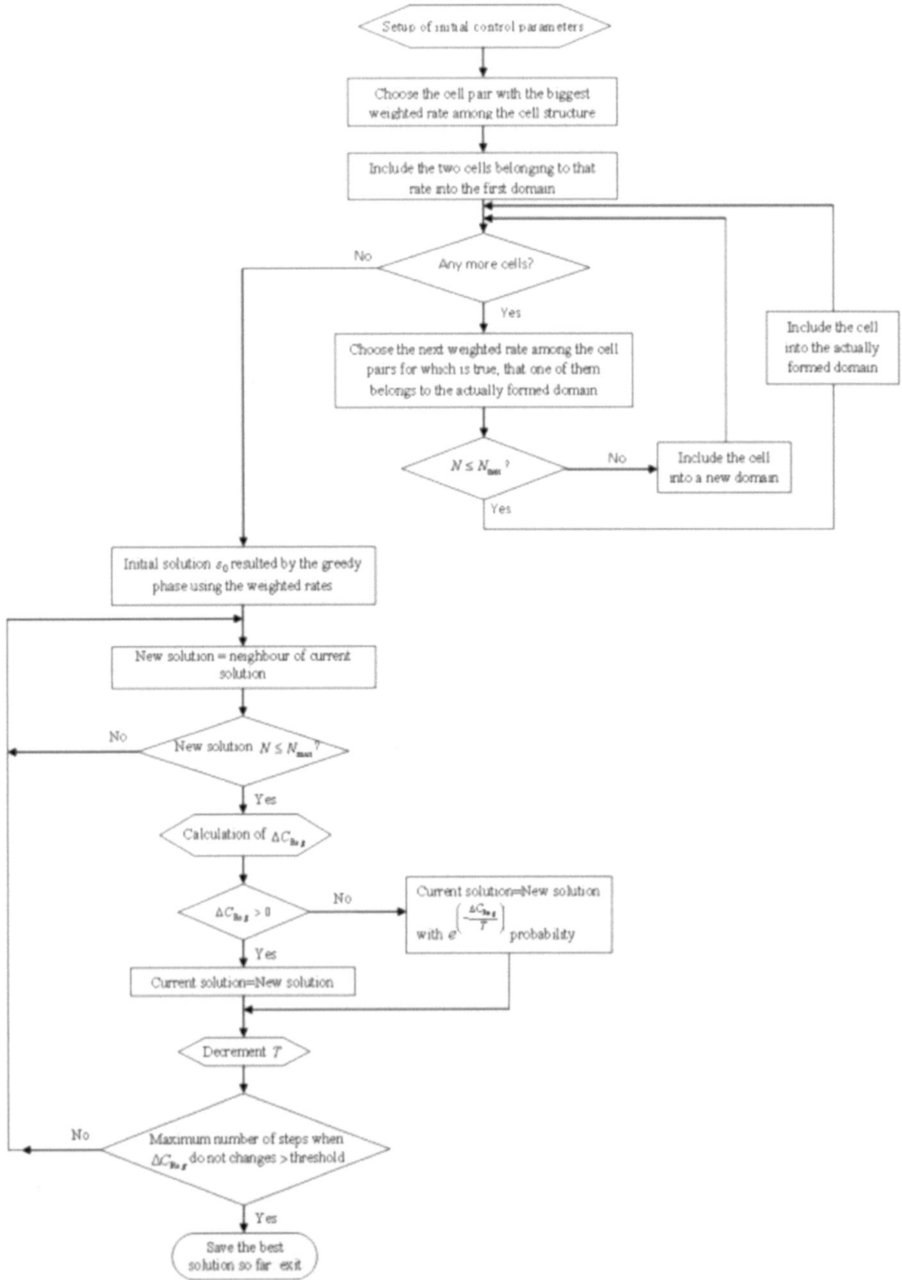

Fig. 1. The detailed flowchart of our proposed location privacy aware domain planning algorithm

4. Evaluation

4.1 The simulation framework

In order to evaluate our algorithm and analyse its performance in real-life scenarios, we designed and implemented a realistic, Java-based mobile environment simulator, which serves a two-fold purpose. On one hand it will generate a realistic cell boundary crossing and incoming call database in a mobile system given by the user with cell, mobile node and movement path placing. It also calculates both the handover rate and the location privacy-weighted rate for each cell pair, defined on the border of these cells. The incoming session statistic can be also generated for every cell; therefore the paging cost and the registration cost can be calculated in the same time for every domain. On the other hand the simulator uses the above produced data as an input for the widest scale of LA and domain planning algorithms, and forms LAs and micromobility domains by running the implemented mathematical functions, e.g., our novel simulation annealing-based, location privacy aware micromobility domain planning algorithm.

As Fig. 2 shows, an arbitrary and customizable road grid can be given and then covered by cells of various access technologies (e.g., WiFi, GSM, UMTS) using the simulator's graphical user interface. The static location privacy significance level of the cells can also be set from 1 to 5 during the cell placement as well as the location type (micro-cell at home, workplace, hospital or hotel). Then the user of the simulator can place communicating mobile nodes firstly by choosing between MNs of different velocities, setting the incoming call arrival parameter (call intensity) and the location privacy profile for different location types to every mobile node.

This way different types of mobility environments with different location privacy characteristics can be designed (rural environment with highways without strict location privacy requirements or a densely populated urban environment with roads and carriageways and the widest scale of location privacy sensitive areas like military facilities, government buildings, etc.,), together with the grids of cells configured and adapted to these environments. The different mobile terminals will move on the defined road grid, continuously choosing randomly a destination point on the road, similarly as in real life. Since typical mobile users are on the move aiming to manage a specific duty or reach a particular destination (e.g., heading to a hotel, a workplace, a hospital, etc.,) and they usually want to arrive in the shortest possible time, therefore the Dijkstra algorithm is used in our simulation framework in order to find the shortest path for mobile hosts towards their selected destination. For every mobile node an incoming call arrival parameter is defined and when an incoming call hits the node, the simulator designates it to the cell where the node is in that moment. When a mobile host changes a cell, the simulator registers that a handover (i.e., cell boundary crossing) happened between the respective cell-pair. When a simulation run ends, the simulator sums the cell boundary crossings and incoming call distribution for every cell in the simulated network, and also calculates the normal and the location privacy-weighted rates for the LA and micromobility domain planning algorithms. The results (road structure, cell structure, call numbers and cell matrix, mobile data) can be saved and opened to easily provide inputs for the Java implementation of our algorithms.

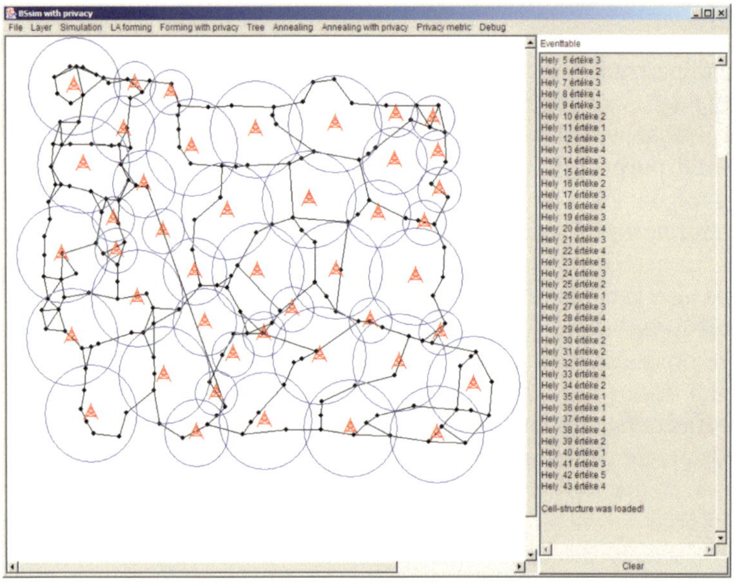

Fig. 2. Initial cell and road structure used for evaluation

Our goal with this mobility simulator was to provide a flexible tool which is able to give the possibility to evaluate Location Area partitioning and micromobility domain planning algorithms for the widest scale of network types, by freely choosing the road grid, communicating mobile hosts and cell structure and characteristics. During our measurements we used our former, simulated annealing based domain optimization method (Bokor, Simon, Dudás, & Imre, 2007) as a basis to compare with the location privacy aware algorithm variant, and also developed a special location privacy metric in the simulator for this comparison.

4.2 Location privacy metric

In order to evaluate the potential and effectiveness of location privacy preserving methods in terms of assessing, quantifying or measuring the abstract concept of location privacy, several metrics are introduced and examined in the literature. (Diaz, Seys, Claessens, & Preneel, 2002) present an information theoretic model that allows to measure the degree of anonymity provided by schemes for anonymous connections. Authors of (Serjantov & Danezis, 2003) introduce an information theoretic measure of anonymity that considers the probabilities of users sending and receiving the messages and also show how to calculate this measure for a message in a standard mix-based anonymity system. The main advantage of this proposal is its capability of not only comparing the effectiveness of different systems, but also evaluating the strength of different attacks. The study of (Shokri, Freudiger, Jadliwala, & Hubaux, 2009) first presents a formal model, which provides an efficient representation of the network users, the bogus entities, the location privacy preserving solutions and the resulting location privacy of users. By using this model, authors provide formal representations of four location privacy metrics among the most relevant categories (uncertainty-based metrics, "clustering error"-based metrics, traceability-based metrics, K-anonymity metrics), and also develop a novel metric for measuring location privacy (called the distortion-based metric), which estimates location privacy as the expected distortion in the reconstructed users' trajectories by an attacker.

Based on the literature we can say that perfect and ideal location privacy metric would capture the exact amount of information that bogus nodes may have about mobile users' actual positions or trajectories. It also means that an ideal location privacy metric should be able to quantify the incapacity of a particular bogus node in localizing or tracking mobile users. Existing location privacy metrics do not utterly capture these attributes of location privacy, often are too specific to particular protocol or scheme, and many times are not able to perfectly represent issues of location privacy because several were not originally designed for mobile networks. Moreover, to the best of our knowledge none of the published location privacy metrics is supposed to help domain or location area planning purposes and none of them focuses on the location privacy peculiarities of micromobility protocols.

It is out of scope of this paper to answer all the above questions and problems and to give a general solution for quantifying location privacy. Our goal, by defining a simple location privacy metric in this section, is to express, that how effectively a given micromobility domain structure takes static location privacy significance of cells and the incoming dynamic location privacy demands of users into account during operation (i.e., how effective could be the protection of users' location privacy while keeping paging and registration costs on a bearable level). In order to achieve this we quantify the inability of non inside-domain attackers in tracking mobile users by computing a weighted number of inter-domain changes of mobile nodes in the network. This is implemented by an extension to our mobility simulator.

During the simulation we track and save movements (i.e., whole paths) of mobile users and also save cell boundary crossings. After running a domain forming algorithm and such creating a domain structure from cells, these savings will help us to localize and count inter-domain changes for every mobile terminal. For every inter-domain handover of a mobile node and for the previous and the next cells of such handovers we sum the value of the cells' static location privacy significance and the squared value of the level of the mobile node's location privacy profile set for the issued location types. We perform the above calculation for every mobile node, and the sum of these values will stand for the location privacy metric of a network containing several micromobility domains. This metric is able to numerically present the location privacy capabilities of a complete network's certain micromobility domain structure: the less the value of the metric is, the higher protection of location privacy will mobile users inherit from micromobility.

4.3 Results

We have tested our novel location privacy aware micromobility domain planning algorithm in a randomly structured complex architecture consisting of 43 cells, 32 mobile nodes and a compound road grid, depicted in Fig. 2. Using this environment we compared our location privacy aware network design scheme with its ancestor which is also a simulated annealing based micromobility domain forming algorithm but without any trace of location privacy awareness (Bokor, Simon, Dudás, & Imre, 2007), (Simon & Imre, A Simulated Annealing Based Location Area Optimization in Next Generation Mobile Networks, 2007).

As an initialization of our experiments we ran the mobility simulator on the example network of Fig. 2 for many thousands of handovers in order to produce all the required realistic input data (e.g., the boundary crossing and incoming session database) for the two solutions we compared and analysed. After that we executed the two algorithms under evaluation (both with parameters $N_{max} = 7$, $T = 100$, and $decr = 2$) on the produced input data and cell structure in order to render the two domain configuration. Fig. 3 shows the generated micromobility domain structure when the location privacy requirement was not taken into consideration (scenario A), while Fig. 4 presents the result after running our location privacy aware micromobility domain planning algorithm (scenario B).

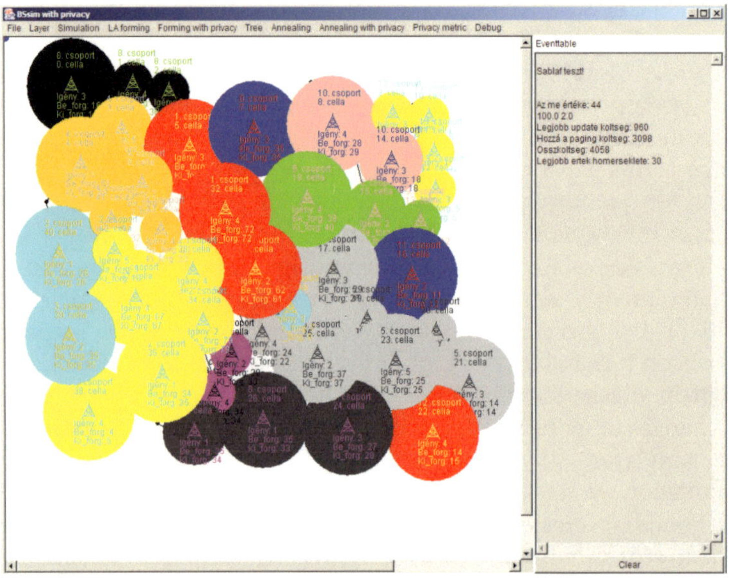

Fig. 3. Micromobility domain structure without taking location privacy into account

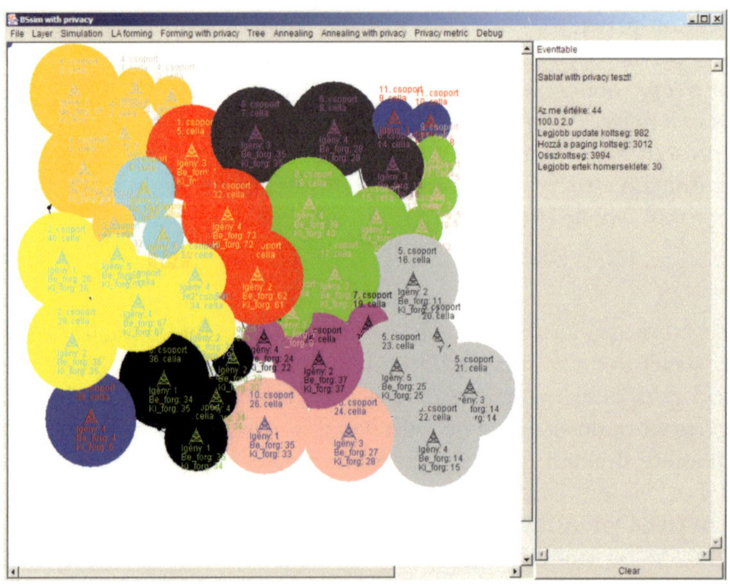

Fig. 4. Micromobility domain structure formed with our location privacy aware design algorithm

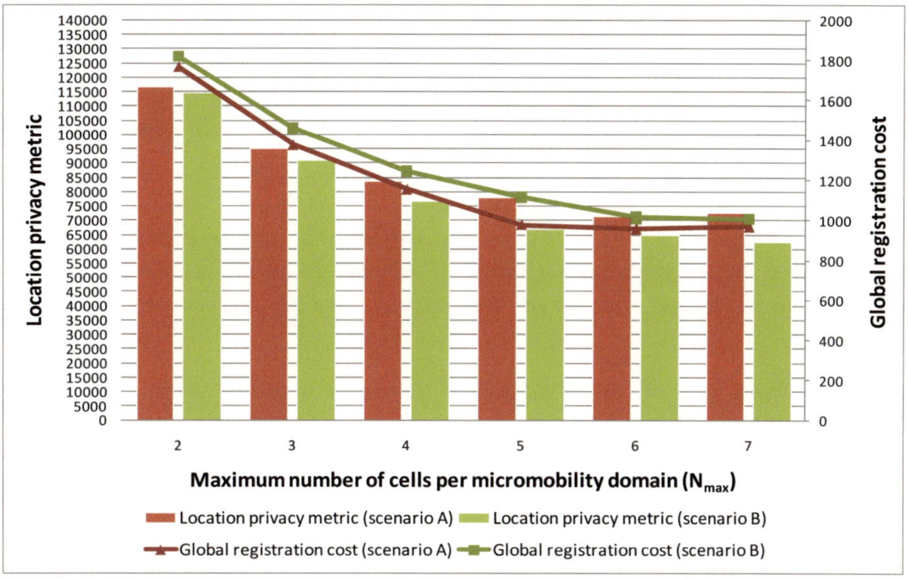

Fig. 5. Comparison of the two scenarios based on location privacy metric and global registration cost

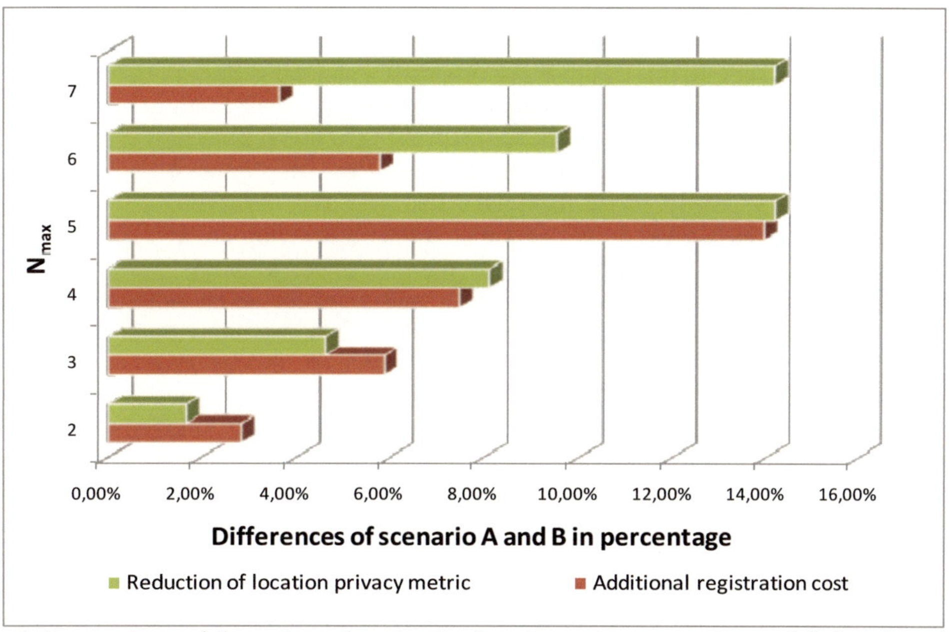

Fig. 6. Comparison of the gain and cost ratio: location privacy metric vs. global registration cost

We examined how the registration cost and the location privacy metric changes by increasing the maximum number of cells in one micromobility domain for each scenario. This way we could check whether the registration cost function is correct, whether it reaches the minimum value when a domain consists of the calculated (15) maximum number of cells

(N_{max}), and how our extended domain forming scheme performs. As Fig. 5 denotes, our simulated annealing based location privacy aware micromobility domain planning algorithm finds a much better solution in means of location privacy support for every value of N_{max} compared to the original scheme which does not care with privacy issues. However, we have to pay the prize of this benefit: the registration cost is slightly higher in scenario B than in scenario A for every domain sizes. This effect is depicted on Fig. 6 which compares the revenue of location privacy support and the accompanied registration cost increment. Fig. 6 shows that our location privacy aware solution responds well to the increasing value of N_{max}, and sees more gain in location privacy metric than loss in registration cost for values $N_{max} \geq 4$.

We can summarize, that our novel algorithm gives much better results than its ancestor when the maximum number of cells is higher ($N_{max} \geq 6$), decreasing the location privacy metric of the network almost for 15% more effective than the former solution, at the expense only of an approximate 4% growth of the global registration cost.

5. Conclusion and future work

In order to design a mobile network that provides location privacy for mobile users in micromobility environments by exploiting inherent properties of micromobility protocols, optimized domain planning is needed, considering the strict constraints like paging service capacity of the network. In this Chapter, we proposed a simulated annealing based location privacy aware micromobility domain planning algorithm for a near-uniform network usage, defining the global registration cost function with the help of the fluid flow model together with a paging constraint. The presented algorithm is a two-step domain forming solution, which consists of a greedy phase that gives the basic cell partitions, and a simulated annealing phase which gives a near-optimal domain structure in acceptable runtime. Aiming to evaluate the performance of our novel method, a simple quantifier for the location privacy ability of micromobility structures was defined and a mobile environment simulator was implemented in Java. Using the input data produced by such a realistic simulation environment, different micromobility planning algorithms were executed. Based on this comprehensive toolset we evaluated our location privacy aware algorithm by examining the global registration cost and the location privacy metric of the network in the function of the maximal number of cells per a micromobility domain. As a result of our evaluation efforts we can say that our algorithm proved its power by significantly reducing the location privacy metric of the network at the expense only of an approximate 4% growth of the global registration cost.

As a part of our future work we plan to extend our algorithms and simulation environment with advanced and more sophisticated location privacy metrics in order to broaden the evaluation of our schemes. We also plan to integrate the concept of location privacy aware network planning into researches relating to personal paging area design.

6. Acknowledgement

This work was made in the frame of Mobile Innovation Centre's 'MEVICO.HU' project, supported by the National Office for Research and Technology (EUREKA_Hu_08-1-2009-0043). The authors also would like to express their appreciation to Krisztián Kovács for his essential work on this research and also to Gábor Gulyás and Iván Székely for raising interest in location privacy studies.

7. References

Baden, R. (2008). IP Geolocation in Metropolitan Area Networks. *Master's Degree Scholarly Paper*. University of Maryland, College Park.

Beresford, A., & Stajano, F. (2003). Location privacy in pervasive computing. *IEEE Pervasive Computing*, 46–55.

Bhattacharjee, P. S., Saha, D., & Mukherjee, A. (1999). Heuristics for assignment of cells to switches in a PCSN. *Proc. IEEE Int. Conf. Personal Comm.*, (pp. 331-334). Jaipur, India.

Bokor, L., Dudás, I., Szabó, S., & Imre, S. (2005). Anycast-based Micromobility: A New Solution for Micromobility Management in IPv6. *in Proceedings of MoMM'05*, (pp. 68-75). Malaysia, Kuala Lumpur.

Bokor, L., Nováczki, S., & Imre, S. (2007). A Complete HIP based Framework for Secure Micromobility. *5th @WAS International Conference on Advances in Mobile Computing and Multimedia*, (pp. 111-122). Jakarta, Indonesia.

Bokor, L., Simon, V., Dudás, I., & Imre, S. (2007). Anycast Subnet Optimization for Efficient IPv6 Mobility Management. *IEEE GIIS'07*, (pp. 187-190). Marrakesh.

Casteluccia, C. (2000). Extending Mobile IP with Adaptive Individual Paging: A Performance Analysis. *Proc. IEEE Symp. Computer and Comm.*, (pp. 113-118).

Cayirci, E., & Akyildiz, I. (2003). Optimal Location Area Design to Minimize Registration Signalling Traffic in Wireless Systems. *IEEE Transactions on Mobile Computing*, *2* (1).

Connolly, G., Sachenko, A., & Markowsky, G. (2003). Distributed traceroute approach to geographically locating IP devices. *Second IEEE International Workshop on Intelligent Data Acquisition and Advanced Computing Systems: Technology and Applications*, (pp. 128 - 131).

Cornelius, C., Kapadia, A., Kotz, D., Peebles, D., Shin, M., & Triandopoulos, N. (2008). Anonysense: privacy-aware people-centric sensing. *International Conference On Mobile Systems, Applications And Services*, (pp. 211-224).

Das, S., Misra, A., Agrawal, P., & Das, S. K. (2000). TeleMIP: telecommunications-enhanced mobile IP architecture for fast intradomain mobility. *IEEE Pers. Commun.*, 50-58.

Diaz, C., Seys, S., Claessens, J., & Preneel, a. B. (2002). Towards measuring anonymity. San Francisco: PET'02.

El-Rabbany, A. (2006). *Introduction to GPS: The Global Positioning System* (2 ed.). Artech House Publishers.

Eriksson, B., Barford, P., Sommersy, J., & Nowak, R. (2010). A Learning-based Approach for IP Geolocation. In *Lecture Notes in Computer Science* (Vol. 6032/2010, pp. 171-180). Berlin / Heidelberg: Springer.

Freedman, M. J., Vutukuru, M., Feamster, N., & Balakrishnan, H. (2005). Geographic Locality of IP Prefixes. *Internet Measurement Conference (IMC)*. Berkeley, CA.

Grilo, A., Estrela, P., & Nunes, M. (2001). Terminal Independent Mobility for IP (TIMIP). *IEEE Communications Magazine* , 34-41.

Gueye, B., Ziviani, A., Crovella, M., & Fdida, S. (2006). Constraint-based geolocation of internet hosts. *IEEE/ACM Transactions on Networking* , *14* (6), 1219-1232.

Gundavelli, S., Leung, K., Devarapalli, V., Chowdhury, K., & Patil, B. (2008, August). Proxy Mobile IPv6. *IETF RFC 5213* .

Haddad, W., Nordmark, E., Dupont, F., Bagnulo, M., & Patil, B. (2006, June 26). Privacy for Mobile and Multihomed Nodes: MoMiPriv Problem Statement. *IETF Internet Draft* .

Haddad, W., Nordmark, E., Dupont, F., Bagnulo, M., Park, S. S., Patil, B., et al. (2006, June 26). Anonymous Identifiers (ALIEN): Privacy Threat Model for Mobile and Multi-Homed Nodes. *IETF Internet Draft* .

He, X., Funato, D., & Kawahara, T. (2003). A dynamic micromobility domain construction scheme. *Personal, Indoor and Mobile Radio Communications (PIMRC'03), 3*, pp. 2495 - 2499.

Helmy, A. A.-G., Jaseemuddin, M., & Bhaskara, G. (2004). Multicast-based mobility: a novel architecture for efficient micromobility. *IEEE Journal on Selected Areas in Communications* , *22* (4).

Hoh, B., & Gruteser, M. (2005). Protecting Location Privacy Through Path Confusion. *First International Conference on Security and Privacy for Emerging Areas in Communications Networks*, (pp. 194 - 205).

Huber, J. (2004). Mobile next-generation networks. *IEEE Multimedia* , *11* (1), 72-83.

Ichikawa, T., Banno, A., & Teraoka, F. (2006). Stealth-Lin6: Anonymizing IPv6 mobility communication. *IPSJ SIG Technical Reports* , *2006 (26)* , 55–60. Japan.

Johnson, D., Perkins, C., & Arkko, J. (2004, June). Mobility Support in IPv6. *IETF RFC 3775* .

Koodli, R. (2007, May). IP Address Location Privacy and Mobile IPv6: Problem Statement. *IETF RFC 4882* .

Kumar, A., Umesh, M. N., & Jha, R. (2000). Mobility modeling of rush hour traffic for location area design in cellular networks. *3rd ACM Int. Workshop Wireless Mobile Multimedia*, (pp. 48-54). Boston, MA.

Kunishi, M., Ishiyama, M., Uehara, K., Esaki, H., & Teraoka, F. (2000). LIN6: A New Approach to Mobility Support in IPv6. *International Symposium on Wireless Personal Multimedia Communication, 455.*

Laarhoven, P. v., & Aarts, E. (1987). *Simulated Annealing: Theory and Applications.* Springer.

Lakhina, A., Byers, J., Crovella, M., & Matta, I. (2003, August). On the Geographic Location of Internet. *IEEE Journal on Selected Areas in Communications* .

Langheinrich, M. (2002). A Privacy Awareness System for Ubiquitous Computing Environments. In G. Borriello, & L. E. Holmquist (Eds.), *Lecture Notes in Computer Science* (Vol. 2498, pp. 237–245). Springer.

Loa, S.-W., Kuo, T.-W., Lam, K.-Y., & Lic, G.-H. (2004). Efficient location area planning for cellular networks with hierarchical location databases. *Computer Networks* , *45* (6), 715-730.

Maekawa, K., & Okabe, Y. (2009). An Enhanced Location Privacy Framework with Mobility Using Host Identity Protocol. *Ninth Annual International Symposium on Applications and the Internet (SAINT'09)*, (pp. 23-29).

Markoulidakis, J., Lyberopoulos, G., Tsirkas, D., & Sykas, E. (1995). Evaluation of location area planning scenarios in future mobile telecommunication systems. *Wireless Networks*, *1*, 17 - 29.

Matos, A., Santos, J., Sargento, S., Aguiar, R., Girao, J., & Liebsch, M. (2006). HIP Location Privacy Framework. *1st ACM/IEEE international workshop on Mobility in the evolving internet architecture* (pp. 57–62). New York, USA: ACM Press.

Moskowitz, R., Nikander, P., Jokela, P., & Henderson, T. (2008, April). Host Identity Protocol. *IETF RFC 5201* .

Pack, S., Choi, Y., & Nam, M. (2006). Design and Analysis of Optimal Multi-Level Hierarchical Mobile IPv6 Networks. *Wireless Personal Communications*, *36*, 95–112.

Pack, S., Nam, M., & Choi, Y. (2004). A Study On Optimal Hierarchy in Multi-Level Hierarchical Mobile IPv6 Networks. *IEEE Globecom*, (pp. 1290-1294).

Prajapati, N. B., Agravat, R. R., & Hasan, M. I. (2010, March). Simulated Annealing for Location Area Planning in Cellular networks. *International journal on applications of graph theory in wireless ad hoc networks and sensor networks (GRAPH-HOC)*, 1-7.

Qian, G., Guang-xia, L., Jing, L., Yi-qun, X., & Ming, Z. (2010). Location Area Design for GEO Mobile Satellite System. *Second International Conference on Computer Engineering and Applications (ICCEA)*, (pp. 525 - 529). Bali Island, Indonesia.

Qiu, Y., Zhao, F., & Koodli, R. (2010, February). Mobile IPv6 Location Privacy Solutions. *IETF RFC 5726* .

Ramjee, R., Porta, T. L., Thuel, S., Varadhan, K., & Wang, S. (1999). HAWAII: A Domain-Based Approach for Supporting Mobility in Wide-area Wireless Networks. *IEEE Int. Conf. Network Protocols.*

Reed, M., Syverson, P., & Goldschlag, D. (1998). Anonymous Connections and Onion Routing. *IEEE Journal on Selected Areas in Communication Special Issue on Copyright and Privacy Protection*, *16*, 482–494.

Reinbold, P., & Bonaventure, O. (2003). IP Micro-Mobility Protocols. *IEEE Communications Surveys & Tutorials*, 40-57.

Rubin, I., & Choi, C. (1997). Impact of the Location Area Structure on the Performance of Signalling Channels in Wireless Cellular Networks. *IEEE Commun. Mag.*, *35* (2).

Serjantov, A., & Danezis, G. (2003). Towards an Information Theoretic Metric for Anonymity. In *Privacy Enhancing Technologies* (Vol. 2482/2003, pp. 259-263). Berlin / Heidelberg: Springer.

Sharma, A., & Ananda, A. L. (2004). A Protocol for Micromobility Management in Next Generation IPv6 Networks. *2nd international workshop on Mobility management & Wireless Access Protocols*, (pp. 72-78).

Shokri, R., Freudiger, J., Jadliwala, M., & Hubaux, J.-P. (2009). A Distortion-Based Metric for Location Privacy. *8th ACM workshop on Privacy in the electronic society*, (pp. 21-30). Chicago, Illinois, USA .

Simon, V., & Imre, S. (2004). A Domain Forming Algorithm for Next Generation, IP Based Mobile Networks. *SOFTCOM'02*, (pp. 289-292). Split, Dubrovnik (Croatia), Venice (Italy).

Simon, V., & Imre, S. (2007). A Simulated Annealing Based Location Area Optimization in Next Generation Mobile Networks. *Journal of Mobile Information Systems* , *3* (3/4), 221-232.

Simon, V., & Imre, S. (2009). Location Area Design Algorithms for Minimizing Signalling Costs in Mobile Networks. In D. Taniar (Ed.), *Mobile Computing: Concepts, Methodologies, Tools, and Applications* (pp. 682-695).

Simon, V., Bokor, L., & Imre, S. (2009). A Hierarchical Network Design Solution for Mobile IPv6. *Journal of Mobile Multimedia (JMM)*, *5* (4), 317-332.

Snekkenes, E. (2001). Concepts for Personal Location Privacy Policies. *3rd ACM Conference on Electronic Commerce* (pp. 48–57). ACM Press.

Soliman, H., Castelluccia, C., Malki, K. E., & Bellier, L. (2005, August). Hierarchical Mobile IPv6 Mobility Management (HMIPv6). *IETF RFC 4140* .

Tabbane, S. (1997). Location Management Methods for Third Generation Mobile Systems. *IEEE Commun. Mag.* , *35* (8).

Valko, A. (1999). Cellular IP: A New Approach to Internet Host Mobility. *ACM SIGCOMM Comp. Commun. Rev.* , *29* (1), 50-65.

Ylitalo, J., & Nikander, P. (2006). BLIND: A Complete Identity Protection Framework for End-Points. In *Lecture Notes in Computer Science* (Vol. 3957, pp. 163–176). Springer Berlin / Heidelberg.

Ylitalo, J., Melen, J., Nikander, P., & Torvinen, V. (2004). Re-thinking Security in IP based Micro-Mobility. *Proc. of the 7th International Conference on Information Security Conference (ISC'04)*, (pp. 318-329). Palo Alto, CA, USA.

5

Simulated Annealing-Based Large-scale IP Traffic Matrix Estimation

Dingde Jiang, Xingwei Wang, Lei Guo and Zhengzheng Xu
Northeastern University
China

1. Introduction

Traffic matrix reflects the volume of traffic that flows between all pairs of sources and destinations in a network. Its element is referred to as an Origin-Destination (OD) pair (or flow). And traffic matrix gives network operators a global aspect of how all the traffic in a large-scale network flows. Thus, with traffic matrix as a key input of traffic engineering and network management, it is very important for network operators to accurately get the traffic matrix in a large-scale network. Unfortunately, as commented in (Papagiannaki et al., 2004), direct measurement of the traffic is not generally practical in the large-scale networks. In 1996, Vardi firstly introduced network tomography method to research the problem that traffic matrix in a network is indirectly measured. Since then, many researchers studied the problem and proposed many solutions(Cao et al., 2000; 2001; Juva, 2007; Soule et al., 2005; 2004; Tan & Wang, 2007; Vardi, 1996; Zhang et al., 2003; 2005). Traffic matrix estimation is so far used by network operators to conduct the network management, network planning, traffic detecting and so on. However, since traffic matrix estimation holds the highly ill-posed properties (Soule et al., 2005; 2004; Tan & Wang, 2007; Vardi, 1996; Zhang et al., 2003; 2005) and especially network traffic is a kind of nonstationary traffic (Cao et al., 2001), this subject is a challenging research problem.

The statistical inference techniques are first used to estimate traffic matrix over local area network (LAN). Authors in (Cao et al., 2000; Vardi, 1996) exploited the statistical model to model the OD flows in order to reduce the ill-posed nature of traffic matrix estimation. Zhang et al. (Zhang et al., 2003; 2005) introduced the gravity model into large-scale IP traffic matrix estimation. By the gravity model, they could obtain the prior information about OD flows and then successfully conduct the large-scale IP traffic matrix estimation. Nevertheless, as mentioned in (Juva, 2007; Soule et al., 2005), the statistical inference techniques are sensitive to the prior information, while the gravity model methods still have the larger estimation errors though it partially reduces the sensitivity to the prior information. Especially when the assumptions about OD flows hold, the gravity model methods are found to be more accurate than the statistical inference techniques, while their estimation accuracy decreases more quickly than that of the statistical inference techniques when the assumptions are not exactly true. Hence, this needs to develop a new method to estimate large-scale IP traffic matrix.

This chapter provides the reader with a method that large scale IP traffic matrix is estimated accurately by, as envisioned by the authors. It begins by explaining the need for using simulated annealing to estimate the traffic matrix, how traffic matrix estimation problem is defined, and possible motivation for using Simulated annealing to solve it. Then the chapter examines how our method is related to, but distinct from, previous work in traffic matrix estimation. The implementation of our method is discussed, and then simulation results and analysis are proposed. Finally, we present the important areas of future work and conclude our work to close the chapter.

1.1 Problem Statement

For a large-scale IP network, assuming there are the n nodes and L links, it will have the $N = n^2$ OD flows. Each of OD flows and link loads is time series. traffic matrix and link loads at time t are denotes as $x(t) = (x_1(t), x_2(t), ..., x_N(t))^T$ and $y(t) = (y_1(t), y_2(t), ..., y_L(t))^T$ čňrespectively. In a large-scale IP network, traffic matrix $x(t)$ and link loads $y(t)$ are correlated by the L by N routing matrix $A = (A_{ij})_{L\times N}$, where A_{ij} is equal 1 if OD flow j traverses link i, or zero. They follow the below constraints:

$$y(t) = Ax(t). \tag{1}$$

Link loads can be attained via the SNMP measurements. Routing matrix can be obtained by the status and configuration information of the network. Therefore, traffic matrix estimation is that, given link loads $y(t)$ and routing matrix A, one seeks to obtain a required solution $x(t)$ satisfied with (1). However, in the large-scale IP network, the number of OD flows is often by far larger than that of links, i.e. $L \ll N$. Eq. (1) denotes a highly under-constrained linear problem. It has the infinite solution for traffic matrix. Hence, large-scale IP traffic matrix estimation is a highly ill-posed inverse problem. How to overcome the ill-posed nature in this problem is the main challenge faced. Network tomography is a good way for this problem (Cao et al., 2000; Tebaldi & West, 1998; Vardi, 1996; Zhang et al., 2003a).
In a large-scale IP network, traffic matrix and link loads vary with time, and are satisfied with the above linear relations. Previous studies show that OD flows, namely elements in traffic matrix, hold strongly daily pattern, and even weekly and monthly pattern. This suggests that OD flows hold the temporal correlations.

1.2 Motivation and Requirements

So far, simulated annealing method is studied extensively and has many successful solutions (Bryan et al., 2006; Hung et al., 2008; Tiwari & Cosman, 2008; Thompson & Bilbro, 2005). It is a non-numerical algorithm which is simple and globally optimal, and is suited well for solving the large-scale combinatorial optimization problems. However, because of the complexity of large-scale IP traffic matrix estimation, it is very difficult to use directly simulated annealing method to estimate it, and even it is not practical. And the solution space of traffic matrix is a continuous real subspace. Hence, due to the randomicity that conventional simulated annealing method generates a new solution, it is difficult to find quickly the globally optimal solution. To solve this problem and attain an accurate estimation of traffic matrix, we consider sufficiently spatial-temporal correlations of OD flows by using covariance matrix about OD flows, and combine partial flow measurement. By covariance matrix, one can quickly choose the direction in which the simulated annealing iterative process advances towards the globally optimal solution.
We investigate large-scale IP traffic matrix estimation problem and present a novel method called the simulated annealing and generalized inference (SAGI). Based on the conventional simulated annealing, we propose a modified simulated annealing process suited for large-scale IP traffic matrix estimation. By the modified simulated annealing, we describe the traffic

matrix estimation into a simulated annealing process. With the temperature dropping slowly, the traffic matrix's estimation gradually approaches to the true value. When temperature declines to the defined value, the estimation is attained. To obtain the accurate estimation, a heuristic method is introduced into the simulated annealing process by using covariance matrix about traffic matrix. Built on this heuristic way, the estimation can be quickly and accurately determined in the simulated annealing process. However, since traffic matrix estimation is a highly ill-posed problem, the estimation sought by simulated annealing may not precisely reflect the traffic matrix's inherent nature. We choose the Euclid and Mahalanobis distances as the optimal metric. This choice is based on the following reasons: (1) Euclid distance computes the whole distance of the vector. It deals with the difference between the elements of the vector in the identical way. (2) Mahalanobis distance can get rid of the disturbance of the correlations between the variables; it is not related with the measurement units; and Mahalanobis distance distinguishes the different characteristics between the variables. By combining these two different distances, a generalized inference is proposed to overcome further the traffic matrix's ill-posed nature. Hence, SAGI can accurately estimate large-scale IP traffic matrix. We use the real data from the Abilene (http://www.cs.utexas.edu, 2004) and GÉANT (Uhlig et al., 2006) networks to validate SAGI. Simulation results show that SAGI exhibits the lower estimation errors and stronger robustness to noise.

2. Related work

Some papers have investigated traffic matrix estimation and proposed some solutions. Vardi (Vardi, 1996), Cao et al. (Cao et al., 2000), and Tebaldi et al. (Tebaldi & West, 1998) used the statistical inference method to estimate traffic matrix only over the local area network. As mentioned in (Soule et al., 2005), these methods are sensitive to the prior, and estimation errors are larger. Medina et al. (Medina et al., 2002) showed that the basic assumptions based on the statistical models are not justified, and they also showed that, when their underlying assumptions are violated, the estimated results are bad. Furthermore, because these methods need to perform the complex mathematical computation, it takes some time to estimate traffic matrix. Hence, it is difficult to scale these methods to large-scale networks.

Zhang et al. (Zhang et al., 2003;a) discussed the problem of large-scale IP traffic matrix estimation by introducing the gravity model. Though, as mentioned in (Soule et al., 2005), their method partially reduced the sensitivity to the prior, it also has the larger errors, because it only considered the spatial correlations among the OD flows. Nucci et al. (Nucci et al., 2004) proposed the method that changed the under-constrained problem into the full rank one by changing the routing and then taking new SNMP measurements under this new routing map. Similarly, Soul et al. (Soule et al., 2004) presented a heuristic algorithm to compute the routing needed in order to obtain a full rank problem. Papagiannaki et al. (Papagiannaki et al., 2004) proposed a data-driven method that depends on measurements alone to obtain traffic matrix, without using the routing matrix and performing the inference, but based on measuring traffic matrix directly. Lakhina et al. (Lakhina et al., 2004) used the Principal Component Analysis to solve the traffic matrix estimation problem. Soule et al. (Soule et al., 2004) introduced the Kalman filtering into traffic matrix estimation. However, all the methods need to establish mathematical model about OD flows and perform the statistical inference, or combine the direct measurement of partial OD flows to infer traffic matrix. Thus, they need the complex mathematical computations. Different from the above methods, SAGI uses simulated annealing to handle large-scale IP traffic matrix estimation problem. By denoting traffic matrix estimation problem into simulated annealing process, we avoid complex mathematical computation and can attain the accurate estimation results.

Liang et al. (Liang et al., 2006), based on game theory, proposed a fast lightweight approach to OD flow estimation. Bermolen et al. (Bermolen et al., 2006) derived analytically the Fisher information matrix under the second moment statistics with the functional mean-variance relationship and then obtained the Cramer-Rao lower bound for the variance of traffic matrix estimator. By this bound, they could attain traffic matrix estimation. Juva (Juva, 2007) studied the sensitivity of the estimation accuracy to those underlying assumptions in the case of the gravity model based and second moment methods. They showed that if the assumptions hold, the gravity model based methods are more accurate, or their accuracy declines faster than that of the second moment methods. However, SAGI does not make any assumption about OD flows. It only sovle traffic matrix estimation problem with simulated annealing method. Due to the capacity of simulated annealing to solve the large-scale combinatorial optimization problems, SAGI is not sensitive to the assumption about OD flows and it is also robust to noise. Because the modified simulated annealing method is simple and fast, this makes it suited for handling the problem of the large-scale IP traffic matrix estimations.

3. Implementation

According to the characteristics of traffic matrix, multi-input and multi-output large-scale IP traffic matrix estimation model based on the modified simulated annealing method is presented in Figure 1, where $y(t) = (y_1(t), y_2(t), ..., y_L(t))^T$ (L is the number of links in a network) is link loads at a particular time t, $x\_0 = (\hat{x}_1^0(t), \hat{x}_x^0(t), ..., \hat{x}_N^0(t))^T$ (N is the number of OD flows in a network) the initial value of traffic matrix, $\hat{x} = (\hat{x}_1(t), \hat{x}_x(t), ..., \hat{x}_N(t))^T$ the estimation of traffic matrix, f cost function, and x_opt, f_min, x_cur, f_cur and x_g denotes optimal solution, minimum of cost function, current solution, current value of cost function and new solution in the iterative process of the modified simulated annealing method, respectively, and "*Stop criterion*" includes the maximum iteration steps and maximum unchanged times of cost function at a certain defined temperature. As showed in Figure 1, the model includes three parts: Initialing, Modified simulated annealing method and IPFP, where Initialing is used for initialing the variable that Modified simulated annealing method needs, Modified simulated annealing method for seeking globally optimal solution, and IPFP for satisfying the estimations of traffic matrix with tomographic constraints.

Generally, simulated annealing method includes generating new solution, computing cost function difference, ascertaining if new solution is accepted, and updating the iterative process. Now, according to the complexity of large-scale IP traffic matrix estimation, simulated annealing method is modified as follows.

3.1 Cost Function

According to Equation (1), cost function used for simulated annealing method is chosen as:

$$f(x(t)) = \|y(t) - Ax(t)\|, \tag{2}$$

where $\|.\|$ is L_2 norm. Assume that the kth iterative result is $x^k(t)$, and the $(k+1)th$ iterative result is $x^{k+1}(t)$. And then cost function difference between the kth result and the $(k+1)th$ one is denoted as:

$$\Delta f^{k+1} = f(x^{k+1}(t)) - f(x^k(t)), \tag{3}$$

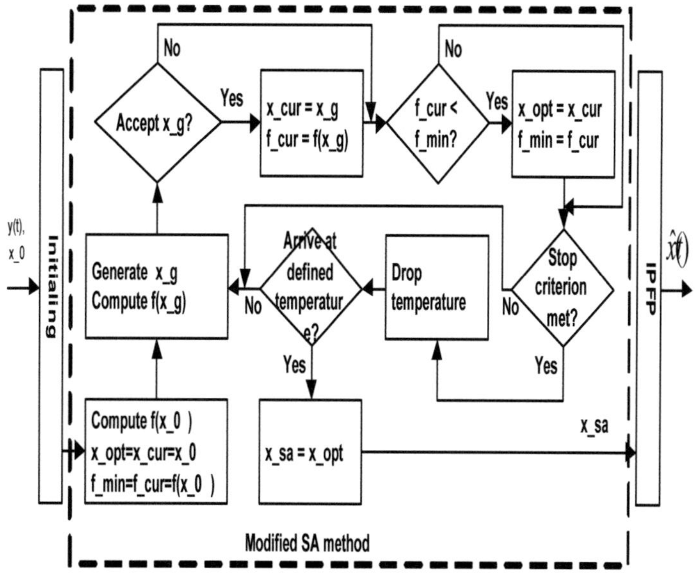

Fig. 1. Architecture representation of multi-input and multi-output large-scale IP traffic matrix estimation model based on the modified simulated annealing method, with the modified simulated annealing method showed in dotted line frame, IPFP used for adjusting the estimation of traffic matrix.

3.2 Generating New Solution

By generating randomly new solution, simulated annealing method makes current solution departing from locally optimal point to globally optimal point. However, the solution space of traffic matrix is a continuous real subspace. Hence, it is difficult of conventional simulated annealing method to find quickly the globally optimal solution. And so covariance matrix about OD flows is introduced to solve this problem.

Firstly, covariance matrix is attained, based on multivariate statistical analysis theory. Assume that traffic matrices of S time plots, which are denoted as $X^S = (x(1), x(2), ..., x(S))$, are known. And then covariance matrix C is represented by the following equation.

$$\begin{cases} U = \sum_{j=1}^{S}(x(i) - \overline{X^S}), \\ C = \frac{1}{S-1}UU^T, \\ \overline{X^S} = \frac{1}{S}\sum_{j=1}^{S} x(i). \end{cases} \quad (4)$$

Equation (4) shows that main diagonal elements of covariance matrix C represent the temporal correlations of traffic matrix sample, and other elements represent spatial-temporal correlations. As mentioned above, OD flows hold strongly daily pattern, and even weekly and monthly pattern, and so covariance matrix C can be used to denote spatial-temporal correlations of traffic matrix. The following simulation results also show this.

According to the characteristics of large-scale IP traffic matrix, new solution in the simulated annealing process, from the kth iterative result $x^k(t)$ to the $(k+1)th$ iterative result $x^{k+1}(t)$, is generated as follows.

$$x^{k+1}(t) = x^k(t) + 2 \times rand \times \Delta x^{k+1}, \quad (5)$$

where "*rand*" is the random number from 0 to 1, and Δx^{k+1} is a direction vector in the $(k+1)th$ iterative process. It is a key problem to ascertain quickly Δx^{k+1}. The following uses the optimal method to attain it. To consider sufficiently spatial-temporal correlations of OD flows and satisfy the estimations of traffic matrix with tomographic constraints, select the objective function:

$$\begin{cases} \min(\|y(t) - Ax^{k+1}(t)\|_2^2 + \lambda\|C \times \Delta x^{k+1}\|_2^2), \\ s.t. \quad \begin{array}{l} y(t) = Ax(t), \\ x_i(t) \geq 0, \quad i = 1, 2, ..., N \end{array} \end{cases} \tag{6}$$

where C is the covariance matrix denoted by equation (4), λ a regularization parameter whose value is generally 0.01 or so.

$$Set \qquad x^{k+1}(t) = x^k(t) + \Delta x^{k+1}, \tag{7}$$

Substitute Equation (7) into Equation (6), and get the below objective function:

$$\begin{cases} \min(\|y(t) - A(x^k(t) + \Delta x^{k+1})\|_2^2 + \lambda\|C \times \Delta x^{k+1}\|_2^2), \\ s.t. \quad \begin{array}{l} y(t) = Ax(t), \\ x_i(t) \geq 0, \quad i = 1, 2, ..., N \end{array} \end{cases} \tag{8}$$

The least square solution of (8) is

$$\Delta x^{k+1} = (A^T A + \lambda \times C^T C)^{-1} A^T (y(t) - Ax^k(t)), \tag{9}$$

According to Equation (5) and (9), get the following new solution in the simulated annealing process.

$$\begin{cases} x^{k+1}(t) = x^k + 2 \times rand \times \Delta x^{k+1}, \\ \Delta x^{k+1} = (A^T A + \lambda \times C^T C)^{-1} A^T Y^k, \\ Y^k = (y(t) - Ax^k(t)). \end{cases} \tag{10}$$

3.3 Accepted Criterion

The modified simulated annealing method uses Metroplis criterion to ascertain if new solution is accepted. Here, Metroplis criterion is denoted by the below equation.

$$P(x^k(t) \Rightarrow x^{k+1}(t)) = \begin{cases} 1 & \Delta f^{k+1} \leq 0, \\ exp(\frac{\Delta f^{k+1}}{T}), & \Delta f^{k+1} > 0. \end{cases} \tag{11}$$

where T is the current temperature value. Equation (11) shows that when $\Delta f^{k+1} \leq 0$, new solution is accepted with probability value 1, or with probability value $exp(\frac{\Delta f^{k+1}}{T})$.

3.4 Updating the Iterative Process

As showed in Figure 1, the modified simulated annealing method firstly computes cost function $f(x\_0)$ by the initial value x_0 of traffic matrix, and then generates new solution x_g in terms of Equation (10). If new solution is accepted, then update x_cur and f_cur, or if $f\_cur < f\_min$, update x_opt and f_min. Now if "*Stop criterion*" is not met, update the corresponding variables, generate the next new solution and repeat the above process, or drop temperature, and ascertain if temperature arrives at the defined value. If temperature arrives

at the defined value, update $x\_sa = x\_opt$. The two variables in the iterative process, namely x_opt and f_min, insure that the met optimal solution is not left out. Thus the modified simulated annealing method holds the memory capability.
Let $x^0(t)$, x_opt, and f_min denote the traffic matrix's prior value, optimal solution, minimum cost function in the iterative process of the simulated annealing, respectively. The traffic matrix's prior value is given by the last moment estimation $\hat{x}(t-1)$. This gives the below iterative equation:

$$\begin{cases} x^{k+1}(t) & = & x^k(t) + 2 \times r \times \Delta x^{k+1}, \\ x^0(t) & = & \hat{x}(t-1). \end{cases} \tag{12}$$

Eqs. (4), (6), and (12) indicate that the modified simulated annealing has built the spatio-temporal model about traffic matrix. This model can accurately capture the traffic matrix's characteristics. However, as time advances forward, this model may not precisely capture the traffic matrix's properties and yields the estimation errors. As mentioned in (Soule et al., 2005), we use the partial flow measurement to calibrate this model. In addition, to follow the constraints in Eq. (6), iterative proportional fitting procedure (IPFP) is used to adjust the estimation obtained.
So far, we have proposed a modified simulated annealing method to attain the traffic matrix's estimation. The following Algorithm 1 proposes the complete steps of this method.
Algorithm 1
Step 1. Give the error ε, ratio factor α, initial temperature T_0, minimum temperature $T_{\min}$, maximum iterative steps K, maximum unchanged times M of cost function at certain temperature, and initial traffic matrix $x^0(t)$. And set temperature $T = T_0$, iterative step $k = 0$, and the variable $m = 0$. Then compute $f(x^0(t))$ by Eq. (1), and set $x\_opt = x^0(t)$, $f\_\min = f(x^0(t))$.
Step 2. Yield random value "r" from 0 to 1. By Eq. (10), get new solution $x^{k+1}(t)$ and compute $f(x^{k+1}(t))$.
Step 3. Compute cost function difference Δf^{k+1} according to Eq. (3). If $\Delta f^{k+1} = 0$, set $m = m + 1$.
Step 4. Generate random value "p_rand" from 0 to 1. If $\Delta f^{k+1} \le 0$ or $\exp(\frac{\Delta f^{k+1}}{T}) > p\_rand$, accept new solution $x^{k+1}(t)$, or discard new solution $x^{k+1}(t)$.
Step 5. If $x^{k+1}(t)$ is accepted and $f(x^{k+1}(t)) < f\_\min$, update $x\_opt = x^{k+1}(t)$ and $f\_\min = f(x^{k+1}(t))$, or If $x^{k+1}(t)$ is not accepted, $x^{k+1}(t) = x^k(t)$.
Step 6. If $k < K$ and $m < M$, set $k = k + 1$ and go back to Step 2.
Step 7. Drop temperature to $T = \alpha T$. if $T \ge T_{\min}$, set $k = 0$, $m = 0$, $x^k(t) = x\_opt$, and go back to Step 2.
Step 8. Adjust x_opt with IPFP and obtain the traffic matrix's estimation $\hat{x}_s(t)$.
Step 9. If $||y(t) - A\hat{x}_s(t)||_2^2 < \varepsilon$, output the result, or directly measure the OD flows and go back to Step 1.

3.5 Generalized Inference

Since traffic matrix estimation is a highly ill-posed problem, how to seek to obtain a solution required is significantly difficult. Here we present a generalized inference method to further overcome the ill-posed nature of this problem. As mentioned in introduction, we choose the Euclid and Mahalanobis distance as the optimal metric. Thus, the objective function is given as follows:

$$\begin{cases} \min((y(t) - Ax(t))^T Q^{-1}(y(t) - Ax(t)) + \\ \qquad ||y(t) - Ax(t)||_2^2 + \alpha||Dx(t)||_2^2) \ , \\ \text{s.t.} \quad \begin{array}{l} y(t) \ = Ax(t), \\ x_i(t) \geq 0, \quad i = 1, 2, ..., N \end{array} \end{cases} \tag{13}$$

where Q is the covariance matrix of link loads, D denotes a smoothing matrix, and α represents a regularization parameter with its value being 0.01 or so.

$$Set \qquad x(t) = x_0(t) + \Delta x(t). \tag{14}$$

By Eqs. (13)-(14), obtain the least square solution:

$$\begin{aligned} \Delta x(t) = (A^T A + A^T Q^{-1} A + \alpha D^T D)^{-1} \times \\ (A^T + A^T Q^{-1})(y(t) - Ax_0(t)). \end{aligned} \tag{15}$$

Accordingly, attain the following iterative equation:

$$\begin{cases} x^{v+1}(t) & = x^v(t) + \Delta x^{v+1}(t), \\ \Delta x^{v+1}(t) & = (A^T A + A^T Q^{-1} A + \alpha D^T D)^{-1} \times \\ & \qquad (A^T + A^T Q^{-1})(y(t) - Ax^v(t)), \\ x^0(t) & = \hat{x}_s(t), \end{cases} \tag{16}$$

where v represents the iterative step and $\hat{x}_s(t)$ is the estimation attained by simulated annealing. Eqs. (13)-(16) represent the generalized inference process. Algorithm 2 gives an overview of the generalized inference process proposed.

Algorithm 2

Step 1. Set the errors ε and δ, give iterative steps V, and let $v = 0$ and $x^0(t) = \hat{x}_s(t)$.
Step 2. According to Eq. (16), perform the generalized inference process.
Step 3. If $||y(t) - Ax^{v+1}(t)||_2^2 \leq \varepsilon$ or $||x^{v+1}(t) - x^v(t)||_2^2$
$\leq \delta$ or $v > V$, exit and output the result, or go back Step 2 otherwise.

Up to now, we propose Algorithms 1 and 2 for the simulated annealing process and generalized inference, respectively. Below we summarize the complete SAGI method proposed.
Step 1. Obtain the traffic matrix $\hat{x}_s(t)$ according to Algorithm 1.
Step 2. By Algorithm 2, attain the optimization solution.
Step 3. Use IPFP to yield a more accurate estimation satisfied with the constraints in Eq. (13).

4. Simulation Results and Analysis

We conduct a series of simulations to validate SAGI, analyzing traffic matrix estimation errors (spatial relative errors (SREs) and temporal relative errors (TREs)) and robustness. Since TomoGravity (Zhang et al., 2003; 2005) and 1-Inverse (Tan & Wang, 2007) is reported as the accurate methods of traffic matrix estimation, SAGI will be compared with them. We use, respectively, the ten-day and twenty-one-day real data from the Abilene (http://www.cs.utexas.edu, 2004) and GÉANT (Uhlig et al., 2006) network to simulate the performance of three methods. The first seven-day and fourteen-day data from the Abilene and GÉANT network are, respectively, used to construct the covariance matrix according to Eq. (4), while the rest are exploited to test three methods.
The SREs and TREs are denoted as follows:

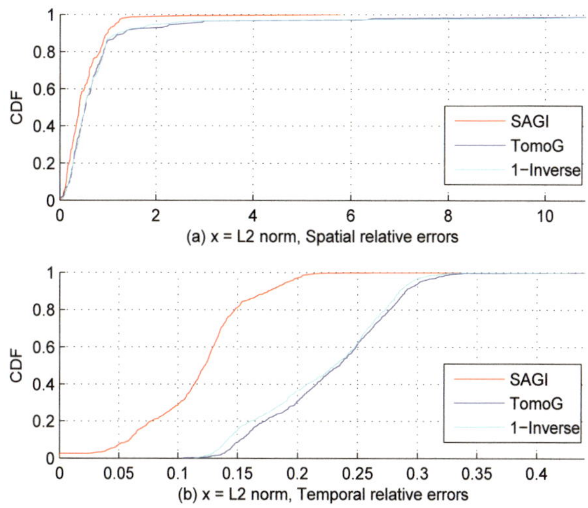

Fig. 2. CDF of spatial and temporal relative errors in Abilene.

$$\begin{cases} err_{sp}(n) = \frac{||\hat{x}_T(n) - x_T(n)||_2}{||x_T(n)||_2}, \\ err_{tm}(t) = \frac{||\hat{x}_N(t) - x_N(t)||_2}{||x_N(t)||_2}, \\ n = 1, 2, ..., N; \quad t = 1, 2, ..., T \end{cases} \tag{17}$$

where N and T are the total number of OD flows and measurement moments, respectively; $||.||_2$ is L_2 norm; $err_{sp}(n)$ and $err_{tm}(t)$ denote the SREs and TREs, respectively. To precisely evaluate the estimation performance of three methods, we examine the cumulative distribution functions (CDFs) of their SREs and TREs. Figs.1 and 2 plot their CDFs in the Abilene and GÉANT network, respectively.

From Figs.1 and 2, we can see that the curves of the SREs' and TREs' CDFs of TomoGravtiy and {1}-Inverse are far below those of SAGI, while TomoGravtiy's and {1}-Inverse's are close. Furthermore, In Fig.1a, for SAGI, about 79% of OD flows are tracked with SREs less than 0.8, while less than 74% for TomoGravity and less than 71% for {1}-Inverse. In Fig.2a, for SAGI, about 86% of OD flows are tracked with SREs less than 0.8, while about 26% for TomoGravity and about 35% for 1-Inverse. This shows that, in Abilene and GÉANT network, the spatial estimation errors of SAGI are far lower than those of other two methods, while those of TomoGravity and {1}-Inverse are close. Analogously, we can also see that, in Fig.1b, about 97% of measurement moments, for SAGI, can be tracked with TREs less than 0.2, while 30.6% for TomoGravity and 36.4% for {1}-Inverse. In Fig.2b, SAGI can track 94% of measurement moments with TREs less than 10.12%, while TomoGravity with TREs less than 50.28% and {1}-Inverse with TREs less than 53.67%. This indicates that in Abilene and GÉANT network, the temporal estimation errors of SAGI are far lower than those of other two methods. However, TomoGravity's is lower than {1}-Inverse's in Abilene network, while {1}-Inverse's is lower than TomoGravity's in GÉANT network. Hence, SAGI can more accurately estimate traffic matrix than TomoGravity and {1}-Inverse.

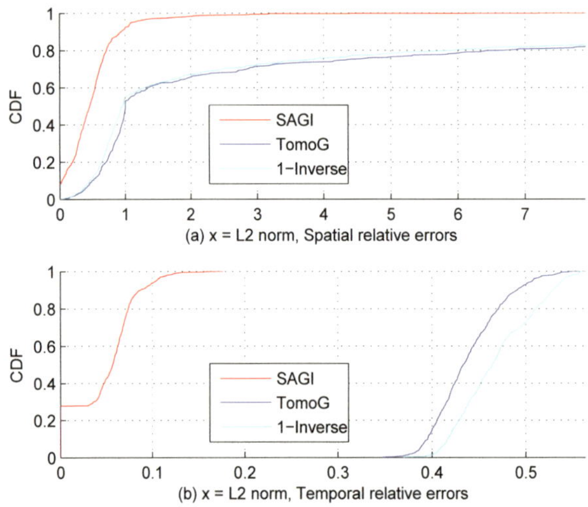

Fig. 3. CDF of spatial and temporal relative errors in GÉANT.

To evaluate the impact of noise on three methods, we introduce an error term $\theta(t)$ to (1) and attain the equation $y_n(t) = Ax(t) + \theta(t)$, where $\theta(t) = y_n(t) \times \eta(0, \zeta)$, and $\eta(0, \zeta)$ denotes a normal distribution with zero mean and standard deviation. We discuss the robustness of three methods in three cases: $\zeta = 0.01$, $\zeta = 0.03$, and $\zeta = 0.05$. We use the following spatial root mean squared relative error (SRMSRE) and temporal root mean squared relative error (TRMSRE) to evaluate the robustness of three methods in the Abilene and GÉANT network.

$$\begin{cases} SRMSRE = \frac{1}{N} \sum_{n=1}^{N} \frac{||\hat{x}_T(n) - x_T(n)||_2}{||x_T(n)||_2}, \\ TRMSRE = \frac{1}{T} \sum_{t=1}^{T} \frac{||\hat{x}_N(t) - x_N(t)||_2}{||x_N(t)||_2}. \end{cases} \quad (18)$$

Tables 1 and 2 show the impact of noise on three methods in the Abilene and GÁENT network, respectively. From both tables, we can see that, in three cases: $\zeta = 0.01$, $\zeta = 0.03$, and $\zeta = 0.05$, the SRMSRE's and TRMSRE's changes of SAGI are lower than those of other two methods. Hence, SAGI is more robust to noise.

5. Future Questions and Research Areas

The previous sections make an investigation for how simulated annealing method is exploited to solve the large-scale traffic matrix estimation. We now examine major issues of the related research for future. With the wireless sensor networks and the Internet of things advancing, IP networks will become more ubiquitous and heterogeneous. Though this chapter exploits the simulated annealing to be able to make the accurate estimation for traffic matrix, SAGI method is only validated in the large-scale IP backbone networks. We do not know if this method is suited for the ubiquitous and heterogeneous networks either. Hence, it is necessary to validate SAGI method in the ubiquitous and heterogeneous networks.

Additionally, there is an implicit assumption in this chapter that the topology of the IP networks keeps up unchanged. In fact, the topology of the networks will change with the environment of networks, for example, when the fault of the networks takes place, their topologies will vary correspondingly. Network topology is related to route matrix. Thus we also consider if SAGI can still estimate accurately traffic matrix when network topology changes.

Table 1. Impact of noise on three methods in Abilene

Noise Level		$\delta = 0.01$	$\delta = 0.03$	$\delta = 0.05$
Link loads	SRMSRE	1.00%	3.01%	5.05%
	TRMSRE	0.98%	2.97%	4.96%
SAGI	SRMSRE	53.10%	53.85%	55.03%
	TRMSRE	13.93%	14.22%	14.75%
TomoG	SRMSRE	96.79%	99.39%	104.66%
	TRMSRE	22.82%	23.48%	24.91%
{1}-Inverse	SRMSRE	99.61%	101.76%	105.76%
	TRMSRE	22.22%	22.87%	24.09%

Table 2. Impact of noise on three methods in GÉANT

Noise Level		$\delta = 0.01$	$\delta = 0.03$	$\delta = 0.05$
Link loads	SRMSRE	0.98%	2.95%	5.00%
	TRMSRE	0.99%	2.97%	5.02%
SAGI	SRMSRE	87.55%	88.30%	89.38%
	TRMSRE	29.05%	29.65%	30.85%
TomoG	SRMSRE	139.03%	141.34%	144.61%
	TRMSRE	42.85%	44.13%	46.51%
{1}-Inverse	SRMSRE	137.99%	139.89%	143.53%
	TRMSRE	45.85%	47.05%	49.27%

6. Conclusion

This chapter has proposed a new method to estimate large-scale IP traffic matrix. By describing the traffic matrix estimation into a modified simulated annealing process and using the generalized inference, we have successfully overcome its ill-posed nature. Simulation results on both real networks show that SAGI exhibits the lower estimation errors and stronger robustness to noise. Although traffic matrix estimation is becoming more and more important, the accurate estimation for it is not becoming increasingly easier. Based on the simulated annealing method, this chapter manages to attain accurately the large-scale IP traffic matrix estimation by considering the spatial and temporal correlations.

7. References

Bryan, K., Cunningham, P., and Bolshakova, N., "Application of simulated annealing to the bi-clustering of gene expression data", IEEE Trans. Inf. Technol. Biomed., Vol. 10, No. 3, pp. 519-525, 2006.

Bermolen P, Vaton S, Juva I. Search for optimality in traffic matrix estimation: A rational approach by cramĺęr-rao lower bounds. In: Proceedings of the 2nd EuroNGI NGI Conf. on Next Generation Internet Design and Engineering; 2006. p. 224-31.

Cao, J.; Davis, D.; Weil, S.; Yu, B. Time-varying network tomography. J. Amer. Stat. Assoc. 2000; 95:1063-75.

Cao, J.; Cleveland, W.; Lin, D. et al. On the nonstationarity of internet traffic. In: Proceedings of ACM SIGMETRICS'01. Cambridge, MA, 2001. p. 102-12.

Hung, M.; Ho, S.; Shu, L.; Hwang, S.; and Ho, S.-Y. "A Novel Multiobjective Simulated Annealing Algorithm for Designing Robust PID Controllers", IEEE Trans. on Systems, Man, and Cybernetics-Part A, Systems and Humans, Vol. 38, No. 2 , pp. 319-330, MARCH. 2008.

http://www.cs.utexas.edu/~yzhang/research/abilene-tm/.

Juva, I. Sensitivity of traffic matrix estimation techniques to their underlying assumption. In: Proceedings of ICC'07. Glasgow, Scotland, 2007. p. 562-8.

Jiang, D.; Wang, X.; and Lei, G. An optimization method of large-scale IP traffic matrix estimation. AEU-International Journal of Electronics and Communications, 2009, In Press.

Jiang, D.; Wang, X.; Lei, G. et al. Accurate estimation of large-scale IP traffic matrix. AEU-International Journal of Electronics and Communications, 2009, In Press.

Jiang, D. and Hu, G. Large-scale IP traffic matrix estimation based on simulated annealing. In Proceedings of the IEEE International Conference on Communications Systems (ICCS'08), Guangzhou, China, 19-21 November. 2008, 1-4.

Lakhina A, Papagiannaki K, Crovella M, et al. Structural analysis of network traffic flows. In Proceedings of ACM Sigmetrics, New York, June 2004.

Liang G, Taft N, Yu B. A fast lightweight approach to origin-destination ip traffic estimation using partial measurements. IEEE Transactions on Information Theory 2006; 52(6): 2634-48.

Medina A, Taft N, Salamatian K, et al. Traffic matrix estimation: Existing techniques and new directions. In Proceedings of ACM SIGCOMM'02, Pittsburgh, USA, August 2002.

Nucci A, Cruz R, Taft N, et al. Design of IGP link weight changes for estimation of traffic matrices. In Proceedings of IEEE Infocom, Hong Kong, March 2004.

Papagiannaki, K.; Taft, N.; and Lakhina, A. A distributed approach to measure traffic matrices. In: Proceedings of ACM Internet Measurement Conference (IMC'04). Taormina, Italy, 2004. p. 161-74.

Soule, A.; Lakhina, A.; Taft, N. et al. Traffic matrices: balancing measurements, inference and modeling. In: Proceedings of ACM SIGMETRICS'05. Banff, Canada, 2005. p.362-73,

Soule, A.; Salamatian, K.; Nucci, A.; and Taft, N.Traffic Matrix tracking using Kalman Filtering. LIP6 Research Report RP-LIP6-2004-07-10, LIP6, 2004.

Soule A, Nucci A, Leonardi E, et al. How to identify and estimate the largest traffic matrix elements in a dynamic environment. In Proceedins of ACM Sigmetrics, New York, June 2004.

Tan, L. and Wang, X. A novel method to estimate IP traffic matrix. IEEE Communications Letters 2007;11: 907-9.

Tebaldi, C. and West, M. "Bayesian inference on network traffic using link count data," Journal of the American Stati-stical Association, vol. 93, no. 442, pp. 557-576, June 1998.

Tiwari, M. and Cosman, P. C. "Selection of Long-Term Reference Frames in Dual-Frame Video Coding Using Simulated Annealing", IEEE Signal Processing Letters. Vol. 15, pp. 249-252, 2008.

Thompson, D. R. and Bilbro, G. L. "Sample-sort simulated annealing", IEEE Transactions on Systems, Man, and Cybernetics - Part B: Cybernetics, vol. 35, no. 3, pp. 625-632, June 2005.

Uhlig S, Quoitin B, Balon S, et al. Providing public intradomain traffic matrices to the research community. ACM SIGCOMM Computer Communication Review 2006;36:83-6

Vardi, Y. Network tomography: estimating source-destination traffic intensities from link data. J. Amer. Stat. Assoc. 1996; 91(433): 365-377.

Zhang ,Y.; Roughan, M.; Duffield, N.; and Greenberg, A. Fast accurate computation of large-scale IP traffic matrices from link loads. In: Proceedings of ACM SIGMETRICS'03. San Diego, California, USA, 2003. p. 206-17.

Zhang, Y.; Roughan, M.; Lund, C.; Donoho, D. Estimating point-to-point and point-to-multipoint traffic matrices: an information-theoretic approach. IEEE/ACM Trans Networking 2005; 13:947-60.

Zhang, Y.; Roughan, M.; Lund, C.; and Donoho, D. "An Information Theoretic Approach to Traffic Matrix Estimation," In ACM SIGCOMM, Karlsruhe, Germany, August 2003.

6

Field sampling scheme optimization using simulated annealing

Pravesh Debba
CSIR Built Environment, Logistics and Quantitative Methods LQM, POBox 395, Pretoria, 0001 South Africa

1. Land characterization: problems in deriving optimal sampling schemes

Land has many components. The various components, such as vegetation, and in the absence of vegetation the rocks and sands with all their minerals make up land cover. To adequately characterize the vegetation components or the mineral components of land, detailed maps describing the spatial distributions of, for example, certain crops or certain minerals are required. The spatial distributions of crops or minerals, however, vary from one place to another according to factors at local settings. Therefore, thorough sampling of land is required to generate detailed maps accurately depicting spatial variability of either crops or minerals and associated metals. Such an undertaking would require money, time, and manpower in order to achieve spatial information of interest at the desired level of accuracy. Therefore, planning *where* and *how many* samples should be collected, in order to map accurately the spatial distributions of either crops or minerals and associated metals, is a non-trivial task.

A sampling plan or scheme refers to positions of samples on the ground. There are two types of sampling schemes, (a) a retrospective scheme, whereby sample locations are either removed from or added to an existing sampling scheme, and (b) a prospective scheme, whereby sample locations are pre-determined before actual sampling in the field. A sampling scheme design is considered optimal if there is (i) a reduction in the number of samples but resulting in estimates of population parameters of interest with the same or similar uncertainty, (ii) a reduction in the variability or mean squared error in estimates of population parameters of interest, (iii) a more correct distribution of samples representing the distribution of the population of interest, or a combination of these criteria. Development of optimal sampling requires *a priori* spatial information about a study area.

Around the mid-20th century and a few decades thereafter, those who studied crops (Driscoll & Coleman, 1974; Everitt et al., 1980; Johnson, 1969) and those who searched for minerals (Allum, 1966; Eardley, 1942; Gilbertson et al., 1976; Laylender, 1956; Longshaw & Gilbertson, 1976) developed their sampling schemes by using geographical information from topographic maps and/or stereoscopic aerial photographs and from visual observations during field reconnaissance surveys. From the 1970s, technological developments in remote sensing resulted in the collection of spaceborne multispectral data, which were to a larger extent useful to derive *a priori* spatial information required in sampling campaigns to study agricultural crops (Everitt et al., 1979; McGraw & Tueller, 1983) but were to a lesser extent useful to derive *a priori* spatial information required in searching for minerals (Houston, 1973; Iranpanah,

1977; Lowman, 1976; Siegal & Abrams, 1976; Siegal & Gillespie, 1980). The reasons for the relative contrast of usefulness spaceborne multispectral data to crop vegetation studies and to search for minerals are that multispectral sensors collect broad wavelength data (a) mostly in the visible to near infrared range of the electromagnetic spectrum, where vegetation has diagnostic spectral features, but (b) partly in the shortwave infrared range of the electromagnetic spectrum, where most minerals have diagnostic spectral features. Multispectral data allow mapping of individual crop species quite accurately (Bouman & Uenk, 1992; Brisco et al., 1989; Richardson et al., 1985), but allow mapping of groups and not individual minerals such as in hydrothermally altered rocks (Abrams, 1984; Carranza & Hale, 2002; Kowalik et al., 1983; Rowan et al., 1977).

From the 1990s, however, advanced technological developments in remote sensing resulted in acquiring airborne hyperspectral data, which are better sources of *a priori* information for those who optimize their respective sampling schemes to study crop vegetation or search for minerals and associated metals. The advantage of hyperspectral data over multispectral data can be attributed to their high spatial resolution and much higher spectral resolutions in the visible to the shortwave infrared regions (Clark, 1999; Polder & van der Heijden, 2001), which allow distinction between plant species (Chang, 2006; Okina et al., 2001; Thenkabail, 2002; Thenkabail et al., 2002) or minerals and associated metals (Cudahy et al., 2000; Martini, 2003; Martini et al., 2003; Papp & Cudahy, 2002). Nevertheless, the ability to process and analyze multi-dimensional hyperspectral data promptly requires improved or novel techniques in order to extract and then further process vital information to derive optimal sampling schemes. The availability of airborne hyperspectral data, therefore, raises two problems in deriving optimal sampling schemes to study crops and to search for minerals and associated metals: (1) how to extract accurate *a priori* information of interest; and (2) how to further process *a priori* information of interest to derive an optimal sampling scheme. The first problem is related to the fact that processing and analysis of hyperspectral data results in only estimates of certain parameters such as (a) vegetation indices, which could reflect crop health (Ausmus & Hilty, 1972; Carter, 1994; Knipling, 1970), and (b) mineral indices, which are estimates of relative abundance of minerals (Chabrillat et al., 1999; Crósta et al., 1998; Resmini et al., 1997; Smith et al., 1985). Accurate estimation of these parameters is undermined by several factors that, for example, distort the spectral signal from materials of interest on the ground to the hyperspectral sensor in the air (Gupta, 2003; Lillesand et al., 1994; Richards, 1993; Sabins, 1996). The second problem is related to the statistical correlation or spatial association between parameters estimated from hyperspectral data and the primary variables of interest, which in this chapter are crops or minerals and associated metals. To investigate potential solutions to these two problems in deriving optimal sampling schemes given hyperspectral data, it is important to first understand hyperspectral remote sensing and optimization of schemes separately and to then merge the disparate knowledge gained. The following two sections provide brief literature reviews on hyperspectral remote sensing and optimization of sampling schemes, respectively.

In this chapter, estimates of parameters of interest derived from hyperspectral data or statistical correlation between parameters estimated from hyperspectral data and the primary variables of interest are here referred to as a model. It is hypothesized that model-based optimal sampling schemes can be derived by (a) improving the precision/accuracy of a model, (b) improving the parameter estimates of a model, (c) reducing the variability of a model, (d) reducing the error of model; or by a combination of any of these aspects. Accordingly, to investigate the hypothesis, the main purpose of this chapter is to use airborne hyperspectral data to obtain models for input into simulated annealing in order to derive optimal sampling schemes.

2. Hyperspectral remote sensing

In the study of electro-magnetic physics, when energy in the form of light interacts with a material, part of the energy at certain wavelength is absorbed, transmitted, emitted, scattered, or reflected due to the property or characteristics of the material (Sabins, 1996). The three most common ways of measuring the reflectance of a material are by (a) using a hand-held spectrometer over the material in the field or laboratory, (b) using a sensor mounted on an aircraft over a land terrain, or (c) using a sensor mounted on a spacecraft over the earth's surface.

Available hyperspectral data are mostly obtained by aircrafts. Hyperspectral data are reflectance measurements at very narrow wavelengths, approximately 10 nm or less, and are acquired simultaneously over a large spectral range, usually between 0.4 μm and 2.5 μm (Chang, 2006). This spectral range includes the visible, near infrared and short wave infrared regions of the electro-magnetic spectrum, resulting in a large number (often > 100) of contiguous spectral bands or channels. Reflectance data in each spectral channel can be pictorially represented as an image, which is composed of discrete picture elements or pixels. The brightness of a pixel represents the reflective value of materials at specific wavelengths of the electro-magnetic spectrum. Every material has unique spectral features (Hapke, 1993), which are distinct arrays of spectral values at certain regions of the electro-magnetic spectrum. Because hyperspectral sensors acquire spectral data from narrow and contiguous bands of the electro-magnetic spectrum, they provide much better capability to identify materials than broad-band sensors (Sabins, 1999). For example, analysis of changes in narrow absorption features (Van der Meer, 2004), which are usually not recorded by broadband sensors, is a powerful tool in remote identification and estimation of individual materials instead of groups of materials.

A vast amount of scientific knowledge has been and is currently being developed in the field of hyperspectral remote sensing of the environment (Chang, 2006; Gupta, 2003; Sabins, 1996). There are several international peer reviewed journals specifically publishing innovative procedures and advancements on hyperspectral remote sensing of the environment. Integration of hyperspectral data or information derived from hyperspectral data into optimization of sampling schemes has been relatively neglected (Stein et al., 1999).

3. Optimization of sampling schemes

Spatial sampling has been addressed by statisticians for many years. In comparing traditional sampling schemes Burgess et al. (1981) found that a regular grid results in only slightly less precise estimates than a triangular grid, for the same sampling density. They concluded that a small loss of precision or small increase in sampling density to achieve a given precision corresponds with a small increase in price to pay for the practical convenience of regular grids. Christakos & Olea (1992) present a case-specific methodology for choosing between different grid designs.

In optimization of model-based sampling schemes, Spruill & Candela (1990) considered the prediction accuracy of chloride concentration in groundwater by removing or adding locations to an existing sampling network. In a similar way, Royle & Nychka (1998) used a geo-

metrical criterion in order to optimize spatial prediction. Brus & de Gruijter (1997) compared design-based and model-based sampling schemes.
With applications of geostatistical methods, it has been previously shown that for spatially correlated data a triangular configuration of sampling points is most efficient and for isotropic variations the grid should be equilateral (Burgess et al., 1981). McBratney et al. (1981) and McBratney & Webster (1981) presented procedures for optimizing the spacing grid of a regular rectangular or triangular lattice design by maximizing the prediction variance, given an *a priori* variogram. If a variogram, however, shows a relatively high nugget and sampling density is relatively scarce, then a hexagonal grid can be most efficient (Yfantis et al., 1987). By removing or adding locations to an existing sampling network, Ben-Jemaa et al. (1995) used ordinary co-kriging between sediment concentration of mercury and a sediment grain size index to maximize the prediction accuracy. Lloyd & Atkinson (1999) used ordinary kriging and ordinary indicator kriging to optimize a sampling scheme. Diggle & Lophaven (2006) used a Bayesian criterion to optimize geo-spatial prediction by (a) deleting locations from an existing sampling design and (b) choosing positions for a new set of sampling locations. Other studies of variogram application to optimize sampling schemes include Russo (1984), Warrick & Myers (1987), Zimmerman & Homer (1991) and Müller & Zimmerman (1999).
With applications of simulated annealing, Sacks & Schiller (1988) presented several algorithms for optimizing a sampling scheme out of a small grid of possible locations. McGwire et al. (1993) investigated the impact of sampling strategies on the stability of linear calibrations by enforcing various sample distance constraints in a Monte Carlo approach. Van Groenigen & Stein (1998) extended this design by presenting the optimal sampling scheme using spatial simulated annealing that could handle earlier data points and complex barriers. Van Groenigen & Stein (1998) also developed further the Warrick & Myers (1987) criterion to optimize sampling schemes. Van Groenigen et al. (1999) used spatial simulated annealing to construct sampling schemes with minimal kriging variance. They found that anisotropy of the variogram had considerable influence on the optimized sampling scheme, with the highest sampling density in the direction of the highest variability. Van Groenigen et al. (1999) used spatial simulated annealing and the criterion for minimizing the maximum kriging variance in obtaining the optimal sampling scheme. Van Groenigen, Pieters & Stein (2000) showed how conditional probabilities of exceeding environmental threshold values of several contaminants could be pooled into one variable, indicating health risk and thereby used simulated annealing to optimize the sampling scheme. Van Groenigen, Gandah & Bouma (2000) used yield maps to optimize, via spatial simulated annealing, soil sampling for precision agriculture in a low-tech environment. Lark (2002) maximized the likelihood estimation for the Gaussian linear model, which results in designs consisting of fairly regular array supplemented by groups of closely spaced locations.
In sampling for field spectral measurements to support remote sensing, Curran & Atkinson (1998) used co-kriging to define the optimal 'multiple' sampling design, which could be used to simultaneously sample ground and remote sensing data. Tapia et al. (2005) applied a multivariate *k*-means classifier to delineate vegetation patterns from remote sensing data together with the Van Groenigen & Stein (1998) criterion in order to prioritize the survey to areas with high uncertainty. In the current chapter, sampling schemes are optimized based on remote sensing data or remotely sensed information and the application of simulated annealing.

4. Simulated Annealing in context of sampling scheme optimization

Simulated annealing is a general optimization method that has been widely applied to find the global optimum of an objective function when several local optima exist. Details on simulated annealing can be found in Kirkpatrick et al. (1983), Bohachevsky et al. (1986) and Aarts & Korst (1989).

In application of simulated annealing to sampling scheme optimization, a fitness function $\phi(\mathbf{S})$ has to be minimized, depending on the sampling configuration $\mathbf{S}$. Starting with a random sampling scheme $\mathbf{S}_0$, let $\mathbf{S}_i$ and $\mathbf{S}_{i+1}$ represent two solutions with fitness $\phi(\mathbf{S}_i)$ and $\phi(\mathbf{S}_{i+1})$, respectively. Sampling scheme $\mathbf{S}_{i+1}$ is derived from $\mathbf{S}_i$ by randomly replacing one of the points of $\mathbf{S}_i$ by a new point not in $\mathbf{S}_i$. A probabilistic acceptance criterion decides whether $\mathbf{S}_{i+1}$ is accepted or not. This probability $P_c(\mathbf{S}_i \to \mathbf{S}_{i+1})$ of $\mathbf{S}_{i+1}$ being accepted can be described as:

$$P_{\mathbf{c}}(\mathbf{S}_i \to \mathbf{S}_{i+1}) = \begin{cases} 1, & \text{if } \phi(\mathbf{S}_{i+1}) \leq \phi(\mathbf{S}_i) \\ \exp\left(\dfrac{\phi(\mathbf{S}_i) - \phi(\mathbf{S}_{i+1})}{\mathbf{c}}\right), & \text{if } \phi(\mathbf{S}_{i+1}) > \phi(\mathbf{S}_i) \end{cases} \quad (1)$$

where $\mathbf{c}$ denotes a positive control parameter (usually called the temperature in simulated annealing problems). Several cooling schedules are possible to reduce the temperature. At each value of $\mathbf{c}$, several transitions have to be made before the annealing can proceed, and $\mathbf{c}$ can take its next value. A transition takes place if $\mathbf{S}_{i+1}$ is accepted. Next, a solution $\mathbf{S}_{i+2}$ is derived from $\mathbf{S}_{i+1}$, and the probability $P_c(\mathbf{S}_{i+1} \to \mathbf{S}_{i+2})$ is calculated according to an acceptance criterion (Equation 1).

Through this and related studies it has been observed that when several local optima exist, as in the case of designing optimal sampling schemes, simulated annealing is superior to gradient based methods.

5. A prospective sampling scheme

Although for this particular case study, a prospective sampling scheme is designed to target a specific mineral, the method is not restrictive to either prospective sampling or in the field of geology (Debba, Carranza, Stein & van der Meer, 2008; Debba et al., 2005). Retrospective sampling schemes can similarly be designed (Debba et al., 2009; Diggle & Lophaven, 2006). Also, these sampling schemes can be applied to various other fields of study, for example, to better estimate certain vegetation parameters (Debba, Stein, van der Meer & Lucieer, 2008).

Hyperspectral imaging systems are useful in identifying individual iron and clay minerals, which can provide details of hydrothermal alteration zoning (Sabins, 1999) based on specific absorption features of these minerals. Thorough discussions on absorption features of hydrothermal alteration minerals can be found in Clark (1999); Hapke (1993); Salisbury et al. (1991); Van der Meer (2004). Various mapping of minerals using hyperspectral data can be found in Crósta et al. (1998); Kruse & Boardman (1997); Rowan et al. (2000); Sabins (1999); Vaughan et al. (2003).

Surface sampling in the field is often advantageous for starting surveys. Identification of hydrothermal alteration minerals like alunite, kaolinite and pyrophyllite, from hyperspectral images leads to a better understanding of the geology and alteration patterns in a region. As such, the analysis of airborne hyperspectral imagery can aid in selecting follow-up targets on the ground before fieldwork is performed. In this study, focus is on the mineral alunite as it is characteristic of hydrothermal alteration zones in the Rodalquilar area in Spain (Arribas et al.,

1995). Alunite has a distinct spectral signature and is often, although not always, related to high sulphidation epithermal gold (Hedenquist et al., 2000). The purpose was to guide field sampling collection to those pixels with the highest likelihood for occurrence of alunite, while representing the overall distribution of alunite. The method offers an objective approach to selecting sampling points in order to, for example, create a mineral alteration map. However, this method can be easily extended to other hydrothermal alteration minerals that have diagnostic absorption features. Combination of several mineral images can then be used in classification of the image to create an alteration map.

The present study aims to use the spectral angle mapper (SAM) and spectral feature fitting (SFF) to classify alunite and obtain rule images. Each pixel in a rule image represents the similarity between the corresponding pixel in the hyperspectral image to a reference spectrum. These rule images are then used to govern sampling to areas with a high probability of alunite occurring and to intensively sample in areas with an abundance of alunite. This effectively delineates favorable areas from unfavorable ones and provides an objective sampling scheme as an initial guideline. The design of the optimal sampling scheme to target these areas of a particular intense hydrothermal alteration mineral is the objective of this study. Such an optimal sampling scheme defies the conventional methods of mineral exploration, which can be time-consuming, cost-prohibitive and involve a high degree of risk in terms of accurate target selection (Srivastav et al., 2000). The study is illustrated with hyperspectral data acquired over the Rodalquilar area.

5.1 Study area

5.1.1 Geology and hydrothermal alteration of the Rodalquilar area

The area of study is located in the Cabo de Gata volcanic field, in the south-eastern corner of Spain (Fig. 1), and consists of calc-alkaline volcanic rocks of the late Tertiary. Volcanic rocks range in composition from pyroxene-bearing andesites to rhyolites. Extensive hydrothermal alteration of the volcanic host rocks has resulted in formation of hydrothermal mineral zones from high to low alteration intensity in the sequence: silica (quartz, chalcedony, and opal) $\rightarrow$ alunite $\rightarrow$ kaolinite $\rightarrow$ illite $\rightarrow$ smectite $\rightarrow$ chlorite. Associated with this mineral alteration are high sulphidation gold deposits and low sulphidation base metal deposits. Gold mineralization is located in the central part of the volcanic field within the Rodalquilar caldera. Arribas et al. (1995) distinguish five hydrothermal alteration zones: silicic, advanced argillic, intermediate argillic and propylitic.

The silicic zone is dominated by the presence of vuggy (porous) quartz, opal and gray and black chalcedony veins. Vuggy quartz (porous quartz) is formed from extreme leaching of the host rock. It hosts high sulphidation gold mineralization and is evidence for a hypogene event. Alteration in the advanced argillic zone is of two types: hypogene and supergene. Alunite, often associated with quartz, kaolinite, illite, jarosite and very rarely pyrophyllite, is the dominant mineral characterizing this zone. The intermediate argillic zone is composed of quartz, kaolinite group minerals, illite, illite-smectite, and minor alunite, diaspore and pyrophyllite. Near the advanced argillic zone, kaolinite is abundant, whereas in the outer zone closer to the propylitic halo illite-smectite becomes the predominant minerals. The propylitic type of alteration is characterized by the presence of chlorite, illite, and smectite. Table 1 presents an overview of the alteration zones and associated alteration minerals. Detection of such minerals is facilitated in the field by hand-held spectrometers.

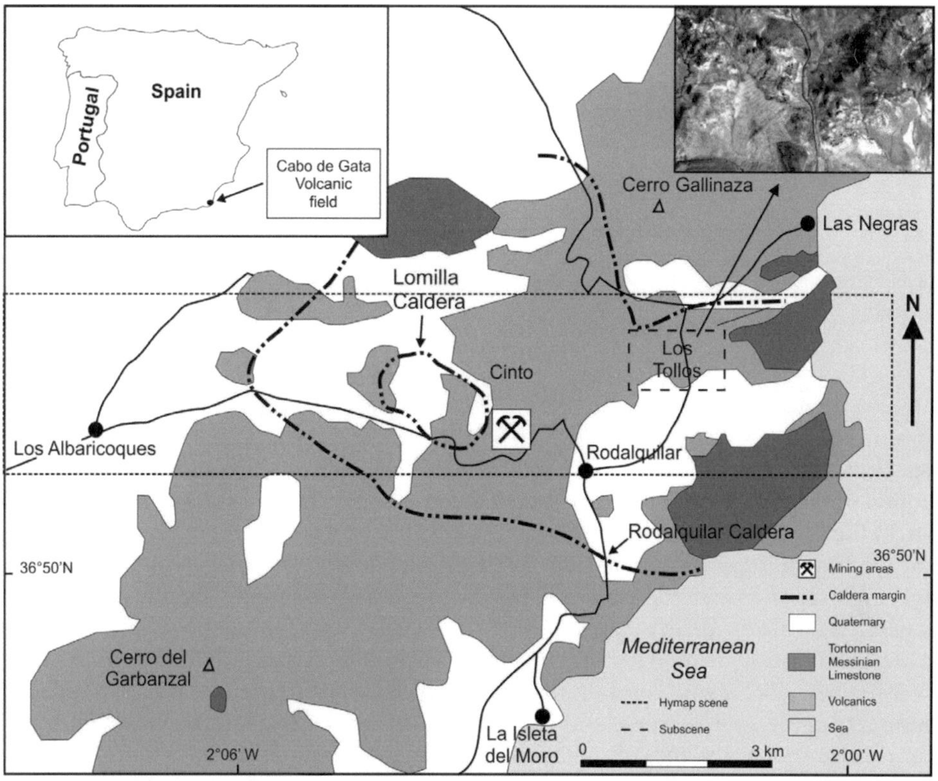

Fig. 1. A generalized geological map (modified after Cunningham et al. (1990)) of the Rodalquilar study area showing the flight line (dotted box) and the hyperspectral data (top right corner and dashed box) used in the present manuscript.

In the Rodalquilar area alunite is associated both with areas of intense hydrothermal alteration that are host to gold mineralization and with barren supergene altered rocks (Arribas et al., 1995; Hedenquist et al., 2000).

5.1.2 Data

We use a sub-scene (350 × 225 pixels) of the airborne imaging spectrometer data acquired by the Hyperspectral Mapper (HyMAP) in July 2003 during the HyEUROPE 2003 campaign (Fig. 1). HyMAP is a 126-channel instrument that collects data in a cross-track direction by mechanical scanning and in an along-track direction by movement of the airborne platform. The instrument acts as an imaging spectrometer in the reflected solar region of the electromagnetic spectrum (0.4–2.5 μm). Spectral coverage is nearly continuous in the SWIR and VNIR regions with small gaps in the middle of the 1.4 and 1.9 μm atmospheric water bands. The spatial configuration of the instrument accounts for an IFOV of 2.5 mrad along track and 2.0 mrad across track resulting in a pixel size on the order of 3–5 m for the data presented in this chapter. Due to instrument failure the SWIR 1 detector did not function during acquisition, thus no data were acquired in the 1.50–1.76 μm window. The HyMAP data were atmospherically and geometrically corrected using the Atmospheric and Topographic Correction (ATCOR 4) model (Richter, 1996).

Alteration Zone	Alteration Minerals
Silicic	quartz; chalcedony; opal
Advanced Argillic	quartz; alunite; kaolinite; pyrophyllite; illite; illite-smectite
Intermediate Argillic	quartz; kaolinite; illite; illite-smectite
Sericitic	quartz; illite
Propylitic	quartz; illite; montmorillonite
Stage 2 Alunite	alunite; kaolinite; jarosite

Table 1. Summary of alteration zones and dominant minerals in the Rodalquilar area (Arribas et al., 1995).

In support of the imaging spectrometer data, field spectra was collected for some of the prospective targets during the over-flight using the Analytical Spectral Device (ASD) fieldspec-pro spectrometer. This spectrometer covers the 0.35–2.50 μm wavelength range with a spectral resolution of 3 nm at 0.7 μm and 10 nm at 1.4 and 2.1 μm. The spectral sampling interval is 1.4 nm in the 0.35–1.05 μm wavelength range and 2 nm in the 1.0–2.5 μm wavelength range.
The SWIR 2, with a spectral range 1.95–2.48 μm (bandwidth 16 nm), is potentially useful for mapping alteration assemblages as well as regolith characterization (Abrams et al., 1977; Cudahy et al., 2000; Goetz & Srivastava, 1985; Kruse, 2002; Papp & Cudahy, 2002). HyMAP has been used successfully to map minerals (Cudahy et al., 2000; Martini, 2003; Martini et al., 2003; Papp & Cudahy, 2002) and detect faults and fractures (Martini et al., 2003). We reduced dimensionality of the data by considering all channels in the spectral range 1.970–2.468 μm. This spectral range covers the most prominent spectral absorption features of hydroxyl-bearing minerals, sulfates and carbonates, which are common to many geologic units and hydrothermal alteration assemblages (Kruse, 2002). These minerals also exhibit distinctive absorption features at wavelengths in the partly missing range of 1.4–1.7 μm, a range also affected by the water absorption features in the atmosphere.
Fig. 2 shows spectral plots of seven of the most prominent alteration minerals in the study area (Arribas et al., 1995), at a spectral resolution coinciding with HyMAP after continuum removal was applied. Continuum removal normalizes the respective spectra to enable comparison of absorption features from a common baseline. The continuum is a function of the wavelength that is fitted over the top of the spectrum between two local spectra maxima. A straight line segment joins the first and last spectral data values taken as the local maxima (Clark & Roush, 1984; Clark et al., 1991). This figure shows differences in absorption features of the different minerals, in terms of shape, size, symmetry, depth and wavelength position. These distinct characteristics enable researchers to identify individual minerals from hyperspectral data. The spectrum of quartz has no distinctive absorption feature (in this spectral range), but the remaining spectra have distinctive absorption features at wavelengths near 2.2 μm, each differing slightly in position and geometry.
Alunite was chosen among the seven most prominent alteration minerals in the area (Hedenquist et al., 2000) because it has distinct absorption characteristics (Clark, 1999; Hapke, 1993; Salisbury et al., 1991; Van der Meer, 2004), which are recognizable from hyperspectral images (Crósta et al., 1998; Kruse & Boardman, 1997; Rowan et al., 2000; Sabins, 1999; Vaughan et al., 2003). Although this study concentrates on one hydrothermal mineral, namely alunite, the method demonstrated can easily be extended to other minerals of interest. The test image

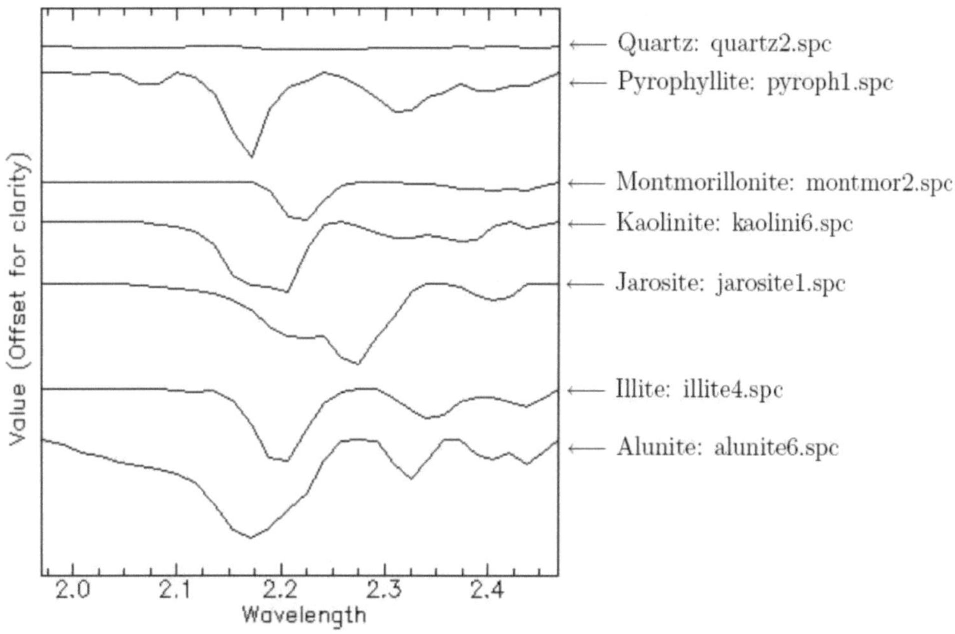

Fig. 2. Plot of 7 endmembers from USGS spectral library (Clark et al., 1993) for the 30 selected channels, enhanced by continuum removal.

selected was in an area that was relatively undisturbed through excavation, hence between 2–3 km from the nearest gold mining area as indicated in Fig. 1.

5.2 Methods

The method for obtaining the optimal sampling scheme commences with application of two classification techniques used, namely, spectral angle mapper (SAM) (Kruse et al., 1993) and spectral feature fitting (SFF) (Clark et al., 1991) to obtain rule images. The digital number (DN) values in a rule image represent similarity between each corresponding pixel's spectrum to a reference mineral spectrum, resulting in one rule image for each mineral considered. Scaled weights are then derived from the rule images. These weights are used in a mathematical objective function (defined in equation 8, see also Van Groenigen, Pieters & Stein (2000)), which is optimized in relation to the spatial distribution of the georeferenced image pixels representing a collection of alunite samples in the field. The aim of optimizing the objective function is to spread the location of the alunite sampling points over the region while targeting pixels that have a high probability of being alunite. In effect, the location of these samples in the field will be dense if distributed in areas with an abundance of alunite and where pixels have a high probability of being alunite. Optimization of the objective function is an exhaustive combinatorial problem. The complexity of the objective function and the iterative process of randomly selecting a pixel in the image as a new sampling point replacing an old one from the collection give rise to many local optima, which is solved through simulated annealing.

5.2.1 Spectral Angle Mapper (SAM) Classifier

SAM is a pixel based supervised classification technique that measures the similarity of an image pixel reflectance spectrum to a reference spectrum from either a spectral library or field spectrum (Kruse et al., 1993). This measure of similarity is the spectral angle (in radians) between the two spectra, where each is an m-dimensional feature vector, with m being the number of spectral channels. Small angles indicate a high similarity between pixel and reference spectra. For an image $\mathbf{I}$, the spectral angle $\theta(\vec{\mathbf{x}})$, for $\vec{\mathbf{x}} \in \mathbf{I}$, is given by

$$\theta(\vec{\mathbf{x}}) = \cos^{-1}\left(\frac{f(\lambda) \cdot e(\lambda)}{||f(\lambda)|| \cdot ||e(\lambda)||}\right), \tag{2}$$

where λ is the wavelength range of the m spectral channels, $f(\lambda)$ is an unclassified m-dimensional image reflectance spectrum under observation and $e(\lambda)$ is an m-dimensional reference spectrum. SAM is directionally dependent, but independent of the length of the spectral vector, thus insensitive to illumination or albedo effects (Crósta et al., 1998). It is also dependent on the user-specified threshold and wavelength range. The result of using equation 2 are grayscale images (SAM's Rule Images), one for each reference mineral, with DN value representing the angular distance in radians between each pixel spectrum and the reference mineral spectrum (see Fig. 3a). Darker pixels in the rule image indicate greater similarity to the reference mineral spectra. Further, if this angular distance is smaller than a user specified threshold, the pixel is assigned to the category of the respective reference mineral, leading to image classification. This algorithm has been implemented in ENVI™ image analysis commercial software.

5.2.2 Spectral Feature Fitting (SFF)

SFF matches the image pixel reflectance spectrum to reference spectrum from either a spectral library or a field spectrum by examining specific absorption features in the spectrum after continuum removal has been applied to both the image and reference spectrum (Clark et al., 1991). Denote the continuum for the image reflectance spectrum as $c_f(\lambda)$ and for the reference spectrum as $c_e(\lambda)$. The continuum is removed (Clark & Roush, 1984) using

$$\begin{aligned} e_c(\lambda) &= e(\lambda)/c_e(\lambda) \\ f_c(\lambda) &= f(\lambda)/c_f(\lambda) \end{aligned} \tag{3}$$

where $e_c(\lambda)$ is the continuum removed reference spectrum and $f_c(\lambda)$ is the continuum removed image reflectance spectrum, respectively. The resulting normalized spectra reflect levels equal to 1.0 if continuum and the spectrum match and less than 1.0 in the case of absorption.

Similarly, the absorption feature depth is defined as

$$\begin{aligned} D[e_c(\lambda)] &= 1 - e_c(\lambda) = 1 - e(\lambda)/c_e(\lambda) \\ D[f_c(\lambda)] &= 1 - f_c(\lambda) = 1 - f(\lambda)/c_f(\lambda) \end{aligned} \tag{4}$$

for each spectrum. The absorption feature depth has a unique magnitude and location, both depending on the mineral and its chemical composition.

Scaling is usually necessary for reference spectra because absorption features in library data typically have greater depth than image reflectance spectra. A simple scaling function of the form $e_c^s(\lambda) = a_0 + a_1 e_c(\lambda)$, where $e_c^s(\lambda)$ is the modified continuum removed reference

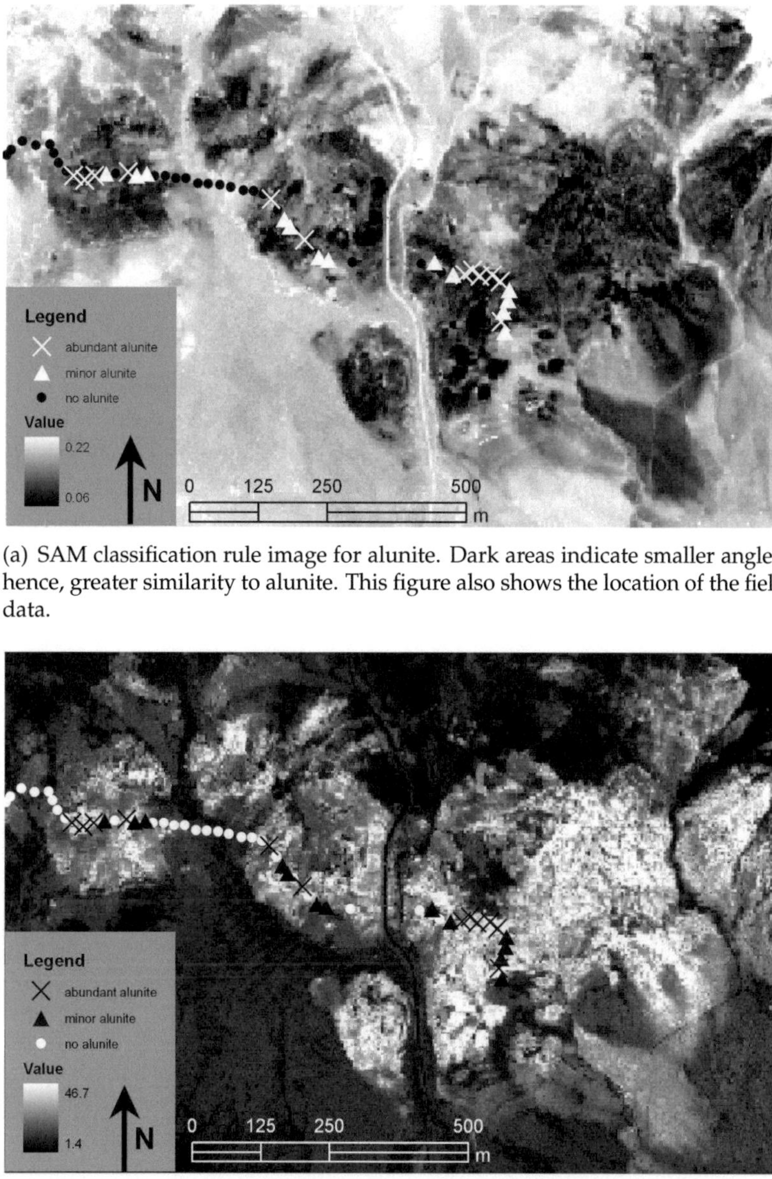

(a) SAM classification rule image for alunite. Dark areas indicate smaller angles, hence, greater similarity to alunite. This figure also shows the location of the field data.

(b) SFF fit image for alunite. Lighter areas indicate better fit values between pixel reflectance spectra and the alunite reference spectrum. This figure also shows the location of the field data.

Fig. 3. SAM and SFF (fit) Rule Images.

spectrum that best matches the image spectra, is useful. For an image **I**, the scale $\tau_S(\overrightarrow{\mathbf{x}})$, for $\overrightarrow{\mathbf{x}} \in \mathbf{I}$, is determined using least squares that gives the best fit to the image spectrum $f_c(\lambda)$

$$D[f_c(\lambda)] = a + \tau_S(\overrightarrow{\mathbf{x}})D[e_c(\lambda)]\,. \tag{5}$$

Hence the scale image, produced for each reference mineral, is the image of scaling factors used to fit the unknown image spectra to the reference spectra. The result is a grayscale scale image, whose DN value corresponds to $\tau_S(\vec{\mathbf{x}})$.
The total root-mean-squares (RMS) errors, $\tau_E(\vec{\mathbf{x}})$, was defined as

$$\tau_E(\vec{\mathbf{x}}) = \sqrt{\frac{1}{m}\sum_b (D[f_c(\lambda_b)] - D[e_c^s(\lambda_b)])^2} \tag{6}$$

where λ_b denotes the wavelength of channel b, $b = 1, \ldots, m$. The result is a grayscale RMS error image, with DN value corresponding to $\tau_E(\vec{\mathbf{x}})$.
The fit image equals

$$\tau_F(\vec{\mathbf{x}}) = \tau_S(\vec{\mathbf{x}})/\tau_E(\vec{\mathbf{x}}) \tag{7}$$

providing a measure of how well image pixel reflectance spectra match reference spectra. A large value of $\tau_F(\vec{\mathbf{x}})$ corresponds to a good match between the image spectrum and the reference spectrum. The fit values are used as a rule image to weigh each pixel to a reference mineral, namely alunite (see Fig. 3b). This algorithm has been implemented in ENVI^{TM} image analysis commercial software. Further details on SFF can be found in (Clark & Swayze, 1995; Clark et al., 1992; 1991; 2003).

5.2.3 Sampling

Sampling by simulation annealing requires definition of a mathematical objective function, called the fitness function.

Fitness function

The Weighted Means Shortest Distance (WMSD)-criterion is a weighted version of the Minimization of the Mean Shortest Distances (MMSD)-criterion (Van Groenigen, Pieters & Stein, 2000). The fitness function is extended with a location dependent weight function that is scaled to $[0,1]$, namely, $w(\vec{\mathbf{x}}) : \mathbf{I} \rightarrow [0,1]$ by

$$\phi_{\text{WMSD}}(\mathbf{S}^n) = \frac{1}{N}\sum_{\vec{\mathbf{x}} \in \mathbf{I}} w(\vec{\mathbf{x}})\, ||\vec{\mathbf{x}} - W_{\mathbf{S}^n}(\vec{\mathbf{x}})||\ , \tag{8}$$

where $W_{\mathbf{S}^n}(\vec{\mathbf{x}})$ is the location vector of the sampling point in $\mathbf{S}^n$ nearest to $\vec{\mathbf{x}}$, N is the number of pixels in the image and $w(\vec{\mathbf{x}})$ is a weight for the pixel with location vector $\vec{\mathbf{x}}$. The weights express knowledge or assumptions about the occurrence of alunite in some parts of the region by controlling the sampling density in these areas. Larger weights result in a higher likelihood of a pixel being selected in the final sampling scheme.
This fitness function also spreads the location of the sampling points over the region classified as alunite. Since these points on the image are georeferenced, they will appropriately serve as target points to be sampled in the field. There will be a high probability that the field sample points suggested are alunite and these points will be spread according to the distribution of alunite as in the classified image. This achieves the purpose of the study of obtaining a collection of sampling points in the field that appropriately represent the distribution of the mineral of interest. A weight function is defined below to meet this objective.
For the weight function, scaled weights are used based on several rule images to guide sampling to areas with a high probability of being alunite and to sample more intensely where

an abundance of alunite occurs. Using SAM's rule image and SFF's rule image, derived by applying equations 2 & 7, thresholds θ^t and τ_F^t are selected for SAM and SFF respectively. Pixels exceeding either of these threshold angles receive zero weight, otherwise the weight is a function of the spectral angle and the fit value. Higher weights will emerge from smaller spectral angle between the image pixel reflectance spectrum and reference alunite spectrum, and a larger fit value between these two spectra. The weight $w(\overrightarrow{\mathbf{x}})$, for each pixel $\overrightarrow{\mathbf{x}}$, scaled to $[0,1]$ is defined as

$$w(\theta(\overrightarrow{\mathbf{x}}),\tau_F(\overrightarrow{\mathbf{x}})) = \begin{cases} \kappa_1 w_1(\theta(\overrightarrow{\mathbf{x}})) + \kappa_2 w_2(\tau_F(\overrightarrow{\mathbf{x}})), \\ \quad \text{if } \theta(\overrightarrow{\mathbf{x}}) \leq \theta^t \text{ and } \tau_F(\overrightarrow{\mathbf{x}}) \geq \tau_F^t \\ 0, \quad \text{if otherwise} \end{cases} \tag{9}$$

where $0 \leq \kappa_1, \kappa_2 \leq 1$ and $\kappa_1 + \kappa_2 = 1$. The weight for SAM: $w_1(\overrightarrow{\mathbf{x}})$, for each pixel $\overrightarrow{\mathbf{x}}$, scaled to $[0,1]$ is defined as

$$w_1(\theta(\overrightarrow{\mathbf{x}})) = \begin{cases} 0, & \text{if } \quad \theta(\overrightarrow{\mathbf{x}}) > \theta^t \\ \dfrac{\theta^t - \theta(\overrightarrow{\mathbf{x}})}{\theta^t - \theta_{\min}}, & \text{if } \quad \theta(\overrightarrow{\mathbf{x}}) \leq \theta^t \end{cases} \tag{10}$$

and the weight for SFF: $w_2(\overrightarrow{\mathbf{x}})$, for each pixel $\overrightarrow{\mathbf{x}}$, scaled to $[0,1]$ is defined as

$$w_2(\tau_F(\overrightarrow{\mathbf{x}})) = \begin{cases} 0, & \text{if } \quad \tau_F(\overrightarrow{\mathbf{x}}) < \tau_F^t \\ \dfrac{\tau_F(\overrightarrow{\mathbf{x}}) - \tau_F^t}{\tau_{F,\max} - \tau_F^t}, & \text{if } \quad \tau_F(\overrightarrow{\mathbf{x}}) \geq \tau_F^t \end{cases} \tag{11}$$

where θ^t is the maximum angle threshold value chosen, $\theta_{\min}$ the minimum spectral angle occurring, τ_F^t is the minimum fit threshold value chosen and $\tau_{F,\max}$ the maximum value.
The weight function if used in the fitness function will be restricted to those pixels with a spectral angle smaller than the threshold chosen and with a fit larger than the chosen threshold. The probability is largest to select a pixel that is most similar to the alunite reference spectrum, in terms of both the angle between these spectra and absorption feature fit. The georeferenced location of each pixel chosen by the algorithm in the final sampling scheme will be a point to be sampled on the ground.
This weight function (equation 9), is based on two rule images. This can easily be extended to more than two rule images, by using different proportions κ_i for each rule image i conditional on $\sum \kappa_i = 1$. Also, in terms of the method of SFF, several absorption features could be considered for a particular mineral, producing a fit image for each feature. These images could be combined in the same way, thereby increasing the weights of image pixels having a spectrum similar to the mineral. This in effect increases the probability of the mineral being selected in the sampling scheme.

5.3 Results

Forty samples were arbitrarily chosen to illustrate the distribution of these points for the proposed sampling scheme. Prior to sampling, isolated segments (< 10 pixels) were removed. This was performed as there was a high chance that they were a result of noise in the image and it seemed impractical to sample in such small areas. However, if these are meaningful targets, with very high probability of alunite, the above procedure can be performed without removal of these pixels.

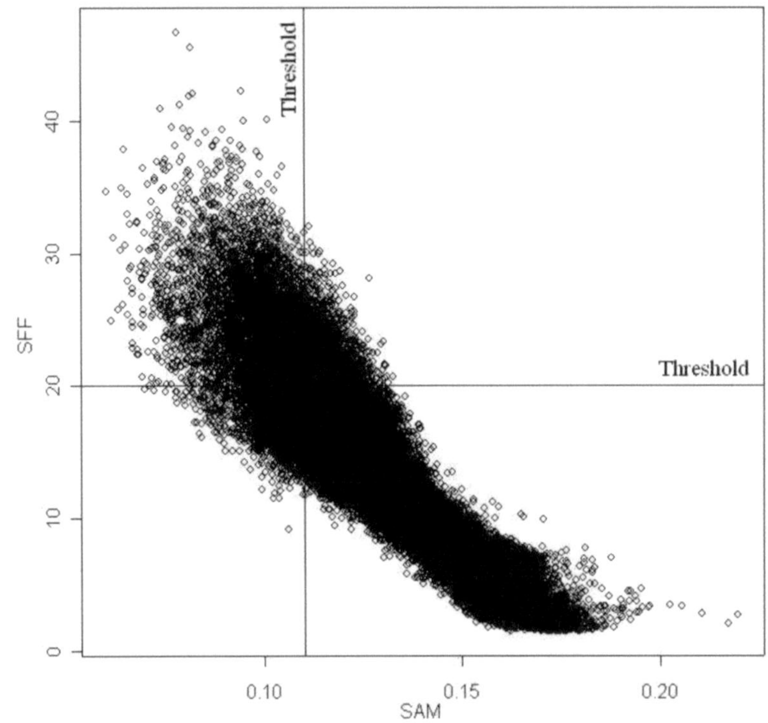

Fig. 4. Scatter plot of values in rule images obtained through SAM and SFF and the respective thresholds chosen to represent similarity or fit to alunite.

The DN values, $\theta(\overrightarrow{\mathbf{x}})$, from SAM's rule image in Fig. 3a were used in equation 10 to obtain scaled weights. We used a threshold, $\theta^t = 0.11$ radians. Pixels lying left of the 0.11 threshold (Fig. 4) correspond to positive weights. The resulting scaled weights correspond to a greater similarity to alunite reference spectrum.

SFF was applied to the alunite reference spectrum, resulting in a scale image and an RMS error image. The ratio of these images, produces a fit image (Fig. 3b). The bright pixels represent the best fit to the alunite reference spectrum. The DN values from the fit image, $\tau_F(\overrightarrow{\mathbf{x}})$, was used in equation 11 to obtain the weights for SFF using a threshold value of 20 for τ_F^t. This threshold was chosen after individual spectral analysis of some pixels and selecting several thresholds. The values of the rule images of SAM and SFF can be seen in Fig. 4. Pixels in the upper left quadrant correspond to positive weights. In equation 9 we have chosen $\kappa_1 = \kappa_2 = \frac{1}{2}$.

Table 2 summaries the weights derived by SAM and the weights derived by SFF. From the first row and first column, 6.5% of the pixels receive zero weight from one classification but weights larger than zero from the other classification. This can also be seen in Fig. 4 corresponding to the pixels in the upper right and lower left quadrants. These weights were then combined using equation 9 and are displayed in Fig. 6. Darker areas have higher weights and hence greater similarity to alunite reference spectrum in terms of both SAM and SFF. The sampling result using this weight function is also displayed in Fig. 6. The sample points are distributed over the alunite region and most of the points are found in the darker areas of the image.

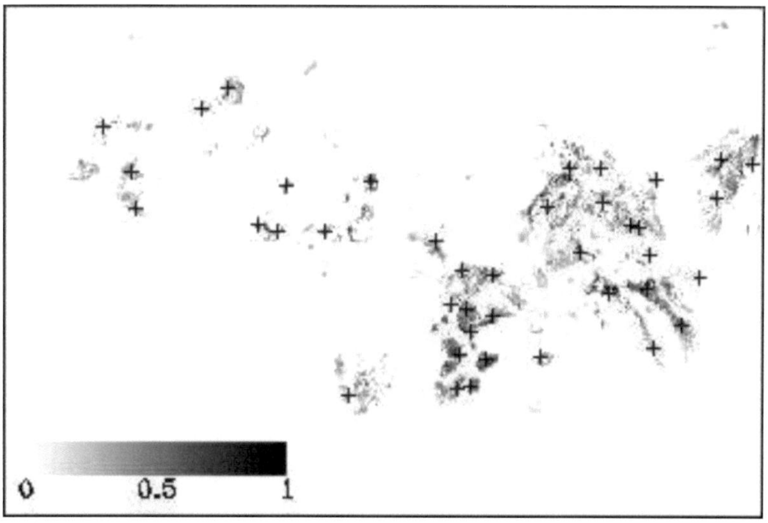

Fig. 5. Weight function: Scaled weights derived using SAM and SFF rule mages for alunite using their respective thresholds. Distribution of 40 sampling points using the weight function. Darker areas indicate greater similarity to alunite.

SFF \ SAM	0.0	(0.0, 0.2]	(0,2, 0.4]	(0.4, 0.6]	(0.6, 0.8]	(0.8, 1.0]
0.0	70603	615	238	84	40	8
(0.0, 0.2]	2546	739	304	126	78	8
(0,2, 0.4]	1183	710	332	111	37	7
(0.4, 0.6]	304	333	156	49	10	1
(0.6, 0.8]	33	42	31	6	1	0
(0.8, 1.0]	4	3	4	4	0	0

Table 2. Weights derived from SAM (column) and SFF (row).Values in the table represent the number (frequency) of pixels that match in a certain range.

Validation

Ground data collected using an ASD fieldspec-pro spectrometer were used to support the proposed sampling schemes by validating the SAM classified image and the images of the weights used in this chapter. Reflectance spectra of 51 ground measurements (see Fig. 3) were analyzed individually for their alunite content and classified into one of three classes, namely, "no alunite", "minor alunite" and "abundant alunite". Using the ground data of those pixels classified as alunite or not, the accuracy of SAM is 78% and for SFF is 79%.

5.4 Discussion and conclusion of the study

Designing sampling schemes that target areas with high probability and in greater abundance of alunite occurring was demonstrated by using a weight function for the WMSD-criterion as an objective function in simulated annealing. Predefined weights allow us to distinguish areas with different priorities. Hence sampling can be focused in areas with a high potential

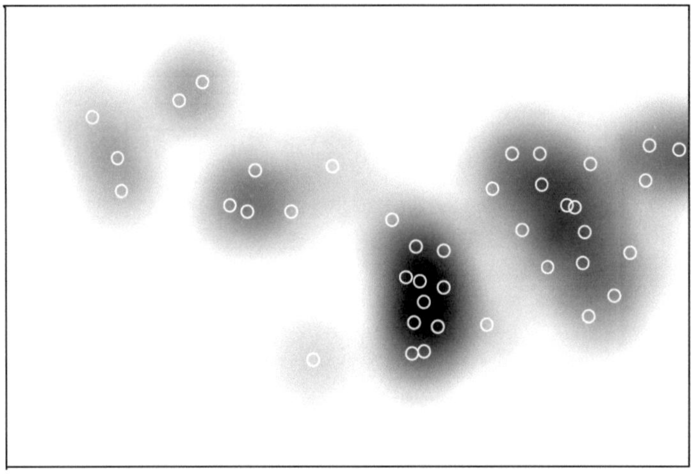

Fig. 6. Distribution of 40 optimized samples with $\theta^t = 0.11$ radians and $\tau_F^t = 20$. Darker patches in the images indicate sampling points are near to each other. This effectively implies greater abundance of alunite.

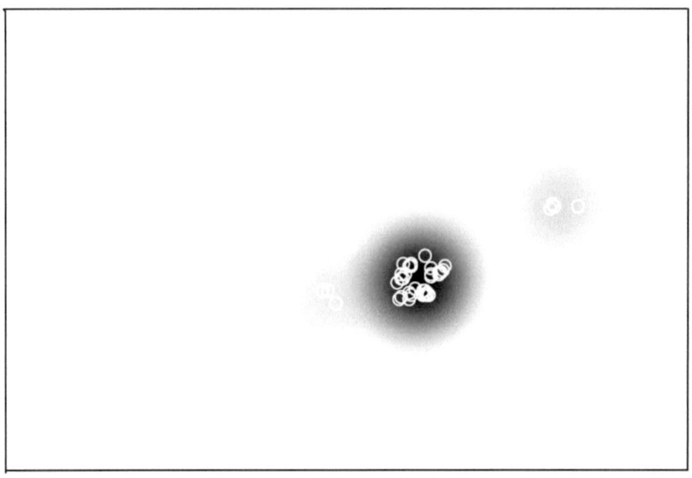

Fig. 7. Distribution of 40 highest weight samples. Darker patches in the images indicate sampling points are near to each other. This effectively implies greater abundance of alunite.

for the occurrence of a mineral of interest and reduces sampling in areas with low potential. This effectively reduces time and costs in the field. Randomly selecting points in the image, as potential sites to sample on the ground, could result in the location of these samples clustered and/or having a low probability of being alunite. Selecting a collection of sampling locations that have the highest probability of being alunite could result in the location of most sampling points clustered in the image (Fig. 7). This implies sampling in a limited area on the ground, and effectively these samples will not represent the overall distribution of alunite over the entire study area. In the proposed sampling schemes there is a balance between selecting samples that have a high probable alunite and the location of samples not to be clustered in

the field. A good sampling scheme will target areas with high probability of alunite and the distribution of sample points will correspond closely to the distribution of alunite. This means intensive sampling in the area with an abundance of alunite.
We used the threshold of 0.11 radians for SAM and a threshold of 20 for SFF. The threshold chosen for SAM in this case can be set higher (similarly the threshold for SFF can be set lower) to include some pixels with a reflectance spectrum similar to that of other minerals, example kaolinite and pyrophyllite. This is not considered to be a major problem, as the scaled weights used by the optimal sampling scheme will be low, thereby reducing the probability of selecting that pixel's location as a point to be sampled on the ground.
The weight function uses two rule images, one derived from SAM and another from SFF. A comparison of the scaled weights derived from SAM and SFF (Table 2), indicates that the methods for SAM and SFF do not always agree. Only the purest pixels classified as alunite have positive weights. The advantage of combining SAM and SFF classification methods in the weights function results in a classified image that is robust for the thresholds and selected channels. The weights derived from SAM and from SFF were then combined into a single weight image, which was used for the design of the optimal sampling scheme. A suitable range for the thresholds has to be known. This can be obtained by observing individual spectra and the purest of these can be selected to train the thresholds. Using the combined weights from SAM and SFF, sample points can be concentrated in the region with a high probability of alunite, which are robust against the thresholds selected. The distribution of sample points corresponds closely to the distribution of alunite (Fig. 6).
The sampling scheme proposed is of interest to (a) exploration geologists for specified target locations of hydrothermally altered minerals (e.g. alunite) with distinct absorption features, (b) researchers trying to understand the geothermal system and hydrothermal zones in a specific region and (c) engineers to better collect field data in relation to flights by improving on ground truthing and calibration measurements. With the aid of new spaceborne launched hyperspectral sensors, e.g. Hyperion and ARIES-1, data are available for most regions and hence will be helpful to geologist's planning phase of selecting important mineral targets in the field. The method presented here could result in reduction of time and effort in the field, but by no means replace the field geologist. It is merely an aid for target selection of minerals as an initial survey, followed by denser surface sampling of interesting anomalies.
Combination of SAM and SFF rule images thus obtained resulted in robust weights to focus sampling in areas of high probability of alunite. Sample points are arranged more intensely in areas with an abundance of alunite. SAM and SFF both lead to a relevant classification of the study area with respect to alunite, as observed from the rule images and validation of the rule images using ground measurements.

6. References

Aarts, E. & Korst, J. (1989). *Simulated Annealing and Boltzmann Machines*, New York: John Wiley.

Abrams, M., Ashley, R., Rowan, L., Goetz, A. F. H. & Kahle, A. (1977). Use of imaging in the .46–2.36 μm spectral region for alteration mapping in the Cuprite mining district, Nevada: USGS OFR-77-585.

Abrams, M. J. (1984). Landsat-4 thematic mapper and thematic mapper simulator data for a porphyry copper, *Photogrammetric Engineering and Remote Sensing* **50**: 1171–1173.

Allum, J. A. E. (1966). *Photogeology and regional mapping*, Oxford : Pergamon Press.

Arribas, Jr., A., Cunningham, C. G., Rytuba, J. J., Rye, R. O., Kelley, W. C., Podwysocki, M. H., McKee, E. H. & Tosdal, R. M. (1995). Geology, geochronology, fluid inclusions, and isotope geochemistry of the Rodalquilar gold alunite deposit, Spain, *Economic Geology* **90**: 795–822.

Ausmus, B. S. & Hilty, J. W. (1972). Reflectance studies of healthy, maize dwarf mosaic virus-infected, and Helminthosporium maydis-infected corn leaves, *Remote Sensing of Environment* **2**: 77–81.

Ben-Jemaa, F., Mariño, M. & Loaiciga, H. (1995). Sampling design for contaminant distribution in lake sediments, *Journal of Water Resource Planning Management* **121**: 71–79.

Bohachevsky, I. O., Johnson, M. E. & Stein, M. L. (1986). Generalized simulated annealing for function optimization, *Technometrics* **28**(3): 209–217.

Bouman, B. A. M. & Uenk, D. (1992). Crop classification possibilities with radar in ERS-1 and JERS-1 configuration, *Remote Sensing of Environment* **40**: 1–13.

Brisco, B., Brown, R. J. & Manore, M. J. (1989). Early season crop discrimination with combined SAR and TM data, *Canadian Journal of Remote Sensing* **15**(1): 44–54.

Brus, D. J. & de Gruijter, J. J. (1997). Random sampling or geostatistical modelling? Choosing between design-based and model-based sampling strategies for soil (with discussion), *Geoderma* **80**: 1–44.

Burgess, T. M., Webster, R. & McBratney, A. B. (1981). Optimal interpolation and isarithmic mapping of soil properties. IV Sampling strategy, *Journal of Soil Science* **32**(4): 643–660.

Carranza, E. J. M. & Hale, M. (2002). Mineral imaging with landsat thematic mapper data for hydrothermal alteration mapping in heavily vegetated terrane, *International Journal of Remote Sensing* **23**(22): 4827–4852.

Carter, G. A. (1994). Ratios of leaf reflectances in narrow wavebands as indicators of plant stress, *International Journal of Remote Sensing* **15**: 697–703.

Chabrillat, S., Goetz, A. F. H., Olsen, H. W., Krosley, L. & Noe, D. C. (1999). Use of AVIRIS hyperspectral data to identify and map expansive clay soils in the front range urban corridor in Colorado, *Proceedings of the 13th International Conference on Applied Geologic Remote Sensing*, I, Vancouver, British Columbia, Canada, pp. 390–397.

Chang, C.-I. (2006). *Hyperspectral Imaging: Techniques for Spectral Detection and Classification*, Springer.

Christakos, G. & Olea, R. A. (1992). Sampling design for spatially distributed hydrogeologic and environmental processes, *Advances in Water Resources* **15**(4): 219–237.

Clark, R. N. (1999). Spectroscopy of rocks and minerals, and principles of spectroscopy, *in* A. Rencz (ed.), *Remote Sensing for the Earth Sciences: Manual of Remote Sensing*, Vol. 3, John Wiley and Sons, New York, chapter 1, pp. 3–58.

Clark, R. N. & Roush, T. L. (1984). Reflectance spectroscopy: Quantitative analysis techniques for remote sensing applications, *Journal of Geophysical Research* **89**: 6329–6340.

Clark, R. N. & Swayze, G. A. (1995). Mapping minerals, amorphous materials, environmental materials, vegetation, water, ice, and snow, and other materials: The USGS Ticorder Algorithm, *Summaries of the Fifth Annual JPL Airborne Earth Science Workshop*, Vol. 1, JPL Publication 95-1, pp. 39–40.

Clark, R. N., Swayze, G. A. & Gallagher, A. (1992). Mapping the mineralogy and lithology of Canyonlands. Utah with imaging spectrometer data and the multiple spectral feature mapping algorithm, *Summaries of the Third Annual JPL Airborne Geoscience Workshop*, Vol. 1, JPL Publication 92-14, pp. 11–13.

Clark, R. N., Swayze, G. A., Gallagher, A. J., King, T. V. V. & Calvin, W. M. (1993). The U. S. Geological survey, digital spectral library: Version 1: 0.2 to 3.0 microns, U.S. Geological Survey Open File Report 93-592.

Clark, R. N., Swayze, G. A., Gorelick, N. & Kruse, F. A. (1991). Mapping with imaging spectrometer data using the complete band shape least-squares algorthm simultaneously fit to multiple spectral features from multiple materials, *Proceedings of the Third Airborne Visible/Infrared Imaging Spectrometer (AVIRIS) workshop*, JPL Publication 91-28, pp. 2–3.

Clark, R. N., Swayze, G. A., Livo, K. E., Kokaly, R. F., Sutley, S. J., Dalton, J. B., McDougal, R. R. & Gent, C. A. (2003). Imaging spectroscopy: Earth and planetary remote sensing with the USGS Tetracorder and expert systems, *Journal of Geophysical Research* **108**(E12): 5–1–5–44.

Crósta, A. P., Sabine, C. & Taranik, J. V. (1998). Hydrothermal alteration mapping at Bodie, California, using AVIRIS hyperspectral data, *Remote Sensing of Environment* **65**(3): 309–319.

Cudahy, T., Okada, K. & Brauhart, C. (2000). Targeting VMS-style Zn mineralisation at Panorama, Australia, using airborne hyperspectral VNIR-SWIR HyMap data, *ERIM Proceedings of the 14th International Conference on Applied Geologic Remote Sensing*, Las Vegas, pp. 395–402.

Cunningham, C. G., Arribas, Jr., A., Rytuba, J. J. & Arribas, A. (1990). Mineralized and unmineralized calderas in Spain; Part I, evolution of the Los Frailes Caldera, *Mineralium Deposita* **25 [Suppl.]**: S21–S28.

Curran, P. J. & Atkinson, P. M. (1998). Geostatistics and remote sensing, *Progress in Physical Geography* **22**(1): 61–78.

Debba, P., Carranza, E. J. M., Stein, A. & van der Meer, F. D. (2008). Deriving optimal exploration target zones on mineral prospectivity maps, *Mathematical Geosciences* **41**(4): 421–446.

Debba, P., Carranza, E. J. M., Stein, A. & van der Meer, F. D. (2009). An optimal spatial sampling scheme to characterize mine tailings, Presented at the 57th Session of the International Statistical Institute (ISI) conference for a special topics contributed paper meeting on Statistical methods applied in GIS and remote sensing, 16-24 August 2009, International Conventional Centre (ICC), Durban, KwaZulu Natal, South Africa.

Debba, P., Stein, A., van der Meer, F. & Lucieer, A. (2008). Field sampling from a segmented image, *in* O. Gervasi, B. Murgante, A. Laganá, D. Taniar, Y. Mun & M. Gavrilova (eds), *Computational Science and Its Applications - ICCSA 2008.*, Vol. 5072 of *LNCS*, Springer, Heidelberg, pp. 756–768.

Debba, P., van Ruitenbeek, F. J. A., van der Meer, F. D., Carranza, E. J. M. & Stein, A. (2005). Optimal field sampling for targeting minerals using hyperspectral data, *Remote Sensing of Environment* **99**: 373–386.

Diggle, P. & Lophaven, S. (2006). Bayesian geostatistical design, *Scandinavian Journal of Statistics* **33**: 53–64.

Driscoll, R. S. & Coleman, M. D. (1974). Color for shrubs, *Photogrammetric Engineering and Remote Sensing* **40**: 451–459.

Eardley, A. J. (1942). *Aerial photographs: their use and interpretation*, New York: Harper.

Everitt, J. H., Gerbermann, A. H., Alaniz, M. A. & Bowen, R. L. (1980). Using 70 mm aerial photography to identify rangeland sites, *Photogrammetric Engineering and Remote Sensing* **46**: 1339–1348.

Everitt, J. H., Richardson, A. J., Gerbermann, A. H., Wiegand, C. L. & Alaniz, M. A. (1979). Landsat-2 data for inventorying rangelands in south Texas, *Proceedings of the 5th Symposium Machine Processing of Remotely Sensed Data. Purdue University, West Lafayette, Ind.*, pp. 132–141.

Gilbertson, B., Longshaw, T. G. & Viljoen, R. P. (1976). Multispectral aerial photography as exploration tool. IV-V - an applications in the Khomas Trough region, South Africa; and cost effective analysis and conclusions (for mineral exploration), *Remote Sensing of Environment* **5**(2): 93–107.

Goetz, A. F. H. & Srivastava, V. (1985). Mineralogical mapping Cuprite mining district, Nevada, *in* G. Vane & A. Goetz (eds), *Proc Airborne imaging spectrometer data analysis workshop*, Jet Propulsion Laboratory Publication 85-41, pp. 22–31.

Gupta, R. P. (2003). *Remote Sensing Geology*, second edn, Springer-Verlag New York, LLC.

Hapke, B. (1993). Combined theory of reflectance and emittance spectroscopy, *in* C. Pieters & P. A. J. Englert (eds), *Remote Geochemical Analysis: Elemental and Mineralogical Composition*, Cambridge University Press, Cambridge, UK, pp. 31–42.

Hedenquist, J. S., Arribas, A. R. & Gonzalez-Urien, E. (2000). Exploration for epithermal gold deposits, *Reviews in Economic Geology* **13**: 245–277.

Houston, R. S. (1973). Geologic mapping using space images, *Contributions to geology* **12**(2): 77–79.

Iranpanah, A. (1977). Geologic applications of Landsat imagery, *Photogrammetric Engineering and Remote Sensing* **43**: 1037–1040.

Johnson, P. L. (1969). *Remote sensing in ecology*, University of Georgia Press, Athens, GA.

Kirkpatrick, S., Gelatt, J. C. D. & Vecchi, M. P. (1983). Optimization by simulated annealing, *Science* **220**(4598): 671–680.

Knipling, E. B. (1970). Physical and physiological basis for the reflectance of visible and near-infrared radiation from vegetation, *Remote Sensing of Environment* **1**: 155–159.

Kowalik, W. S., Lyon, R. J. P. & Switzwe, P. (1983). The effect of additive reaidance terms on ratios of Landsat data (for mineral exploration), *Photogrammetric Engineering and Remote Sensing* **49**: 659–669.

Kruse, F. A. (2002). Comparison of AVIRIS and Hyperion for hyperspectral mineral mapping, *SPIE Aerospace Conference, 9-16 March 2002, Big Sky, Montana, published on CD-ROM, IEEE Catalog Number 02TH8593C, Paper 6.0102*, pp. 1–12.

Kruse, F. A. & Boardman, J. W. (1997). Characterization and mapping of Kimberlites and related diatremes in Utah, Colorodo, and Wyoming, USA, using the airborne visible/ infrared imaging spectrometer (AVIRIS), *ERIM Proceedings of the 12th International Conference on Applied Geologic Remote Sensing*, Colorado, pp. 21–28.

Kruse, F. A., Lefkoff, A. B., Boardman, J. W., Heidebrecht, K. B., Shapiro, A. T., Barloon, P. J. & Goetz, F. H. (1993). The spectral image processing system (SIPS) - interactive visualization and analysis of imaging spectrometer data, *Remote Sensing Environment* **44**: 145–163.

Lark, R. M. (2002). Optimized spatial sampling of soil for estimation of the variogram by maximum likelihood, *Geoderma* **105**: 49–80.

Laylender, P. A. (1956). A performance estimate comparing conventional geologic mapping with that accomplished with the aid of color photographs, *Photogrammetric engineering* p. 953.

Lillesand, T. M., Kiefer, R. W. & Chipman, J. W. (1994). *Remote Sensing and Image Interpretation*, New York, John Wiley & Sons.

Lloyd, C. D. & Atkinson, P. M. (1999). Designing optimal sampling configurations with ordinary and indicator kriging, in proceedings of the 4th international conference on geocomputation, Virginia, USA, *GeoComputation 99* .

Longshaw, T. G. & Gilbertson, B. (1976). Multispectral aerial photography as exploration tool - III two applications in the North-Western Cape Province, South Africa (for mineral exploration), *Remote Sensing of Environment* **5**(2): 79–92.

Lowman, P. D. (1976). Geologic structure in California: three studies with Landsat-1 imagery, *California Geology* **29**: 75–81.

Martini, B. A. (2003). Assessing hydrothermal system dynamics and character by coupling hyperspectral imaging with historical drilling data: Long Valley Caldera, CA, USA, *Proceedings 25th New Zealand Geothermal Workshop*, Vol. 25, pp. 101–106.

Martini, B. A., Silver, E. A., Pickles, W. L. & Cocks, P. A. (2003). Hyperspectral mineral mapping in support of geothermal exploration: Examples from Long Valley Caldera, CA and Dixie Valley, NV, USA, *Geothermal Resources Council Transactions*, Vol. 27, pp. 657–662.

McBratney, A. B. & Webster, R. (1981). The design of optimal sampling schemes for local estimation and mapping of regionalized variables - II: Program and examples, *Computers & Geosciences* **7**(4): 335–365.

McBratney, A. B., Webster, R. & Burgess, T. M. (1981). The design of optimal sampling schemes for local estimation and mapping of regionalized variables - I: Theory and method, *Computers & Geosciences* **7**(4): 331–334.

McGraw, J. F. & Tueller, P. T. (1983). Landsat computer-aided analysis techniques for range vegetation mapping, *Journal of Range Management* **36**: 627–631.

McGwire, K., Friedl, M. & Estes, J. E. (1993). Spatial structure, sampling design and scale in remotely-sensed imagery of a California Savanna Woodlands, *International Journal of Remote Sensing* **14**(11): 2137–2164.

Müller, W. G. & Zimmerman, D. L. (1999). Optimal designs for variogram estimation, *Environmetrics* **10**(23–37).

Okina, G. S., Roberts, D. A., Murraya, B. & Okin, W. J. (2001). Practical limits on hyperspectral vegetation discrimination in arid and semiarid environments, *Remote Sensing of Environment* **77**: 212–225.

Papp, É. & Cudahy, T. (2002). Geophysical and remote sensing methods for regolith exploration, *in* É. Papp (ed.), *Hyperspectral remote sensing*, CRCLEME Open File Report 144, pp. 13–21.

Polder, G. & van der Heijden, G. W. A. M. (2001). Multispectral and hyperspectral image acquisition and processing, *in* Q. Tong, Y. Zhu & Z. Zhu (eds), *Proceedings of SPIE*, Vol. 4548.

Resmini, R. G., Kappus, M. E., Aldrich, W. S., Harsanyi, J. C. & Anderson, M. (1997). Mineral mapping with hyperspectral digital imagery collection experiment (HYDICE) sensor at Cuprite, Nevada, U.S.A., *International Journal of Remote Sensing* **18**(7): 1553–1570.

Richards, J. A. (1993). *Remote Sensing Digital Image Analysis: An Introduction*, second edn, Springer-Verlag, Berlin.

Richardson, A. J., Menges, R. M. & Nixon, P. R. (1985). Distinguishing weed from crop plants using video remote-sensing, *Photogrammetric Engineering & Remote Sensing* **51**(11): 1785–1790.

Richter, R. (1996). Atmospheric correction of DAIS hyperspectral image data, *SPIE Proceedings*, Vol. 2756, Orlando, pp. 390–399.

Rowan, L. C., Crowley, J. K., Schmidt, R. G., Ager, C. M. & Mars, J. C. (2000). Mapping hydrothermally altered rocks by analyzing hyperspectral image (AVIRIS) data of forested areas in the Southeastern United States, *Journal of Geochemical Exploration* **68**(3): 145–166.

Rowan, L. C., Goetz, A. F. H. & Ashley, R. P. (1977). Discrimination of hydrothermally altered and unaltered rocks in visible and near infrared multispectral images, *Geophysics* **42**(3): 522–535.

Royle, J. A. & Nychka, D. (1998). An algorithm for the construction of spatial coverage designs with implementation in S-PLUS, *Computational Geoscience* **24**: 479–488.

Russo, D. (1984). Design of an optimal sampling network for estimating the variogram, *Soil Science Society American Journal* **52**: 708–716.

Sabins, F. F. (1996). *Remote Sensing: Principles and Interpretation*, third edn, W.H. Freeman and Company, New York.

Sabins, F. F. (1999). Remote sensing for mineral exploration, *Ore Geology Reviews* **14**(Issues 3–4): 157–183.

Sacks, J. & Schiller, S. (1988). Spatial designs, *in* S. Gupta & J. Berger (eds), *Statistical Decision Theory and Related Topics*, Vol. 2 of *Papers from the forth Purdue symposium*, Springer-Verlag, New York, pp. 385–399.

Salisbury, J. W., Walter, L. S., Vergo, N. & D'Aria, D. M. (1991). *Infrared (2.1-2.5 μm) spectra of minerals*, Johns Hopkins University Press, Baltimore, MD.

Siegal, B. S. & Abrams, M. J. (1976). Geologic mapping using Landsat data, *Photogrammetric Engineering and Remote Sensing* **42**: 325–337.

Siegal, B. S. & Gillespie, A. R. (1980). *Remote sensing in geology*, New York : Wiley.

Smith, M. O., Johnston, P. E. & Adams, J. B. (1985). Quantitative determination of mineral types and abundances from reflectance spectra using principal component analysis, *Journal of Geophysical Research* **90**: 797–804.

Spruill, T. B. & Candela, L. (1990). Two approaches to design of monitoring networks, *Ground Water* **28**: 430–442.

Srivastav, S. K., Bhattacharya, A., Kamaraju, M. V. V., Reddy, G. S., Shrimal, A. K., Mehta, D. S., List, F. K. & Burger, H. (2000). Remote sensing and GIS for locating favourable zones of lead-zinc-copper mineralization in Rajpura-Dariba area, Rajasthan, India, *International Journal Remote Sensing* **21**(17): 3253–3267.

Stein, A., van der Meer, F. & Gorte, B. (eds) (1999). *Spatial Statistics for Remote Sensing*, Vol. 1 of *Remote Sensing and Digital Image Processing*, Kluwer Academic Publishers.

Tapia, R., Stein, A. & Bijker, W. (2005). Optimization of sampling schemes for vegetation mapping using fuzzy classification, *Remote Sensing of Environment* pp. 425–433.

Thenkabail, P. S. (2002). Optimal hyperspectral narrowbands for discriminating agricultural crops, *Remote Sensing Reviews* **20**(4): 257–291.
URL: *http://www.yale.edu/ceo/Projects/swap/pubs/ optimal_bands_text.pdf*

Thenkabail, P. S., Smith, R. B. & De-Pauw, E. (2002). Evaluation of narrowband and broadband vegetation indices for determining optimal hyperspectral wavebands for agricultural crop characterization, *Photogrammetric Engineering and Remote Sensing* **68**(6): 607–621.

Van der Meer, F. D. (2004). Analysis of spectral absorption features in hyperspactral imagery, *JAG: International Journal of Applied Earth Observation and Geoinformation* **5**(1): 55–68.

Van Groenigen, J. W., Gandah, M. & Bouma, J. (2000). Soil sampling strategies for precision agriculture research under Sahelian conditions, *Soil Science Society American Journal* **64**: 1674–1680.

Van Groenigen, J. W., Pieters, G. & Stein, A. (2000). Optimizing spatial sampling for multivariate contamination in urban areas, *Environmetrics* **11**: 227–244.

Van Groenigen, J. W., Siderius, W. & Stein, A. (1999). Constrained optimisation of soil sampling for minimisation of the kriging variance, *Geoderma* **87**: 239–259.

Van Groenigen, J. W. & Stein, A. (1998). Constrained optimization of spatial sampling using continuous simulated annealing, *Journal Environmental Quality* **27**: 1078–1086.

Vaughan, R. G., Calvin, W. M. & Taranik, J. V. (2003). SEBASS hyperspectral thermal infrared data: surface emissivity measurement and mineral mapping, *Remote Sensing of Environment* **85**(1): 48–63.

Warrick, A. W. & Myers, D. E. (1987). Optimization of sampling locations for variogram calculations, *Water Resources Research* **23**(3): 496–500.

Yfantis, E. A., Flatman, G. T. & Behar, J. V. (1987). Efficiency of kriging estimation for square, triangular, and hexagonal grids, *Mathematical Geology* **19**(3): 183–205.

Zimmerman, D. L. & Homer, K. E. (1991). A network design criterion for estimating selected attributes of the semivariogram, *Environmetrics* **4**: 425–441.

Customized Simulated Annealing Algorithm Suitable for Primer Design in Polymerase Chain Reaction Processes

Luciana Montera[1], Maria do Carmo Nicoletti[2],
Said Sadique Adi[1] and Maria Emilia Machado Telles Walter[3]
[1]*Federal University of Mato Grosso do Sul*
[2]*Federal University of São Carlos*
[3]*University of Brasília*
Brazil

1. Introduction

The investigation of functionalities and other biological characteristics of proteins can be carried out from their corresponding gene sequence (DNA). The development of a process named PCR (Polymerase Chain Reaction) (Mullis & Faloona, 1987), based on an enzyme named DNA polymerase, was decisive for establishing a laboratorial procedure for generating thousands to millions of copies of a particular DNA sequence (amplification). Besides amplification, PCR-based techniques can also be employed in a variety of processes with different purposes, such as DNA sequencing and molecular evolution.

A basic PCR set up requires several components and reagents as described in (Sambrook & Russel, 2001). Among the components, the two most relevant for the *in silico* proposal and the experiments described in this chapter are the DNA fragment to be amplified (referred to as template) and a primer sequence pair. Primers are appropriate short nucleotide sequences added to the reaction in order to mark the limits of the target region, i.e., the region of the template to be amplified. Commonly two primers are used namely forward, for flanking the beginning of the target region, and reverse, for flanking its end. The primer pair is one of the most important parameters for a successful PCR. Its design involves several variables whose values, generally, are determined via extensive calculations. Also, primer design requires several issues; for instance, it should not be easy for primers to anneal with other primers in the mixture neither should they be biased to anneal among themselves, which would prevent them to anneal with the DNA template.

It is worth mentioning that although many different software systems are available for assisting primer design, such as those described in (Contreras-Moreira et al., 2009; Boyce et al., 2009; Mann et al., 2009; Kalendar et al., 2009; Gatto & Schretter, 2009; Piriyapongsa et al., 2009; You et al., 2008; Christensen et al., 2008; Tsai et al., 2007; Schretter & Milinkovitch, 2006; Liang et al., 2005; Boutros & Okey, 2004; Gordon & Sensen, 2004; Rose et al., 2003; Rozen & Skaletsky, 2000), the design process itself is still not well defined. This is mainly due to the number of variables involved and the lack of consensus in relation to their adequate values. This adds an extra degree of uncertainty to the process which, by its own nature, is already prone to some uncertainty. Additionally, several available software systems have not been developed for general use; they have been designed to find primers in specific situations such as gene identification (Giegerich et al., 1996), measurement of eukaryotic gene expression (Gunnar et al., 2004), novel gene characterization (Costas et al., 2007), genetic disease diagnosis (Frech et al., 2009), detection of variations and mutations in genes (Evans & Liu, 2005; Haas et al., 2003; Ke et al., 2002) and molecular evolution (Lahr et al., 2009; Oliveira et al., 2006; Pusch et al., 2004; Antia et al., 2003; Patten et al., 1996). Besides, it must be mentioned that, undoubtedly useful, *in silico* primers must be sometimes adjusted in real experiments (Morales & Holben, 2009).

This chapter is an extension of a previous work (Montera & Nicoletti, 2008) where the design of a primer pair is approached as a search process based on a customized simulated annealing, implemented by an interactive software named SAPrimer[1]. After this Introduction the chapter is organized into four more sections as follows.

Section 2 contextualizes the application area (Molecular Biology) by introducing a few important definitions and processes relevant to the understanding of the work described in the chapter. It presents an up-to-date review of the state-of-the-art relative to PCR. PCR based methods such as real-time PCR, multiplex PCR and InterAlu-PCR will be briefly mentioned since they deal with important issues related to the process. The section also describes in detail the basic three steps composing a PCR process namely, (1) DNA denaturing, (2) primer and DNA template annealing and (3) primer extension. The three iterative steps are temperature-dependent and cyclically executed. The amplification process is responsible for producing a vast amount of copies from a small amount of DNA sequences (template). Critical to the amplification process is the adequate choice of a pair of primes. Considerations focusing on the importance of a well designed primer pair for the success of a PCR process as well as the main difficulties to design them are also presented.

Section 3 specifies and details the main variables to be considered when designing primers. Particular attention is given to the values assigned to the variables as well as their impact on the results.

Section 4 deals specifically with the use of a heuristic search method known as Simulated Annealing (SA) for solving the problem of finding an adequate pair of primes for a PCR process. As it is well known, the definition of a suitable objective (or fitness) function is a critical aspect when using SA for solving a problem. Aiming at promoting readability, Section 4 has been divided into two subsections. Subsection 4.1 presents the construction of the function in a systematic objective and didactic way, taking into account the variables and parameters listed in Section 3. It describes how they are combined into a function to be used to direct the search process conducted by the proposed customized version of SA. For a proper evaluation of a primer pair, the fitness function is defined considering how each variable value (size, composition, annealing temperature, etc.), calculated for each primer in a pair, differs from a pre-established set of values.

Subsection 4.2 focuses on the description of two releases of SAPrimer software, which implements an user-friendly computational environment to search for optimal pair of primers. Details of the main common functionalities of both releases (SAPrimer (R1) and

---

[1] http://www.facom.ufms.br/~montera/SAPrimer

SAPrimer (R2)) are presented, including a description of how a primer pair is found, evaluated and chosen (Montera & Nicoletti, 2008). Subsection 4.2 also discusses some new features incorporated to SAPrimer (R2). Particularly the search process was modified so that instead of keeping only one primer pair as a candidate solution, a list of the best primer pairs found so far during the iterative process is kept and, as final result, the list of selected pairs, ordered by their fitness values, is returned to the user. Other new functionalities included in SAPrimer (R2) are also discussed, such as finding primers for any user-defined frame size and finding degenerate primers for a given protein sequence.

Finally, Section 5 presents the final considerations and highlights the main contributions that the proposal and the available software can offer to those who need assistance for conducting PCR-related experiments.

2. The Role of Polymerase Chain Reaction (PCR) in Molecular Evolution and the Role of Primers in PCR

Directed molecular evolution (or *in vitro* evolution) is a laboratorial procedure that attempts to simulate the Darwinian evolution. One of its main goals is to obtain proteins with certain properties enhanced. The process starts with a pool of DNA (or RNA) molecules and, by implementing an iterative process of recombination, tries to construct new functional sequences from the previous ones.

The literature brings several directed molecular evolution methods such as error-prone polymerase chain reaction (epPCR) (Cadwell & Joyce, 1992), Stemmer's DNA shuffling (Stemmer, 1994a; Stemmer, 1994b), staggered extension (StEP) (Zhao et al., 1998), heteroduplex recombination (Volkov et al., 1999), degenerate homoduplex recombination (DHR) (Coco et al., 2002), assembly of designed oligonucleotides (ADO) (Zha et al., 2003) and codon shuffling (Chopra & Ranganathan, 2003). A review of some molecular evolution methods for enzymes can be found in (Lutz & Patrick, 2004). Usually, directed molecular evolution methods share the common goal of generating new sequences that encode functionally interesting proteins.

The process of *in vitro* evolution, as described in (Sun, 1999) and schematically shown in Fig. 1, starts by constructing a library of (DNA, RNA or protein) molecules using (1) random molecules of peptides or oligonucleotides or (2) variants of one or more parent molecule(s) obtained through mutagenesis, as described next. Usually option (1) is not appealing due to the vast amount of resulting molecules and their high diversity. However, a library built using a process of mutation (mutagenesis) from one or a few molecules, which are already known to have some desired property, can be more appealing, since diversity can be kept under control. The initial library (Pool 1 in Fig. 1) is then input to a process that selects potentially relevant molecules (i.e., those that can have a desired function) - generally only a small number of molecules are selected. Next a process of mutation (mutagenesis) is used in order to increase the number of the selected molecules, as well as their diversity. After mutation, the resulting molecules undergo to an amplification process, to have their numbers increased. The sequence selection, mutagenesis and amplification constitute a cycle of the *in vitro* evolution process. The cycle is repeated until molecules having the desired properties are finally selected.

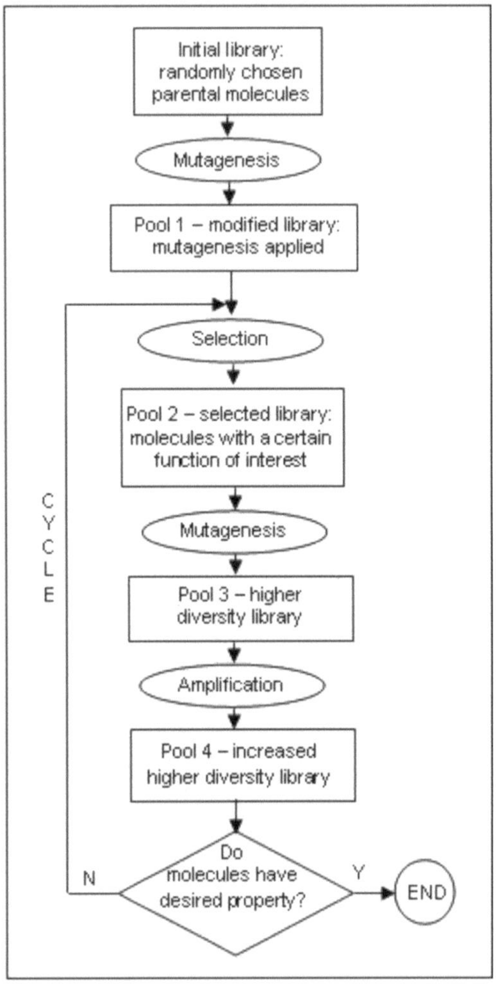

Fig. 1. General *in vitro* evolution scheme

Both mutagenesis and amplification are basic processes in *in vitro* evolution experiments. Mutagenesis can be used either for creating the initial molecular library or for increasing the molecular diversity, after a selection process took place, as shows Fig. 1. The amplification process allows the production of multiple copies of chosen target molecules and can be implemented by Polymerase Chain Reaction (PCR), that can be improved by using the primer search strategy described in the following sections of this chapter.

As defined in (Metzker & Caskey, 2001), "PCR is an elegant but simple technique for the *in vitro* amplification of target DNA using DNA polymerase and two specific oligonucleotide or primer sequences flanking the region of interest". The DNA polymerase synthesizes a new double-stranded of DNA from a single-stranded template. So that, it is necessary a $3' \rightarrow 5'$ primer (reverse) to make a complementary strand from a template in $5' \rightarrow 3'$ direction, and a $5' \rightarrow 3'$ primer (forward) to make a complementary strand from a template in $3' \rightarrow 5'$ direction. In a PCR cycle, the three temperature-controlled steps pictorially shown in Fig. 2 are:

(1) *Denaturing*: double-stranded DNA molecules are heated so that each double-stranded DNA molecule is completely separated into two single-stranded molecules;
(2) *Annealing*: the temperature is lowered such that primers anneal to their complementary single-stranded sequences;
(3) *Extension*: the temperature is raised up achieving an optimum point for the polymerase to react. DNA polymerases use the single-stranded molecules as templates to extend the primers that have been annealed to the templates in the previous step.

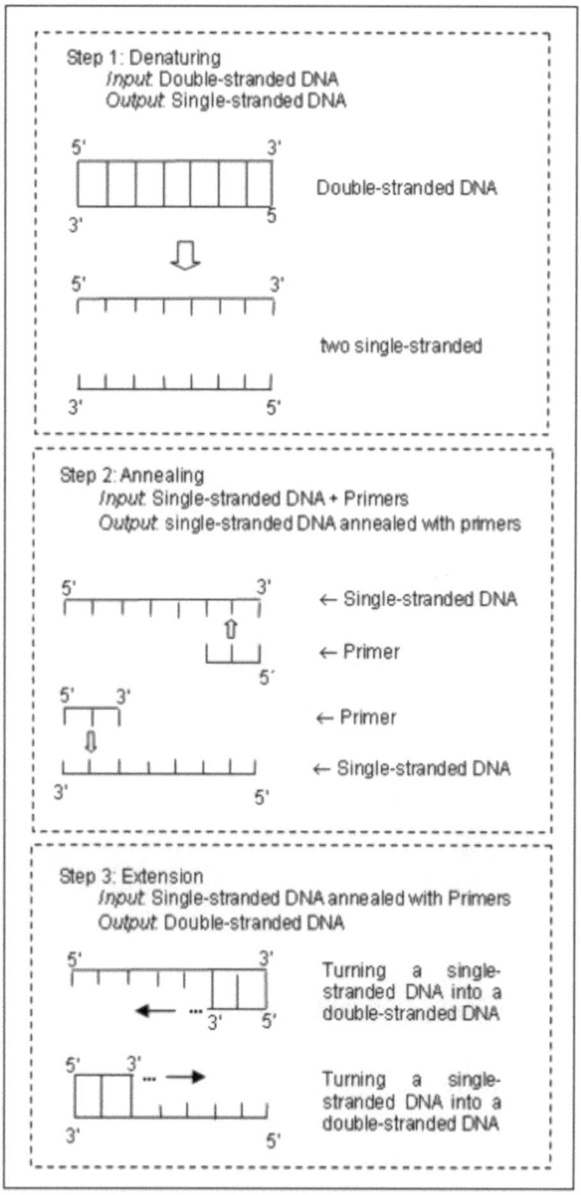

Fig. 2. The three temperature-controlled steps of a PCR process

PCR-based DNA technology can be used to perform mutation and recombination. As stated in (Tait & Horton, 1998), "The application of PCR techniques has blurred the distinctions among mutagenesis, recombination, and synthesis of genes. The product of PCR-based manipulations is really a mosaic in which sequences derived from natural sources are connected by sequences derived from the synthetic oligonucleotide primers used to direct the amplification; essentially any desired gene sequence can be constructed by combining natural, mutant, and synthetic regions".

The success of a PCR is highly dependent on the primer pair chosen and on the experimental conditions in which the reaction occurs, such as the number of cycles, the temperature and the time involved in each individual step as well as the quality and the volume of primers used in the annealing step. The denaturation and the annealing temperatures are directly dependent on the primers used. An exhaustive list of variables and parameters that interfere in a PCR experiment as well as a discussion about PCR techniques, its results, limitations and applications can be found in (Hugles & Moody, 2008; Dieffenbach & Dveksler, 2003; Kanagawa, 2003; Metzker & Caskey, 2001; He et al., 1994; Nuovo, et al., 1993; Innis & Gelfand, 1990; Allawi & SantaLucia, 1998a; Allawi & SantaLucia, 1998b; Allawi & SantaLucia, 1998c; Allawi & SantaLucia, 1997). Of particular interest for the work described in this chapter is the adequate choice of a pair of primes.

It is important to mention, as pointed out in (Hassibi et al., 2004), that "while in theory one would expect an exponential growth for the target as a function of PCR cycles (i.e., 2^n times the original DNA number, after n cycles), in practice, replication processes measured by different real-time PCR systems show varying yields, suggesting a biochemical random process. In addition to variable gains and inconsistent amplification levels within a PCR process, there is also the likelihood of creating non-specific byproducts (i.e., DNA strands different from the target) as well as of inserting mutations into the product, which further degrades the quality of the PCR product".

Besides DNA amplification and molecular evolution, PCR-based methods have been associated to a variety of processes. Studies of gene expression level (Isenbarger et al., 2008; Dixon et al., 2007), loss of allelic heterozygosity (LOH) (Vladušić et al., 2010; Chih-Ming et al., 2009; Franko et al., 2008; Saelee et al., 2008), microsatellite instability (MSI) (Eveno et al., 2010; Bertagnolli et al., 2009), microdeletions (Kolb et al., 2010; Pasmant et al., 2009), quantification of small ncRNAs (Ro et al., 2006; Berezikov et al., 2006) and detection of low-level mutations (Milbury et al., 2009) are a few examples of the popularity, success and diversity of uses of PCR. Some of the examples can be characterized as quantitative PCR or Real Time PCR (Lan et al., 2009; Roux, 2009; VanGuilder et al., 2008; Pattyn et al., 2003; Vandesompele et al., 2002) or quantitative multiplex PCR (Sasaki et al., 2010; Wang et al., 2009; Castellsagué et al., 2008), Inter-Alu PCR (Bonafè et al., 2001; Srivastava et al., 2005), or COLD-PCR (Milbury et al., 2009) and miniprimer PCR (Isenbarger et al., 2008).

3. Primers and Their Main Characteristics

The primer pair that can be used in the annealing step of a PCR is not unique, since forward and reverse primers with different sizes are possible. This poses a non-deterministic aspect to the process. The pair of primers that promotes the best results of a PCR (i.e., the pair that optimizes the amount and the specificity of the product) is named optimum pair.

Finding the optimum pair involves the simultaneous analysis of many parameters like primer size, primer contents of cytosine and guanine bases, melting temperature of the DNA strands, 3′ end composition, specificity, formation of secondary structure between forward and reverse primers or between two forward or two reverse primers, and several others. Since there is not a unique value that defines the proper value for each one of these variables, generally a range of values is considered. For example, the goal could be to find a primer whose length is in the interval 18-30 bp having its cytosine and guanine composition (%CG) between 40-60%.
Frequently value restrictions imposed on some variables can conflict with values assigned to other variables. In spite of the non-existence of a consensus for the exact values of several parameters, studies can be found in the literature establishing values, or intervals of values for them (Apte & Daniel, 2009; Vikalo et al., 2006; Yu et al., 2006; Acinas et al., 2005; Abd-Elsalam, 2003; Kanagawa, 2003; Sommer & Tautz, 1989).
Each of the next four subsections groups important primer characteristics which will be used to create specific metrics to be incorporated into the objective function used by the SA (described in Section 4). The criterion used for grouping them is identified in the title of the corresponding subsection.

3.1 Repeats, runs and secondary structures

The repetition of nucleotide sequences (named *repeat*) inside of a primer sequence should be avoided since the occurrence of repeats can favor the occurrence of *misprimes*, i.e., a misplaced annealing between the template and the primer sequence that causes the amplification of a region different from the target region. The occurrence of a long repetition of one single base in the primer sequence is named *run*. Runs should be avoided because they can favor misprimes.
Another important characteristic that should be avoided during a primer design is their *self-complementarity*, which promotes the primer-primer annealing. Self-complementary primer sequences can affect the PCR efficiency by reducing the concentration of single-stranded primers since some annealed primer-primer could be extended by the polymerase, resulting in an unwanted non-specific product. Three distinct primer-primer annealing situations can occur, promoting the construction of secondary structures known as *self-dimer* (annealing between two forward or two reverse primer sequences), *hetero-dimer* (annealing between one forward and one reverse primer sequence), and *hairpins* (annealing of a primer sequence, to itself).

3.2 Specificity and primer length

A forward primer is considered specific if it anneals to the template just at the beginning of the target region. A reverse primer is considered specific if it anneals to the template just at the ending of the target region. The specificity of a primer is highly important to assure that the PCR product will correspond exactly to the target region, that is, to the region to be amplified. A way to evaluate the specificity of a primer sequence is by 'sliding' it along the length of the template, trying to detect alternative priming sites, other than the target region. Clearly, primers that promote alternative annealing sites are not a good choice. The specificity is closely related to the primer length.

The choice of primer lenght involves at least three parameters: specificity, annealing stability and cost. The longer is the primer, the smaller are the chances of existing alternative priming sites, i.e., the longer the primers, the more specific they are. Longer primers are more stable due to the greater number of hydrogen bonds they form with the template. Longer primers, however, are more biased to the formation of secondary structures and are financially more expensive to be produced. Shorter primers, in spite of their lower cost, are prone to anneal outside the target region, resulting in non-specific product, lowering the quality of the PCR product. There is no single optimum length for a primer. A rule-of-thumb suggested in (Abd-Elsalam, 2003) is "primers of 18–30 nucleotides in length are the best".

3.3 The %CG content and the 3′ end

The percentage of cytosine (C) and guanine (G) bases (%CG) in a primer sequence is very important because these numbers provide information about the annealing stability/strength. The binding between thymine (T) and adenine (A) bases occurs due to the formation of two hydrogen bonds; the binding between cytosine (C) and guanine (G) bases occurs due to the formation of three hydrogen bonds, making the latter more stable and more difficult to be formed and broken. As a consequence, the CG content of a primer directly influences the temperature in which the annealing between the primer and the template will occur. In general, primers with a CG content varying between 40% and 60% are preferred.

Mismatches can occur during the annealing between a primer and a template. They can be located anywhere (inside or at the end of the primer–template complex) and can affect the stability of the complex, causing undesirable side effects as far as the efficiency of the polymerase extension process is concerned. A mismatch located at (or near) the 3′ end of a primer (where the extension by polymerase starts) has a greater damaging effect than those located at other positions (Kwok et al., 1990). Based on this information, it can be inferred that the 3′ end of a primer should be well "stuck" to the template, so that the polymerase can start and conduct the extension process efficiently. Due to the strong binding between the C and G bases, the presence of either at the 3′ end of a primer should be preferred (over the occurrence of a T or A) since this will (potentially) assure more stability to the primer-template complex.

3.4 Melting and annealing temperatures

The melting temperature (T_m) is the temperature at which 50% of the DNA molecules are in duplex form and the other 50% are in denaturated form. In a PCR, it is expected that while the template molecules denature, the primer molecules anneal to the single-stranded resulting sequences (templates). The temperature at which the annealing between the primer and the template occurs is defined as the annealing temperature (T_a). The T_m value can be defined in relation to both the product (amplified templates) and the primers; the T_a calculation is particularly dependent on both. There are several different methods to estimate the T_m value, which can be broadly classified according to the adopted methodology: *Basic* (only considers the %CG content), *Salt Adjusted* (takes into account the salt concentration at the solution) and *Thermodynamic* (uses the Nearest Neighbor model).

The most basic formula for the T_m calculation was given in (Wallace et al., 1979) and is shown in eq. (1) in Table 1, where $|C|$, $|G|$, $|A|$ and $|T|$ represent, respectively, the number of cytosine, guanine, adenine and thymine bases present in the DNA sequence. Eq. (1) establishes that value of T_m is directly related to the length and contents of a DNA sequence. Another basic formulation, proposed in (Marmur & Doty, 1962), is given by eq. (2) in Table 1, which assumes that the reaction occurs at the standard conditions of pH = 7.0, 50mM Na^+ and 50nM of primer concentration. The salt adjusted formulation proposed in (Howley et al., 1979), considering the same values for the pH and sequence concentration as in (Marmur & Doty, 1962), is given by eq. (3), in Table 1.

$$T_m = 2*(|A|+|T|)+4*(|C|+|G|) \quad (1)$$

$$T_m = \frac{64.9+41*(|C|+|G|-16.4)}{(|A|+|T|+|C|+|G|)} \quad (2)$$

$$T_m = 100.5+41*\frac{|C|+|G|-6.4}{|A|+|T|+|C|+|G|} - \frac{820}{|A|+|T|+|C|+|G|} + 16.6*\log[Na^+] \quad (3)$$

Table 1. Basic and salt adjusted T_m formulas

Formulations dependent on the Nearest Neighbor (NN) model are widely used; one of the reasons is due to "the stability of a DNA duplex appears to depend primarily on the identity of the nearest neighbor bases", as stated in (Breslauer et al., 1986). Considering the four bases, there are sixteen different pairwise nearest neighbor possibilities that can be used to predict the stability and the T_m of a duplex. The NN model establishes values for the enthalpy and entropy variation (represented by ΔH and ΔS, respectively) to each one of the sixteen pairs. Several studies propose different values for ΔH and ΔS, as those ones described in (Breslauer et al., 1986) , (Sugimoto et al., 1996) and (SantaLucia et al., 1996). The ΔH and ΔS values for a DNA sequence $X = x_1x_2 \ldots x_n$ are calculated using eq. (4).

$$\Delta H = \sum_{i=1}^{n-1} \Delta H(x_i, x_{i+1}) \qquad \Delta S = \sum_{i=1}^{n-1} \Delta S(x_i, x_{i+1}) \quad (4)$$

A commonly used formulation to calculate the T_m value considering the contribution of the NN model was proposed in (Rychlik et al., 1990) and is given by eq. (5), where R = 1.987 cal/°C*mol is the molar gas constant, γ is the primer concentration in the solution, $[Na^+]$ is the salt concentration, and ΔH and ΔS the enthalpy and entropy variation of the primer sequences, respectively.

$$T_m = \frac{\Delta H}{\Delta S + R*\ln\frac{\gamma}{4}} - 273.15 + 16.6*\log[Na^+] \quad (5)$$

A few other proposals to calculate T_m can be found in the literature. It is important to mention, however, that all the attempts to define a proper value for T_m are only an approximation of the real melting temperature since, as commented in (Kämpke et al., 2001), "A proper computation of the primer melting temperature does not appear to exist". a comparative study of different melting temperature calculation methods as well as the influence of the different NN interaction values available for the T_m calculations is presented in (Panjkovich & Melo, 2005).
Although there have been some attempts to estimate T_a (such as in (Rychlik et al., 1990)), it seems that there is a consensus in the literature that the T_a value should be empirically determined (see (Innis & Gelfand, 1990)).

4. A Customized Simulated Annealing Algorithm for PCR Primer Design

Generally speaking, simulated annealing (Kirkpatrick et al., 1983) is a probabilistic algorithm suitable for finding a good approximation to a global optimum of a given function in a large search space. It is based on successive steps, which depend on an arbitrarily set parameter named temperature (T).
In this chapter the design of a primer pair has been approached as an optimization problem, using a customized SA to conduct a search process throughout the space of all possible primer pairs, trying to find an optimal solution (i.e., a primer pair) to a function. The SA technique is heavily dependent on an appropriate choice of the function to be optimized. For this particular domain, the function was constructed based on the primer relevant characteristics for a successful PCR when amplifying a given DNA target, as described in Section 3. The next two subsections focus, respectively, on the construction of the objective function and on the description and use of the two releases of the SAPrimer software, that implement the search for an optimal pair of primers using the objective function previously constructed.

4.1 Constructing the objective function

Before presenting and discussing the function used in the experiments, the basic metrics implemented for evaluating primer characteristics are described in Table 2, where *fp* and *rp* represent the forward and reverse primer in a primer pair, respectively.
In order to "measure" how "good" a primer pair (fp, rp) is (relative to the probability of a successful PCR), it is mandatory to evaluate its conformity to a pre-established (user-defined) range of values, as well as to check the occurrence of any of unwanted characteristics, such as runs, repeats, secondary structures and non-specificity. The range of parameter values that should be defined by the user are listed in Table 3.
In Table 3, the parameter MAX_DIF establishes the allowed maximum T_m difference ($T_m$dif) between the forward and the reverse primer. Both T_m and T_m difference are measured in Celsius degree (°C). The 3'_END is a Boolean parameter that specifies the user preference (or not) for the occurrence of base C or G at the 3' end of the primer sequences.
As there is no agreement about the best T_m formula to be used, the T_m value is estimated by the average of all T_m values calculated using all distinct formulas described in Table 1 of Section 3.4. When T_m uses the enthalpy and entropy contribution, a calculation is done for each distinct NN interaction values proposed in (Breslauer et al., 1986), (Sugimoto et al., 1996) and (SantaLucia et al., 1996).

The function to evaluate a primer pair (*fp*, *rp*) used for implementing the SA algorithm is given by eq. (6). It "measures" how well the argument pair fits the pre-established range of values (for the characteristics given in Table 3) and how "good" it is, concerning others (e.g. absence of repeats, runs, etc.), by associating a "cost"to the unwanted values of the characteristics. The highest is the function value, the less suitable is the primer pair given as its argument, since costs indicate how far the characteristics of a primer pair are from those pre-established by the user.

Metric	Type	Description
len(*fp*), len(*rp*)	integer	Gives the length of the argument sequence
CG(*fp*), CG(*rp*)	real	Gives the % of C and G bases in the argument sequence
T_m(*fp*), T_m(*rp*)	real	Gives the T_m of the argument sequence
$T_m$dif(*fp*, *rp*)	real	Gives the T_m difference between the argument sequences
3'_end(*fp*), 3'_end(*rp*)	Boolean	Checks the existence of a C or G base at the 3' end of the argument sequence
run(*fp*), run(*rp*)	Boolean	Checks the existence of runs in the argument sequence
repeat(*fp*), repeat(*rp*)	Boolean	Checks the existence of repeats in the argument sequence
spec(*fp*), spec(*rp*)	Boolean	Checks the specificity of the argument sequence
sec(*fp*, *rp*)	Boolean	Checks the existence of secondary structures in the argument sequences

Table 2. Basic metrics for evaluating a primer

Parameter	Range of values/Type
LENGTH_INTERVAL	[MIN_LEN, MAX_LEN] / both integer
%CG_CONTENT	[MIN_CG, MAX_CG] /both real
Tm	[MIN_Tm, MAX_Tm] / both real
MAX_DIF	- / real
3'_END	- / Boolean

Table 3. User-defined parameter values

$$\text{fitness}\,(fp, rp) = \text{len\_cost}(fp) + \text{len\_cost}(rp) + \%\text{CG\_cost}(fp) +$$
$$+ \%\text{CG\_cost}(rp) + 3*(T_{m}\text{\_cost}(fp) + T_{m}\text{\_cost}(rp)) +$$

$$+ T_m\text{dif\_cost}(fp, rp) + 3'\text{\_end\_cost}(fp) + \tag{6}$$
$$+ 3'\text{\_end\_cost}(rp) + \text{run\_cost}(fp) + \text{run\_cost}(rp) +$$
$$+ \text{repeat\_cost}(fp) + \text{repeat\_cost}(rp) + \text{spec\_cost}(fp) +$$
$$+ \text{spec\_cost}(rp) + \text{sec\_struc\_cost}(fp, rp)$$

Taking sq as *fp* or *rp*, each individual cost function is defined as:

$$\text{len\_cost}(sq) = \begin{cases} 0 \text{ if } MIN\_LEN \le len(sq) \le MAX\_LEN \\ MIN\_LEN - len(sq) \text{ if } len(sq) < MIN\_LEN \\ len(sq) - MAX\_LEN \text{ if } len(sq) > MAX\_LEN \end{cases}$$

$$\%CG\_cost(sq) = \begin{cases} 0 \text{ if } MIN\_CG \le CG(sq) \le MAX\_CG \\ MIN\_CG - CG(sq) \text{ if } CG(sq) < MIN\_CG \\ CG(sq) - MAX\_CG \text{ if } CG(sq) > MAX\_CG \end{cases}$$

$$T_m\_cost(sq) = \begin{cases} 0 \text{ if } MIN\_T_m \le T_m(sq) \le MAX\_T_m \\ MIN\_T_m - T_m(sq) \text{ if } T_m(sq) < MIN\_T_m \\ T_m(sq) - MAX\_T_m \text{ if } T_m(sq) > MAX\_T_m \end{cases}$$

$$T_m dif\_cost(fp, rp) = \begin{cases} 0 \text{ if } T_m dif(fp, rp) \le MAX\_DIF \\ T_m dif(fp, rp) - MAX\_DIF \text{ otherwise} \end{cases}$$

$$3'\_end\_cost(sq) = \begin{cases} 0 \text{ if } 3'\_end(sq) = \text{true} \\ 5 \text{ otherwise} \end{cases}$$

$$run\_cost(sq) = \begin{cases} 0 \text{ if } run(sq) = \text{false} \\ 5 * \text{number of runs otherwise} \end{cases}$$

$$repeat\_cost(sq) = \begin{cases} 0 \text{ if } reapet(sq) = \text{false} \\ 5 * \text{number of repeats otherwise} \end{cases}$$

$$spec\_cost(sq) = \begin{cases} 0 \text{ if } spec(sq) = \text{true} \\ 5 * \text{number of alternative priming sites otherwise} \end{cases}$$

$$sec\_struc\_cost(fp, rp) = \begin{cases} 0 \text{ if } sec(fp, rp) = \text{false} \\ \sum_{i=1}^{5} highest\_cost(G_i) \text{ otherwise} \end{cases}$$

The first three cost functions assign a cost to a primer (forward or reverse) whose values for primer length, %CG content and melting temperature, respectively, are outside the pre-established limits given in Table 3. The fourth cost function ($T_m$dif_cost) assigns a cost to a primer pair depending on its temperature difference be higher than the user-defined parameter MAX_DIF.
The inclusion of the fifth cost function for the calculation of the value of fitness is dependent on the information given by the user regarding his/her preference (or not) for a base C or G at the 3′ end of the primers. If the user has no preference, 3′_end_cost(*sq*) is not included in the fitness calculation. Otherwise, the non-existence of a C or G base at the 3′ end of a primer adds the arbitrary cost of 5 to the fitness value. The cost associated to the presence of runs and repeats is given by the functions run_cost and repeat_cost, respectively, which add a cost of 5 to each time a run or a repeat is found. The spec_cost function is similar to the two previous cost functions.
The last cost function assigns a cost to the possible secondary structures that may be formed in each of the following five groups (G_i, i = 1,...,5): hetero-dimer, self-dimer (forward), self-dimer (reverse), hairpin (forward) and hairpin (reverse). In each group, different annealing situations can happen. The sec_struc_cost function takes into consideration only the annealing situation with the highest cost per group (highest_cost(G_i)). The cost of any annealing situation is given as the sum of the numbers of A-T matches (costs 2 each) and C-G matches (costs 4 each), as suggested in (Kämpke et al., 2001).
The pseudocode of the implemented SA algorithm is given in Fig. 3. The algorithm starts by randomly choosing a pair of primers (referred to as current) *fp_cur* and *rp_cur*, such that |*fp_cur*| = m and |*rp_cur*| = n with MIN_LEN ≤ m, n ≤ MAX_LEN; the first m bases and the last n complementary bases of the target DNA sequence are the *fp_cur* and *rp_cur* respectively and their cost is evaluated.

```
procedure SAPrimer
 begin
  fp_cur = find_primer(MIN_LEN, MAX_LEN)
  rp_cur = find_primer(MIN_LEN, MAX_LEN)
  cost_cur = tot_cost(fp_cur, rp_cur)
  T = 200
  decreasing_factor = 0.999
  while (T > 0.01)
     fp_new = find_primer_neighbor (len(fp_cur))
     rp_new = find_primer_neighbor (len(rp_cur))
     cost_new = tot_cost (fp_new, rp_new)
     if (cost_new < cost_cur) then
          // change the current primer pair
          fp_cur = fp_new
          rp_cur = rp_new
          cost_cur = cost_new
     else
          num = random( )
          if (num < exp(-ΔE/T)) then
               fp_cur = fp_new
               rp_cur = rp_new
               cost_cur = cost_new
     T = T * decreasing_factor
 end
```

Fig. 3. Pseudocode of the customized SA algorithm used by SAPrimer

At each step, the algorithm randomly chooses a new candidate-pair (fp_new, rp_new) in the neighborhood of the current pair; any primer pair such that |fp_cur|- 3 ≤ |fp_new| ≤ |fp_cur| + 3 and |rp_cur| - 3 ≤ |rp_new| ≤ |rp_cur| + 3 has its cost evaluated. The cost value of the new candidate solution is then compared with the cost of the current solution. The primer pair with the smaller cost becomes the current pair. Notice, however, that even if the new candidate has a bigger fitness value, it can be chosen as the current pair, depending on a probability function based on both the T parameter and the ΔE parameter (where ΔE is the difference between the new and current solution cost). The acceptance of a solution with a higher cost is an attempt to prevent local minima. The value of 200 assigned to the T parameter was empirically determined as well the decreasing_factor of 0.999.

4.2 The SAPrimer – An automatic environment for searching an optimal pair of primers

Both releases of SAPrimer were developed using Builder C++ environment and run under the Windows operating system or under the Linux operating system with an appropriated emulator. They are user-friendly and do not require in-depth knowledge of primer design or heuristic methods.

SAPrimer (R2) takes as input a DNA or a protein sequence, which can be described in fasta or text plain format, and find a primer pair that amplifies the input sequence. If not modified by the user, default values are used for all parameters involved in the primer search: minimum and maximum values for T_m, %CG, primer length, T_m difference and 3' end preference, besides those ones that control the SA algorithm: initial temperature and decreasing factor. SAPrimer (R1) takes as input only DNA sequences.

Fig. 4 shows the use of the SAPrimer (R2) when searching for a suitable primer pair to amplify the DREB1A gene from *Arabidopsis thaliana* (NCBI Reference Sequence: NC_003075.4). Genes from this family exhibit tolerance to abiotic stresses such as low temperatures and drought. The parameters in Fig. 4 are shown with their default values. SAPrimer (R2) prompts the best primer pair found (forward and reverse), showing its length, %CG, T_m and fitness. The list of the best ten primer pairs found is given by clicking on the button "See best 10 primer pairs". A graphic is plotted showing, at each iteration, the fitness of the current solution as evidence of the process convergence (or not).

Notice in Fig. 4, that the optimal primer pair found does not conform to the %CG restriction once the reverse primer has only 20.83% of bases C and G in its composition. Furthermore, the reverse primer does not include a C or G base at its 3′ end. These restrictions fail due to the low GC content at the 3′ extremity of the DREB1A gene sequence (among the last 45 bases, only 4 are C and 8 are G). As explained in Subsection 4.1, an optimal primer pair is a pair that deviates the least from the user-defined parameter values; a solution will always be found, even in cases where there is no primer pair satisfying all restrictions. This decision prevents the user from not obtaining results; them results that do not entirely conform to the user's specifications are taken into account. This is not the case of a few computational systems; as an example, the online available software Primer3[2] (Rozen & Skaletsky, 2000) could not find any solution under the same entries used in the example given in Fig. 4.

---

[2] http://frodo.wi.mit.edu/primer3/

With SAPrimer (R2), the user can also perform a search taking into account only a frame of the input sequence. In order to do this, the value of parameter Product size (whose default value is the size of the input sequence) should be modified to the size of the frame.

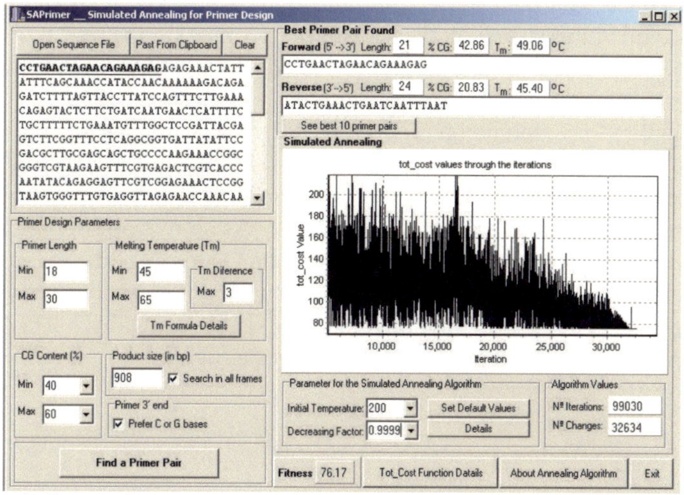

Fig. 4. SAPrimer (R2) interface

In Fig. 5 for example, the input DNA sequence has 908 bp (NC_003075.4), but a primer pair is desired for amplifying any portion of 897 bp. To provide more precise results, this search can be performed in two different ways: 1) looking for all frames having the specified size or 2) looking for a primer pair with the specified size at some frames. The user can choose the first (or second) search mode by clicking (or not) the "Search in all frames" button on the SAPrimer graphic interface. Generally, considering a sequence $S = s_0, s_1, ..., s_n$ to perform the search mode 1) for a frame of size k, $k < n$, the SA (as described in Fig. 3) must be executed n-k times, one for each possible frame of length k (frames starting at position 1, 2, 3 until n-k).

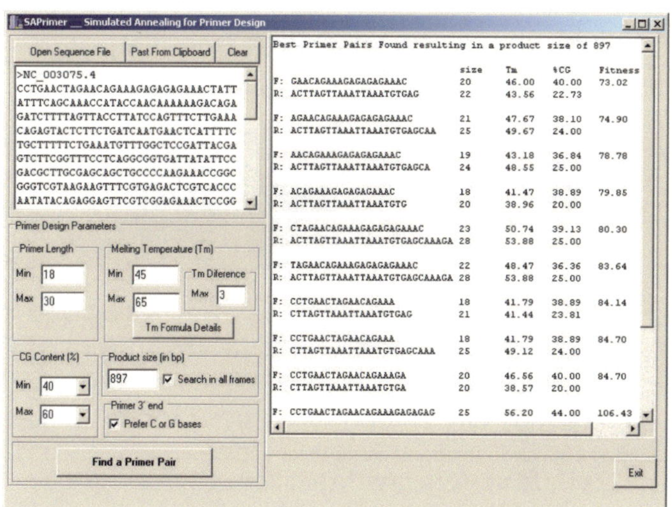

Fig. 5. Optimal primer pairs found for all frame sizes having 897 bp

To implement the search mode 2) the SA presented in Fig. 3 was slightly modified. It also differs from the first implementation of the search mode 1), that has a fixed frame to search. In the search mode 2), the SA randomly chooses a frame at each step. For each chosen frame, a primer pair conforming to the size restrictions (min and max) is randomly chosen and its fitness is calculated. At the end of this search mode, the results prompted to the user show the primer pair with the smaller fitness score, its size, T_m and %CG. Fig. 5 shows the results of SA, when search mode 2) is chosen, for the NC_003075.4 sequence and a frame of size 897 bp.
Another functionality implemented in SAPrimer (R2) allows the use of a protein sequence as input. In this case, the protein must be first translated into its corresponding DNA sequence. However, as it is known, an amino acid sequence can correspond to more than one DNA sequence, due to the degeneracy of the Genetic Code. As an example, consider the sequence CWY (C - cysteine, W - thryptofan, Y - tyrosine). The C amino acid has two corresponding codons: UGU and UGC, the amino acid W has only one corresponding codon: UGG and the amino acid Y has also two corresponding codons: UAU and UAC. This results in four possible translations of the sequence CWY, as shown below:

C W Y
UGU UGG UAU
UGC UGG UAU
UGU UGG UAC
UGC UGG UAC

As can be inferred, the number of possible DNA sequences that can result from the translation of a specific protein sequence grows fast with the size of the protein and the number of codons associated to each amino acid. The total number of possible DNA sequences that corresponds to a specific protein sequence is given by the product of the number of distinct corresponding codons to each amino acid that composes the sequence[3].

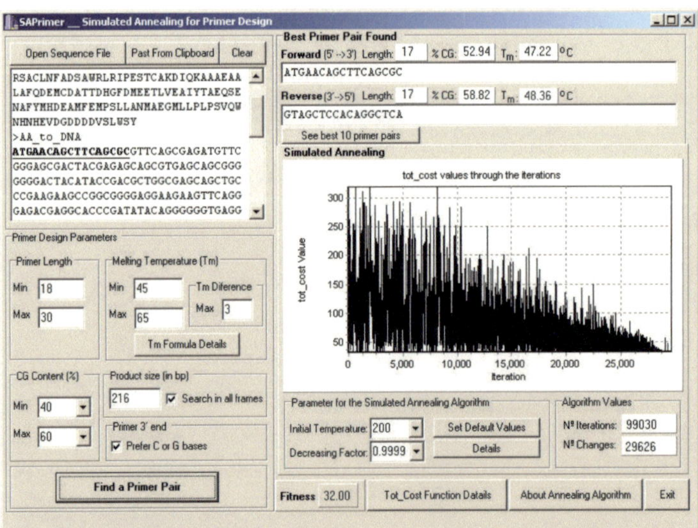

Fig. 6. Optimal primer pair found for a protein sequence given as input

[3] In the presented example, CWY has 2*1*2 = 4 possible corresponding DNA sequences.

Calculating all possible corresponding DNA sequence for a given protein sequence and finding the best primer pair for each one do not lead to a feasible solution to the problem because is highly time-consuming. The adopted strategy randomly chooses only one possible translation and finds the best primer pair for it. Notice that this strategy can produce different results, i.e., different primer pairs each time SAPrimer is run. So, the primers found for a particular SAPrimer run are called degenerated primers.
The DREB1A protein sequence (NCBI Reference Sequence: NP_567720.1) was used to exemplify the use of SAPrimer for proteins, and the results are shown in Fig. 6.

5. Conclusions

PCR is an important laboratorial process that can amplify a specific DNA sequence. Of crucial relevance for a successful PCR process is the identification of a suitable pair of primers. Due to the many variables and the range of values that can be assigned to them, the identification of a suitable pair of primes is a hard task, subject to a few uncertainties. A way to find out suitable primers is *via* a search process throughout the space defined by all possible pairs. By nature such spaces are quite vast preventing the use of exhaustive search methods. An efficient alternative is to use heuristic based methods such as simulated annealing.
This chapter describes the use of simulated annealing for primer design. Initially it details the relevant variables and their possible values as a first step to show how they can be combined into an objective function that "measures" the quality of a given primer pair. This function is used by the SA algorithm.
The chapter also describes the main aspects of two releases of an user-friendly software named SAPrimer, which implements the SA search, among other features. The SAPrimer software, as discussed in (Montera & Nicoletti, 2008) always finds the best possible primer pair to amplify a specific DNA sequence, even when some restrictions can not be satisfied, for example, when the given DNA sequence does not have an appropriated %CG or when the T_m value of a primer (forward or reverse) does not respect user-defined range of values. The second release, named SAPrimer (R2), is more flexible in the sense of offering to the user the possibility of finding primers to amplify any portion of the input sequence, defined by a fixed frame size and finding degenerated primer pair for a protein sequence.
The work will proceed by implementing other heuristic search strategies (starting with genetic algorithm) in an attempt to identify the most suitable type of search for dealing with the problem of primer design.

Acknowledgements

The authors thank the financial support received from the Brazilian agencies CNPq (Proc. no. 620080/2008-6) and Capes.

6. References

Abd-Elsalam, K.A. (2003). Bioinformatics tools and guidelines for PCR primer design. African Journal of Biotechnology, Vol. 2, No. 5, pp 91-95.

Acinas, S.G.; Sarma-Rupavtarm, R.; Klepac-Ceraj, V. & Polz, M.F. (2005). PCR-induced sequence artifacts and bias: insights from comparison of two 16S rRNA clone libraries constructed from the same sample. Applied Environmental Microbiology, Vol. 71, pp. 8966-8969.

Allawi, H.T. & SantaLucia, J.J. (1997) Thermodynamics and NMR of internal G*T mismatches in DNA. Biochemistry, Vol. 36, pp. 10581–10594.

Allawi, H.T. & SantaLucia, J.J. (1998a) Nearest neighbor thermodynamic parameters for internal G*A mismatches in DNA. Biochemistry, Vol. 37, pp. 2170–2179.

Allawi, H.T. & SantaLucia, J.J. (1998b) Nearest-neighbor thermodynamics of internal A*C mismatches in DNA: sequence dependence and pH effects. Biochemistry, Vol. 37, pp. 9435–9444.

Allawi, H.T. & SantaLucia, J.J. (1998c) Thermodynamics of internal C*T mismatches in DNA. Nucleic Acids Research, Vol. 26, pp. 2694–2701.

Antia, R.; Regoes, R.R; Koella, J.C. & Bergstrom, C.T. (2003). The role of evolution in the emergence of infectious diseases. Nature, Vol. 426, pp. 658-661.

Apte, A. & Daniel, S. (2009). PCR Primer Design. Cold Spring Harb Protoc.

Berezikov, E.; Cuppen, E. & Plasterk, R.H. (2006). Approaches to microRNA discovery. Nature Genetics, Vol. 38, S2-S7.

Bertagnolli, M.M.; Niedzwiecki, D.; Compton, C.C.; Hahn, H.P.; Hall, M.; Damas, B.; Jewell, S.D.; Mayer, R.J.; Goldberg, R.M.; Saltz, L.B.; Warren, R.S. & Redston, M. (2009). Microsatellite instability predicts improved response to adjuvant therapy with irinotecan, fluorouracil, and leucovorin in stage III colon cancer: Cancer and Leukemia Group B Protocol 89803. J. Clin Oncol., Vol. 27, pp. 1814-1821.

Bonafè, M.; Cardelli, M.; Marchegiani, F.; Cavallone, L.; Giovagnetti, S.; Olivieri, F.; Lisa, R.; Pieri, C. & Franceschi, C. (2001). Increase of homozygosity in centenarians revealed by a new inter-Alu PCR technique. Experimental Gerontology, Vol. 36, pp. 1063-1073.

Boutros, P.C. & Okey, A.B. (2004). PUNS: transcriptomic- and genomic-in silico PCR for enhanced primer design. Bioinformatics, Vol. 20, No. 15, pp. 2399–2400.

Boyce, R.; Chilana, P. & Rose, T.M. (2009). iCODEHOP: a new interactive program for designing COnsensus-DEgenerate Hybrid Oligonucleotide Primers from multiply aligned protein sequences. Nucleic Acids Research, Vol. 37, Web Server issue, W222-8.

Breslauer, K.J.; Frank, R.; Blocker, H. & Marky, L.A. (1986). Predicting DNA duplex stability from the base sequence, Proc. Natl. Acad. Sci. USA 83, pp. 3746-3750.

Cadwell, R.C. & Joyce, G.F. (1992). Randomization of genes by PCR. PCR Methods and Applications, Vol. 2, pp. 28-33.

Castellsagué, E.; González, S.; Nadal, M.; Campos, O.; Guinó, E.; Urioste, M.; Blanco, I.; Frebourg, T. & Capellá G. (2008). Detection of APC gene deletions using quantitative multiplex PCR of short fluorescent fragments. Clinical Chemistry, Vol. 54, pp. 1132-1140.

Chih-Ming, H.; Ming-Chieh, L.; Shih-Hung, H.; Chi-Jung, H.; Hung-Cheng, L.; Tsai-Yen, C. & Shwu-Fen, C. (2009). PTEN promoter methylation and LOH of 10q22–23 locus in PTEN expression of ovarian clear cell adenocarcinomas. Gynecologic Oncology, Vol. 112, pp. 307-313.

Chopra, S. & Ranganathan, A. (2003). Protein evolution by 'codon shuffling': a novel method for generating highly variant mutant libraries by assembly of hexamer DNA duplexes. Chem. Biol., Vol. 10, pp. 917-926.

Christensen, H.; Larsen, J. & Olsen, J. E. (2008). Bioinformatical design of oligonucleotides - design of PCR primers and hybridization probes including a summary of computer-programs. http://www.staff.kvl.dk/~hech/PrimerDesign.pdf

Coco, W.M.; Encell, L.P.; Levinson, W.E.; Crist, M.J.; Loomis, A.K.; Licato, L.L.; Arensdorf J.J.; Sica, N.; Pienkos, P.T. & Monticello, D.J. (2002). Growth factor engineering by degenerate homoduplex gene family recombination. Nature Biotechnology, Vol. 20, pp. 1246-1250

Contreras-Moreira, B.; Sachman-Ruiz, B.; Figueroa-Palacios, I. & Vinuesa, P. (2009). primers4clades: a web server that uses phylogenetic trees to design lineage-specific PCR primers for metagenomic and diversity studies. Nucleic Acids Research, Vol. 37, Web Server issue, W95-W100.

Costas, B.A.; McManus, G.; Doherty, M. & Katz, L.A. (2007). Use of species-specific primers and PCR to measure the distributions of planktonic ciliates in coastal waters. Limnol. Oceanogr. Methods, Vol. 5, pp. 163-173.

Dieffenbach, C.W. & Dveksler, G.S. (2003). PCR Primer: A Laboratory Manual, (2nd. ed.), Cold Spring Harbor Laboratory Press, New York.

Dixon, A.L.; Liang, L.; Moffatt, M.F.; Chen, W.; Heath, S.; Wong, K.C.; Taylor, J.; Burnett, E.; Gut, I.; Farrall, M.; Lathrop, G.M.; Abecasis, G.R. & Cookson, W.O. (2007). A genome-wide association study of global gene expression. Nature Genetics, Vol. 39, No. 10, pp. 1202-1207.

Evans, P. M. & Liu, C. (2005). SiteFind: a software tool for introducing a restriction site as a marker for successful site-directed mutagenesis. BMC Mol. Biol., Vol. 6, No. 22,

Eveno, C.; Nemeth, J.; Soliman, H.; Praz, F.; de The, H.; Valleur, P.; Talbot, Ian-C.& Pocard, M. (2010). Association between a high number of isolated lymph nodes in T1 to T4 N0M0 colorectal cancer and the microsatellite instability phenotype. Arch. Surg., Vol. 145, No. 1, pp. 12-17.

Franko, J.; Krasinskas, A.M.; Nikiforova, M.N.; Zarnescu, N.O.; Lee, K.K.W.; Hughes, S.J.; Bartlett, D.L.; Zeh III, H.J. & Mose, A.J. (2008). Loss of heterozygosity predicts poor survival after resection of pancreatic adenocarcinoma. J. Gastrointest. Surg., Vol. 12, pp. 1664-1673.

Frech, C.; Breuer, K.; Ronacher, B.; Kern, T.; Sohn, C. & Gebauer, G. (2009). hybseek: Pathogen primer design tool for diagnostic multi-analyte assays. Computer Methods and Programs in Biomedicine, Vol. 94, Issue 2, pp. 152-160.

Gatto, L. & Schretter, C. (2009). Designing Primer Pairs and Oligos with OligoFaktorySE. journal.embnet.org. Technical Notes. EMBnet.news 15.3, pp. 22-24.

Giegerich, R.; Meyer, F. & Schleiermacher, C. (1996). GeneFisher - software support for the detection of postulated genes. Proc. Int. Conf. Intell. Syst. Mol. Biol., Vol. 4, pp. 68-77.

Gordon, P.M.K. & Sensen, C.W. (2004). Osprey: a comprehensive tool employing novel methods for the design of oligonucleotides for DNA sequencing and microarrays. Nucleic Acids Research, Vol. 32, No. 17, e133.

Gunnar, W.; Kokocinsky, F. & Lichter, P. (2004). AutoPrime: selecting primers for expressed sequences. Genome Biology, Vol. 5, P11.

Haas, S.A.; Hild, M.; Wright, A.P.H.; Hain, T.; Talibi, D. & Vingron, M. (2003). Genome-scale design of PCR primers and long oligomers for DNA microarrays. Nucleic Acids Research, Vol. 31, No. 19, pp. 5576-5581.

Hassibi, A.; Kakavand, H. & Lee, T.H. (2004). A stochastic model and simulation algorithm for polymerase chain reaction (PCR) systems. Proc. of Workshop on Genomics Signal Processing and Statistics (GENSIPS).

He, Q.; Marjamäki, M.; Soini, H.; Mertsola, J. & Viljanen, M.K. (1994). Primers are decisive for sensitivity of PCR. BioTechniques, Vol. 17, No. 1, pp. 82-87.

Howley, P.M.; Israel, M.F.; Law, M-F. & Martin, M.A. (1979). A rapid method for detecting and mapping homology between heterologous DNAs. Journal of Biological Chemistry, Vol. 254, pp. 4876-4883.

Hugles, S. & Moody, A. (2008). PCR. Scion Publishing. Oxfordshire, England.

Innis, M.A. & Gelfand, D.H. (1990). Optimization of PCRs. In: PCR Protocols (Innis, Gelfand, Sninsky and White, eds.), Academic Press, New York.

Isenbarger, T.A.; Finney, M.; Ríos Velázquez, C.; Handelsman, J. & Ruvkun, G. (2008). Miniprimer PCR, a new lens for viewing the microbial world. Applied Environmental Microbiology, Vol. 74, No. 3, pp. 840-849.

Kalendar, R.; Lee, D. & Schulman, A.H. (2009) FastPCR Software for PCR Primer and Probe Design and Repeat Search. Genes, Genomes and Genomics. Vol. 3, No. 1, pp. 1-14.

Kämpke, T.; Kieninger, M. & Mecklenbug, M. (2001). Efficient primer design algorithms. Bioinformatics, Vol. 17, No. 3, pp. 214-225.

Kanagawa, T. (2003). Bias and artifacts in multitemplate polymerase chain reactions (PCR). J. Biosci. Bioeng., Vol. 96, pp. 317-323.

Ke, X; Collins, A.R. & Ye, S. (2002). PCR designer for restriction analysis of various types of sequence mutation. Bioinformatics, Vol. 18, No. 12, pp. 1688-1689.

Kirkpatrick, S.; Gelatt, C.D. & Vecchi, M.P. (1983). Optimization by simulated annealing. Science, Vol. 220, pp. 671-680.

Kolb, L.E.; Arlier, Z.; Yalcinkaya, C.; Ozturk, A.K.; Moliterno, J.A.; Erturk, O.; Bayrakli, F.; Korkmaz, B.; DiLuna, M.L.; Yasuno, K.; Bilguvar, K.; Ozcelik, T.; Tuysuz, B.; State, M.W. & Gunel, M. (2010). Novel VLDLR microdeletion identified in two Turkish siblings with pachygyria and pontocerebellar atrophy. Neurogenetics, Jan. 15, pp. 1364-6745.

Kwok, S.; Kellogg, D.E.; McKinney, N.; Spasic, D.; Goda, L.; Levenson, C. & Sninsky, J. (1990). Effects of primer-template mismatches on the polymerase chain reaction: human immunodeficiency virus 1 model studies. Nucleic Acids Research, Vol. 18, pp. 999-1005.

Lahr, D.J.G. & Katz, L.A. (2009). Reducing the impact of PCR-mediated recombination in molecular evolution and environmental studies using a new-generation high-fidelity DNA polymerase. BioTechniques, Vol. 47, pp. 857-866.

Lan, C.-C.; Tang, R.; Un San Leong, I & Love, D. R. (2009). Quantitative Real-Time RT-PCR (qRT-PCR) of Zebrafish Transcripts: Optimization of RNA Extraction, Quality Control Considerations, and Data Analysis. Cold Spring Harb Protoc., Vol. 10, pp. pdb.prot5314 - pdb.prot5314.

Liang, H.-L.; Lee, C. & Wu, J.-S. (2005). Multiplex PCR primer design for gene family using genetic algorithm, GECCO'05, June 25-29, Washington DC, USA. pp. 67-74.

Lutz, S. & Patrick, W.M. (2004). Novel methods for directed evolution of enzymes: quality, not quantity. Current Opinion in Biotechnology, Vol. 15, pp. 291-297.

Mann T.; Humbert, R.; Dorschner, M.; Stamatoyannopoulos, J. & Noble, W.S. (2009). A thermodynamic approach to PCR primer design. Nucleic Acids Research, Vol. 37, No. 13, e95.

Marmur, J. & Doty, P. (1962). Determination of the base composition of deoxyribonucleic acid from its thermal denaturation temperature. Journal of Molecular Biology, Vol. 5, pp. 109-118.

Metzker, M.L. & Caskey, T.C. (2001). Polymerase Chain Reaction (PCR), Encyclopedia of Life Science. Nature Publishing Group.

Milbury, C.A.; Li, J. & Makrigiorogs, G.M. (2009). PCR-based methods for the enrichment of minority alleles and mutations. Clinical Chemistry, Vol. 55, No. 4, pp. 632-640.

Montera, L. & Nicoletti, M.C. (2008). The PCR primer design as a metaheuristic search process. Lecture Notes in Artificial Intelligence, Vol. 5097, pp. 963-973.

Montera. L.; Nicoletti, M.C. & Silva, F.H. (2006). Computer assisted parental sequence analysis as a previous step to DNA Shuffling process. Conference on Evolutionary Computation (CEC 2006) in IEEE Congress on Computational Intelligence - Vancouver, Canada, pp. 8079-8086.

Morales, S.E. & Holben, W.E. (2009). Empirical testing of 16S rRNA gene PCR primer pairs reveals variance in target specificity and efficacy not suggested by in silico analysis. Applied and Environmental Microbiology, Vol. 75, No. 9, pp. 2677–2683.

Mullis, K.B. & Faloona, F. (1987). Specific synthesis of DNA in vitro via a polymerase-catalyzed chain reaction. Methods Enzymology, Vol. 155, pp. 335-350.

Nuovo, G.J.; Gallery, F.; Hom, R.; MacConnell, P. & Bloch, W (1993). Importance of different variables for enhancing in situ detection of PCR-amplified DNA. Genome Research, Vol. 2, pp. 305-312.

Oliveira, E.J.; Pádua, J.G.; Zucchi, M.I.; Vencovsky, R. & Vieira, M.L.C. (2006). Origin, evolution and genome distribution of microsatellites. Genetics and Molecular Biology, Vol. 29, No. 2, pp. 294-307.

Panjkovich, A. & Melo, F. (2005). Comparison of different melting temperature calculation methods for short DNA sequences. Bioinformatics, Vol. 21, No. 6, pp. 711-722.

Pasmant, E.; Sabbagh, A.; Masliah-Planchon, J.; Haddad, V.; Hamel, M-J.; Laurendeau, I.; Soulier, J.; Parfait, B.; Wolkenstein, P.; Bièche, I.; Vidaud, M. & Vidaud D. (2009). Detection and characterization of NF1 microdeletions by custom high resolution array CGH. Journal of Molecular Diagnostics, Vol. 11, No. 6, pp. 524-529.

Patten, P.A.; Gray, N.S.; Yang, P.L.; Marks, C.B.; Wedemayer, G.J.; Boniface, J.J.; Stevens, R.C. & Schultz, P.G. (1996). The immunological evolution of catalisis. Science, Vol. 271. No. 5252, pp. 1086-1091.

Pattyn, F.; Speleman, F.; Paepe, A. & Vandesompele, J. (2003). RTPrimerDB: the Real-Time PCR primer and probe database. Nucleic Acids Research. Vol. 31, No. 1, pp. 122-123.

Piriyapongsa, J.; Ngamphiw, C.; Assawamakin, A.; Wangkumhang, P.; Suwannasri, P.; Ruangrit, U.; Agavatpanitch, G. & Tongsima, S. (2009). RExPrimer: an integrated primer designing tool increases PCR effectiveness by avoiding 3' SNP 3'-in-primer and mis-priming from structural variation. BMC Genomics, 10(Suppl 3):S4.

Pusch, C.M.; Broghammer, M.; Nicholson, G.J.; Nerlich, A.G.; Zink, A.; Kennerknecht, I.; Bachmann, L. & Blin, L. (2004). PCR-induced sequence alterations hamper the typing of prehistoric bone samples for diagnostic achondroplasia mutations. Mol. Biol. Evol., Vol. 21, No. 11, pp. 2005–2011.

Ro, S.; Park, C.; Jin, J.; Sanders, K.M. & Yan, W. (2006) A PCR-based method for detection and quantification of small RNAs. Biochem. Biophys. Res. Commun., Vol. 315, No. 3, pp. 756-763.

Rose, T.M.; Henikoff, J.G. & Henikoff, S. (2003). CODEHOP (COnsensus-DEgenerate Hybrid Oligonucleotide Primer) PCR primer design. Nucleic Acids Research, Vol. 31, No. 13, pp. 3763-3766.

Roux, K. H. (2009). Optimization and Troubleshooting in PCR. Cold Spring Harb Protoc., Vol. 4, pp. pdb.ip66 - pdb.ip66.

Rozen, S. & Skaletsky, H.J. (2000). Primer3 on the WWW for general users and for biologist programmers. In: Krawetz S, Misener S (eds), Bioinformatics Methods and Protocols: Methods in Molecular Biology. Humana Press, Totowa, NJ, pp. 365-386.

Rychlik, W.; Spencer, W.J. & Rhoads, R.E. (1990). Optimization of the annealing temperature for DNA amplification in vitro. Nucleic Acids Research, Vol. 18, pp. 6409-6412.

Saelee, P.; Wongkham, S.; Bhudhisawasdi, V.; Sripa, B.; Chariyalertsak, S. & Petmitr, S. (2008). Allelic loss on chromosome 5q34 is associated with poor prognosis in hepatocellular carcinoma. Cancer Research Clinical Oncology, Vol. 134, No. 10, pp. 1135-1141.

Sambrook. J. & Russel, D.W. (2001). Molecular Cloning: A Laboratory Manual (3rd ed.). Cold Spring Harbor, N.Y.: Cold Spring Harbor Laboratory Press.

SantaLucia, J.Jr.; Allawi, H.T. & Seneviratne, P.A. (1996). Improved Nearest-Neighbor parameters for predicting DNA duplex stability. Biochemistry, Vol. 35, pp. 3555-3562.

Sasaki, T.; Tsubakishita, S.; Tanaka, Y.; Sakusabe, A.; Ohtsuka, M.; Hirotaki, S.; Kawakami, T.; Fukata, T. & Hiramatsu, K. (2010). Multiplex-PCR method for species identification of coagulase-positive staphylococci. Journal of Clinical Microbiology, Vol. 48, No. 3, pp. 765-769.

Schretter, C.; & Milinkovitch, M.C. (2006) OLIGOFAKTORY: a visual tool for interactive oligonucleotide design. Bioinformatics, Vol. 22, No. 1, pp. 115–116.

Sommer, R. & Tautz, D. (1989). Minimal homology requirements for PCR primers. Nucleic Acids Research. Vol. 17, No.16, pp. 6749.

Srivastava, T.; Seth, A.; Datta, K.; Chosdol K.; Chattopadhyay, P. & Sinha, S. (2005). Inter-alu PCR detects high frequency of genetic alterations in glioma cells exposed to sub-lethal cisplatin. Int. J. Cancer, Vol. 117, No. 4, pp. 683-689.

Stemmer, W.P.C. (1994a). DNA Shuffling by random fragmentation and reassembly: In vitro recombination for molecular evolution. Proc. Natl. Acad. Sci., Vol 9, pp. 10747-10751.

Stemmer, W.P.C. (1994b). Rapid evolution of a protein in vitro by DNA shuffling. Nature, Vol. 370, pp. 389–391.

Sugimoto, N.; Nakano, S.; Yoneyama, M. & Honda, K. (1996). Improved thermodynamic parameters and helix initiation factor to predict stability of DNA duplexes. Nucleic Acids Research, Vol. 24, pp. 4501-4505.

Sun, F. (1999). Modeling DNA Shuffling. J. Comp. Biol., Vol. 6, pp. 77-90.

Tait, R.C. & Horton, R.M. (1998). Genetic engineering with PCR. Horizon Scientific Press, Norwich.

Tsai, M.-F.; Lin, Y.-J.; Cheng, Y.-C.; Lee, K.-H.; Huang, C.-C.; Chen, Y.-T. & Yao, A. (2007). PrimerZ: streamlined primer design for promoters, exons and human SNPs. Nucleic Acids Research. pp. (Web Server issue): W63–W65.

Vandesompele, J.; Preter, K.; Pattyn, F.; Poppe, B.; Van Roy, N.; Paepe, A. & Speleman, F. (2002). Accurate normalization of real-time quantitative RT-PCR data by geometric averaging of multiple internal control genes. Genome Biology, Vol. 3, pp. research0034.1-0034.11.

VanGuilder, H.D.; Vrana, K.E. & Freeman, W.M. (2008). Twenty-five years of quantitative PCR for gene expression analysis. BioTechniques, Vol. 44. No. 5, pp. 619-626.

Vikalo, H.; Hassibi, B. & Hassibi, A. (2006). On Joint Maximum-Likelihood Estimation of PCR Efficiency and Initial Amount of Target. Proc. IEEE Workshop on Genomic Signal Processing and Statistics (GENSIPS), pp. 688-695.

Vladušić, T.; Hrašćan, R.; Vrhovac, I.; Krušlin, B.; Gamulin, M.; Grgić, M.; Pećina-Šlaus, N. & Čolić, J.F. (2010). Loss of heterozygosity of selected tumor suppressor genes in human testicular germ cell tumors. Pathology - Research and Practice, Vol. 206, pp. 163-167.

Volkov, A.A.; Shao, Z. & Arnold, F. H. (1999). Recombination and chimeragenesis by in vitro heteroduplex formation and in vivo repair. Nucleic Acids Research, Vol. 27, No. 18, e18.

Wallace, R.B.; Shaffer, J.; Murphy, R.F.; Bonner, J.; Hirose, T. & Itakura, K. (1979). Hybridization of synthetic oligodeoxyribonucleotides to phi chi 174 DNA: the effect of single base pair mismatch. Nucleic Acids Research, Vol. 6, pp. 3543-3557.

Wang, R.; Morris, D.S.; Tomlins, S.A.; Lonigro, R.J.; Tsodikov, A.; Mehra, R.; Giordano, T.J.; Kunju, L.P.; Lee, C.T.; Weizer A.Z. & Chinnaiyan A.M. (2009). Development of a multiplex quantitative PCR signature to predict progression in non-muscle-invasive bladder cancer. Cancer Research, Vol. 69, pp. 3810-3818.

You, F.M.; Huo, N.; Gu, Y.Q.; Luo, M.C.; Ma, Y.; Hane, D.; Lazo G.R.; Dvorak, J. & Anderson, O.D. (2008). BatchPrimer3: a high throughput Web application for PCR and sequencing primer design. BMC Bioinformatics, Vol. 9, pp. 253.

Yu, W.; Rusterholtz, K.J.; Krummel, A.T. & Lehman, N. (2006). Detection of high levels of recombination generated during PCR amplification of RNA templates. BioTechniques, Vol. 40, pp. 499-507.

Zha, D.; Eipper, A. & Reetz, M.T. (2003). Assembly of designed oligonucleotides as an efficient method for gene recombination: a new tool in directed evolution. ChemBioChem, Vol. 4, pp. 34–39.

Zhao, H.; Giver, L.; Shao, Z.; Affholter, A. & Arnold, F. H. (1998). Molecular evolution by staggered extension process (StEP) in vitro recombination. Nature Biotechnology, Vol. 16, pp. 258–261.

8

Network Reconfiguration for Reliability Worth Enhancement in Distribution System by Simulated Annealing

Somporn Sirisumrannukul
Department of Electrical Engineering, Faculty of Engineering
King Mongkut's University of Technology North Bangkok
Thailand

1. Introduction

The distribution system is an important part that provides the final links between the utility and the customers. Most distribution systems in practice have a single-circuit main feeder and are radially configured. The radial distribution system is widely used because of its simple design, generally low cost and supportive protection scheme. This configuration suggests from a reliability point of view that all components between a load point and the supply point must work and therefore poor reliability can be expected as the failure of any single component causes the load point to be disconnected.

The reliability in a distribution system can be improved by network reconfiguration, which is accomplished by closing normally-open switches and opening normally closed switches (Brown, 2001). These switches play an important role in reducing interruption durations in the event of a system failure. Two types of switches are normally installed along the main feeders and laterals: sectionalizing switch (normally closed switch) and tie switch (normally open switch). The former is a device that isolates a faulted part from the system so that the healthy part can still be electrically supplied. The latter is a device that recovers loads that has been disconnected by transferring some of the loads to other supporting distribution feeders without violating operation and engineering constraints (Chowdhury, 2001). Apparently, different network configurations due to an alteration of the switch statuses provide different services to the customers.

A great deal of work has been done on network reconfiguration (also known as feeder reconfiguration) in distribution systems mainly in the context of active power loss reduction because the cost of MW loss occupies considerable amount of operating cost in the system and therefore small amount achieved from loss reduction is still attractive for electric power utilities. A number of methods have been proposed to solve feeder reconfiguration for loss minimization, such as integer programming (Sarma & Prakasa Rao, 1995) and artificial neural network (Kashem et al., 1998) and simulated annealing (Chang & Kuo, 1994). The reconfiguration problem in this case are normally subject to power balance equations, bus voltage upper and lower limits, line carrying capability of the feeders and radial topology of the network. Other constraints may be taken into account, for example, load balancing

(Zhou et al., 1997), introduction of distributed generation (Nathachot & Sirisumrannukul, 2009) and capacitor placement (Su & Lee, 2001).
Very little has been paid attention to reliability improvement by feeder reconfiguration. Tsai, L. H. presented a model for improving the reliability of electric distribution systems through network reconfiguration. Two main reliability indices are targeted to be minimized: system average interruption frequency (SAIFI) and the system average interruption duration (SAIDI). The mathematical formulations for calculating the change of SAIDI and SAIFI as a result of reconfiguration were developed to identify beneficial load transfers. However, his method did not take into account reliability worth, which can be described in terms of customer interruption costs.
Ye Bin et. al proposed network reconfiguration to increase reliability worth by an improved genetic algorithm. The mathematical model is formuated in which its objective function is to minimize customer interruption costs. The procedure was illustrated by the distribution system connected at bus 2 of the 6-bus Roy Billitton Test System (RBTS). It is shown from their studies that their developed methodology permits flexible use of sectionalizing and tie switches without introducing additional costs while being able to achieve large possible economic benefit.
The emphasis of this chapter is given to reliability worth enhancement in distribution systems, where a good network topology can significantly improve load point reliability. However, a good connection is not straightforward to be identified as the large number of on/off switch statuses needs to be determined. In addition, some configurations are not allowed because they lead either to an isolated system or to a non-radial system. Theoretically, the complete enumeration can be used to arrive at an optimal solution while satisfying the constraints. Nevertheless, such an exhaustive technique would be practically impossible. Alternatively, simulating annealing (SA), which is one of powerful searching techniques for combinatorial optimization problems, can be served as a tool for on/off decision making of the switches in the system. This technique imitates the behavior of a set of atoms in the annealing of metals. The cooling procedure goes gradually from a high temperature to a freezing point, where the energy of the system has acquired the globally minimal value. This physical annealing process is analogous to the determination of near-global or global optimum solutions for optimization problems.
A SA algorithm for network reconfiguration is developed to identify the most appropriate topology that gives the lowest customer interruption cost. Customer interruption costs are calculated from load point reliability indices and their customer damage functions. The developed algorithm is tested with a distribution system connected at bus 2 of the RBTS, which consists of 4 feeders and 22 load points, and a 69-bus distribution system, which consists of 7 feeders and 69 load points.

2. Simulated Annealing

Simulated annealing is physically referred to the process of heating up a solid with a high temperature. The molten solid is then gradually cooled until it is solidified at a low temperature. At each step of the cooling, the temperature is kept constant for a period of time in order to allow the solid to reach thermal equilibrium where the solid could have many configurations.

This physical annealing process is analogous to the determination of near-global or global optimum solutions for optimization problems. The underlying idea is to begin with a current atomic configuration. This configuration is equivalent to the current solution of an optimization problem. The energy of the atoms is analogous to the cost of the objective function and the final ground state corresponds to the global minimum of the cost function (Aarts, 2001) (Winton, 2003). The analogy between physical system and optimization problem is shown in Table 1.

Physical system	Optimization problem
State	Feasible solution
Energy	Cost
Ground state	Optimal solution
Rapid quenching	Local search
Careful annealing	Simulated annealing

Table 1. Analogy between simulated annealing and optimization

On the basis of the above analogy, the main idea of the SA algorithm is to initialize randomly a feasible solution, x_0. The energy $E(x_0)$, which is equivalent to objective function, of the initial solution will be evaluated. A new candidate solution is randomly generated in the neighborhood of the current one. The move to the new candidate feasible solution is accepted if it is superior in the objective value to the current one (i.e., a reduction in the objective function for a minimization problem). Nevertheless, an inferior candidate solution has a chance of acceptance with a probability, p, given by the Boltzmann distribution.

$$p = \exp(-\Delta E / kT) \tag{1}$$

where ΔE = change in objective value

k = Boltzmann's constant

T = current temperature

A uniformly distributed random number, r, is drawn in the range [0, 1]. The move to the inferior solution is accepted if the random number is less than p; otherwise the move is discarded. Such an acceptance avoids getting trapped on a local optimal solution and therefore expands the search space. The last accepted solution for each temperature T_i forms the initial solution of the next stage. The temperature is gradually lowered (e.g., $T_{i+1} = \alpha T_i$, where α is a constant between 0 and 1) and the algorithm proceeds until a stopping criterion (say, temperature is less than a minimum specified temperature $T_{\min}$) or another preset stopping criteria are satisfied. A flowchart for simulated annealing algorithm is shown in Fig. 1 (Weck, 2004).
For a constrained optimization problem, its solutions can be obtained from penalty function methods. The main idea behind these methods is to convert a constrained optimization problem into an unconstrained one, whose objective function is formed by attaching the constraints to the original objective function. The unconstrained problem with the

augmented objective function can be solved by SA. With a penalty function method, infeasible solutions will be penalized by a penalty factor multiplied by their degree of violation.

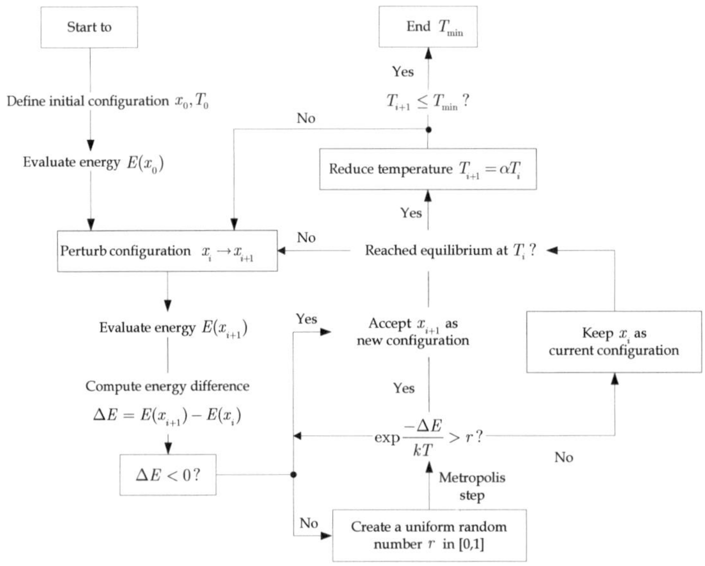

Fig. 1. Simulated annealing algorithm

3. Distribution Reliability Indices

A distribution circuit normally uses primary or main feeders and lateral distributions. A primary feeder originates from a substation and passes through major load centers. The lateral distributors connect the individual load points to the main feeder with distribution transformers at their ends. Many distribution systems used in practice have a single-circuit main feeder and defined as radial distribution system. A radial distribution system consists of series components (e.g., lines, cables, transformers) to load points. This configuration requires that all components between a load point and the supply point operate; and hence the distribution system is more susceptible to outage in a single event. There are two types of reliability indices evaluated in the distribution system: load point reliability indices and system reliability indices (Billinton & Allan,1996).

3.1 Load Point Reliability Indices

The basic distribution system reliability indices of a load point p are average failure rate λ_p, average outage duration r_p and annual outage time U_p. These three basic indices are calculated using the priciple of series systems and given by

$$\lambda_p = \sum_{i=1}^{n} \lambda_i \tag{2}$$

$$U_p = \sum_{i=1}^{n} \lambda_i r_i \tag{3}$$

$$r_p = \frac{U_p}{\lambda_p} = \frac{\sum_{i=1}^{n} \lambda_i r_i}{\sum_{i=1}^{n} \lambda_i} \tag{4}$$

where n = number of outage events affecting load point p
λ_i = failure rate of component i (failure/yr or, in short, f/yr)
r_i = repair time of component i (hr)

3.2 Customer Oriented Reliability Indices

With the three basic load point indices and energy consumption at load points, system average interruption frequency index (SAIFI), system average interruption duration index (SAIDI), average service availability (ASAI), average service unavailability (ASUI), energy not supplied (ENS) and average energy not supplied (AENS) can be calculated. These six customer oriented reliability indices are obtained from

$$\text{SAIFI} = \frac{\sum_{j=1}^{nl} \lambda_j N_j}{\sum_{j=1}^{nl} N_j} \quad \text{(interruptions/customer)} \tag{5}$$

$$\text{SAIDI} = \frac{\sum_{j=1}^{nl} U_j N_j}{\sum_{j=1}^{nl} N_j} \quad \text{(hours/customer)} \tag{6}$$

$$\text{ASAI} = \frac{\sum_{j=1}^{nl} N_j \times 8760 - \sum_{j=1}^{nl} U_j N_j}{\sum_{j=1}^{nl} N_j \times 8760} \tag{7}$$

$$\text{ASUI} = 1 - \text{ASAI} \tag{8}$$

$$\text{ENS} = \sum_{j=1}^{nl} L_{a(j)} U_j \quad \text{(kWh)} \tag{9}$$

$$\text{AENS} = \frac{ENS}{\sum_{j=1}^{nl} N_j} \quad \text{(kWh/customer)} \tag{10}$$

where nl = number of load points

λ_j = failure rate of load point j (f/yr)

N_j = number of customer connected at load point j

U_j = unavailability of load point j (hr/yr)

$L_{a,(j)}$ = average connected load at load point j (kW)

4. Quantification of Reliability Worth

Reliability worth can be quantified in forms of customer interruption costs. Customer interruption costs provide an indirect measure of monetary losses associated with a power failure and are served as input data for cost implications and worth assessments of system planning and operational decisions. The calculation of customer interruption costs requires distribution reliability indices of the load points and customer interruption cost data.

Customer interruption cost data, compiled from customer surveys, are used to develop a sector customer damage function (SCDF). The SCDF is a function of customer class and outage duration, which can be used to estimate monetary loss incurred by customers due to power failure. Table 2 shows the SCDF for seven sectors of customers for five discrete outage durations (Goel et al., 1991). The outage cost data in the table is plotted as shown in Fig. 2. Using interpolation or extrapolation techniques, the cost of interruption for any other duration is determined by interpolation.

User sector	**Interruption duration (minutes)**				
	1	**20**	**60**	**240**	**480**
Large users	1.005	1.508	2.225	3.968	8.24
Industrial	1.625	3.868	9.085	25.16	55.81
Commercial	0.381	2.969	8.552	31.32	83.01
Agricultural	0.06	0.343	0.649	2.064	4.12
Residential	0.001	0.093	0.482	4.914	15.69
Goverment and institute	0.044	0.369	1.492	6.558	26.04
Office and building	4.778	9.878	21.06	68.83	119.2

Table 2. Sector customer damage cost ($/kW)

The contingency enumeration method (Geol & Billinton, 1994) estimates the expected interruption cost (ECOST). This method considers each outage event in association with the interruption cost data of the customers. The system model consists of relevant reliability parameters of all components such as the main and lateral feeders, factors such as the inclusion or not of disconnects on the main feeders, fuses in the lateral sections, alternate back-fed supply, replacing a failed low voltage transformer or using a spare instead of repairing it, etc. The $ECOST$ of load point p is evaluated by

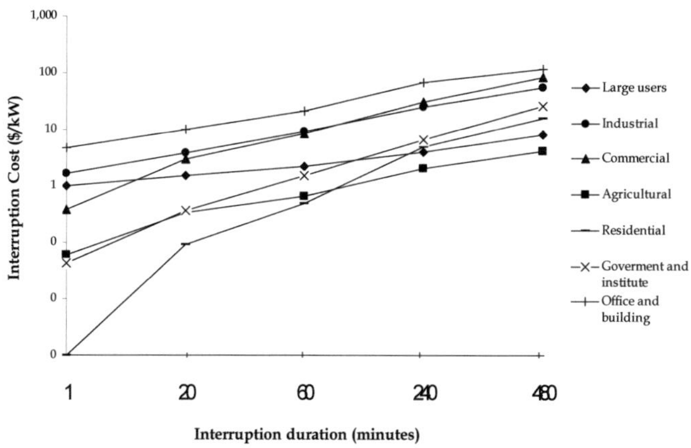

Fig. 2. Section customer damage function

$$ECOST_p = \sum_{k=1}^{nc} C_{k,p}(r_k) L_{av,p} \lambda_k \qquad (\$) \qquad (11)$$

where $ECOST_p$ = expected interruption cost of load point p ($)

$L_{av,p}$ = average connected load at load point p (kW)

$C_{k,p}(r_k)$ = cost for contingency k of load point p with an outage duration of r_k ($/kW)

r_k = average outage time of contingency k

λ_k = failure rate of contingency k (f/yr)

nc = number of contingencies that isolate load point p

5. Optimization of Network Reconfiguration

The objective function is to minimize the total interruption cost given in (11), subject to the following two constraints: the system is still radially operated and all the load points are still electrically supplied.

$$\text{minimize} \sum_{j=1}^{nl} ECOST_j \qquad (12)$$

The optimal or near optimal solution of (12) can be found by the following simulated annealing algorithm.

Step 1: Read the feeder length, statistical operating data and customer damage function of the distribution network.

Step 2: Specify sufficiently high temperature, cooling schedule, initial network configuration, minimum temperature and penalty factor and set i =0.

Step 3: Initialize feasible statuses of the switches x_i and calculate the associated interruption cost $ECOST(x_i)$. Feasible statuses can be found from an existing configuration.

Step 4: Generate new statuses of the switches x_{i+1}. If the new configuration satisfies the two system constraints, a new interruption cost $ECOST(x_{i+1})$ is calculated, or a penalty factor is applied to the objective function.

Step 5: Perform an acceptance test for the new solution in step 4. If $\Delta ECOST = ECOST(x_{i+1}) - ECOST(x_i) < 0$, the new interruption cost is accepted as it is superior to the previous one, otherwise go to step 5.

Step 6: Generate a uniform random number in the range [0, 1] and calculate the probability of acceptance $p = \exp(-\Delta ECOST / kT)$. If $r < p$, the interruption cost obtained in step 6 is accepted and proceed to step 7; if not, return to step 3.

Step 7: Decrease the temperature in the next iteration by setting $T_{i+1} = \alpha T_i$, where $0 < \alpha < 1$.

Step 8: Terminate the calculation process if $T \leq T_{\min}$ where $T_{\min}$ is minimum specified temperature; otherwise $k = k + 1$ and repeat steps 2-7.

6. Case Study

The developed methodology is tested with bus 2 of the RBTS (Allan et al., 1991) and a 69-bus distribution system (Chiang & Jean-Jameau, 1990).

6.1 RBTS

The 33 kV distribution system at bus 2 of the RBTS is employed in this case study, as shown in Fig. 3. The reliability data of the components are provided in Table A. 1 of Appendix. Feeder and transfomer are listed in Tables A.2 and A.3 respectively. The average and maximum loads of this system are 12.291 MW and 20.00 MW (i.e., the system load factor is 0.61455). The feeders are operated as radial feeders but connected as a mesh through normally open sectionalizing points in the event of system failure. The system has sectionalizing switches in the main feeders, fuses in each lateral branch and an alternative supply at the end of each feeder. Note that there is only one sectionalizing switch installed at one side of each lateral branch tapped from the main feeder. The recovery of a failed transformer is replaced by a spare one. The distribution system has 2 tie switches, 14 sectionalizing switches, 22 load points, 22 transformers and 6 circuit breakers.
The customer and loading data are provided in Table A.4. The SCDF for this system is shown in Fig. 1. These studies consider the 11kV feeders only and ignore any failures in the 33 kV system, the 33/11kV substation and the 11kV breakers. It is assumed that the 11 kV source breaker operates successfully when required, sectionalizing switches are opened whenever possible to isolate a fault, and the supply restored to as many load points as possible using appropriate disconnects and the alternative supply if available (Allan et al., 1991). Feeder and transformer section numbers are circled in Fig. 3.

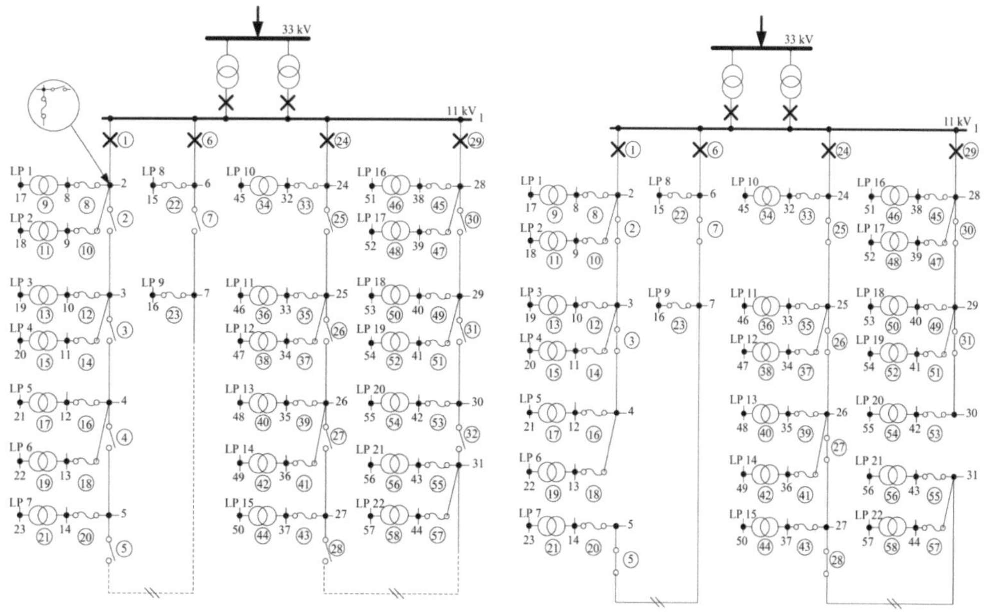

a) before reconfiguration b) after reconfiguration

Fig. 3. Distribution system of bus 2 of RBTS

A SA-based computer program for distribution network reconfiguration was developed on and tested on Intel Processor Core (TM) Duo CPU 2.4 GHz, RAM 3 GB. The maximum number of temperatures is specified at 3,000 with a step size (α) of 0.00025 for temperature scaling. The annealing process will be terminated if the maximum number of temperatures has been reached.

The algorithm starts with tie switches No. 5 and No. 28 left open while all sectionalizing switches are closed (designated as pattern 1). This initial configuration gives load point reliability indices listed in Table 3 and a system interruption cost of $199,680 as shown in Table 4. The optimal solution obtained from the simulated annealing algorithm is to open sectionalizing switches No. 4 and No. 32 and to close tie switches No. 5 and No. 28 (pattern 2), giving an ECOST of $197,360. Such switch statuses satisfy the two system constraints and make an annual saving of $2,320. For a practical distribution system with thousands of feeders, the annual saving will be much more significant. If the two tie switches remains closed, Table 5 shows moves from the optimal solution to two other neighborhood solutions (patterns 3 and 4) of sectionalizing switches, which produce higher ECOSTs compared with that of the optimal one. The convergence report of the simulated annealing algorithm is shown in Fig. 4, from which the solution remains unchanged after 1,700 drops in the temperature. This system takes about 4 seconds to converge.

It is very interesting to note that if we consider minimizing the system ENS, instead of the system ECOST, the result is shown in Table 6. It can be seen that setting the system ENS as the objective function yields different switch statuses because the SCDF fails to be realized in the later case. In other words, 1 MWh for energy not served for one load point does not produce the same effect as the others. In short, as far as monetary matter is of priority, the ECOST minimization would be more appropriate. In this case, not only is the system ECOST reduced, but also the system reliability indices like SAIFI, SAIDI, ASAI and ENS are seen improved, signifying the benefit of network or feeder reconfiguration.

Load Point	λ (f/yr)	r (hr)	U (hr/yr)	Load Point	λ (f/yr)	r (hr)	U (hr/yr)
1	0.240	14.90	3.58	12	0.256	14.29	3.66
2	0.253	14.40	3.64	13	0.253	14.19	3.59
3	0.253	14.40	3.64	14	0.256	14.08	3.61
4	0.240	14.90	3.58	15	0.243	14.73	3.58
5	0.253	14.40	3.64	16	0.253	14.40	3.64
6	0.250	14.51	3.63	17	0.243	14.78	3.59
7	0.253	14.24	3.60	18	0.243	14.73	3.58
8	0.140	3.89	0.54	19	0.256	14.24	3.65
9	0.140	3.60	0.50	20	0.256	14.24	3.65
10	0.243	14.73	3.58	21	0.253	14.19	3.59
11	0.253	14.40	3.64	22	0.256	14.08	3.61

Table 3. Initial load point relaibility indices of bus 2 of RBTS

Reliability indices	Before reconfiguration	After reconfiguration
SAIFI (failure/customer/yr)	0.248	0.222
SAIDI (hr/customer/yr)	3.612	3.584
ASUI	0.00041	0.00040
ASAI	0.99959	0.99960
ENS (MWh/yr)	37.745	37.254
ECOST (k$/yr)	199.68	197.35
AENS (MWh/customer/yr)	19.78	19.52
Sectionalizing switches to be opened	-	4, 32
Tie switches to be closed	-	5, 28

Table 4. Simulation results before and after reconfiguration for RBTS

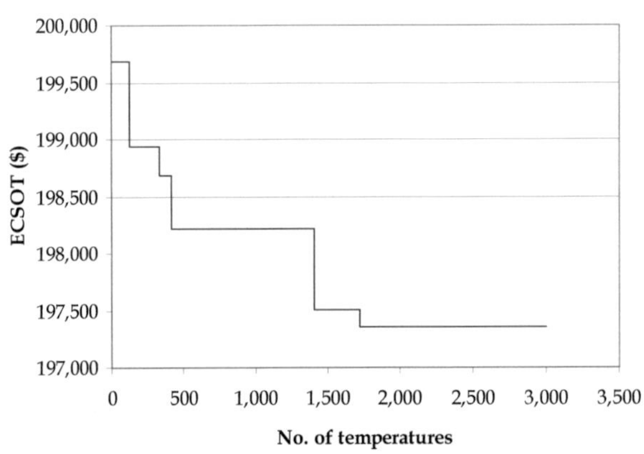

Fig. 4. Convergence report for customer interruption cost of RBTS

Pattern	Sectionalizing switch No.	ECOST ($)
1	-	199,677
2	4, 32	197,358
3	3, 32	197,668
4	4, 27	197,511

Table 5. Simulation results for ECOST minimization

Pattern	Sectionalizing switch No.	ENS (MWh)
1	-	37.7457
2	4, 32	37.2546
3	3, 32	37.1023
4	4, 27	37.2883

Table 6. Simulation results for ENS minimization

6.2 69-Bus System

The test system is a 12.66 kV radial distribution system with 69 buses, 7 laterals and 5 tie-lines (looping branches). The single line diagram of this system is shown in Fig. 5. Each branch in the system has a sectionalizing switch for reconfiguration purpose. There are 69 load points, 69 fuses, 69 transformers and 1 circuit breaker at the substation. As in the case of RBTS, the circuit breaker, the sectionalizing switches, and the fuses are all considered fully reliable and only one sectionalizing switch is installed on one side of each lateral. The statistical data of system equipment are given in Table A.5. The feeder and transformer data are provided in Tables A.6 and A.7. All the feeders and laterals are considered as overhead lines. The customer damage function is shown in Table 7, the data of which is plotted as shown in Fig. 6. The system has an average demand of 52.613 MW, a load factor of 0.63, and 6,120 customers. The maximum number of temperature is set at 100,000.

Figures 7, 8 and 9 show, respectively, three basic load point reliability indices for this system; namely, average failure rate (λ), average outage duration (r) and annual outage time (U). Compared with the RBTS, this system has higher failure rates and hence annual outage times mainly because there are more components in series that affect the load points. The initial configuration states that the tie switches located on branch No. 208-212 are open while all the sectionalizing switches are closed. With this configuration, the initial ECOST is $159,672. The optimal solution for this system, as shown in Fig. 10, indicates that tie switch No. 209, 210, 212 remains open and the statuses of tie switch No. 208 and 211 are changed from 'open' to 'closed', giving a ECOST of $27,799. Only two sectionalizing switches are required to be opened: switch No. 43 and No. 59. This system sees a reduction in ECOST of $27,799, accounting for 17.41%. The computation time is 80 seconds. A summary of simulation results before and after reconfiguration is given in Table 8.

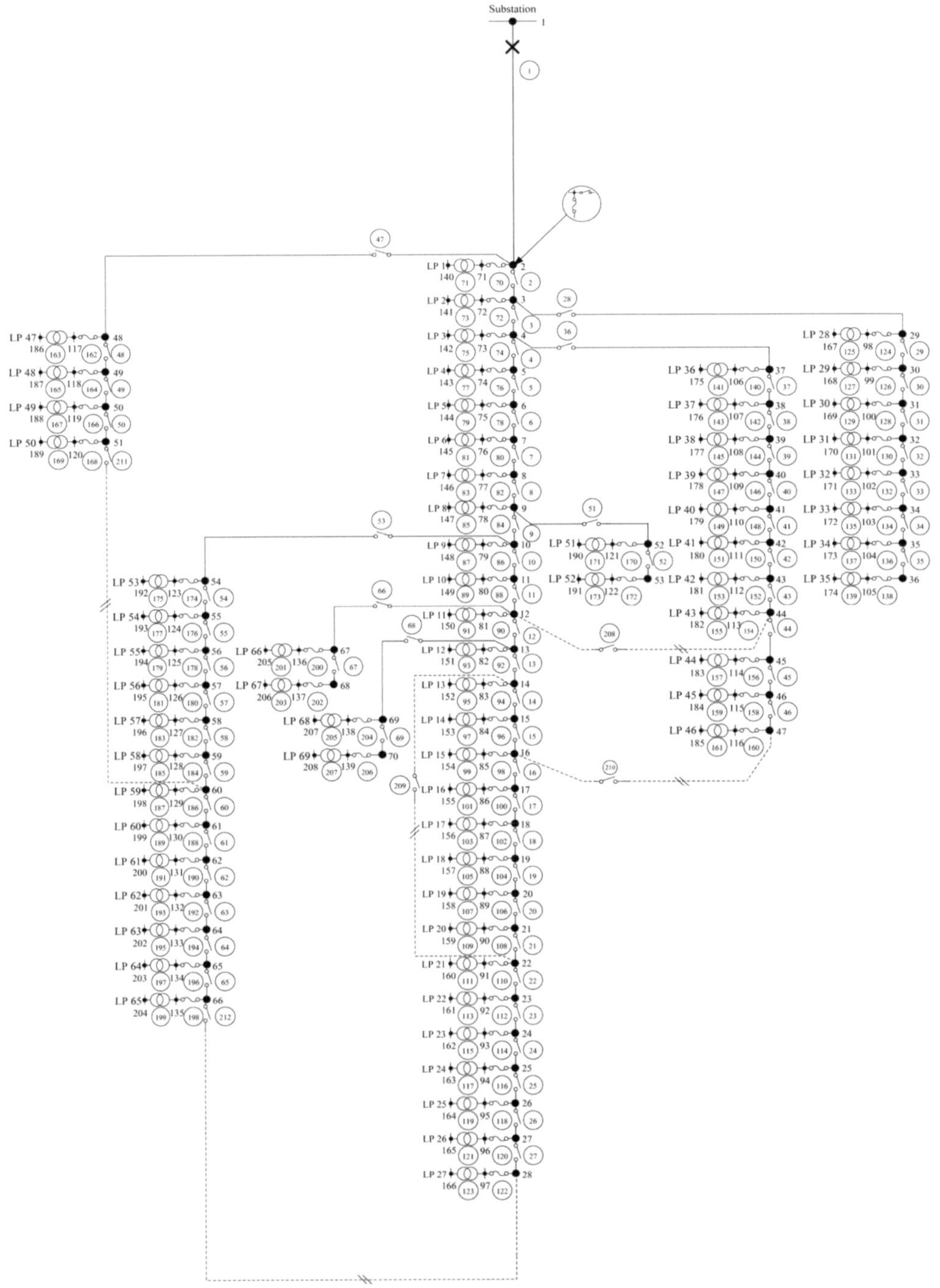

Fig. 5. 69-bus system before reconfiguration

User sector	Interruption duration (minutes)				
	1	20	60	240	480
Commercial	0.130	0.143	0.148	0.173	0.381
Educational	0.018	0.025	0.027	0.044	0.054
Office and building	0.248	0.287	0.351	0.494	4.778
Residential	0.001	0.005	0.008	0.020	0.033
Small industrial	0.105	0.116	0.151	0.193	1.626
Large industrial	1.005	1.508	2.225	3.968	8.240

Table 7. Sector customer damage cost for 69-bus system ($/kW)

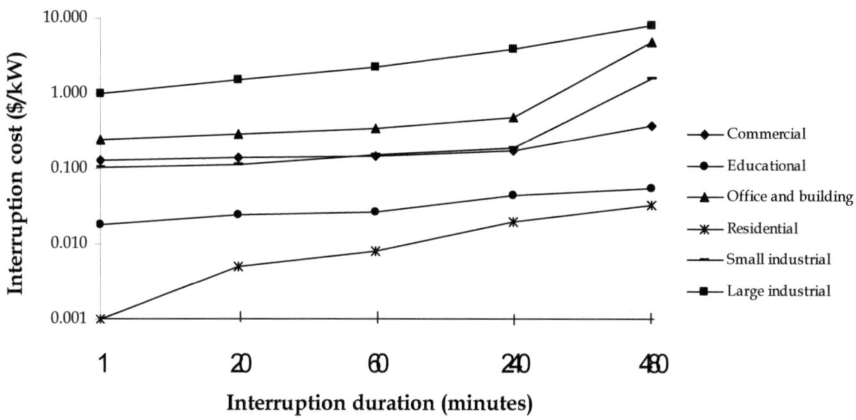

Fig. 6. Sector customer damage cost of 69-bus system

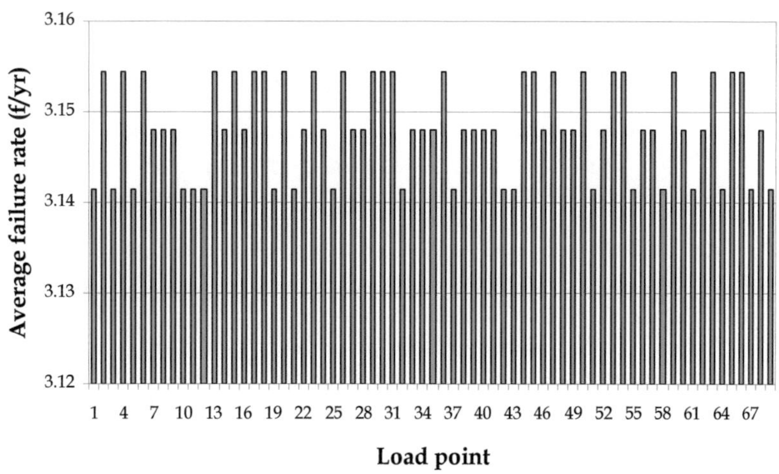

Fig. 7. Average failure rate of load points of 69-bus system

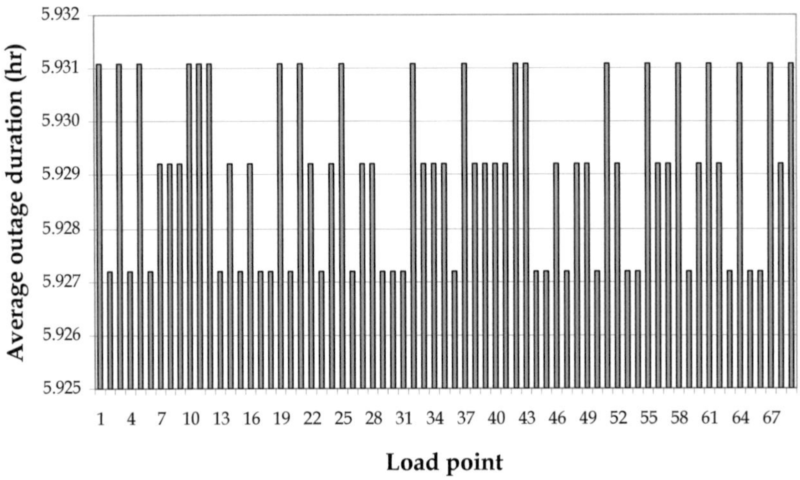

Fig. 8. Average outage duration of load points of 69-bus system

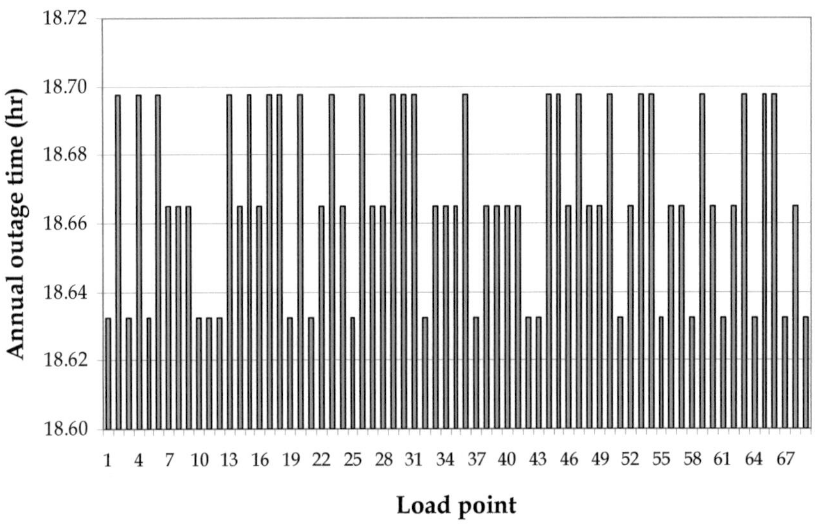

Fig. 9. Annual outage time of load points of 69-bus system

In fact, feeder reconfiguration attempts to balance the risk of losing customer load points with high interruption costs and those with low interruption costs so that the total customer interruption cost is minimized. With this logical idea, feeder reconfiguration can, therefore, result in overall reliability improvement.

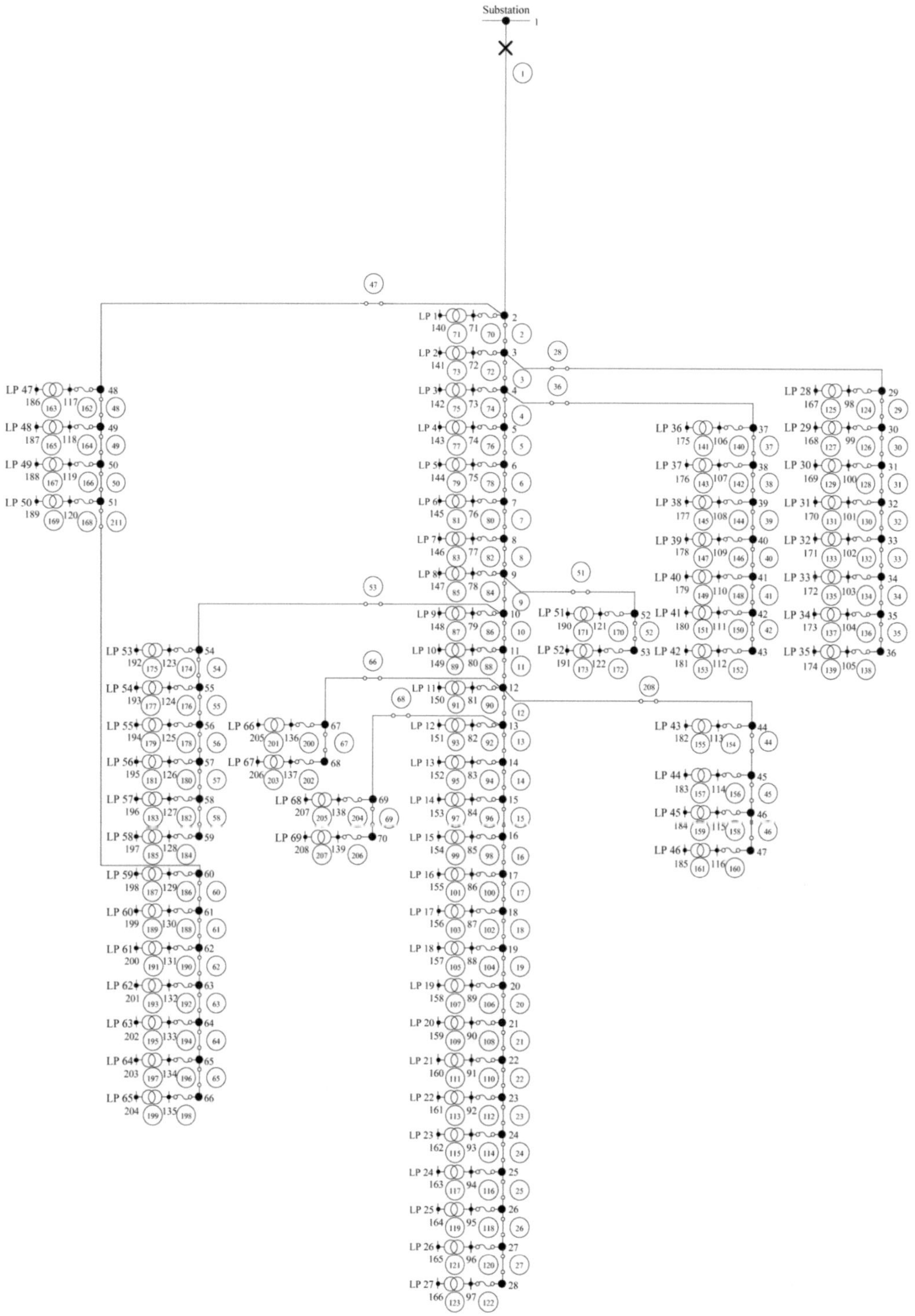

Fig. 10. 69-bus system after reconfiguration

	Before reconfiguration	After reconfiguration
SAIFI (failure/customer/yr)	3.1478	3.0568
SAIDI (hr/customer/yr)	18.664	16.860
ASUI	0.002131	0.001925
ASAI	0.997869	0.998075
ENS (MWh/yr)	0.982128	0.88387
AENS (MWh/customer/yr)	0.160478	0.14442
ECOST ($/yr)	159,672	131,873
Sectionalizing switches to be open	-	43, 59
Tie switches to be closed	-	208, 211

Table 8. Simulation results before and after reconfiguration for 69-bus system

7. Conclusion

The network reconfiguration problem for reliability enhancement is solved by the developed simulated annealing in conjunction with reliability worth analysis that provides an indirect measure for cost implication associated with power failure. The objective is to minimize customer interruption cost with the constraints that all load points have to be electrically supplied and radially connected. It can be seen from the results of the RBTS and the 69-bus system that the total customer interruption cost can be reduced (i.e., the system reliability worth is enhanced) and system reliability indices are improved if the network is properly configured. Some other benefits that can be obtained from the network configuration could also be taken into account such as loss reduction and load balancing. In such case, a multi-objective optimization problem will result where achieving one objective usually comes at the expense of the others and therefore a priority ranking is generally required. Other constraints may be included such as the number of switching operations of sectionalizing and tie switches.

8. References

Brown, R. E. (2001). Distribution Reliability Assessment and Reconfiguration Optimization, *IEEE Transmission and Distribution Conference and Exposition,* Vol. 2, pp. 994-999, ISBN 0780372859, USA, October 2001, Atlanta.

Chowdhury, A. A. & Koval, D. O. (2001). Application of Customer Interruption Costs in Transmission Network Reliability Planning, *IEEE Transactions on Industry Application* (November/December 2001), Vol. 37, No. 6, pp. 1590-1596.

Sarma, N. D. R. & Prakasa Rao, K. S. (1995). A New 0-1 Integer Programming Method of Feeder Reconfiguration for Loss Minimization in Distribution Systems, *Electric Power Systems Research,* (May 1995), Vo. 33, No. 2, pp. 125-131.

Kashem, M. A.; Jlasmon G. B.; Mohamed A. & Moghavvemi M. Artificial Neural Network Approach to Network Reconfiguration for Loss Minimization in Distribution Networks, *Electrical Power and Energy Systems,* (May 1998), Vol. 20, No. 4, pp. 247-258.

Chang, H. & Kuo, C. (1994). Network Reconfiguration in Distribution Systems Using Simulated Annealing, *Electric Power Systems Research,* (May 1994), Vo. 29, No. 3,pp. 227-238.

Zhou, Q.; Shirmohammadi, D., & Liu, E. (1997). Distribution Feeder Reconfiguration for Service Restoration and Load Balancing, *IEEE Transactions on Power Systems*, (May 1997), Vol. 12, No. 2, pp. 724-729.

Rugthaicharoencheep, N. & Sirisumrannukul, S. (2009). Feeder Reconfiguration for Loss Reduction in Distribution System with Distributed Generators by Tabu Search. *The Greater Mekong Subregion Academic and Research Network International Journal*, (March 2009), Vol. 3, No. 2., pp. 47-54.

Su, C. & Lee, C. (2001). Feeder Reconfiguration and Capacitor Setting for Loss Reduction of Distribution Systems, *Electric Power Systems Research*, (June 2001), Vol. 58, No. 2, pp. 97–102.

Tsai, L. (1993). Network Reconfiguration to Enhance Reliability of Electric Distribution Systems, *Electric Power Systems Research*, (July 1993), Vol. 27, No. 2, pp. 135-140.

Bin, Y.; Xiu-Li W.; Bie Zhao-Hong, B. & Xi-Fan, W. (2002). Distribution Network Reconfiguration for Reliability Worth Enhancement, *Proceedings of International Conference on Power System Technology*, Vol. 4, pp. 2547-2550, ISBN 978-0-852-96748-5 , China, October 2002, Kunming.

Aarts, E. & Korst, J. (1991). *Simulated Annealing and Boltzmann Machines: A Stochastic Approach to Combinatorial Optimization and Neural Computing*, Wiley Publishers, ISBN 978-0-471-92146-2, United States of America.

Winton, W. & Venkataramanan, M. A. (2003). *Introduction to Mathematical Programming*, Thomson, ISBN 978-0-534-35964-5, United States of America.

Weck, O. & Jilla, C. (2004). *Simulated Annealing a Basic Introduction*, http://ocw.mit.edu/NR/rdonlyres/Aeronauticsand-Astronautics/16-888Spring-2004/5F6CFF91-524F-4792-859D-98331A73AC7C/0/l10a_sa.pdf

Billinton, R. & Allan, R. N. (1996). *Reliability Evaluation of Power Systems*, Plenum Press, ISBN 978-0-306-45259-8, United States of America.

Geol, L.; Billinton, R. & Gupta R. (1991). Basic Data and Evaluation of Distribution System Reliability Worth, *Proceedings of IEEE Western Canada Conference on Computer, Power and Communications Systems in a Rural Environment*, pp. 271-277, ISBN 0-87942-594-6, Canada, May 1991, Regina.

Geol, L. & Billinton, R. (1994). Determination of Reliability Worth for Distribution System Planning, *IEEE Transactions on Power Delivery*, (July 1994), Vol. 9, No. 3, pp. 1577-1583.

Allan, R. N.; Billinton, R.; Sjarief, I.; Goel, L. & So, K. S. (1991). A Reliability Test System for Educational Purposes-Basic Distribution System Data and Results, *IEEE Transactions on Power Systems*, (May 1991), Vol. 6, No. 2, pp. 813-820.

Chiang H.D. & Jean-Jameau R.M. (1990). Optimal Network Reconfigurations in Distribution Systems, Part 2. Solution Algorithms and Numerical Results, *IEEE Transactions on Power Delivery*, (July 1990) Vol. 5, No. 3, pp. 1568-1574.

Acknowledgement

The assistance from Mr. Sakulpong, A. and Mr. Rugthaicharoencheep, N. is sincerely acknowledged.

Appendix A
A.1 Roy Billinton Test System (RBTS)

Component	λ	r	s
Transformer	0.0150	200	-
Line	0.0650	5	1.0

λ = failure rate (f/km-yr)
r = repair time and replacement time (hr)
s = switching time (hr)

Table A.1. Component reliability data

Feeder type	Length (km)	Feeder section numbers
1	0.60	4, 7, 8, 14, 26, 32, 33, 43, 47, 49
2	0.75	1, 2, 3, 6, 18, 24, 27, 30, 31, 35, 39, 45, 55
3	0.80	10, 12, 16, 20, 22, 23, 25, 29, 37, 41, 51, 53, 57

Table A.2. Feeder data

Tranformer section numbers
9, 11, 13, 15, 17, 19, 21, 22, 23, 34, 36, 38, 40, 42, 44, 46, 48, 50, 52, 54, 56, 58

Table A.3. Tranformer data

Number of load points	Load points (LP)	Customer type	Average load (MW)	Peak load (MW)	Number of customers per load point
5	1, 2, 3, 10, 11	Residential	0.535	0.8668	210
4	12, 17, 18, 19	Residential	0.450	0.7291	200
1	8	Small industrial	1.00	1.6279	1
1	9	Small industrial	1.15	1.8721	1
6	4, 5, 13, 14, 20, 21	Government	0.566	0.9167	1
5	6, 7, 15, 16, 22	Commercial	0.454	0.7500	10
Total			12.291	20.00	1,908

Table A.4. Customer and loading data

A.2 69-Bus System

Component	λ	r	s
Transformer	0.0150	200	-
Line	0.0650	5	1.0

λ = failure rate (f/km-yr)
r = repair time and replacement time (hr)
s = switching time (hr)

Table A.5. Component reliability data

Length (km)	Feeder section numbers
0.60	3, 5, 6, 7, 9, 14, 16, 17, 19, 21, 23, 24, 27, 28, 33, 35, 37, 41, 45, 46, 48, 51, 55, 57, 60, 62, 63, 66, 67, 70, 74, 78, 88, 90, 92, 106, 110, 118, 132, 142, 152, 154, 170, 178, 184, 190, 196, 202, 206
0.70	2, 4, 12, 13, 18, 20, 26, 30, 31, 32, 36, 38, 43, 47, 54, 59, 64, 65, 68, 82, 84, 86, 96, 100, 112, 116, 122, 124, 134, 136, 138, 144, 146, 148, 150, 160, 164, 166, 172, 180, 182, 188, 192, 204
0.80	1, 8, 10, 11, 15, 22, 25, 29, 34, 39, 40, 42, 44, 49, 50, 52, 53, 56, 58, 61, 69, 72, 76, 80, 94, 98, 102, 104, 108, 114, 120, 126, 128, 130, 140, 156, 158, 162, 168, 174, 176, 186, 194, 198, 200

Table A.6. Feeder data

Tranformer section numbers
71, 73, 75, 77, 79, 81, 83, 85, 87, 89, 91, 93,95, 97, 99, 101, 103, 105, 107, 109, 111, 113, 115, 117, 119, 121, 123, 125, 127, 129, 131, 133, 135, 137, 139, 141, 143, 145, 147, 149, 151, 153, 155, 157, 159, 161, 163, 165, 167, 169, 171, 173, 175, 177, 179, 181, 183, 185, 187, 189, 191, 193, 195, 197, 199, 201, 203, 205, 207, 208, 209, 210, 211, 212

Table A.7. Transformer data

Number of load points	Load points (LP)	Customer type	Average load (MW)	Peak load (MW)	Number of customers per load point
12	1, 2, 13, 14, 25, 26, 37, 38, 49, 50, 60, 61	Commercial	0.574	0.950	200
11	3, 4, 15, 16, 27, 28, 39, 40, 51, 52, 62	Educational	0.632	0.825	1
10	5, 6, 17, 18, 29, 30, 41, 42, 53, 54	Office and building	0.988	1.412	10
17	7, 8, 19, 20, 31, 32, 43, 44, 55, 56, 63, 64, 65, 66, 67, 68, 69	Residential	1.200	1.934	210
10	9, 10, 21, 22, 33, 34, 45, 46, 57, 58	Small industrial	0.555	0.878	3
9	11, 12, 23, 24, 35, 36, 47, 48, 59	Large industrial	0.327	0.798	1
Total			52.613	83.435	6,120

Table A.8. Customer and loading data

9

Optimal Design of an IPM Motor for Electric Power Steering Application Using Simulated Annealing Method

Hamidreza Akhondi, Jafar Milimonfared and Hasan Rastegar
Amirkabir University of Technology
Iran

1. Introduction

Electric power steering (EPS) in newer vehicles is becoming an alternative to the hydraulic power steering (HPS) because of the recent advances in electrical motors, power converters , sensors and digital control systems (Mir et al., 2003). In the EPS system, an electric motor is connected to the steering rack via a gear mechanism. Some sensors measure the torque on the steer and the angular position of the hand wheel. A control system receives these signals from the sensors, together with vehicle speed, turning rate, and gives operating commands to the electric motor drive, controlling steering direction and dynamics and driver effort. The control unit determines the amount of steering assist torque, which has to be also modified according to vehicle speed to maintain good steering feel.

Electric power steering eliminates the need for a hydraulic power steering pump, hoses, hydraulic fluid, drive belt and pulley on the engine, therefore the total system is lighter than a comparable hydraulic system through the use of compact system units (Mir et al., 2003). Also, since EPS is an on-demand system that operates only when the steering wheel is turned, the fuel efficiency of vehicle equipped with such system is better than that of automotive equipped with an equivalent-output hydraulic system (Liao & Isaac, 2003). As a result, Electric power steering systems have many advantages over traditional hydraulic power steering systems in engine efficiency, space efficiency, and environmental compatibility. This motivates the great increase of EPS-equipped automotive recently (wilson, 2005).

Electric power steering basically consists of a torque sensor and motor actuator couple. The sensor is attached to the steering column and measures the torque applied by the driver for moving the steering wheel. This torque signal is transmitted to a control power card that sends an amplified proportional power signal to the electric motor (in this paper we use interior permanent magnet (IPM) synchronous motor), which is engaged to the steering rack bar.

An EPS system has the following two functions. First, it can reduce steering torque and present various steering feels. The steering torque (or driver torque) is defined as the one which a driver experiences (or a driver applies to the steering column) when turning the steering wheel. When an appropriate assist torque from an EPS system is applied in the same direction as the driver's steering direction, the amount of steering torque required by a driver for steering can be significantly relieved. In addition, adjustment of the characteristics of assist torque allows the driver to experience various steering feels. Second, the EPS system can improve return to center performance of a steering wheel when it is steered. While the steering wheel is turned and then released during cornering, it returns to the center position by the so-called self-aligning torque exerted on the tires by the road. Since this torque increases with vehicle speed, at high vehicle speeds the steering wheel may exhibit excessive overshoot and subsequent oscillation. The EPS system can eliminate this phenomenon by providing active damping capability, thus enhance return ability characteristics.

This paper presents an Electric Power Steering system using IPM motor and drive system which is widely being applied in automotive applications. Due to factors such as high power density and efficiency, maintenance, and extremely wide operating speed range, permanent magnet synchronous motors (PMSM) are the subject of development for traction drive applications (Jahns et al., 1986).

Optimization with Simulated Annealing (Ingber, 1993) method is done on the IPM motor structure considering the EPS requirements and constraints to obtain the motor parameters. So the paper deals with the design and performance evaluation of an IPM motor for EPS system. The components of system such IPMSM electrical and mechanical parts, power electronic converter, steering mechanism and controller are integrated as entire model of EPS using Simulink environment for analyzing the system performance with interactions between each component. The block diagram of EPS with IPMSM drive system is shown in Fig. 1.

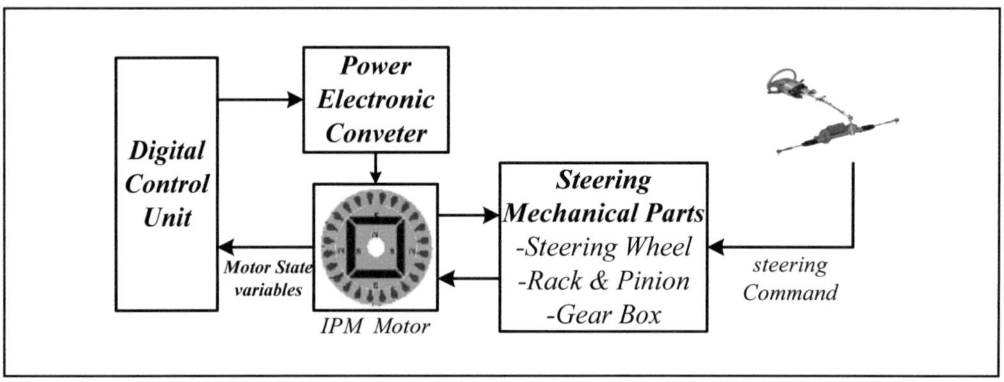

Fig. 1. Block Diagram of Overall EPS System

2. Optimization of the IPM Motor Parameters

The IPM motor presents many advantages over the other motors. Among them, it exhibits high torque density, yielding a minimum size and weight, good power to weight ratio as demanded in automotive applications (Chedot & Friedrich, 2003) and a high efficiency, even under reduced loads. In addition, its manufacture is easy, because the PMs are simply introduced in suitable holes in the rotor and the motor has capability to operate in flux weakening region. So for the IPMSM, the magnetic circuit has been fully designed using the optimization from analytic and finite-element based software.

In this design, the objectives to be reached are the reduction of the volume and total weight as well as the reduction of the size of the magnets to decrease the cost (Sebastian et al., 2004). An easiness of the manufacturing process must be kept in mind for a future industrial application. Other objectives as the dynamic behavior and the torque ripple will be examined in the future with the power electronic and control interactions.

Taking into account the important number of design variables, an optimization under constraints is chosen. Variables are classified into discrete and continuous one. If discrete variables are fixed (for example number of stator slots) a non-linear mathematic algorithm can be used to optimize the machine structure with geometrical constraints. A number of optimization variables noted U are selected in order to find optimal values noted U* as shown below.

U* minimizes an objective function F and verifies the feasibility domain under constraints:

Minimize F(U)

$$U^* \in U$$

Subject to

$$H_i(U^*)=0$$
$$G_i(U^*)\geq 0$$
$$U_{\ell i} \leq U_i \leq U_{ui}$$

U* must permit to reach the desired goal with the minimization criterion. It must also verify the equality and inequality constraints while keeping in the range of allowed values. For example, if the power to weight ratio has to be limited, it is necessary to choose:

$U \rightarrow$ motor parameter (magnet flux linkage & dimensions)

$F(U) \rightarrow$ power to weight ratio

$G_1(U) \rightarrow$ external diameter $\leq D_{max}$

…

$G_i(U) \rightarrow$ motor torque $\geq T_{min}$

The method is based on an analysis and optimization parts. The analysis part uses the parametric model with the variables U to calculate the energetic values of the machine according to design specifications. The analysis part treats three domains (Fig.2). The magnetic domain is the first and the central one because it is coupled with the two others. It allows the evaluation of inductance and back-*emf*. This brings to electromechanical performances. The thermal domain gives temperature of magnets and copper to estimate flux density and resistances. The electrical domain gives the relationship between the current reference and the real current according to the voltage limit.

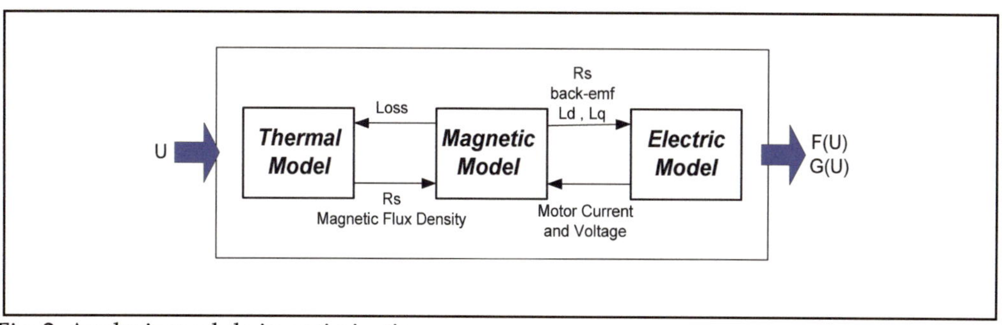

Fig. 2. Analysis module in optimization process

The optimization part manages the variables U on the basis of F(U) and G(U) information given by the analysis part. In this paper the Simulated Annealing Method (SA) is used in optimization part. The SA algorithm mainly consists of repeating a sequence of iterations. Given an optimization problem, at a selected initial temperature, the SA starts off with the initial solutions: current and trial, randomly selected from two points within the search space. Two energy level sets of current solution and trial solution, Ei and Ej respectively, are obtained. The Metropolis algorithm, generation and acceptance is then applied. If Ej - Ei <0, then the trial solution is accepted and replaces the current solution. Otherwise, the acceptance or rejection is based on Boltzmann's probability acceptance, which is $PA = \exp\left(-\frac{Ei - Ej}{KT}\right)$ where T denotes the temperature, k is Boltzmann's constant. If PA is higher than R, where R is a random value (0-1), the trial solution is accepted and replaces the current solution. If PA is less than R then the current solution remains and a new trial solution is generated. The generation mechanism and acceptance criterion are then repeated. After a certain amount of iterations, the temperature is reduced by multiplying its value by a factor slightly below one. With reduced temperature, these two processes are repeated again until the criterion of execution is achieved (Ingber, 1993).
The final machine parameters after optimization with this method is given in table 1.

3. Modelling of EPS with IPM Motor and Drive

Typical EPS system is shown in Fig. 3. The major components are a torque sensor, an electric motor, a reduction gear and control unit. Torque sensor is located between steering wheel and steering column and measures the applied torque by converting difference of twisted angle to electric signal. The electric motor is attached in steering column through reduction gear box. Control unit calculates motor target torque and current from the signal of torque sensor and vehicle velocity. So the calculated torque is applied to steering column by motor through reduction gear.
There are four different type of EPS, column, pinion and rack-assisted or a fully steer by wire type (Mohammadi & Kazemi, 2003). In this paper, a column-assist-type EPS shown in Fig. 3 is used for modeling and simulation. The equilibrium equations of steering wheel, pinion, rack and motor are:

$$J_{sw}\ddot{\theta}_{sw} + B_{sw}\dot{\theta}_{sw} + K_{sc}(\theta_{sw} - \theta_{sc}) = T_{sw} \tag{1}$$

$$J_p\ddot{\theta}_p + B_p\dot{\theta}_p + K_{sc}(\theta_p - \theta_{sw}) = N\,T_m - T_p \tag{2}$$

$$M_R\ddot{X}_R + B_R\dot{X}_R + F_t = \frac{T_p}{R_p} \quad , \quad X_R = R_p \cdot \theta_p \tag{3}$$

$$J_m\ddot{\theta}_m + B_m\dot{\theta}_m + T_m = T_e \quad , \quad \theta_m = N \cdot \theta_p \tag{4}$$

Once the Equations (3) and (4) are rearranged about θ_P and substitute it to Equation (2), we can get new equations as below:

$$(J_p + R_p^2 M_R + N^2 J_m)\ddot{\theta}_p + (B_p + R_p^2 B_R + N^2 B_m)\dot{\theta}_p = K_{sc}(\theta_{sw} - \theta_p) + T_e - R_p F_t \quad (5)$$

If $J_{eq} = J_p + R_p^2 M_R + N^2 J_m$, $B_{eq} = B_p + R_p^2 B_R + N^2 B_m$ then we have below equation:

$$J_{eq}\ddot{\theta}_p + B_{eq}\dot{\theta}_p = K_{sc}(\theta_{sw} - \theta_p) + T_e - R_p F_t \quad (6)$$

The equation of wheel and tire loads is the same as:

$$F_t = J_w \ddot{X}_R + B_w \dot{X}_R + K_w X_R + CF_w \, sign(\dot{X}_R) \quad (7)$$

Where CF_w is Coulomb friction breakout force on road wheel. Thus final equation is expressed as:

$$(J_p + R_p^2(M_R + J_w) + N^2 J_m)\ddot{\theta}_p + (B_p + R_p^2(B_R + B_w) + N^2 B_m)\dot{\theta}_p + R_p^2 K_w \theta_p + R_p CF_w \, sign(\dot{\theta}_p) = K_{sc}(\theta_{sw} - \theta_p) + T_e \quad (8)$$

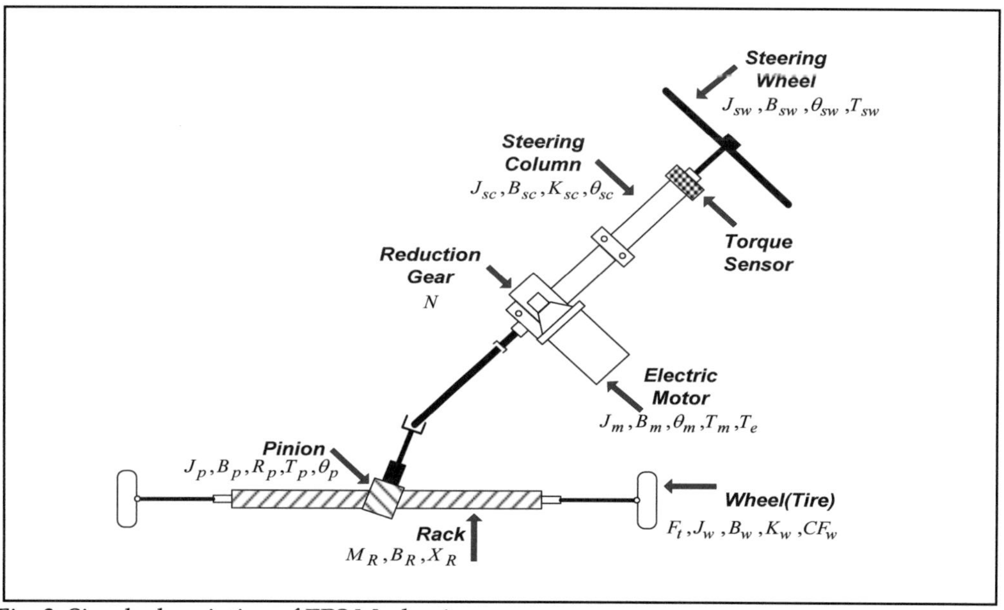

Fig. 3. Simple description of EPS Mechanism

Using these equations, the mechanical part of EPS which incorporates the mechanical part of PMSM is modeled. The block diagram of EPS system with IPM motor and drive is shown in Fig. 4. In this block diagram the motor parameters is obtained from design and optimization procedure that mentioned in previous section. The voltage source inverter is constructed with IGBT for more accurate simulation. A current phase control technique with simple PI controller is used for simulation including a PWM module. SVPWM model is implemented by unified voltage modulation techniques (Mohan et al, 1997) And a dead time function is implemented using delay block. The control strategy which is applied to IPM motor is maximum torque per ampere up to rated speed and maximum torque per voltage (flux) over the rated speed (Lee & Hong, 2006).

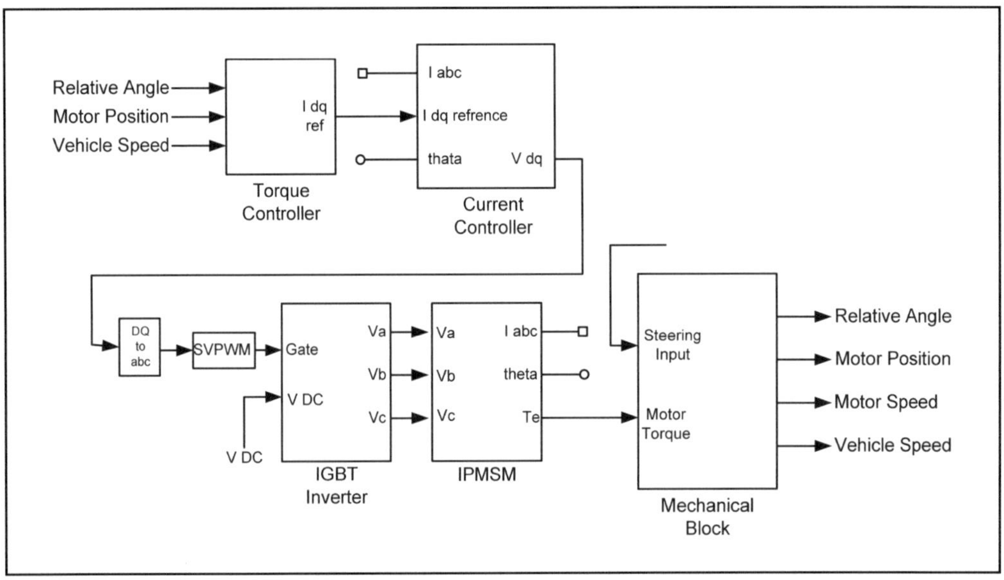

Fig. 4. A model of EPS with IPMSM Drive System

4. System Simulation and Results

Table 1 shows the parameters of IPMSM for EPS system simulation. These parameters are obtained by the information of motor structure, dimension and material that obtained in optimization procedure and FEM (Finite Element Method) analysis is done to obtain parameters. Stator resistance is depends on winding turns and material.

Motor Parameter	VALUE
Magnet Flux Linkage (Wb)	0.105
Stator Resistance (Ω)	0.02
d-Axis Inductance (mH)	8.6
q-Axis Inductance (mH)	22.5

Table 1. Motor Parameters Obtained from Optimization

In simulation of electric power steering system with mechanical parts, the torque controller is simple PI controller which uses relative angle (difference between steering angle and rotor angle), motor position and vehicle speed to generate the reference value of q-axis current. d-axis current is generated from q-axis current and maximum torque per ampere or maximum torque per flux (voltage). The current controller uses this reference values to generate d-q reference voltages. Using these reference voltages, switching signals for IGBT inverter is constructed and system can control the IPM motor torque in order to produce needed assisted torque. DC voltage link in inverter is 12V as in vehicle.

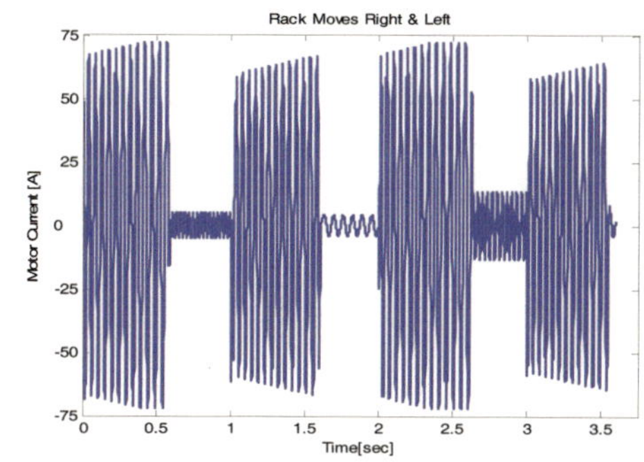

(a)

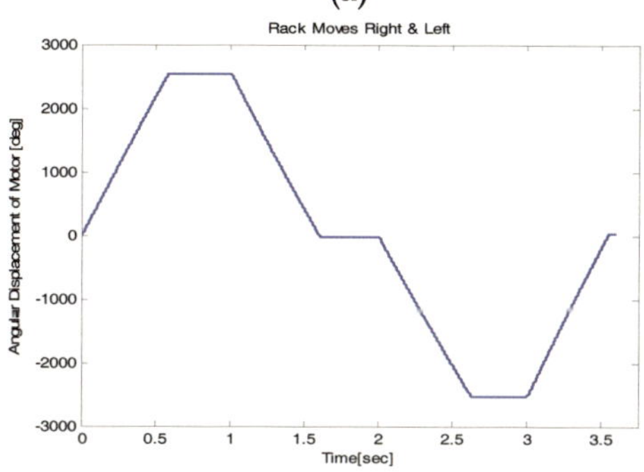

(b)

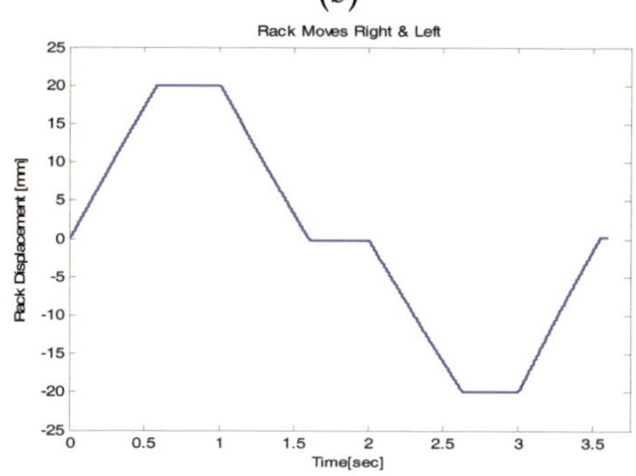

(c)

Fig. 4. Rack moves right, return back, moves left and finally return to primary position. (a) Motor Current. (b) Motor angular displacement. (c) Rack displacement.

In the following simulations, the goal is to control the rack displacement. For example Fig 5 shows simulation results when left and right movement of rack is desired. The rack moves right up to 20mm, return back, moves left up to 20mm and finally back to its first position. We can notify that this modeling of EPS system facsimiles the characteristics and behavior of system very similar to which we desire and command.

5. Conclusion

In this paper, design and optimization of interior permanent magnet motor for electric power steering application is studied. IPM motors advantages in automotive systems are discussed. Optimization is done with different objective function such as power to weight and magnet volume. After obtaining the motor parameters, we evaluate the performance of entire system through some different tests. Simulation results show that the system performance can improved using an IPM motor and drive because of its high torque density and capability of flux weakening operation. With the EPS logic for the reduction in steering torque, the driver can turn the steering wheel with a significantly reduced steering torque. With the EPS control to return to center performance, a quick response of steering wheel without overshoot after cornering can be obtained by proper control of assist motor.

6. References

Dave Wilson, "Electric power steering: one good turn deserves another", "Bush: No quick energy fix" Associated Press article, The Arizona Republic, pp 1, A9, Thursday, April 28, 2005.

Hooman Mohammadi and Reza Kazemi, "Simulation of Different Types of Electric Power Assisted Streering (EPS) to Inverstigate Applied Torque Positions' Effects", *SAE paper* No. 2003-01-0585, 2003.

L.Ingber, "Simulated annealing : practice versus theory,"*Mathematical and Computer Modeling,* vol.18, pp.29-57, 1993

L. Chédot, G. Friedrich, "Optimal control of interior permanent magnet synchronous integrated starter-generator," *Eur. Power Elec. Drives Conf. (EPE'2003),* CD Proceedings, Toulouse (France), 2003.

N. Mohan and et al., "*Power Electronics and Variable Frequency Drives*", IEEE PRESS, pp400-453, 1997.

S. Mir, M. Islam, and T. Sebastian, "Role of electronics and controls in steering system," in *Proc. 29th IEEE IECON,* Roanoke, VA, Nov. 2–6, 2003, pp. 2859–2864.

T. Jahns, G. Kliman, and T. Neumann, "Interior pm synchronous motors for adjustable speed drives," *IEEE Trans. Ind. Appl.,* vol. IA-22, no. 4, pp. 738–747, 1986.

T. Sebastian, S. Mir, M. Islam, "Electric Motors for Automotive Applications," *EPE Journal,* Vol.14, No.1, February 2004, pp..

Wootaik Lee, Jung-Pyo Hong, "Object oriented modeling of an Interior Permanent Magnet Synchronous Motor Drives for Dynamic Simulation of Vehicular Propulsion", *IEEE Vehicle Power and Propulsion Conference,* paper No. SNO-b109x, 2006.

Y. Gene Liao ,H. Isaac Du, "Modeling and analysis of electric power steering system and its effect on vehicle dynamic behavior", *Int. J. of Vehicle Automotive System*(IJVAS), Vol. 1, No. 2, pp. 153-166, 2003.

10

Using the simulated annealing algorithm to solve the optimal control problem

Horacio Martínez-Alfaro
hma@itesm.mx
Tecnológico de Monterrey, Campus Monterrey
México

1. Introduction

A lot of research has been done in Automatic Control Systems during the last decade and more recently in discrete control systems due to the popular use of powerful personal computers. This work presents an approach to solve the Discrete-Time Time Invariant Linear Quadratic (LQ) Optimal Control problem which minimizes a specific performance index (either minimum time and/or minimum energy). The design approach presented in this paper transforms the LQ problem into a combinatorial optimization problem. The Simulated Annealing (SA) algorithm is used to carry out the optimization.
Simulated Annealing is basically an iterative improvement strategy augmented by a criterion for occasionally accepting configurations with higher values of the performance index (Malhorta et al., 1991; Martínez-Alfaro & Flugrad, 1994; Martínez-Alfaro & Ulloa-Pérez, 1996; Rutenbar, 1989). Given a performance index $J(z)$ (analog to the energy of the material) and an initial configuration z_0, the iterative improvement solution is seeked by randomly perturbing z_0. The Metropolis algorithm (Martínez-Alfaro & Flugrad, 1994; Martínez-Alfaro & Ulloa-Pérez, 1996; Rutenbar, 1989) was used for acceptance/rejection of the perturbed configuration.
In this design approach, SA was used to minimized the performance index of the LQ problem and as result obtaining the values of the feedback gain matrix $\mathbf{K}$ that make stable the feedback system and minimize the performance index of the control system in state space representation (Ogata, 1995). The SA algorithm starts with an initial feedback gain matrix $\mathbf{K}$ and evaluates the performance index. The current $\mathbf{K}$ is perturbed to generate another $\mathbf{K}_{new}$ and the performance index is evaluated. The acceptance/rejection criteria is based on the Metropolis algorithm. This procedure is repeated under a cooling schedule. Some experiments were performed with first through third order plants for Regulation and Tracking, Single Input - Single Output (SISO) and Multiple Input - Multiple Output (MIMO) systems. Matlab and Simulink were used as simulation software to carry out the experiments.
The parameters of the SA algorithm (perturbation size, initial temperature, number of Markov chains, etc.) were specially tunned for each plant.
Additional experiments were performed with non-conventional performance indices for tracking problems (Steffanoni Palacios, 1998) where characteristics like maximum overshoot $\max(y(k) - r(k))$, manipulation softness index $|\mathbf{u}(k+1) - \mathbf{u}(k)|$, output softness index $|\mathbf{y}(k+1) - \mathbf{y}(k)|$, and the error magnitude $|\mathbf{r}(k) - \mathbf{y}(k)|$.

The proposed scheme with the use of the SA algorithm showed to be another good tool for discrete optimal control systems design even though only linear time invariant plants were considered (Grimble & Johnson, 1988; Ogata, 1987; 1995; Salgado et al., 2001; Santina et al., 1994). A large CPU time was involved in this scheme in order to obtain similar results to the ones by LQ. The design process is simplified due to the use of gain matrices that generate a stable feedback system. The equations required are those use for the simulation of the feedback system which are very simple and very easy to implement.

2. Methodology

The procedure is described as follow:

1. Propose a initial solution $\mathbf{K}_{initial}$.
2. Evaluate the performance index and save initial cost $J_{initial}(\mathbf{K}_{initial})$. $\mathbf{K}_{initial}$ needs to be converted to matrices $\mathbf{K}_1$ and $\mathbf{K}_2$ for tracking systems.
3. Randomly perturb $\mathbf{K}_{initial}$ to obtain a $\mathbf{K}_{new}$.
4. Evaluate the performance index and save initial cost $J_{new}(\mathbf{K}_{new})$.
5. Accept or reject $\mathbf{K}_{new}$ according to the Metropolis criterion.
6. If accepted, $\mathbf{K}_{initial} \leftarrow \mathbf{K}_{new}$, decrement temperature according to $J_{new}/J_{initial}$.
7. Repeat from step 3.

Once a Markov chain is completed, decrement the temperature, $T_{i+1} = \alpha T_i$, where T_i represents the current temperature and $\alpha = 0.9$ (Martínez-Alfaro & Flugrad, 1994). The procedure ends when the final temperature or a certain number of Markov chains has been reached.

3. Implementation

The code was implemented in Matlab, and the models were design for Regulation and Tracking, SISO and MIMO systems.
A discrete optimal control system can be represented as follows (Ogata, 1995):

$$\mathbf{x}(k+1) = \mathbf{G}\,\mathbf{x}(k) + \mathbf{H}\,\mathbf{u}(k) \tag{1}$$

$$\mathbf{y}(k) = \mathbf{C}\,\mathbf{x}(k) + \mathbf{D}\,\mathbf{u}(k) \tag{2}$$

where $\mathbf{x}^{(n\times 1)}$ is the state vector, $\mathbf{y}^{(m\times 1)}$ is the output vector, $\mathbf{u}^{(r\times 1)}$ is the control vector, $\mathbf{G}^{(n\times n)}$ is the state matrix, $\mathbf{H}^{(n\times r)}$ is the input matrix, $\mathbf{C}^{(m\times n)}$ is the output matrix, and $\mathbf{D}^{(m\times r)}$ is the direct transmission matrix.
In an LQ problem the solution determines the optimal control sequence for $\mathbf{u}(k)$ that minimizes the performance index (Ogata, 1995).

3.1 Regulation

The equation that define the performance index for a Regulator is (Ogata, 1987):

$$J = \frac{1}{2}\sum_{k=0}^{N-1}\left[\mathbf{x}'(k)\,\mathbf{Q}\,\mathbf{x}(k) + \mathbf{u}'(k)\,\mathbf{R}\,\mathbf{u}(k)\right] \tag{3}$$

where $\mathbf{Q}^{(n\times n)}$ is positive definite or positive semidefinite Hermitian matrix, $\mathbf{Q}^{(n\times n)}$ is positive definite or positive semidefinite Hermitian matrix, and N is the number of samples. Equation 3 represents the objective function of the SA algorithm.

3.2 Tracking

A tracking system can be represented as follows (Ogata, 1987):

$$\begin{aligned} \mathbf{x}(k+1) &= \mathbf{G}\,\mathbf{x}(k) + \mathbf{H}\,\mathbf{u}(k), & \mathbf{u}(k) &= \mathbf{K}_1\,\mathbf{v}(k) - \mathbf{K}_2\,\mathbf{x}(k) \\ \mathbf{y}(k) &= \mathbf{C}\,\mathbf{x}(k), & \mathbf{v}(k) &= \mathbf{r}(k) - \mathbf{y}(k) + \mathbf{v}(k-1) \end{aligned} \tag{4}$$

where $\mathbf{x}$ is the state vector, $\mathbf{u}$ is the control vector, $\mathbf{y}$ is the output vector, $\mathbf{r}$ is the input reference vector, $\mathbf{v}$ is the speed vector, $\mathbf{K}_1$ is the integral control matrix, $\mathbf{K}_2$ is the feedback matrix, $\mathbf{G}$ is the state matrix, $\mathbf{H}$ is the input matrix, and $\mathbf{C}$ is the output matrix.
The representation used in this work was a Regulator representation (Ogata, 1987):

$$\xi(k+1) = \hat{\mathbf{G}}\,\xi(k) + \hat{\mathbf{H}}\,\mathbf{w}(k), \qquad \mathbf{w}(k) = -\hat{\mathbf{K}}\,\xi(k) \tag{5}$$

where:

$$\begin{aligned} \xi(k) &= \begin{bmatrix} \mathbf{x}_e(k) \\ \mathbf{u}_e(k) \end{bmatrix}, & \hat{\mathbf{G}} &= \begin{bmatrix} \mathbf{G} & \mathbf{H} \\ \mathbf{0} & 0 \end{bmatrix} \\ \hat{\mathbf{H}} &= \begin{bmatrix} \mathbf{0} \\ \mathbf{I}_m \end{bmatrix}, & \hat{\mathbf{K}} &= (\mathbf{R} + \hat{\mathbf{H}}'\,\hat{\mathbf{P}}\,\hat{\mathbf{H}})^{-1}\hat{\mathbf{H}}'\,\hat{\mathbf{P}}\,\hat{\mathbf{G}}, \\ [\mathbf{K}_2\ \ \mathbf{K}_1] &= (\hat{\mathbf{K}} + [\mathbf{0}\ \ \mathbf{I}_m])\mathbf{R}\begin{bmatrix} \mathbf{G}-\mathbf{I}_n & \mathbf{H} \\ \mathbf{C}\mathbf{G} & \mathbf{C}\mathbf{H} \end{bmatrix}^{-1} \end{aligned} \tag{6}$$

and the states are defined as

$$\mathbf{x}_e(k) = \mathbf{x}(k) - \mathbf{x}(\infty), \qquad \mathbf{u}_e(k) = \mathbf{u}(k) - \mathbf{u}(\infty) \tag{7}$$

The performance index is:

$$J = \frac{1}{2}\sum_{k=0}^{\infty}\left[\xi'(k)\,\hat{\mathbf{Q}}\,\xi(k) + \mathbf{w}'(k)\,\mathbf{R}\,\mathbf{w}(k)\right] \quad \text{with} \quad \hat{\mathbf{Q}} = \begin{bmatrix} \mathbf{Q} & \mathbf{0} \\ \mathbf{0} & \mathbf{0} \end{bmatrix} \tag{8}$$

Since our simultaion is finite, the performance index should be evaluated for N samples:

$$J = \frac{1}{2}\sum_{k=0}^{N}\left[\xi'(k)\,\hat{\mathbf{Q}}\,\xi(k) + \mathbf{w}'(k)\,\mathbf{R}\,\mathbf{w}(k)\right] \tag{9}$$

3.2.1 Non-conventional performance index

Non-conventional performance indexes are specially good when we desire to include certain output and/or vector control characteristics in addition to the ones provided by a standard LQ problem.
The propose performance index is (Steffanoni Palacios, 1998):

$$J = C_1\,\zeta + C_2\,\vartheta + C_3\,\varphi + \sum_{k=0}^{N}\left[C_4\,\xi'(k)\,\hat{\mathbf{Q}}\,\xi(k) + C_5\,\mathbf{w}'(k)\,\mathbf{R}\,\mathbf{w}(k) + C_6\,\varepsilon(k)\right] \tag{10}$$

where

- ζ is the softness index of $\mathbf{u}(k)$ defined by $|\mathbf{u}(k+1) - \mathbf{u}(k)|$.
- ϑ is the maximum overshoot defined by $\max(\mathbf{y}(k) - \mathbf{r}(k))$.
- φ is the output softness index defined by $|\mathbf{y}(k+1) - \mathbf{y}(k)|$.
- $\varepsilon(k)$ is the error defined by $|\mathbf{r}(k) - \mathbf{y}(k)|$.

- $\xi(k)$ is the augmented state vector.
- $\mathbf{w}(k)$ is the augmented state-input vector for the control law.
- $\hat{\mathbf{Q}}$ and $\mathbf{R}$ are the weighting matrices for quadratic error.
- $C_i, i = 1, \ldots, 6$ are weighting constants. C_4 y C_5 take 0 or 1 values wheather or not to include the quadratic error.

This description is valid only for SISO systems. The changes for MIMO systems (we consider just n inputs and outputs) are:

Softness index in vector $\mathbf{u}(k)$

$$\zeta = \max(\max(|u_i(k+1) - u_i(k)|),\ i = 1, \ldots, n) \quad (11)$$

Maximum overshoot

$$\vartheta = \max(\max(y_i(k) - r_i(k)),\ i = 1, \ldots, n) \quad (12)$$

Output softness index

$$\varphi = \max(\max(|y_i(k+1) - y_i(k)|),\ i = 1, \ldots, n) \quad (13)$$

Error

$$\varepsilon(k) = \max(\max(|r_i(k) - y_i(k)|),\ i = 1, \ldots, n) \quad (14)$$

The SA algorithm is based on the one used by (Martínez-Alfaro & Flugrad, 1994).

4. Experiments and Results

For SISO systems, many experiments were performed for regulator and tracking systems. In this work we present just the experiments with third order plants. Very similar experiments were performed with MIMO systems (regulator and tracking), but we only work with two-input-two-output plants.

4.1 SISO systems

4.1.1 Regulator

The following values for a third order system were:

$$\mathbf{G} = \begin{bmatrix} 0 & 0 & -0.25 \\ 1 & 0 & 0 \\ 0 & 1 & 0.5 \end{bmatrix}, \quad \mathbf{H} = \begin{bmatrix} 1 \\ 0 \\ 1 \end{bmatrix}, \quad \mathbf{Q} = \begin{bmatrix} 1 & 0 & 0 \\ 0 & 1 & 0 \\ 0 & 0 & 1 \end{bmatrix},$$

$$\mathbf{R} = 1, \quad \mathbf{x}(0) = \begin{bmatrix} -5 \\ 4.3 \\ -6.8 \end{bmatrix}$$

The SA algorithm parameters were: initial solution $= \mathbf{0}$, maximum perturbation $= 1$, initial temperature $= 100$, number of Markov chains $= 100$, percentage of acceptance $= 80$. The SA algorithm found a $J = 68.383218$ and LQ a $J = 68.367889$. Table 1 shows the gains.
Figure 1, presents the SA behavior. The states of both controllers performed similarly, Figure 3; but we can appreciate that exist a little difference between them, Figure 2.

	J	$\mathbf{K}$
LQ	$J = 68.367889$	$[-0.177028 \quad -0.298681 \quad -0.076100]$
SA	$J = 68.383218$	$[-0.193591 \quad -0.312924 \quad -0.014769]$

Table 1. Controller gains

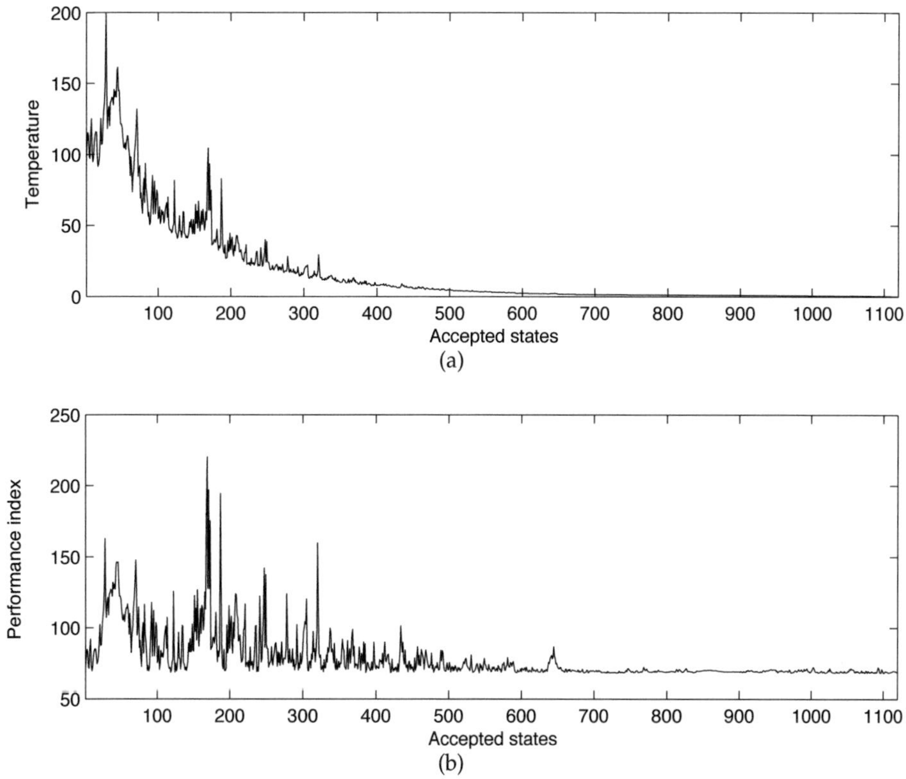

Fig. 1. Behavior of the SA algorithm

According to Section 3.2, the tracking system experiment is next with is $N = 100$.

$$\mathbf{G} = \begin{bmatrix} 0 & 1 & 0 \\ 0 & 0 & 1 \\ -.12 & -.01 & 1 \end{bmatrix}, \quad \mathbf{H} = \begin{bmatrix} 0 \\ 0 \\ 1 \end{bmatrix}, \quad \mathbf{C}^T = \begin{bmatrix} 0.5 \\ 1 \\ 0 \end{bmatrix},$$

$$\mathbf{Q} = \begin{bmatrix} 1 & 0 & 0 \\ 0 & 1 & 0 \\ 0 & 0 & 1 \end{bmatrix}, \quad \mathbf{R} = 10$$

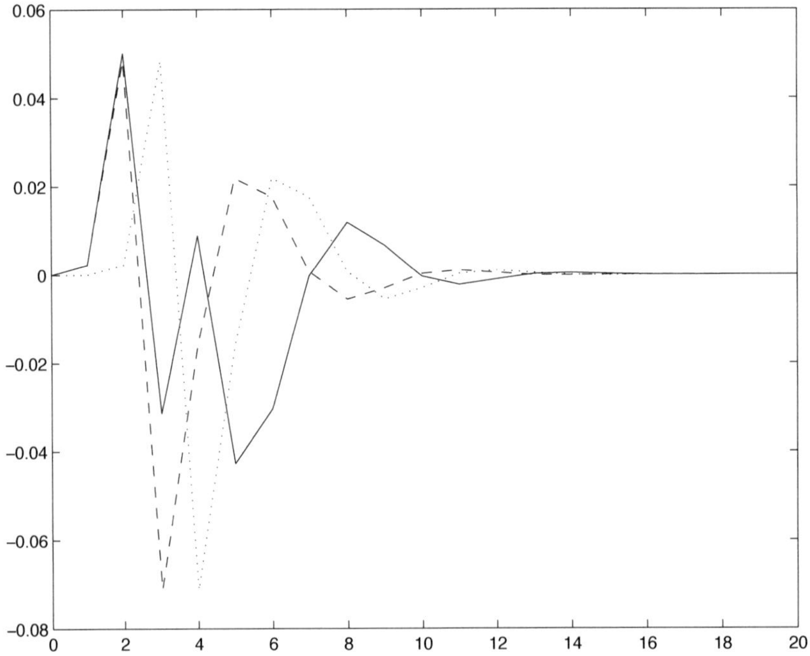

Fig. 2. Behavior of the state difference using LQ and SA.

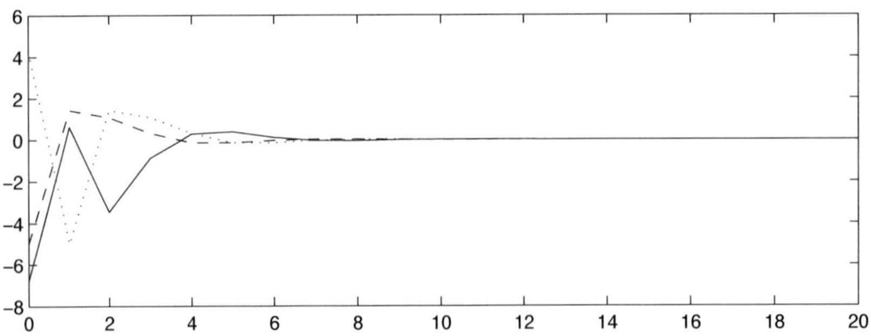

Fig. 3. Behavior of the states using LQ.

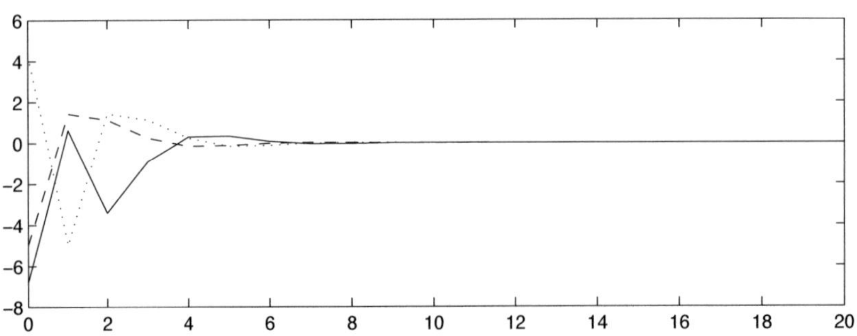

Fig. 4. Behavior of states using SA.

Yielding

$$\hat{\mathbf{G}} = \begin{bmatrix} 0 & 1 & 0 & 0 \\ 0 & 0 & 1 & 0 \\ -0.12 & -0.01 & 1 & 1 \\ 0 & 0 & 0 & 0 \end{bmatrix}, \quad \hat{\mathbf{H}} = \begin{bmatrix} 0 \\ 0 \\ 0 \\ 1 \end{bmatrix}$$

The SA algorithm parameters were: initial solution = 0, maximum perturbation = 0.01, initial temperature = 100, number of Markov chains = 100, percentage of acceptance = 80. LQ obtained a $J = 2.537522$ and SA a $J = 2.537810$. Although the indexes are very similar, gain matrices differ a little bit (shown in Table 2). Figure 6 shows the states and Figure 7the input.

	$\mathbf{K}_1$	$\mathbf{K}_2$
LQ	0.290169	$[-0.120000 \quad 0.063347 \quad 1.385170]$
SA	0.294318	$[-0.107662 \quad 0.052728 \quad 1.402107]$

Table 2. Controller gain

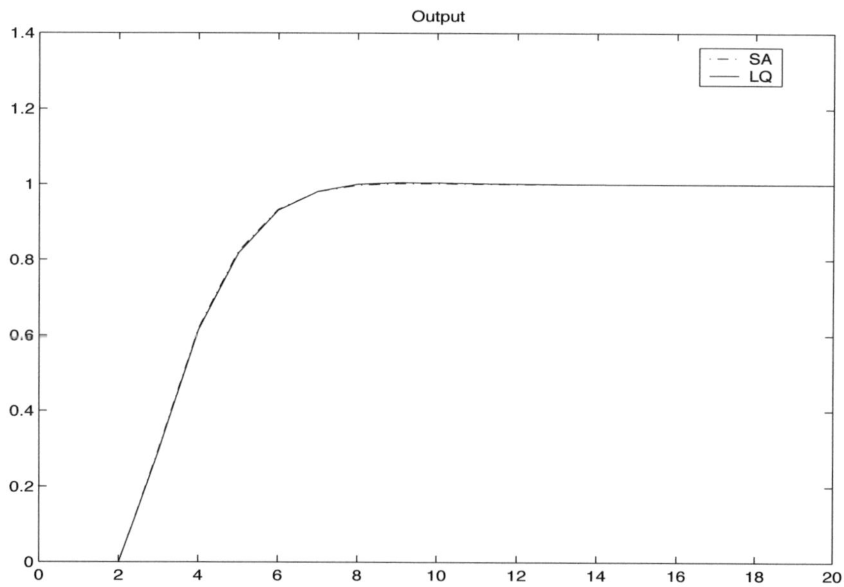

Fig. 5. Output

4.1.2 Tracking with non-conventional performance index

Several experiments were perform with type of index. This experiment was a third order plant, the same of previous section. The coefficient values for the performance index were: $C_1 = 10$, $C_2 = 10$, $C_3 = 20$, $C_4 = 1$, $C_5 = 1$, and $C_6 = 10$. The SA algorithm parameters were: initial solution = 0, maximum perturbation = 1, initial temperature = 100, number of Markov chains = 100, and the percentage of acceptance = 80. SA obtained a $J = 46.100502$, with $\mathbf{K}_1 = 0.383241$, and $\mathbf{K}_2 = [-0.108121,\ 0.189388,\ 1.424966]$. Figure 8 shows the response of the system and Figures 9 and 10 show the states and input, respectively.

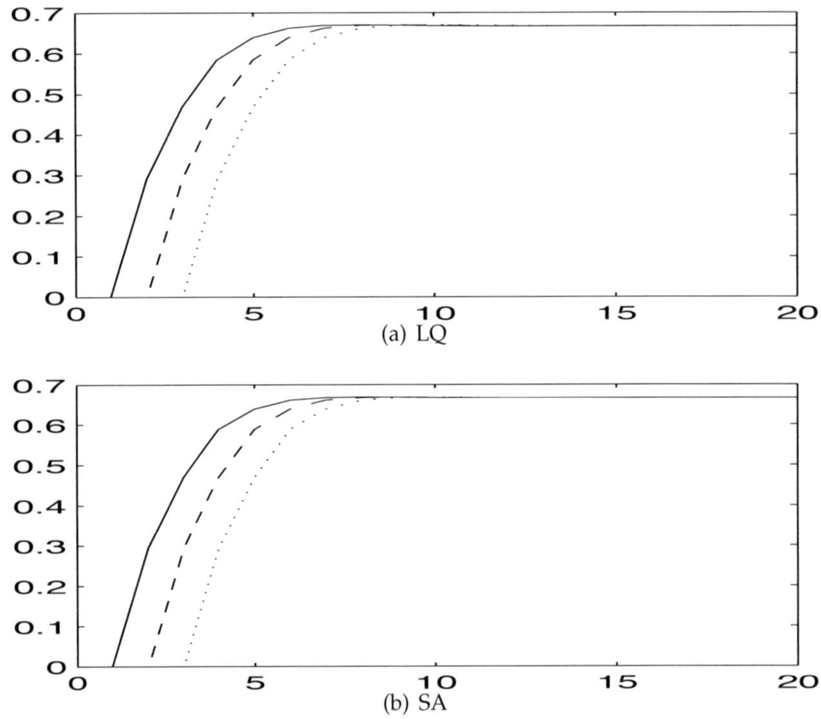

Fig. 6. States behavior

4.2 MIMO systems

4.2.1 Regulator

The system used was:

$$\mathbf{G} = \begin{bmatrix} 3.5 & 0.5 & 0.5 \\ 1 & 2.5 & 0 \\ 1.5 & -1 & 4 \end{bmatrix}, \quad \mathbf{H} = \begin{bmatrix} 1 & 0 & 0 \\ 0 & 1 & 0 \end{bmatrix}, \quad \mathbf{Q} = \begin{bmatrix} 1 & 0 & 0 \\ 0 & 1 & 0 \\ 0 & 0 & 1 \end{bmatrix},$$

$$\mathbf{R} = \begin{bmatrix} 1 & 0 \\ 0 & 1 \end{bmatrix}, \quad \mathbf{x}(0) = \begin{bmatrix} 5 \\ -1 \\ 3 \end{bmatrix}$$

The SA algorithm parameters were: initial solution = 0, maximum perturbation = 5, initial temperature = 100, number of Markov chains = 100, and percentage of acceptance = 80. LQ obtained a $J = 732.375702$ and SA a $J = 733.428460$. Gain matrices are very similar. Figure 11 shows the states.

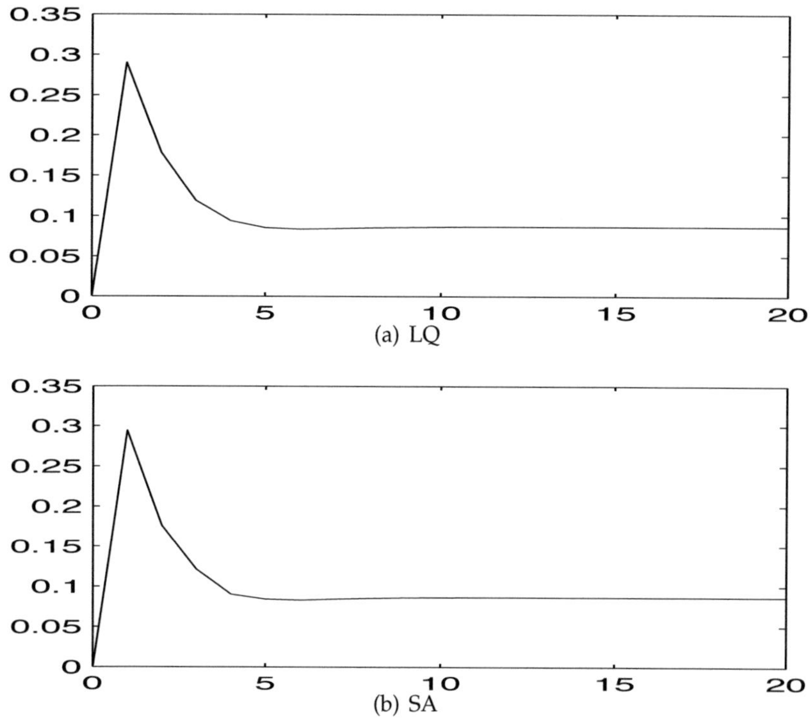

Fig. 7. Input behavior

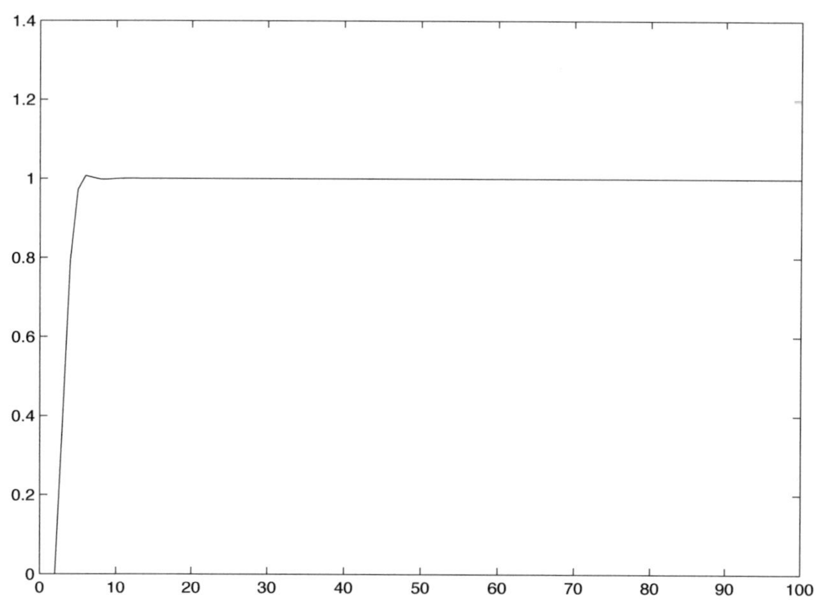

Fig. 8. Tracking with Non-conventional index: unit step response.

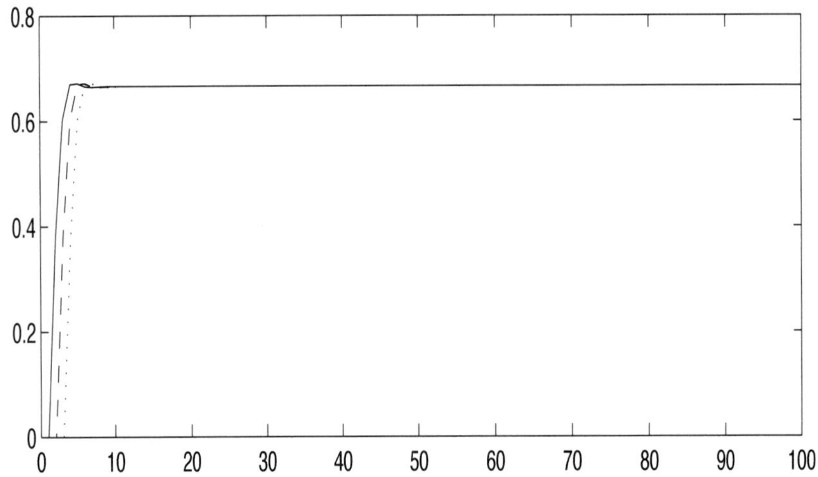

Fig. 9. Tracking with Non-conventional index: states behavior.

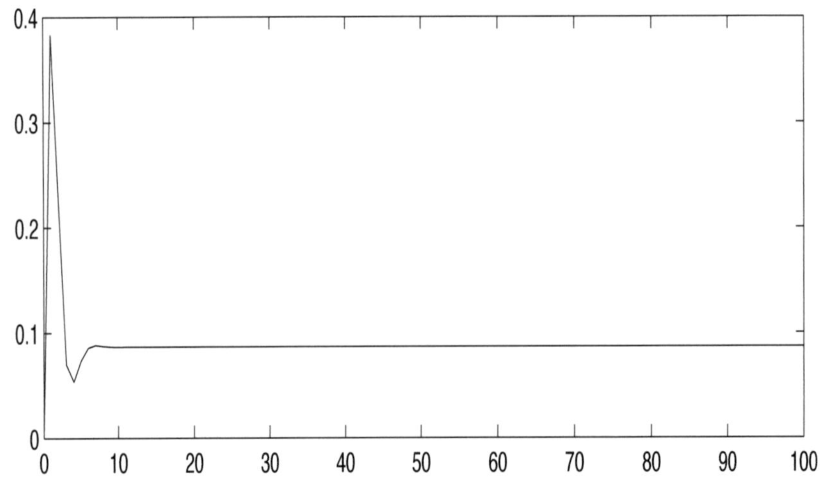

Fig. 10. Tracking with Non-conventional index: input behavior.

4.2.2 Tracking

The number of samples was 100.

$$\mathbf{G} = \begin{bmatrix} -\frac{1}{3} & 0 & 0 \\ 0 & \frac{1}{2} & 0 \\ 0 & 0 & \frac{1}{2} \end{bmatrix}, \quad \mathbf{H} = \begin{bmatrix} 2 & 3 \\ 1 & 0 \\ 0 & 1 \end{bmatrix}, \quad \mathbf{C}^T = \begin{bmatrix} 4 & -1 \\ 1 & 0 \\ 0 & 1 \end{bmatrix},$$

$$\mathbf{Q} = \begin{bmatrix} 1 & 0 & 0 \\ 0 & 1 & 0 \\ 0 & 0 & 1 \end{bmatrix}, \quad \mathbf{R} = \begin{bmatrix} 1 & 0 \\ 0 & 1 \end{bmatrix}$$

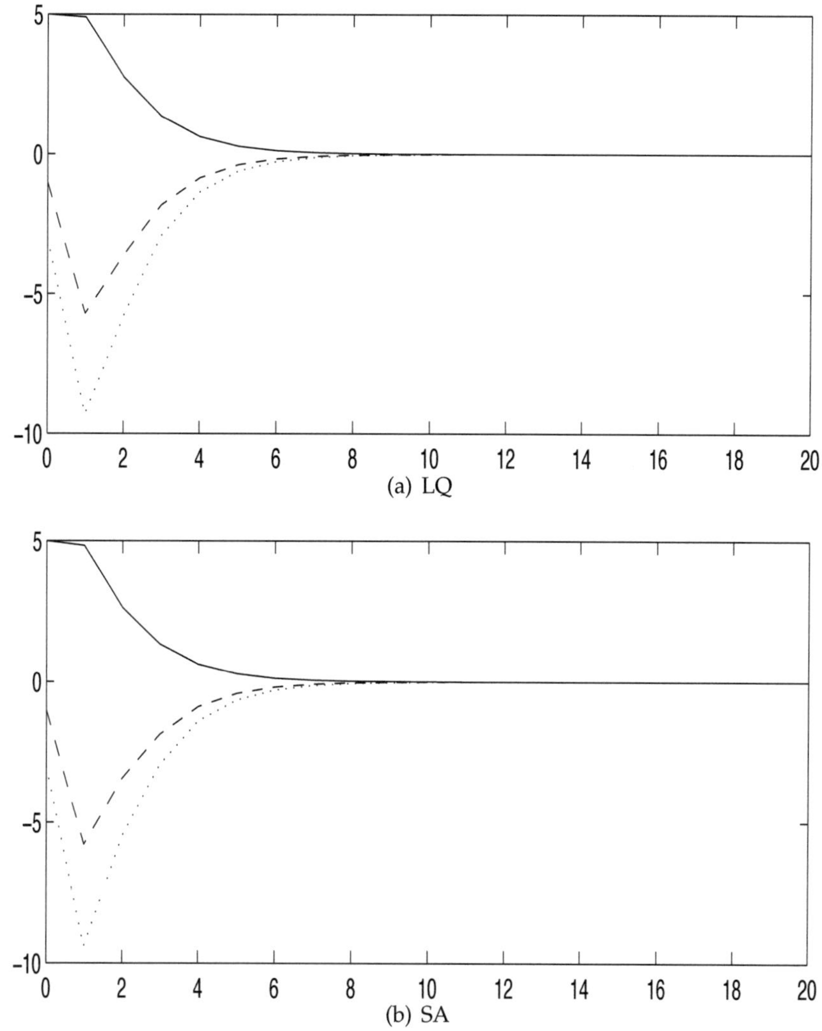

Fig. 11. MIMO Regulator system.

Converting the tracking system to regulator

$$\hat{\mathbf{G}} = \begin{bmatrix} -\frac{1}{3} & 0 & 0 & 2 & 3 \\ 0 & \frac{1}{2} & 0 & 1 & 0 \\ 0 & 0 & \frac{1}{2} & 0 & 1 \\ 0 & 0 & 0 & 0 & 0 \\ 0 & 0 & 0 & 0 & 0 \end{bmatrix}, \quad \hat{\mathbf{H}} = \begin{bmatrix} 0 & 0 \\ 0 & 0 \\ 0 & 0 \\ 1 & 0 \\ 0 & 1 \end{bmatrix}$$

The SA algorithm parameters were: initial solution $= \mathbf{0}$, maximum perturbation $= 0.02$, initial temperature $= 100$, number of Markov chains $= 100$, percentage of acceptance $= 80$. LQ obtained a $J = 6.132915$ and SA a $J = 6.134467$. The value entries obtained for the gain matrix differ a little bit from the ones obtained by SA; however, the performance indexes are very similar. Figure 12 shows the controller response.

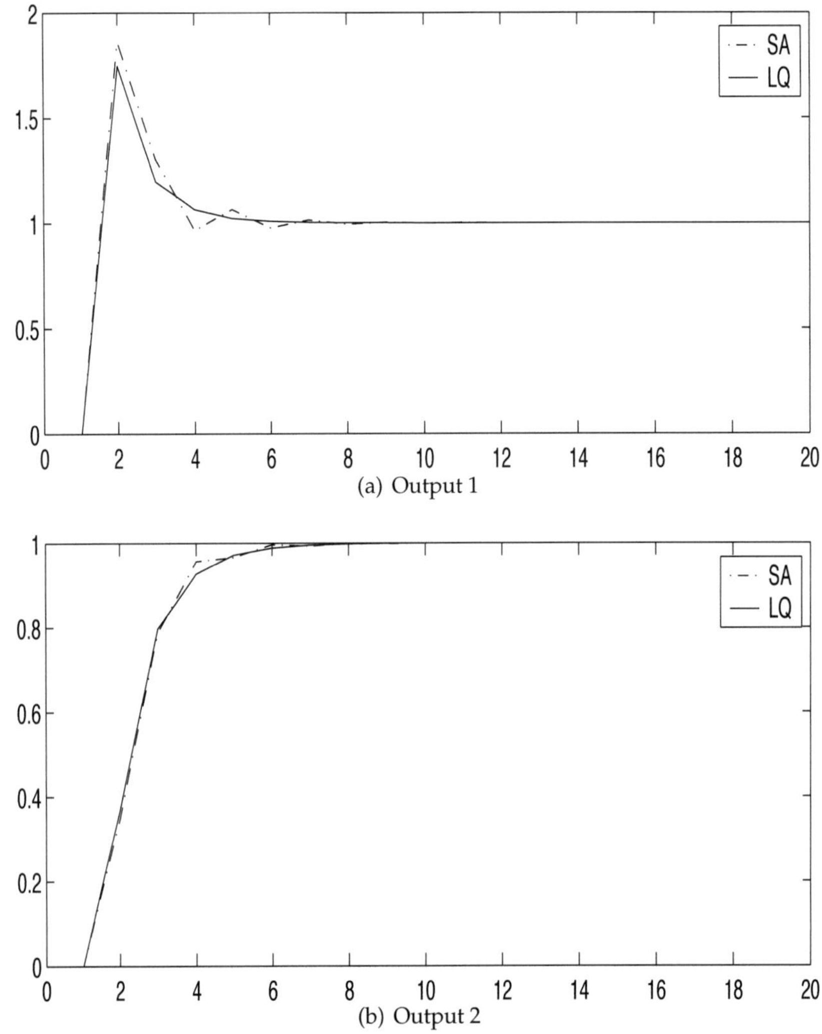

Fig. 12. MIMO tracking outputs.

4.2.3 Tracking with non-conventional performance index

Although several experiments were performed, only one is shown here. The plant used for this experiment is the same as in the previous example and the performance index is the same as the tracking for the SISO system example. The coefficient values were: $C_1 = 30$, $C_2 = 20$, $C_3 = 50$, $C_4 = 1$, $C_5 = 1$, and $C_6 = 30$. The SA algorithm parameters were: initial solution $= \mathbf{0}$, maximum perturbation $= 0.1$, initial temperature $= 100$, number of Markov chains=100, percentage of acceptance = 80. The results are:

$$J = 128.589993$$

$$\mathbf{K}_1 = \begin{bmatrix} -0.029799 & -0.874366 \\ 0.152552 & 0.560652 \end{bmatrix}$$

$$\mathbf{K}_2 = \begin{bmatrix} -0.279253 & 0.165710 & -0.398472 \\ -0.007700 & -0.132882 & 0.272621 \end{bmatrix}$$

The controller response is shown in Figure 13. The states are shown in Figure 14.

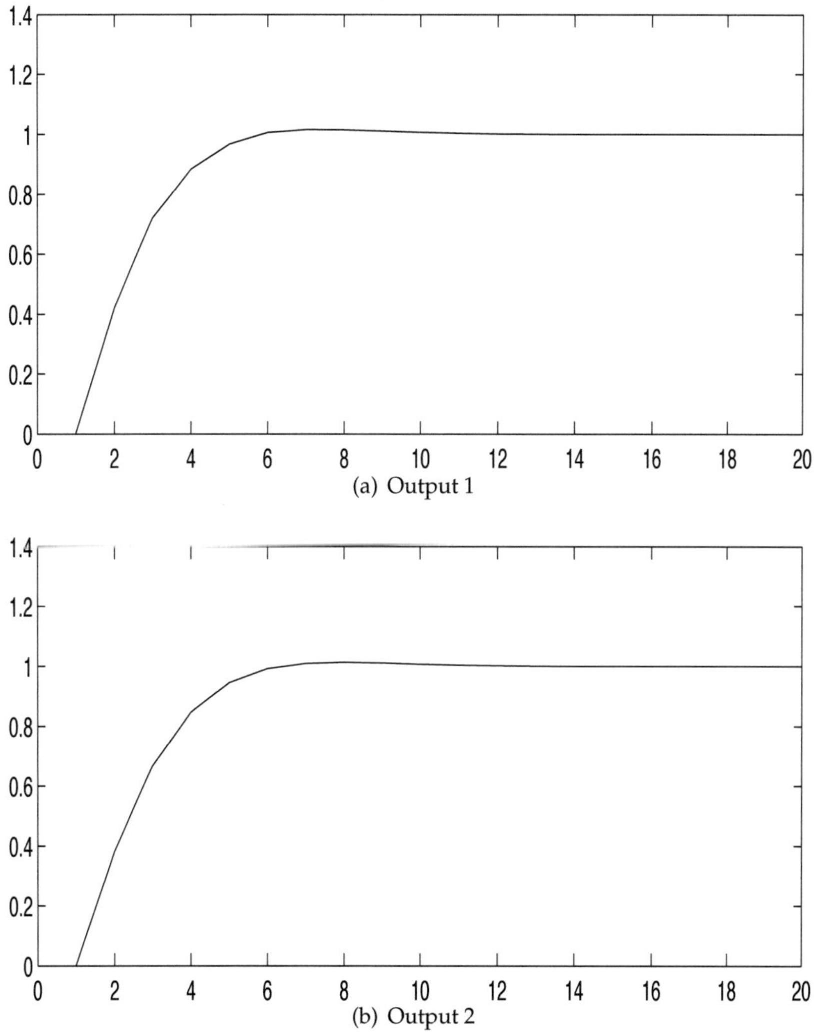

Fig. 13. MIMO tracking with non-conventional index.

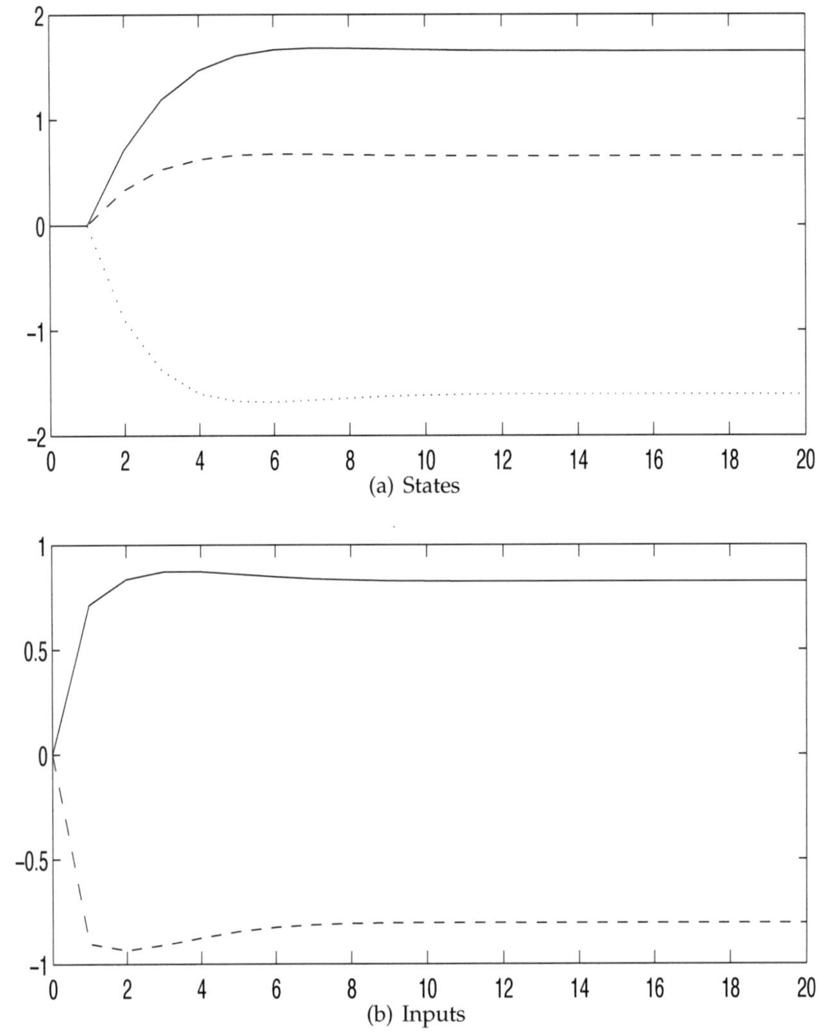

Fig. 14. MIMO tracking with non-conventional index: States and inputs behavior.

5. Conclusions

The results presented here, show that this kind of algorithms and the SA technique used work well. However, it is not possible to generalize the use of this scheme because the order of the models for the plants used were just first, second, and third. SA is an algorithm whose objective function must be adapted to the problem, and doing so (tuning), is where the use of heuristics is required. Through these heuristics, we can propose the values for the algorithm parameters that are suitable to find good solutions, but this is a long trial and error procedure. The CPU time that SA algorithm takes for finding a good solution is larger than the time we require to calculate LQ controller. But, in the case of tracking with non-conventional performance index, the method provided with SA algorithm works very well, and this is the main idea, to provide a good tool for discrete-time optimal control systems design.

6. References

Grimble, M. J. & Johnson, M. A. (1988). *Optimal Control And Stochastic Estimation: Theory and Applications, Volume 1*, John Wiley and Sons.

Malhorta, A., Oliver, J. H. & Tu, W. (1991). Synthesis of spatially and intrinsically, constrained curves using simulated annealing, *ASME Advances in Design Automation*.

Martínez-Alfaro, H. & Flugrad, D. (1994). Collision-free path planning of an object using B-splines and simulated annealing, *IEEE International Conference on Systems, Man, and Cybernetics*, IEEE International Conference on Systems, Man, and Cybernetics.

Martínez-Alfaro, H. & Ulloa-Pérez, A. (1996). Computing near optimal paths in C-space using simulated annealing, *ASME Design Engineering Technical Conference/Mechanisms Conference*.

Ogata, K. (1987). *Discrete-time Control Systems*, Prentice-Hall.

Ogata, K. (1995). *Sistemas de Control en Tiempo Discreto*, Pearson Educación.

Rutenbar, R. (1989). Simulated annealing algorithms: An overview, *IEEE Circuit and Devices* **JAN**: 19–26.

Salgado, M. E., Goodwin, G. C. & Graebe, S. F. (2001). *Control System Design*, Prentice-Hall.

Santina, M. S., Stubberud, A. R. & Hostetter, G. H. (1994). *Digital Control System Design*, Sanders College Publishing.

Steffanoni Palacios, J. A. (1998). *Diseño de sistemas de control óptimo en espacio de estado utilizando algoritmos genéticos*, Master's thesis, Tecnológico de Monterrey.

11

A simulated annealing band selection approach for high-dimensional remote sensing images

Yang-Lang Chang and Jyh-Perng Fang
Department of Electrical Engineering National Taipei University of Technology,Taipei Taiwan

1. Introduction

State-of-the-art sensors can make use of a growing number of spectral bands. Data initially developed in a few multispectral bands today can be collected from several hundred hyperspectral and even thousands of ultraspectral bands. This recent technology finds application in many domains, including satellite based geospatial technology, monitoring systems, medical imaging, and industrial product inspection. High-dimensional images provide large spectral information for subsequent data analysis. While images are continuously being acquired and archived, existing methods have proved inadequate for analyzing such large volumes of data. As a result, a vital demand exists for new concepts and techniques for treating high-dimensional datasets.

A common issue in hyperspectral image classification is how to improve class separability without incurring the curse of dimensionality Bellman (1961). This problem has occupied various research communities, including statistics, pattern recognition, and data mining. Researchers all describe the difficulties associated with the feasibility of distribution estimation. Accordingly, selecting the most valuable and meaningful information has become ever more important. Numerous techniques were developed for *feature extraction* and *band selection* to reduce dimensionality without loss of class separability for dealing with high-dimensional datasets Bruce et al. (2002); Jimenez & Landgrebe (1999); Jimenez-Rodriguez et al. (2007); Plaza et al. (2005); Tu et al. (1998); Wang & Chang (2006). The most widely used approach is the *principal components analysis* (PCA) which reorganizes the data coordinates in accordance with data variances so that features are extracted based on the magnitudes of their corresponding eigenvalues Richards & Jia (1999). Further *Fisher discriminant analysis* uses the between-class and within-class variances to extract desired features and reduce dimensionality Duda & Hart (1973). They focus on the estimation of statistics at full dimensionality to extract classification features. For example, conventional PCA assumes the covariances of different classes are the same. It treats the data as if it is a single distribution of different classes. The potential differences between class covariances are not explored.

In our previous work, a *greedy modular eigenspace* (GME) Chang, Han, Fan, Chen, Chen & Chang (2003) approach was proposed to solve this problem. The GME *band selection* (GMEBS) was developed by clustering highly correlated bands into a smaller subset based on the *greedy algorithm* and was proved to be a fast and effective method for *supervised-band-subset selection* (also named *feature selection*). It divides the data into different classes and overcomes the dependency on global statistics, while preserving the inherent separability of different classes. Most classifiers seek only one set of features that discriminates all classes simultaneously. This not only requires a large number of features, but also increases the complexity of the potential decision boundary. GMEBS method solves this problem and speeds up the feature extraction processes significantly. Although GMEBS can provide acceptable results for *feature selection* and *dimensionality reduction*, it consumes a large amount of computation to obtain a solution by a *greedy algorithm*. Unfortunately, it is also hard to find the optimal (maximum) or near-optimal (near-maximum) set by *greedy algorithm* except by exhaustive iteration. The long execution time of this exhaustive iteration has been the major drawback in practice. Accordingly, finding the optimal or near-optimal solution is very expensive.

Correspondingly, finding an efficient alternative has become necessary to overcome the above mentioned drawback of GMEBS. One consequence is the development of a technique known as *simulated annealing* (SA) Greene & Supowit (1984); Kirkpatrick et al. (1983) for feature extraction of high- dimensional datasets. Instead of adopting the band-subset-selection paradigm underlying the *greedy optimization* approach of GMEBS, we introduce *simulated annealing band selection* (SABS), which makes use of the *heuristic optimization algorithm* to collect the subsets of non-correlated bands for hyperspectral images to overcome this disadvantage. SA optimization has been widely adopted in fields such as electronics design automation Fang et al. (2004; 2006). The proposed SABS can readily select each band and sort different classes into the most common band subset. It can not only speed up the procedure to simultaneously select the most significant features according to the SA *optimization scheme*, but also make use of the hyperspatial characteristics embedded in GME features.

The performance of the proposed SABS is evaluated by fusing *MODIS/ASTER airborne simulator* (MASTER), a hyperspectral sensor, and airborne *synthetic aperture radar* (SAR) images for land cover classification during the Pacrim II campaign. Experimental results demonstrated that the proposed SABS approach is an effective method for dimensionality reduction and feature extraction. Compared to GMEBS, SABS can not only effectively group highly correlated bands, but also consume less resources. This chapter is organized as follows. In Section 2, the proposed SABS is described in detail. In Section 3, a set of experiments is conducted to demonstrate the feasibility and utility of the proposed SABS approach. Finally, in Section 4, some conclusions are outlined.

2. Methodology

2.1 Review of GMEBS

A visual *correlation matrix pseudo-color map* (CMPM) which was proposed by Lee & Landgrebe (1993) is used in Fig. 1 to emphasize the second-order statistics in hyperspectral data and to illustrate the magnitude of correlation matrices in the GMEBS method. Also shown in Fig. 1 is GME set $\mathbf{\Phi}^k$, $\mathbf{\Phi}^k = (\Phi_1^k, \ldots \Phi_l^k, \ldots \Phi_{n_k}^k)$, for class $\mathbf{W}_k$, which we previously proposed Chang, Han, Fan, Chen, Chen & Chang (2003); Chang et al. (2004). It illustrates the original CMPM and the reordered one after GMEBS. Each modular eigenspace Φ_l^k, subset of GME, includes a subset of highly correlated bands. Each ground cover type or material class has a distinct set

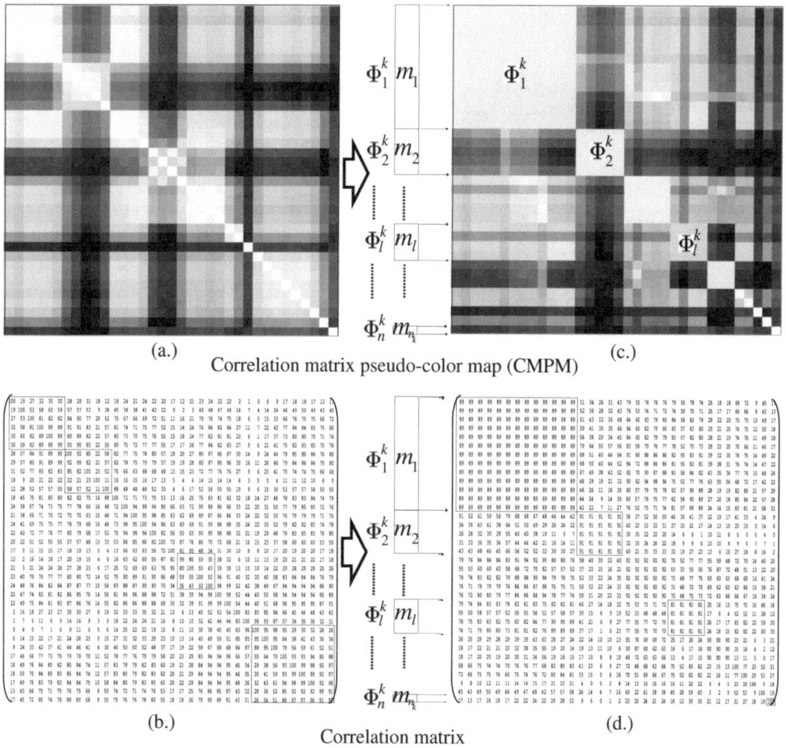

Fig. 1. An example illustrating (a) an original CMPM, (b) its corresponding correlation matrix for class k, (c) the GME set for class k, and (d) its corresponding correlation matrix after SA band selection.

of GME-generated *feature eigenspaces*.

GMEBS is a spectral-based technique that explores the correlation among bands. It utilizes the inherent separability of different classes in high-dimensional data to reduce dimensionality and formulate a unique GME feature. GMEBS performs a *greedy* iteration searching algorithm which reorders the correlation coefficients in the data correlation matrix row by row and column by column simultaneously, and groups highly correlated bands as GME *feature eigenspaces* that can be further used for *feature extraction* and *selection*. Reordering the bands in terms of wavelengths in high-dimensional data sets, without regard for the original order, is an important characteristic of GMEBS. Fig. 2 shows the graphical mechanism of GMEBS spectral band reordering. After finding GME sets $\mathbf{\Phi}^k$ for all classes $\mathbf{W}_k$, $k \in \{1, \ldots, N\}$, a fast and effective *feature scale uniformity transformation* (FSUT) Chang, Chen, Han, Fan, Chen & Chang (2003); Chang et al. (2004) is performed to unify the feature scales of these GME sets into an *identical* GME (IGME) set $\mathbf{\Phi}_I$. It uses *intersection* (AND) operations applied to the band numbers inside each GME module $\mathbf{W}_k$ to unify the feature scales of different classes. The concept block diagram of GMEBS is shown in Fig. 3 (a). Every different class has the same IGME set $\mathbf{\Phi}_I$ after GMEBS.

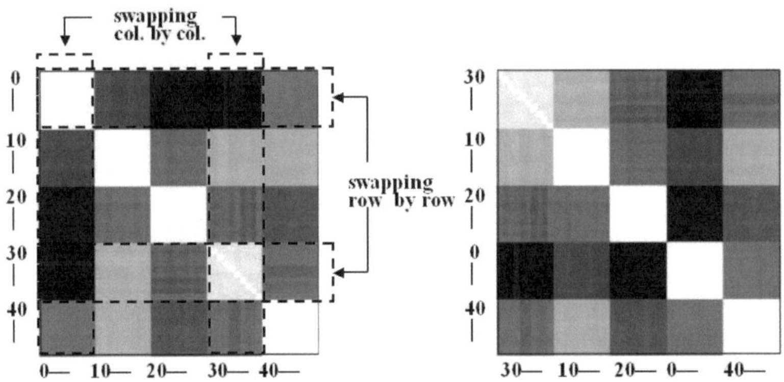

Fig. 2. The original CMPM (White=1 or -1; black=0) and the CMPM after reordering band Nos.0-9 and 30-39.

GMEBS defines a correlation submatrix $\mathbf{c}_{\Phi_l^k}[m_l][m_l]$ which belongs to the lth modular eigenspace (Φ_l^k) of GME $\mathbf{\Phi}^k$, $\mathbf{\Phi}^k = (\Phi_1^k, \ldots \Phi_l^k, \ldots \Phi_{n_k}^k)$, for a land cover class $\mathbf{W}_k$ in the dataset, where m_l and n_k respectively represent the number of bands (features) in the modular eigenspace Φ_l^k, and the total number of modular eigenspaces in the GME set $\mathbf{\Phi}^k$, i.e. $l \in \{1, \ldots, n_k\}$, as shown in Fig. 1. The original correlation matrix $\mathbf{c}_{X^k}[m_t][m_t]$, where m_t is the total number of original bands (i.e. $m_t = \sum_{l=1}^{n_k} m_l$), is decomposed into n_k correlation submatrices $\mathbf{c}_{\Phi_1^k}[m_1][m_1], \ldots \mathbf{c}_{\Phi_l^k}[m_l][m_l], \ldots \mathbf{c}_{\Phi_{n_k}^k}[m_{n_k}][m_{n_k}]$ to build the GME set $\mathbf{\Phi}^k$ for the class $\mathbf{W}_k$. There are $\frac{m_t!}{2}$ (a half factorial of m_t) possible combinations to construct a GME candidate $\mathbf{\Phi}^k$. It is computationally expensive to make an exhaustive search to find the optimal GME set $\mathbf{\Phi}^k$ if m_t is a large number. In order to find the near-optimal GME set $\mathbf{\Phi}^k$ of class $\mathbf{W}_k$, a *heuristic optimization algorithm* of SA-based band reordering algorithm is therefore applied to SABS method.

2.2 SABS

A common technique in metallurgy, SA denotes the slow-cooling melt behavior in the formation of hardened metals. Two decades ago scientists recognized the similarities between a simulated annealing process and a best-solution search for a combinatorial optimization problem Kirkpatrick et al. (1983). SA provides an *annealing schedule* that starts at an effective high temperature and gradually decreases until it slightly above zero. The *heuristic optimization algorithm* is performed in a nested loop fashion at various designated temperatures. Advantages of SA include escape from local minima at non-zero temperatures, early appearance of gross features of final state at highest temperatures, and emergence of some finer details at lower temperatures.

SABS collects GME sets $\mathbf{\Phi}^k$ from high-dimensional images of different classes simultaneously based on the *simulated annealing optimization algorithm*. Each modular eigenspace Φ_l^k includes a subset of highly correlated bands. SABS scheme has a number of merits. 1.) GMEBS tends to collect the bands into a subset with highly correlated covariance to avoid a potential bias

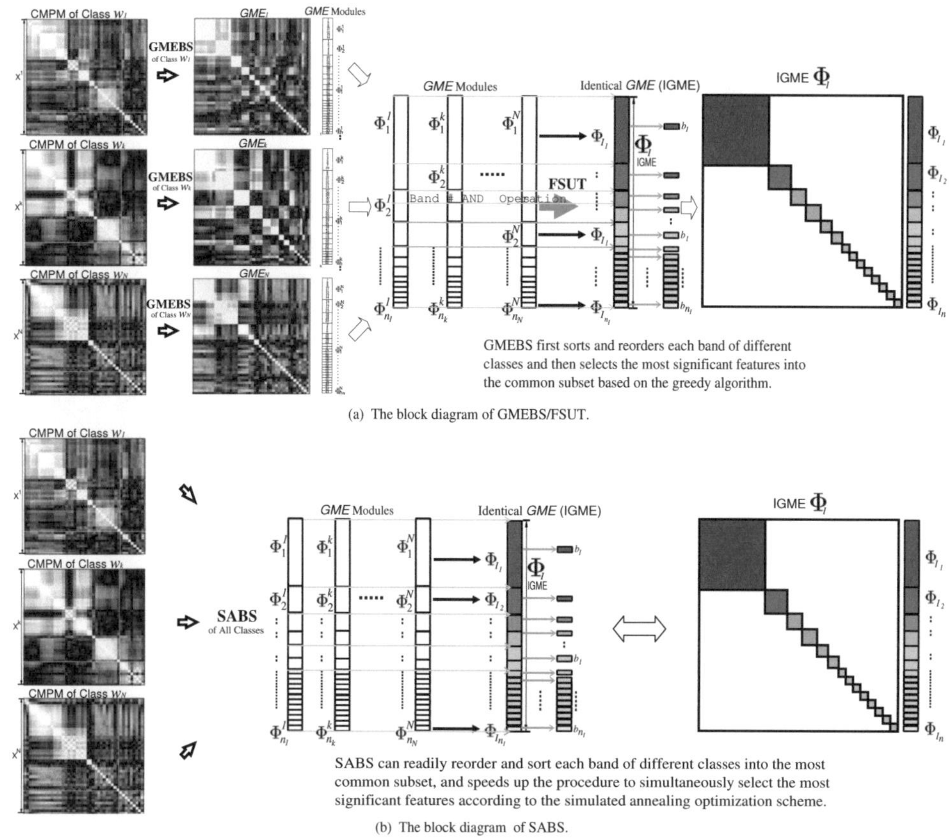

Fig. 3. An illustration of the differences between (a) FSUT/GMEBS and (b) the proposed SABS methods.

problem that may occur in PCA Jia & Richards (1999). 2.) Unlike traditional PCA, it avoids the bias problems that arise from transforming the information into linear combinations of bands. 3.) In addition, it can further extend the search and convergence abilities in the solution space based on *simulated annealing method* to reach the global optimal or near-optimal solution and escape from local minima. 4.) Finally, it takes advantage of the special characteristics of GME to readily reorder and sort each band of different classes into the most common feature subspaces according to the SA *optimization scheme*.

For each class $\mathbf{W}_k$, $k \in \{1, \ldots, N\}$, SABS performs SA-based iterations to build an IGME set $\mathbf{\Phi}_I^k$. Unlike GMEBS that first sorts and reorders each band of different classes based on the *greedy* algorithm and then selects the significant features IGME set $\mathbf{\Phi}_I^k$ by FSUT Chang, Chen, Han, Fan, Chen & Chang (2003); Chang et al. (2004), the proposed SABS can readily reorder and sort each band of different classes into the most common subset, and speeds up the procedure to simultaneously select IGME set $\mathbf{\Phi}_I^k$ based on SA *optimization scheme*. An illustration of the differences between GMEBS/FSUT and SABS methods is shown in Fig. 3. SABS collects the same band numbers located in each modular eigenspace Φ_l^k of all different classes

$\mathbf{W}_k$ ($k \in \{1, \ldots, N\}$) simultaneously.

The proposed SABS scheme is as follows:

1) Perturbation: SABS optimization algorithm is performed in two nested loops. They are Markov chains and temperature reduction cycles. After initialization, the cost can be produced by the permutation as shown in Fig. 4. Two bands associated with correlation matrix $\mathbf{c}_{X^k}[m_t][m_t]$ are randomly swapped (switched) for all classes, $\mathbf{W}_k$, $k \in \{1, \ldots, N\}$, where m_t is the total number of original bands for all of different classes $\mathbf{W}_k$, $k \in \{1, \ldots, N\}$, at the same time.

2) Cost function: After each perturbation, the cost is obtained by accumulating the *values of correlation coefficient* $VCC_{\Phi_l^k}[i][j]$ for the corresponding correlation submatrices $\mathbf{c}_{\Phi_1^k}[m_1][m_1]$, $\ldots \mathbf{c}_{\Phi_l^k}[m_l][m_l], \ldots \mathbf{c}_{\Phi_{n_k}^k}[m_{n_k}][m_{n_k}]$ of modular eigenspaces Φ_l^k, $i, j \in \{1, \ldots, m_l\}$, $l \in \{1, \ldots, n_k\}$ and $k \in \{1, \ldots, N\}$, as shown in Eq. 1,

$$cost = \frac{1}{\sum_{k=1}^{N} \sum_{l=1}^{n_k} \sum_{i=1}^{m_l} \sum_{j=1}^{m_l} |VCC_{\Phi_l^k}[i][j]|}, \tag{1}$$

where m_l and n_k represent the number of bands (feature spaces) in modular eigenspaces Φ_l^k, and the total number of modular eigenspaces of GME set Φ^k, $l \in \{1, \ldots, n_k\}$, respectively. $VCC_{\Phi_l^k}[i][j]$ is located at the ith row and the jth column of the lth correlation submatrix $\mathbf{c}_{\Phi_l^k}[m_l][m_l]$ for all of the class $\mathbf{W}_k$, $k \in \{1, \ldots, N\}$.

3) Annealing schedule: At the initial temperature T_0, the annealing starts with the original correlation matrix $\mathbf{c}_{X^k}[m_t][m_t]$ for all of the class $\mathbf{W}_k$, $k \in \{1, \ldots, N\}$. The temperature decreases steadily, $T_x = r^x T_0$, where $r = 0.85$ and $x = 1, 2, 3, \cdots$. Band-swapping is performed at each temperature K, where $5 \leq K \leq 10$. The *annealing process* terminates when number of accepted swapping is smaller (< 0.05) or temperature is low enough.

The operations of proposed SA band swapping algorithm is shown in Fig. 4, wherein P, ε, r, K are parameters for tuning the SA band swapping algorithm. T_0, reported in Line 2, is an initial temperature and Δavg is an average of cost change after a sequence of random band swapping. Parameter P is chosen such that $P = e^{-\Delta avg/T_0} \approx 1$ and consequently enables a higher probability of accepting *uphill* at high temperatures. The rest of the parameters are given empirically. Parameter ε is the terminated temperature, r is the decreasing rate of temperature, and K is used to control the counts of perturbation at each temperature. The *Markov chain MT* is determined by parameter K and the problem size N. The variables *uphill*, and *reject* are used to control the numbers of perturbation at each temperature. In addition, both variables are used to observe the performance of proposed SABS and consequently to help constructing an effective *annealing schedule.*

In the pseudo code, *Random* shown in Line 8 is a floating number generated from a random function, which ranges between 0 and 1. The probabilities of going *uphill* (paying higher costs) decrease as temperatures fall in *the annealing schedule*, which is controlled by the Boltzmann factor $e^{-\Delta cost/T}$. At each temperature, the band swappings (perturbations) are repeated until either there are n downhill perturbations or the total number of perturbations exceeds 2n

```
SA_Band_Swapping Algorithm (P, ε, r, K)
CM ← original correlation matrix;
Best ← CM;  T ← Δavg / log(P); MT ← uphill ← 0;  n ← KN;
repeat - // Temperature reduction cycles
  MT ← uphill ← reject ← 0;
  repeat - // Markov chains
     New_CM ← band_swapping(CM);
     MT ← MT + 1;  Δcost ← cost(New_CM) - cost(CM);
     if (Δcost ≤ 0) or (Random < e^(-Δcost/T)) then
        if (Δcost > 0) then uphill ← uphill + 1;
        CM ← New_CM;
        if cost(CM) < cost(Best) then Best ← CM;
     else reject ← reject + 1;
   until (uphill > n) or (MT > 2n);
   T ← rT;
until (reject / MT > 0.95) or (T < ε);
```

Fig. 4. SA band swapping algorithm.

where n is the number of spectral bands. The annealing process is terminated either when the number of accepted perturbations is less than 5% of all perturbations occurring at a certain temperature or when the temperature is low enough.

The basic components for the SA algorithm include solution space, neighborhood structure, cost function, and annealing schedule. To solve an optimization problem using SA, proper arrangement of these components is necessary. The solution space is defined by all possible combinations of swapping rows and columns in the original CMPM spaces. The modular eigenspace Φ_l^k is constructed by randomly swapping two bands among the associated correlation matrices of different classes. SABS makes use of the SA cost function to constrain the values of *correlation coefficients VCCs* within a threshold range of 0.70 to 0.92. The cost function is obtained by accumulating the $VCCs$ inside the modular eigenspaces Φ_l^k of different classes.

Eventually, an IGME set $\mathbf{\Phi}_I$ is composed. For convenience, we sort these IGME feature modules Φ_{I_l}, where $l \in \{1, \ldots, n_I\}$, according to the number of their feature bands, i.e. the number of feature spaces in descending order. Each IGME feature module Φ_{I_l} has a unique band set inside a modular eigenspace Φ_l^k box as illustrated in Fig. 3. Compared to the GMEBS/FSUT, the proposed SABS can not only speed up the computation by taking into account the IGME feature module Φ_{I_l} of different classes at the same time, but also improve the features extracted from the most common GME $\mathbf{\Phi}^k$ of different classes simultaneously. Furthermore, SABS provides a quick procedure for band selection to find the most significant hyperspectral features compared to GMEBS and the other conventional feature extraction methods.

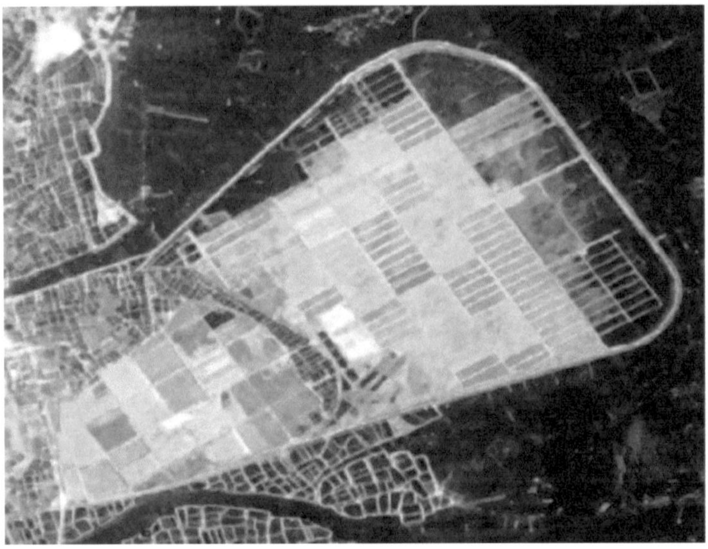

Fig. 5. The map of the Au-Ku test site used in the experiment.

3. Experimental Results

A plantation area in Au-Ku on the east coast of Taiwan as shown in Fig. 5 was chosen for investigation. The image data was obtained by the MASTER and SAR instrument as part of the PacRim II project Hook et al. (2000). A ground survey was made of the selected six land cover types at the same time. The proposed SABS was applied to 35 bands selected from the 50 contiguous bands (excluding the low signal-to-noise ratio mid-infrared channels) of MASTER Hook et al. (2000) and nine components of AIRSAR. Nine components in the polarimetric SAR covariance matrix are preprocessed Lee et al. (1999). Six land cover classes, sugar cane A, sugar cane B, seawater, pond, bare soil and rice ($N = 6$) are used in the experiment. The *k-nearest neighbor* (KNN) classifier was used to test the effectiveness of SABS. The criterion for calculating the classification accuracy of experiments was based on exhaustive test cases. One hundred and fifty labeled samples were randomly collected from ground survey datasets by iterating every fifth sample interval for each class. Thirty labeled samples were chosen as training samples, while the rest were used as test samples, i.e. the samples were partitioned into 30 (20%) training and 120 (80%) test samples ($M = 120$) for each test case. Eighteen correlation coefficient thresholds, $VCCs = 0.70 \sim 0.92$ with a offset of 0.01, were selected to carry out the experiments.

The parameters used for SABS are initialized as follows. The probability to accept higher cost is decreased following the decreased temperature, and the decreasing rate of temperature is 0.95, the terminating temperature is 100 Celsius degree (^oC), while the factor deciding the number of perturbation at a specified temperature is 20. We examined the effectiveness and robustness of the SABS with initial temperatures differentiating from 100,000Ű900,000 degrees Celsius. Finally, all of the multiple combinations of parameters stated above are averaged to obtain the experimental results. Table 1 summarizes the evaluation of classification accuracy under a different initial temperature to illustrate the validity of these unique properties of

Initial temperature	offset (%) 50	60	70	80	90
10000	99.67%	91.28%	100.00%	90.84%	100.00%
30000	93.31%	100.00%	99.84%	91.00%	94.68%
50000	100.00%	92.93%	100.00%	92.38%	99.89%
70000	100.00%	100.00%	89.80%	92.38%	99.78%
90000	95.45%	99.40%	89.42%	100.00%	91.01%

Table 1. Summary evaluation of classification accuracy for SABS scheme.

proposed SABS method. These encouraging results showed that satisfactory classification accuracy could be achieved with only a few computational time and small training samples.

Interestingly, two comparisons of both *dimensionality reduction rate* (DRR) and *variance of classification accuracy* (VCA) according to different $VCCs$ are also illustrated. The DRR and VCA are used to validate the performances of the proposed SABS as shown defined in Eq. 2 and Eq. 4 respectively.

$$DRR = \frac{m_t - n_k}{m_t} \times 100\%, \tag{2}$$

where m_t and n_k represent the total number of original bands (i.e. $m_t = \sum_{l=1}^{n_k} m_l$), and the total number of modular eigenspaces in the GME set $\mathbf{\Phi}^k$ respectively Chang, Han, Fan, Chen, Chen & Chang (2003).

$$VCA = \frac{\sum_{i=1}^{n}(Acc_i - \mu_i)^2}{n}, \tag{3}$$

where n represents the number of times to arbitrarily choose three bands respectively from the three larger SABS modular eigenspace Φ_l^k for the classification operations. Acc_i is the corresponding classification accuracy of the above operations. The mean μ is equal to $\frac{\sum_{i=1}^{n} Acc_i}{n}$.

Fig. 6 summarizes the evaluation results that have the same *costs*, namely *quality of solutions*, to illustrate the validity of proposed SABS. The criteria for the SABS performance evaluations in Fig. 6 (a.) and (b.) are based on different experimental benchmarks with the same *quality of solution*. Furthermore, an evaluation of classification efficiency ($CE = \xi$),

$$\xi = \frac{DRR}{VCA}, \tag{4}$$

as shown in Fig. 7, is also designed to validate the contributions of proposed SABS. The results appearing in Fig. 7 show that an *efficient critical point* around $VCC = 0.91$ can be reached to obtain a high DRR accompanied with a low VCA impact when SABS is applied to the high-dimensional datasets.

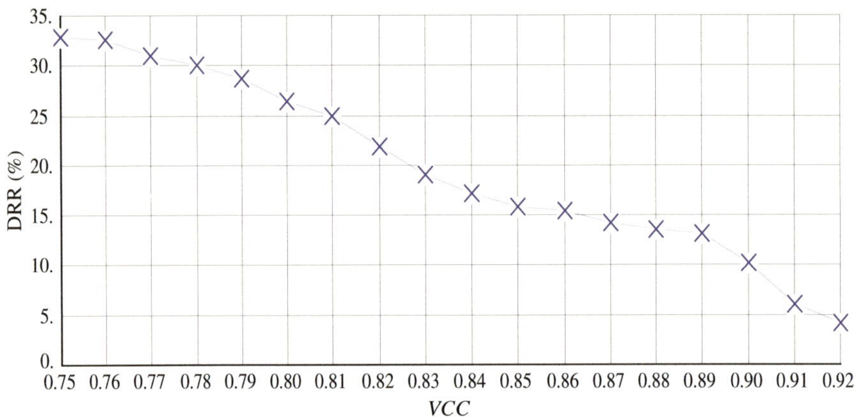

(a). SABS DRR comparison

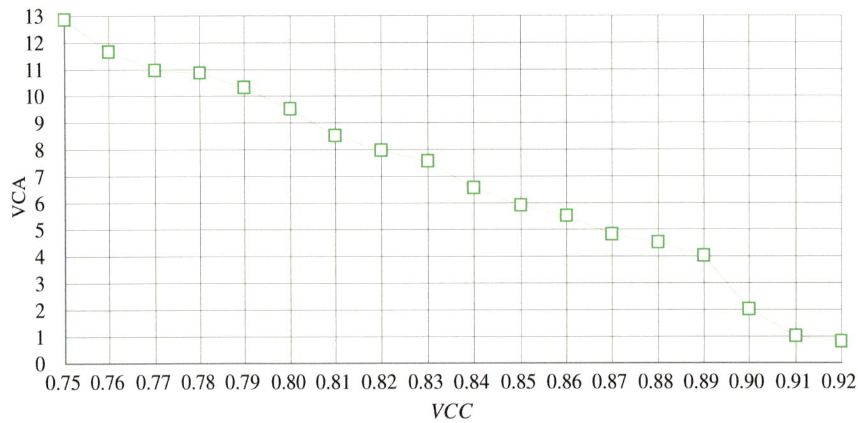

(b). SABS VCA comparison

Fig. 6. Two SABS performance comparisons of (a.) DRR and (b.) VCA with different thresholds of VCCs.

4. Conclusions

This chapter presents a novel SABS technique for *feature selection* and *dimensionality reduction* of hyperspectral and SAR images. Reordering the bands regardless of the original order in terms of wavelengths in high-dimensional datasets is an important characteristic of SABS. It is proposed to overcome the drawback of GMEBS which has a long execution time during the exhaustive iteration to obtain a solution by the *greedy algorithm*. By adopting the band-subset-selection paradigm underlying the *heuristic optimization algorithm*, the proposed SABS can not only readily find the most significant GME subsets, but also further extend the search abilities in the solution space to reach the global optimal or near-optimal solution and escape from local minima based on *simulated annealing method*.

Encouraging experimental results showed that the feature bands selected by SABS algorithm from high-dimensional remote sensing images contain robust discriminatory properties cru-

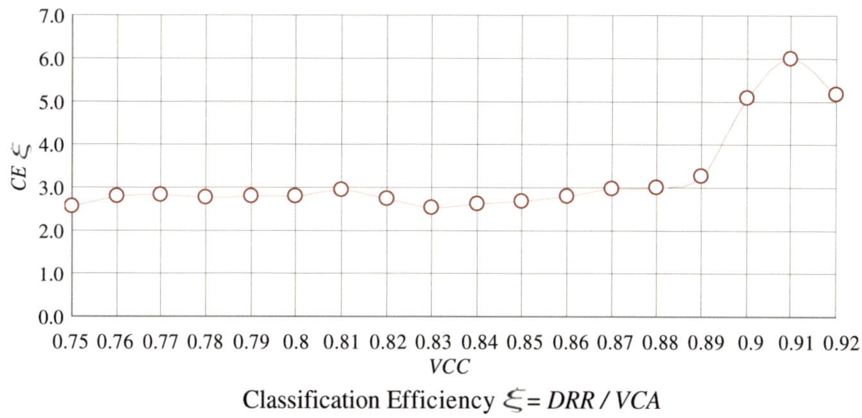

Fig. 7. The SABS classification efficiency comparison with different thresholds of VCCs.

cial to subsequent classification. They make use of the potential significant separability embedded in GME to select a unique set of most important feature bands in high-dimensional datasets. The experimental results also demonstrated that the proposed SABS can significantly improve the computational loads and provide a more reliable quality of solution compared to the GMEBS method. The proposed evaluation of $CE(\xi)$ provides an objective criterion to determine a suitable and appropriate value of VCC, and to obtain a high quality DRR accompanied with a lower VCA impact. Besides the subjects discussed in this chapter, how to find the best tradeoff among the global search, accuracy, and computational cost will be the issues of our future studies.

Acknowledgment

This work was supported by the National Science Council, Taiwan, under Grant Nos. NSC 98-2116-M-027-002 and NSC 99-2116-M-027-003, and Ministry of Economic Affairs, Taiwan, under Grant No. 98-EC-17-A-02-S2-0021.

5. References

Bellman, R. E. (1961). *Adaptive Control Processes: A Guided Tour*, Princeton University Press, New Jersey, NJ.

Bruce, L. M., Koger, C. H. & Li, J. (2002). Dimensionality reduction of hyperspectral data using discrete wavelet transform feature extraction, *IEEE Trans. Geosci. Remote Sensing* **40, Issue: 10**: 2331–2338.

Chang, Y. L., Chen, C. T., Han, C. C., Fan, K. C., Chen, K. S. & Chang, J. H. (2003). Hyperspectral and sar imagery data fusion with positive boolean function, Vol. 5093 of *Proc. SPIE*, pp. 765–776.

Chang, Y. L., Han, C. C., Fan, K. C., Chen, K. S., Chen, C. T. & Chang, J. H. (2003). Greedy modular eigenspaces and positive boolean function for supervised hyperspectral image classification, *Optical Engineering* **42, no. 9**: 2576–2587.

Chang, Y. L., Han, C. C., Ren, H., Chen, C.-T., Chen, K. S. & Fan, K. C. (2004). Data fusion of hyperspectral and sar images, *Optical Engineering* **43, no. 8**: 1787–1797.

Duda, R. & Hart, P. (1973). *Pattern Classification and Scene Analysis*, John Wiley & Sons, New York.

Fang, J. P., Tong, Y. S. & Chen, S. J. (2004). Simultaneous routing and buffering in floorplan design, Vol. 151, no. 1 of *IEE Proc. Computers and Digital Techniques*, pp. 17–22.

Fang, J. P., Tong, Y. S. & Chen, S. J. (2006). An enhanced bsa for floorplanning, *IEICE Trans. Fundamentals* **E89-A, no. 2**: 528–534.

Greene, J. & Supowit, K. (1984). Simulated annealing without rejected moves, Proc. Int'l Conf. on Computer Designs, pp. 658–663.

Hook, S. J., Myers, J. J., Thome, K. J., Fitzgerald, M. & Kahle, A. B. (2000). The modis/aster airborne simulator (master) - a new instrument for earth science studies, *Remote Sensing of Environment* **76, Issue 1**: 93–102.

Jia, X. & Richards, J. A. (1999). Segmented principal components transformation for efficient hyperspectral remote-sensing image display and classification, *IEEE Trans. Geosci. Remote Sensing* **37, no. 1**: 538–542.

Jimenez, L. O. & Landgrebe, D. A. (1999). Hyperspectral data analysis and supervised feature reduction via projection pursuit, *IEEE Trans. Geosci. Remote Sensing* **37, Issue: 6**: 2653–2667.

Jimenez-Rodriguez, L. O., Arzuaga-Cruz, E. & Velez-Reyes, M. (2007). Unsupervised linear feature-extraction methods and their effects in the classification of high-dimensional data, *IEEE Trans. Geosci. Remote Sensing* **45, Issue: 2**: 469–483.

Kirkpatrick, S., Gelatt, C. D. & Vecchi, M. P. (1983). Optimization by simulated annealing, *Science* **220, no. 4598**: 671–680.

Lee, C. & Landgrebe, D. A. (1993). Analyzing high-dimensional multispectral data, *IEEE Trans. Geosci. Remote Sensing* **31, no. 4**: 792–800.

Lee, J. S., Grunes, M. R., Ainsworth, T. L., Du, L. J., Schuler, D. L. & Cloude, S. R. (1999). Unsupervised classification using polarimetric decomposition and the complex wishart classifier, *IEEE Trans. Geosci. Remote Sensing* **37, no. 5**: 2249–2258.

Plaza, A., Martinez, P., Plaza, J. & Perez, R. (2005). Dimensionality reduction and classification of hyperspectral image data using sequences of extended morphological transformations, *IEEE Trans. Geosci. Remote Sensing* **43, Issue: 3**: 466–479.

Richards, J. A. & Jia, X. (1999). *Remote Sensing Digital Image Analysis, An Introduction, 3rd ed.*, Springer-Verlag, New York.

Tu, T.-M., Chen, C.-H., Wu, J.-L. & Chang, C.-I. (1998). A fast two-stage classification method for high-dimensional remote sensing data, *IEEE Trans. Geosci. Remote Sensing* **36, Issue: 1**: 182–191.

Wang, J. & Chang, C.-I. (2006). Independent component analysis-based dimensionality reduction with applications in hyperspectral image analysis, *IEEE Trans. Geosci. Remote Sensing* **44, Issue: 6**: 1586–1600.

12

Importance of the initial conditions and the time schedule in the Simulated Annealing

K. Shojaee[1], H. Shakouri G[2] and M. Behnam Taghadosi[3]

A Mushy State SA for TSP

Abstract

It is a long time that the Simulated Annealing (SA) procedure is introduced as a non-derivative based optimization for solving NP-hard problems. Improvements from the original algorithm in the recent decade mostly concentrate on combining its initial algorithm with some heuristic methods. This is while modifications are rarely happened to the initial condition selection methods from which the annealing schedules starts or the time schedule itself. There are several parameters in the process of annealing the adjustment of which affects the overall performance. This paper focuses on the initial temperature and proposes a lower temperature with low energy to speed up the process, while using an auxiliary memory to buffer the best solution. Such an annealing indeed starts from a mushy state rather than a quite liquid molten material. The mushy state characteristics depends on the problem that SA is being applied to solve. In this paper the Mushy State Simulated Annealing (MSSA) is applied to the Traveling Salesman Problem (TSP). The mushy state may be obtained by some simple methods like crossover elimination. A very fast version of a Wise Traveling Salesman, who starts from a randomly chosen city and seeks for the nearest one as the next, is also applied to initiate SA by a low-energy-low-temperature state. This fast method results in quite accurate solutions compared to other recent novel methods.

Keywords
Combinatorial Optimization, Traveling Salesman, Initial Condition

---

[1] Low-Power High-Performance Nanosystems Laboratory, School of Electrical and Computer Engineering, University of Tehran, Tehran, Iran (email:k.shojaee@ece.ut.ac.ir)
[2] Industrial Engineering Department, University of Tehran, Tehran, Iran (email: hshakouri@ut.ac.ir)
[3] Mechatronics Laboratory (LIM) , politecnico di Torino, Torino, Italy (email:mojtaba.behnam@polito.it)

1. Introduction

Simulated Annealing (SA) is one of the earliest methods for derivative-free optimization such as Tabu Search (TS) [1]. Although it was introduced first to solve combinatorial discrete problems [2], it has recently shown a high attitude for solution of continuous problems as well [3]-[5]. SA is derived from physical behaviour of molten metals when the temperature is slowly falling to form a regular crystalline solid structure. There are two key parameters in the cooling process that determine how firm or amorphous will be the result for the metal in its frozen state. The first one is the initial temperature from which the cooling starts; and the second is the rate by which the temperature is falling.

Concerning the rate of decay, it should be low enough to allow the atoms in the molten metal to line them up and give enough time to form a crystal lattice with the minimum internal energy.

Evidently, a slow decay will lead to a long time for the solidifying process. To reduce the time, one may think of a low initial temperature. However, on the other hand, if the initial temperature is not high enough, atoms of the molten metal would not have enough freedom to rearrange their positions in a very regular minimum energy structure.

Although there are some theoretical limits and formulations to choose a proper cooling rate [6]-[22], there is not any deterministic criterion to set the initial pseudo-temperature in the literature. For instance, applying SA to the travelling salesman problem (TSP), one may set it to 0.5 and change by 10% at each step [9], while some other prefer 1000 reducing by a factor of 0.99, i.e. 1% [10]. Moreover, the concept is a case dependent one and even may not fit to a bounded range, e.g. in some articles it is even initialized in a range from 0.001 to 100 [11].

There are a few research papers that suggest a formulation to relate the initial temperature to particular characteristics of the problem. Pao et al. considered an initial temperature such that the initial acceptance rate is about 70% [12]. Feng-Tse Lin, et al. proposed an Annealing-Genetic approach and use the following formula [13]:

$T_0 = \Delta E$ / (Population Size/2),

where ΔE is the difference between the highest cost and the lowest cost found for the first generation of the randomly generated population.

Thompson and Bilbro set the initial temperature by defining a probability function for energy change in continuous problems. The probability of accepting a higher cost solution was set to 0.75. Then, the following probability distribution is solved to find T_0 [14]:

$p = \exp(\Delta E / T)$,

where ΔE is the average cost of the random solutions plus its standard deviation.

Hao Chen et al. set the initial temperature such that the initial acceptance probability for an average uphill move is 0.97 [15].

Although SA algorithms are conceptually simple, finding optimal parameters such as initial temperature, the annealing schedule, the acceptance function parameters, etc., is by no means simple or straightforward. First of all, setting parameters for SA is problem dependent, and it is best accomplished through trial and error. Furthermore, many studies have demonstrated that SA algorithms are very sensitive to parameters, and their performances are largely dependent on fine tuning of the parameters [16]. The problem dependent nature of setting parameters for SA and its sensitivity to parameters limit the effectiveness and robustness of SA algorithms. SA possesses a formal proof of convergence to the global optima. This convergence proof relies on a very slow cooling schedule of setting the initial condition to a sufficiently large temperature and let it decay by $T_k = T_0$ /

log(*k*), where *k* is bound by the number of iterations[17]. While this cooling schedule is impractical, it identifies a useful trade-off where longer cooling schedules tend to lead to better quality solutions.

Also, the stochastic simulated annealing (SSA) [7] tends to find a global optimum if the annealing process is carried out sufficiently slowly. It means that SSA is able to find high-quality solutions (global optima or near-global-optima), if the temperature is reduced exponentially but with a sufficiently small exponent. For many applications, this may mean prohibitively long relaxation time in order to find solutions of acceptable quality, and conversely, reasonably long periods of time may still result in poor solutions. Lipo Wang et al. have used chaotic neural networks to be combined with the best features of SSA and have shown the effectiveness of this new stochastic chaotic simulated annealing (SCSA) [18]. However there is not any especial idea on the initializing or the cooling schedule in this approach. Before, Yuyao He had applied a chaotic noise to a Hopfield neural network and had set the annealing process such that the chaotic noise gradually reduced. Hence, it was initially chaotic but eventually convergent, and, thus, had shown richer and more flexible dynamics [19].

In brief, we observe that there is a trade off between choosing a high initial temperature or choosing a low rate of cooling, and gaining a short processing time or finding the minimum energy structure.

Exactly similar to such a trade off exists when applying SA to any optimization problem such as TSP. Assuming the objective function of an optimization problem to be an energy function, and the initial guesses for the unknown variables to be the initial problem, the above mentioned trade off appears as shown by the following notation:

Initial temperature $\uparrow$	$\Rightarrow$ Optimization time $\uparrow$
Initial temperature $\downarrow$	$\Rightarrow$ Final energy $\uparrow$ (Local minima)
Rate of cooling $\uparrow$	$\Rightarrow$ Final energy $\uparrow$ (Local minima)
Rate of cooling $\downarrow$	$\Rightarrow$ Optimization time $\uparrow$

It is easy to deduce that selection of a proper set of optimization parameters for SA itself is a multi-objective decision making (optimization) problem. In this paper we have discussed the first one, i.e. the initial temperature, and propose an approach to speed up the algorithm while obtaining accurate solutions for the chosen case study, which is TSP.

It is usual to select a very high temperature that provides a suitable initial condition with enough mobility for the atoms to move freely to new locations faraway enough in order to form as possible as minimum-energy structures. A certain criterion is to set it large enough that almost any trial point (state) will be acceptable.

This may cause the SA process to experiment new accepted points with even higher energy states. As the temperature decays, the probability to accept states that do not reduce the energy decreases.

Since the cooling process that starts from a high temperature in a liquid-like state is a time consuming, this paper proposes to start annealing from a state in a lower temperature with a lower internal energy. Such a state may be called a mushy state, rather than a liquid state. In such reduced temperatures with low energy, the ratio of acceptable states to the total trials may be less than 10%, compared to that of usual high temperatures.

After that the state is set to a lower energy state in a lower initial temperature, the annealing process can bring us the benefit of a faster local search and find the optimal state with the minimum energy. Starting from a very high temperature the metal should be cooled slowly, otherwise the atoms do not have time to orient themselves into a regular structure, but if the initial state is imposed to the atoms in a low energy low temperature, we can adjust the cooling rate to be faster.

Perhaps there are many optimization methods, even direct (random search methods) that can be applied as a prelude for SA. A simple algorithm that is used in this paper is to eliminate all intersecting paths in an initially selected random tour. A second simple method is also applied to show independence of the proposed method to the method that the initial tour is found.

The paper is organized in six sections. After this section we will have short introductions to both the SA and the TSP in sections 2 and 3. Section 4 describes how we chose the initial conditions and how schedule the annealing. The results obtained applying the proposed method are given in section 5, where we have compared the best, the worst and the average error in the final solution (if available) with some recent works. Finally, section 6 concludes the paper.

2. A short overview on the SA

Rather than giving a detailed description of SA, herein the fundamental terminology of SA is explained shortly [8][21]. The method consists of four main parts.

2.1 Objective function

An objective function $f(.)$ is a mapping from an input vector x into a scalar E:

$$E = f(x), \tag{1}$$

where each x is assumed as a point in an input space. The SA is to sample the input space effectively to find an x that minimizes E. The input vector may be the structure of the atoms and/or their movements limited to that structure, and E may be the internal energy of the metal. In TSP, x is the tour sequence and E is the total cost (distance) of travelling.

2.2 Generating function

A generating function $g(.,\ .)$ specifies the probability density function of the difference between the current point and the next point to be visited. Specifically, Δx (= $x_{new} - x$) is a random variable with probability density function $g(\Delta x, T)$, where T is the pseudo-temperature. If E is the internal energy of the metal, T is the real temperature, however, in TSP can be interpreted as percentage of the new points that can reduce the total cost. Clearly, if the number of intersecting paths in a tour x is high, we can assume that the pseudo-temperature is high. Usually $g(.,\ .)$ is independent of the temperature. However, in conventional SA, also known as Boltzmann machines, the generating function is a Gaussian probability density function:

$$g(\Delta x, T) = (2\pi T)^{-n/2} \exp[-|\Delta x|^2 /(2T)], \tag{2}$$

where n is the dimension of the space under exploration. The fatter tail of the Cauchy distribution gives the chance to explore new points in the space farther from the current point while searching the space.

For discrete or combinatorial optimization problems, like TSP, each x is not necessarily an n-vector with unconstrained values. Instead, each x is restricted to be one of N points that comprise the solution space or the input space. Usually N is very large but finite such that reduces probability of a time consuming search without any result. Since, adding randomly generated Δx to a current point x may not generate another legal point in the solution space, instead of using generating functions , *a move set* is usually defined to find the next legal point, denoted by $M(x)$. This creates the set of legal points available for exploration after x. Usually the move set, $M(x)$, is chosen in the sense that the objective function at any point of the move set, i.e. a set of *neighbouring* points $x+\Delta x$, will not differ too much from the objective function at x. The definition of the move set is problem dependent. For TSP there are at least three kinds of move sets that are defined and used by researchers: *Inversion*, *Translation*, and *Switching* [21]. An especial variant of inversion is the simple idea of *Crossover elimination*.

Once the move set is defined, x_{new} is usually selected at random from the move set, such that all neighbouring points have an equal probability of being chosen. In this paper, we have fixed the move set to the inversion, which has shown better performance compared to the others.

2.3 Acceptance function

After that the objective is evaluated for a new point x_{new}, SA decides whether to accept or reject it based on the value of an acceptance function $h(.,.)$. The most frequently used acceptance function is the *Boltzmann probability distribution*:

$$h(\Delta E, T) = \frac{1}{1 + \exp(\Delta E/(cT))} \tag{3}$$

where c is a constant, T is the temperature, and ΔE is the energy difference between x_{new} and x:

$$\Delta E = f(x_{new}) - f(x) \tag{4}$$

Usually x_{new} is accepted with probability $h(\Delta E, T)$. If ΔE is negative, SA tends to accept the new point to reduce the energy. Nevertheless, if ΔE is positive SA may also accept the new point and move to a higher energy state. It means, SA can move uphill or downhill; but the lower the temperature, the less likely to accept any significant upward change.

There are several alternatives for the acceptance function. A simple alternative with approximately the same behaviour is:

$$h(\Delta E, T) = \exp(-\frac{\Delta E}{cT}) \tag{5}$$

where there is no need to check for the sign of ΔE. Instead, if $h(\Delta E, T)$ is greater than a uniformly distributed random number, the new point is accepted. A deterministic alternative method is to use *Threshold Accepting*, where x_{new} is accepted just if $\Delta E<T$ [22].

2.4 Annealing schedule

An annealing or cooling schedule regulates how rapidly the temperature T goes from high to low values, as a function of time or iteration counts. There are not so many works discussing the initial temperature selection or even the cooling schedule. Indeed, the exact interpretation of *high* and *low* and the specification of a good annealing schedule require certain problem-specific physical insight and/or trial-and-error. The easiest way of setting an annealing schedule is to decrease the temperature T by a certain percentage at the kth iteration:

$$T_{k+1} = a\, T_k \tag{6}$$

where $0 < a < 1$ is an adjusting parameter. It is proved that a *Boltzmann machine* using the aforementioned generating function can find a global optimum of $f(x)$ if the temperature T is reduced not faster than T_0 / $\log(k)$ [17]. Researchers have used various cooling strategies, among which we choose the following:

$$T_{k+1}=T_k/\log(k^{1/D}), \tag{7}$$

where D is set to two.

3. The Traveling Salesman Problem (TSP)

The Travelling Salesman Problem (TSP) seems to be the most well-known typical NP-hard problem. Given a set of nodes and a set of weights specifying cost to travel between each two nodes, the optimal solution is to find a closed loop of the paths with minimal total weights in a finite complete graph.

Lets denote the set of "cities" in TSP as $C = \{c_1 , c_2 ,..., c_n\}$ in company with a matrix D_T an element of which is called d_{ij} that gives the distance or cost function (weight) for going from t_i, to t_j. In real problems, usually the coordinates of the cities are given, by which the matrix D_T can be easily computed.

The path linking the two cities here is called a "link". A sequence of cities $C^* = [c_{s1}, c_{s2}, \ldots, c_{sn}]$ denotes a legal solution of TSP (the salesman must visit each city once and only once), where $\{s_1, s_2, ..., s_n\}$ is a sequence of $\{1, ..., n\}$. Then the Travelling Salesman Problem's optimal goal can be expressed as minimizing the following objective function that can be interpreted as energy function:

$$E(C) = d_{s_1 s_n} + \sum_{i=1}^{n-1} d_{s_i s_{i+1}} \;. \tag{8}$$

where $C = [s_1, s_2, ..., s_n]$ is the travelling tour. If all the costs between any two cities are equal in both directions, i.e. D_T is a symmetric matrix, the problem is called symmetric TSP; otherwise, it is called asymmetric [23].

Sometimes D_T is calculated based on the coordinates of the cities that may generate real numbers. Normally d_{ij}'s are rounded to integer numbers to standardize the results according to the standard code proposed in [23]. Generation of the distance matrix, D_T, given the coordinates is a straight forward procedure. However, the reverse process is not possible for all cases.

Suppose the coordinates are given by two vectors namely X and Y. There are $2n$ elements in the vectors X and Y, while a symmetric D_T contains $\frac{1}{2}\, n \times (n - 1)$ elements. Each equation can be written as:

$$(x_i - x_j)^2 + (y_i - y_j)^2 = d_{ij}^2;\ i = 1, \ldots, n;\ j = i + 1, \ldots, n - 1; \qquad (9)$$

where xi , yi , xj and yj are the ith and jth elements in X and Y respectively. Therefore, solution of $n\ (n - 1)/2$ nonlinear equations available from D_T to find the $2n$ unknown coordinates in X and Y requires:

$2n \leq \frac{1}{2}\, n \times (n - 1)$,

or equivalently:

$n \geq 5$.

Thus, there will not be a unique solution for cases with more than 5 cities. However, a feasible solution will suffice to apply the above modification to all cases with $n \geq 5$. Note that the nonlinear equations should be solved just once to find the feasible solution for the coordinates X and Y. It is obvious that for an asymmetric D_T there is no solution without any extra information.

4. Initializing and annealing schedule

As mentioned, there are not many articles talking about the initial condition when the annealing process starts. The main idea proposed in this paper is originated from the behaviour of the metal during the annealing process. The cooling schedule is an exponential shape function of the time that can be divided into three parts. The first part is a rapidly decaying curve with a high slope in average and the last one is the ending part of the exponential function with almost frozen state. The first part should be passed as fast as possible, while complying the lower bound on the rate of cooling. And the last part has almost no significant effect on the final result. Therefore, none of these two states are of interest in this paper. The initial temperature is proposed to be selected within the middle of the curve, as shown typically in Fig. 1.

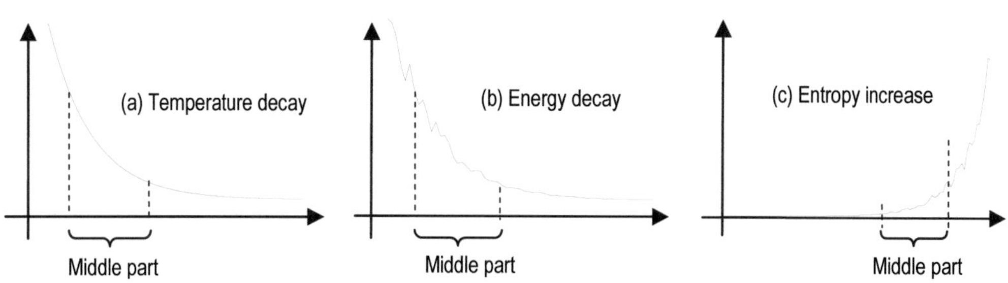

(a) Temperature decay, (b) Energy decay, (c) Entropy increase

Fig. 1. Typical behaviour of an annealing schedule; the mushy state falls in the middle;

To assign a proxy for the temperature, we may use a ratio named γ defined as follows:
γ = the ratio of accepted new points to the total trials.
If the ratio is high, it means that the internal energy is high enough that many of motions by the atoms in a way that reduce the energy are possible. The ratio should be close to one, say 90%. Conversely, if the ratio is low, say 10%, the metal is nearby to become frozen; there are not so many new structures that reduce the energy. We propose to start annealing from such an initial condition in the middle zone, i.e. a mushy or doughty state, rather than liquid or firm states.

4.1 Initiating temperature and energy

We have applied two different methods to initialize both the temperature and energy in the mushy state. The first one is a simple algorithm for crossover elimination and the second one is an efficient fast simple method derived from a rough behaviour of a Wise Travelling Salesman (WTS), who seeks for the next nearest city. The following subsections describe the two methods.

4.1.1 Crossover Elimination

In the special case of TSP, knowing that the optimal tour will not contain any intersection of the paths, a simple fast algorithm of intersection detection and elimination is applied. Starting from a randomly generated initial tour, every couple of links with crossover should be deleted and replace by swapping the two links. Figure 2 easily illustrates this idea.
To do so, without lacking generality, let's continue describing the algorithm for the case that the input data is given in terms of the co-ordinates. Based on this assumption, we assume that the co-ordinates are arranged in two vectors named X and Y. Now, let's assume that the initial random tour is named C_0. This vector is a sequence of the city indexes:

$$C_0 = [1, \ldots, c_i, c_{i+1}, \ldots, c_j, c_{j+1}, \ldots].$$

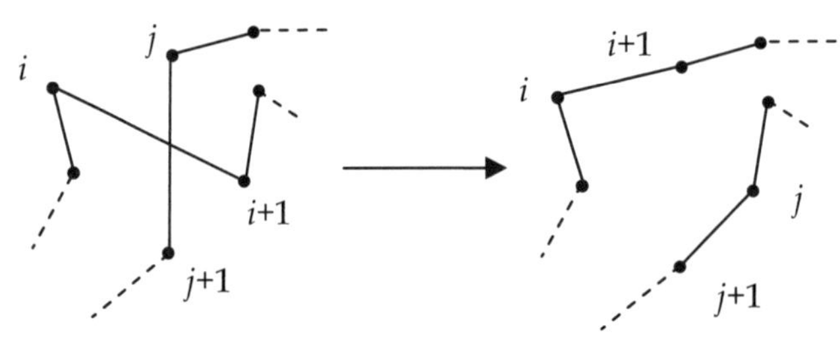

(a) Tour C_n (b) Tour C_m

Fig. 2. Intersected Links Elimination

Suppose the subscripts of the elements of the sequence be the same shown in Fig. 2. Therefore, the line equations for all links of the tour can be calculated, by which it is possible to check that if each of the two paths are intersected or not. We need to solve $\frac{1}{2} n \times (n - 3)$ linear equations, where any valid solution should be in range of the coordinates X and Y, subsequently requiring:

$$x_{\min} < x_c < x_{\max}$$

$$y_{\min} < y_c < y_{\max}$$

where, x_c and y_c are coordinates of the intersection point of each pair of links with non-common ends, and x_{min}, x_{max}, y_{min} and y_{max} are the minimum and maximum coordinates found on the two links. Note that checking one of the above two conditions suffices to ensure intersection occurrence. Then, if there is a cross over, like in Fig. 2 (a), the sequence should be modified to generate T_m as follows:

$$C_m = [1, \ldots, c_i, c_j, \ldots, c_{i+1}, c_{j+1}, \ldots].$$

which is shown in Fig. 2 (b). It means that the $(i+1)^{th}$ element should be exchanged with the jth element. Then it is clear that the total cost will be reduced, i.e.:

$$E(C_m) < E(C_0).$$

Once that crossover occurrence is checked $\frac{1}{2}\, n \times (n - 3)$ times for a tour and resolved by swapping the links, there may be new intersections generated. Therefore, the algorithm is iterated until no crossover is found in the final tour.

The algorithm is summarized in the following:

(a) Generate an initial tour randomly;
(b) Check for intersection of each path with all other non-neighbouring paths;
(c) If there is a crossover, remove it by swapping the paths;
(d) Repeat steps (b) and (c) until there is no crossover in the tour.

4.1.2 The Wise Traveling Salesman (WTS)

The basis thought beyond this algorithm is the way that a normal wise person may roughly decide on its next destination at each current position. For the first time that a normal human starts his/her travel, he/she may guess that a good path perhaps can continue from the nearest city. Indeed, at each step, the next city to travel is chosen among the nearest cities to the current city. Besides this original idea, one may apply a random walk process to let the traveler experience new experiments while using his/her wisdom to choose its next destination. It means that he/she examines other paths in the next experimental tour by changing some of the cities in the sequence randomly. Finally, he/she will give a weighting for his/her previously experienced tours in the next travel. However, in this paper we have not applied these two factors for initializing the SA. Thus, the simplest version of this method can be summarized in the following steps:

(a) Select the starting city randomly;
(b) Compute the cost from the current city to all unvisited cities in a vector;
(c) Sort the resulting vector elements and choose the next city with the less cost;
(d) After completing the tour, calculate the total cost (distance).

This way, the initial energy, and consequently the initial temperature when starting SA, will be much lower than what is usual.

4.2 Annealing schedule

The proposed method also includes modifications to the annealing schedule to compensate side effects of shortening the annealing process. The first modification is to repeat generation of new points at each temperature until the acceptance is A_{Max}. The maximum iterations, sometimes called the Markov chain length, is initially considered such that $A_{Max} = 100 \times n$, where n is number of the cities in TSP. Since acceptance probability exponentially decreases, at each temperature we may reduce A_{Max} by a constant ratio, say 0.9. However, in

very low temperatures the acceptance probability is very low and there should be a criterion to agree that it is the freezing temperature. In this research, if the total iterations at each temperature, i.e. the Markov chain length, exceed $A_{Max} \times n$, we stop the annealing process and call the current temperature as the freezing point.
Furthermore, in a normal SA, if the optimum solution is lost once that the algorithm faces an uphill acceptance there is enough opportunity to recover it in the future steps. When starting the annealing from low temperatures the expected time to find the global optima is shorter. Therefore, the first modification is a memory of the latest minimum energy solution found during all steps passed in the annealing. The best tour found is saved and inserted once to the process at each temperature to be compared with the current situation. This will resolve the probability of missing the best previously obtained solution.
This way the annealing process is summarized to the following steps:

(a) Employing a simple locally optimizing algorithm, set the initial temperature to a mushy state temperature, where the acceptance ratio, γ, is about 10%;
(b) Set maximum acceptance to $A_{Max} = 100 \times n$;
(c) Start annealing as usual, while:
    i. Changing A_{Max} to $0.9 \times A_{Max}$;
    ii. Saving the best solution found up to now;
    iii. Inserting the best solution to each Markov chain;
(d) Stop annealing if the current Markov chain length is greater than $A_{Max} \times n$.

5. The Results

The proposed initializing method, so called Mushy State Simulated Annealing (MSSA), is applied to many benchmarks listed in TSPLIB [23]. MSSA is run 40 times: 20 runs with an initial condition obtained by crossover elimination and 20 runs initialized by WTS. The initial conditions, i.e. the initial pseudo-temperature and the initial energy are case dependent parameters. As mentioned in Section 4, we used the ratio of accepted motions (new points), which are found based on an acceptance function like (5), to the total number of tried motions (γ). If this ratio tends to zero, the case is in its solid state, and if it is very high (near 1), then it is in the liquid state.
Figure 3 shows relation between the pseudo-temperature and the acceptance-trial ratio for the case of **eli51**. It is seen that in high temperatures the ratio saturates to about 1, and in low temperatures the case has reached to its solid state with the minimum energy. Therefore, the best initial condition to start annealing is a temperature close to the melting point or the take off point in the curve, which is about the pseudo-temperature of 30 in this case.
The results for cases with below 1432 cities are given below in Table 1, through which it will be easy to realize that the method has improved SA significantly. The optimal values given by the TSBLIB site, for each case are listed in the second column of the table. We have compared the best, the worst and the average of the error in the results obtained by the new approach with other results given by recent novel works (if the best and/or the worst cases are available). The error percentage is calculated by:
$\delta = 100\,(E - E^*) / E^*$
where E^* is the optimal (minimum) energy.

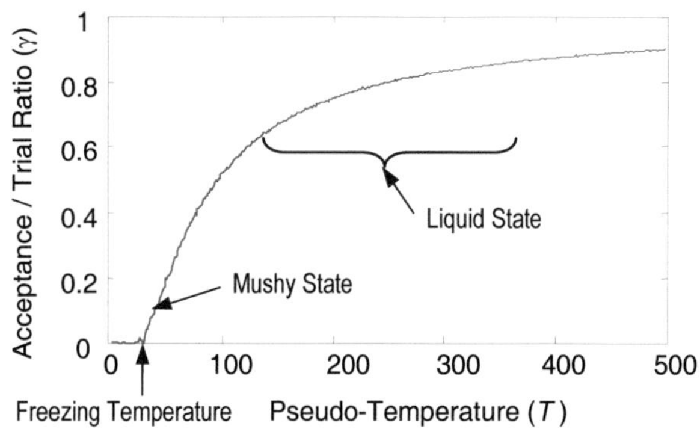

Fig. 3. Relation between the Pseudo-Temperature and the Acceptance-Trial Ratio, for the case of eli51.

The first method chosen for comparison is the Constructive Optimizing Neural Network (CONN) proposed in [24], for which it is claimed that all runs has led to the same results, so that the best, the worst and the average of the solutions are the same. The second one is a Kohonen-Like decomposition method [25], in its three different versions abbreviated by KD, KL and KG. The third is a Genetic Algorithm-Based Clustering [26]. Four variants of this method are introduced and tested, the results of which are given as EER, SE, ECER and SP. The fourth collection of the methods compared in the table are categorized under the column entitles Self-Organizing neural networks. Four versions are given in the table namely KNIES-global, KNIES-local, Budinich and ESOM [27]. The results for the normal SA are also taken from the same reference. A set of enhanced methods called Self-Organizing Map designed by Genetic Algorithms is the fifth set. There also four columns quoted for this category from [16][28]. Finally, we have compared our results with the best and the average error percentages of the results given in [29] for its memetic neural network.
It is easy to deduce that MSSA by both initializing methods has led to very accurate results, with slightly weaker characteristics for WTS as a cost of speeding up the algorithm. The proposed method has shown superiority to all other competing methods, though they are not tested for the last benchmark, **u1432**, which perhaps will lead to more inaccurate results, if tested. To accomplish our comparison, we have added another set of methods from [8], in which 11 methods are run on 30 benchmarks from **lin105** to **u1432**. For brevity purpose, the problems are categorized into 3 groups, namely: small, medium and large size benchmarks. The results are given in Table 2, where the average of the average error in each group is shown. For detailed explanation of each method see [8].

Algorithms in [7]	Average Error in			Total Average Error
	Small Size	Medium Size	Large Size	
SA (Simulated Annealing)	2.76	3.25	3.7	3.09
TA (Threshold Accepting)	5.37	4.18	9.95	5.75
RRT (Record-to-Record Travel)	4.22	6.79	13.96	6.78

BD (Bounded Demon)	5.26	4.44	7.73	5.4
RBD (Randomized Bounded Demon)	4.33	9.38	13.59	7.66
AD (Annealed Demon)	3.24	3.27	10.4	4.49
RAD (Randomized Annealed Demon)	2.82	4.38	10.94	4.76
ABD (Annealed Bounded Demon)	2.65	2.77	9.15	3.81
RABD (Randomized Annealed Bounded Demon)	2.63	3.64	4.13	3.24
ADH (Annealed Demon Hybrid)	2.97	2.95	9.19	4.03
ABDH (Annealed Bounded Demon Hybrid)	2.69	2.89	8.52	3.76
MSSA (the proposed method)				
By Crossover Elimination	1.10	2.22	2.63	1.63
By WTS	1.24	2.42	2.88	1.81

Table 2. Comparison of MSSA with other methods given in [8] for 29 benchmarks (the average of the average error in 25 runs)

To have a better feeling from the speed of the algorithms, let's first have a look at the fig. 4. As explained before, if annealing starts from a very high temperature, say 500 or more for the case of **eli51**, with more than 90% for the ratio γ (or an alternative parameter like the initial acceptance probability for an average uphill move [15]), it may take more than 8000 evaluations of the energy function to reach the minimum, while starting from a mushy state will lead to convergence in less than 2000 iterations. This means 4 times faster, as is observed in Figure 4, where it is shown how the annealing schedule would be and from which point it is started in this method. It should be added here that the total calculation time to find a mushy state with about γ =10%, done by any algorithm like the crossover elimination or the WTS, is less than one tenth of the total iteration time needed for SA to slow down its initially high temperature within 6000 = 8000 - 2000 iterations.
As the final point, it is worthy to mention that comparison of the speed of calculation for different methods is not accurate unless the methods are run on one computer in the same condition. Since the speed of an algorithm is dependent to the properties of the computer by which the algorithm is being run, the number of *floating point operation* (*fpo*) is a proper alternative to compare the speeds. However, for the fact of randomness, it is almost impossible to compute and compare the right number of *fpo* for each algorithm. As it is observed in this paper, we compared the proposed method with a normal SA and approved analytically that an MSSA is much faster. Comparing the method with other methods we could just refer to the average (minimum/maximum) error in the final results of each algorithm.

TSP Benchmark	Optimal Solution	MSSA By Crossover Elimination			MSSA By WTS			CONN [24]			KOHONEN-LIKE Decomposition [25] (Average δ)			Genetic Algorithm-Based Clustering [26] (Average δ)				Self-Organizing neural networks [27] (Average δ)					Self-Organizing Map designed by Genetic Algorithms [28] (Average δ)				Memetic neural network [29]	
																							Enhanced SOMs					
		Best δ	Average δ	Worst δ	Best δ	Average δ	Worst δ	Best δ	Average δ	Worst δ	KD	KL	KG	EER	SE	ECER	SP	KNIES-global	KNIES-local	SA	Budinich	ESOM	CEN	Budinich	ESOM	EISOM	Best δ	Average δ
eil51	426	0	0.36	0.94	0	0.79	1.88	2.58	2.58	2.58	3.50	2.86	2.86	1.16	7.19	0.23	0.23	2.86	2.86	2.33	3.10	2.10	1.88	2.48	0.93	1.97	1.64	2.14
st70	675	0	1.02	1.63	0	0.90	1.48	2.96	2.96	2.96	3.67	1.51	2.33	-	-	-	-	2.33	1.51	2.14	1.70	2.09	-	-	-	-	0.59	0.99
eil76	538	0	0.82	1.67	0	0.70	2.04	5.02	5.02	5.02	6.49	4.98	5.48	4.27	3.41	0.92	2.18	5.48	4.98	5.54	5.32	3.89	-	-	-	-	2.04	2.88
gr96	514	0	0.83	1.36	0	0.53	1.17	3.61	3.61	3.61	-	-	-	10.62	8.07	3.09	2.46	-	-	4.12	2.09	1.03	4.39	0.46	0.46	0.53	-	-
kroA100	21282	0	0.52	0.93	0.28	0.65	2.04	2.57	2.57	2.57	-	-	-	16.54	6.70	3.81	2.41	-	-	5.94	3.68	1.01	1.60	0.93	0.81	0.54	0.24	1.14
rd100	7910	0.01	1.40	1.96	0.01	1.42	3.12	3.59	3.59	3.59	4.89	2.09	2.62	11.10	8.93	3.23	3.81	2.62	2.09	3.26	3.16	1.96	-	-	-	-	0.99	2.65
eil101	629	0	0.90	1.91	0	1.97	3.34	4.61	4.61	4.61	6.84	4.66	5.63	17.99	8.71	4.55	4.12	5.63	4.66	5.74	5.24	3.43	2.07	4.31	2.72	2.92	2.07	3.15
lin105	14379	0	0.52	1.00	0	0.33	0.77	0.38	0.38	0.38	2.18	1.98	1.29	22.55	2.85	2.31	3.10	1.29	1.98	1.87	1.71	0.25	-	-	-	-	0.00	0.34
pr107	44303	0	0.14	0.30	0	0.13	0.30	2.77	2.77	2.77	10.83	0.73	0.42	20.46	5.79	2.11	2.98	0.42	0.73	1.54	1.32	1.48	-	-	-	-	0.14	0.67
pr124	59030	0	0.25	0.60	0	0.21	0.45	1.74	1.74	1.74	3.22	0.08	0.49	30.51	3.75	2.93	3.02	0.49	0.08	1.26	1.62	0.67	-	-	-	-	0.26	1.52
bier127	118282	0.12	0.37	0.68	0.04	0.58	1.12	2.45	2.45	2.45	5.82	2.76	3.08	9.49	4.39	3.56	2.21	3.08	2.76	3.52	3.61	1.70	-	-	-	-	1.25	2.78
pr136	96772	0.35	1.05	1.97	0.55	1.43	2.89	2.27	2.27	2.27	1.93	4.53	5.15	26.50	12.54	12.43	6.19	5.15	4.53	4.90	5.20	4.31	-	-	-	-	0.73	3.10
gr137	698	0.14	0.63	1.29	0	0.92	2.00	4.69	4.69	4.69	-	-	-	23.85	6.58	2.54	4.22	-	-	8.45	8.61	4.27	3.29	4.51	2.52	2.18	-	-
kroA150	26524	1.36	2.18	3.37	0.48	1.47	2.22	4.78	4.78	4.78	-	-	-	29.15	7.10	8.01	5.17	-	-	-	-	-	2.90	2.23	1.69	1.26	1.64	2.73
kroA200	29368	0.48	1.22	2.50	1.03	1.49	2.30	4.40	4.40	4.40	5.66	5.72	6.57	40.97	10.46	7.72	5.91	6.57	5.72	5.61	6.13	2.91	3.22	2.67	1.96	1.21	1.08	2.20
pr226	80369	0.90	1.48	2.85	1.34	1.96	2.21	1.93	1.93	1.93	-	-	-	57.09	5.52	4.71	5.05	-	-	-	-	-	-	-	-	-	-	-
pr264	49135	0.85	2.91	5.55	1.66	2.83	4.49	3.58	3.58	3.58	-	-	-	54.08	10.26	10.49	9.37	-	-	-	-	-	-	-	-	-	-	-
lin318	42029	0.53	1.34	1.90	0.70	1.79	2.56	-	-	-	-	-	-	53.18	12.06	12.49	12.99	-	-	7.56	8.19	4.11	4.67	2.81	2.89	1.96	3.63	5.51
rd400	15281	1.90	2.48	2.85	2.30	2.54	2.80	5.77	5.77	5.77	-	-	-	56.83	17.25	14.33	15.95	-	-	-	-	-	-	-	-	-	-	-

pcb442	50778	2.04	2.26	2.68	1.78	2.46	3.09	5.56	5.56	5.56	8.00	11.07	10.45	60.29	14.11	19.80	12.76	10.45	11.07	9.15	8.43	7.43	5.31	6.88	5.11	5.67	3.57	6.08
att532	87550	1.56	1.96	2.37	1.92	2.52	3.37	5.66	5.66	5.66	6.15	6.74	6.80	67.58	17.72	16.18	18.41	6.80	6.74	5.38	5.67	4.95	5.81	4.76	3.54	2.39	3.29	4.21
rat783	8806	1.46	1.90	2.43	1.44	2.27	3.45	7.59	7.59	7.59	9.11	-	9.53	72.88	19.89	25.96	23.28	-	-	-	-	-	-	-	-	-	5.46	5.95
pr1002	259045	2.07	2.27	2.48	2.33	2.57	2.73	6.94	6.94	6.94	7.08	-	7.60	-	-	-	-	-	-	6.03	8.75	5.93	6.99	7.44	5.07	4.01	4.75	6.11
u1432	152970	2.04	2.99	3.96	1.97	3.18	4.28	-	-	-	-	-	-	-	-	-	-	-	-	-	-	-	-	-	-	-	-	-
Average		0.66	1.33	2.05	0.74	1.48	2.34	4.00	4.00	4.00	5.69	3.82	4.69	32.72	9.20	7.69	6.94	4.09	3.82	4.69	4.64	2.97	3.83	3.59	2.52	2.24	1.94	3.04
*MSSA By Crossover Elimination		-	-	-	0.66	1.33	2.05	0.66	1.33	2.06	1.10	0.94	1.10	1.22	1.22	1.22	1.22	0.94	0.94	0.99	0.99	0.99	1.32	1.32	1.32	1.32	0.63	1.24
*MSSA By WETS		0.74	1.48	2.34	-	-	-	0.75	1.47	2.33	1.32	1.15	1.32	1.38	1.38	1.38	1.38	1.15	1.15	1.19	1.19	1.19	1.56	1.56	1.56	1.56	0.66	1.41

* The last two rows contain average of the cases for which the corresponding method is run and the results are given.

Table 1. Comparison between MSSA and other new methods for 24 benchmarks

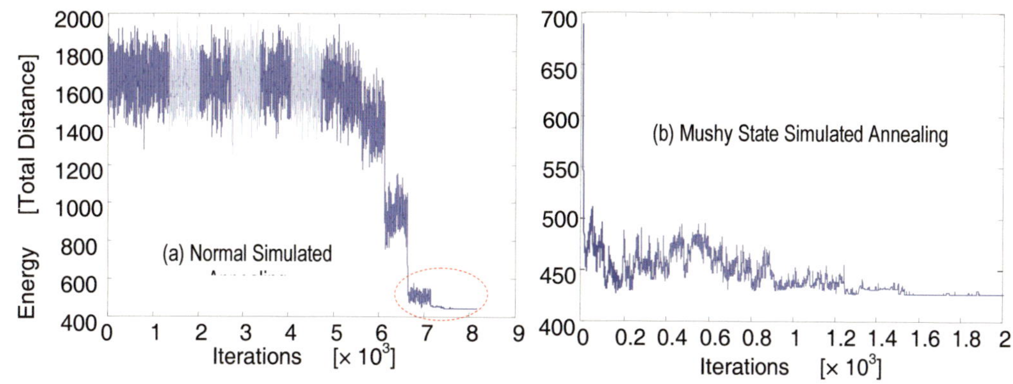

(a) Normal Simulated Annealing, (b) Mushy State Simulated Annealing

Fig. 4. Energy decay in the annealing process for eli51;

6. Conclusion

Simulated annealing is one of the top ten methods of non-derivative based optimization methods, various versions of which are proposed by researchers during the two last decades. Focusing on the initial condition by which the annealing starts, this paper proposes a novel variant of the original SA named mushy state simulated annealing (MSSA). In this method we start annealing not from a high temperature in a liquid state, but from a low temperature in a mushy state. Moreover, we use a memory to save the best solution found previously. This technique has speeded up the optimization process while achieving to quite accurate optimum solutions. For the case study of TSP, two simple algorithms including crossover elimination and the shortly introduced method of WTS are used to initiate the MSSA. Results are compared to many recent new optimization methods that are applied to solve TSP. Despite of its higher speed compared to the normal SA, superiority of the proposed method is observed in all cases with less than 1432 cities. The average error obtained by MSSA for the 24 benchmarks is much less than all other methods compared to this method.

7. References

[1] S. Kirkpatrick, C. D. Gelatt, and M. P. Vecchi, “Optimization by simulated annealing,” Science, vol. 220, pp. 671–680, 1983.

[2] M. R. Garey and D. S. Johnson, "Computers and Intractability: A Guide to the Theory of NP-Completeness", *New York: Freeman*, 1979.

[3] Herbert H. Tsang, and Kay C. Wiese "The Significance of Thermodynamic Models in the Accuracy Improvement of RNA Secondary Structure Prediction Using Permutation-based Simulated Annealing", *IEEE Congress on Evolutionary Computation* (CEC), 2007.

[4] Ming-Hao Hung, Li-Sun Shu, Shinn-Jang Ho, Shiow-Fen Hwang, and Shinn-Ying Ho, “A Novel Intelligent Multiobjective Simulated Annealing Algorithm for Designing Robust PID Controllers”, *IEEE Transactions on Systems, Man, and Cybernetics—PART A: Systems and Humans*, Vol. 38, No. 2, pp. 319-330, March 2008.

[5] Kevin I. Smith, Richard M. Everson, Jonathan E. Fieldsend , Chris Murphy, and Rashmi Misra, "Dominance-Based Multiobjective Simulated Annealing", *IEEE Transactions On Evolutionary Computation, vol. 12, no. 3, pp. 323-341, June 2008.*

[6] S. A. Kravitz and R. A. Rutenbar, "Placement by simulated annealing on a multiprocessor," *IEEE Transactions Computer-Aided Design Integr. CircuitsSyst.*, vol. 6, no. 4, pp. 534–549, Jul. 1987.

[7] E. Aarts and J. Korst, "Simulated Annealing and Boltzmann Machines: A Stochastic Approach to Combinatorial Optimization and Neural Computing", *New York: Wiley, 1989.*

[8] Joshua W. Pepper, Bruce L. Golden, and Edward A. Wasil, "Solving the Traveling Salesman Problem With Annealing-Based Heuristics: A Computational Study", *IEEE Transactions on Systems, Man, and Cybernetics – PART A: Systems and Humans,* Vol. 32, No. 1, Jan. 2002.

[9] Hyeon-Joong Cho, Se-Young Oh and Doo-Hyun Choi, "Population-oriented simulated annealing technique based on local Temperature concept", *Electronics Letters, vol. 34, no. 3, pp.312-313,* 5th February 1998.

[10] Percy P. C. Yip, and Yoh-Han Pao, "Combinatorial Optimization with Use of Guided Evolutionary Simulated Annealing", *IEEE Transactions on Neural Networks, vol. 6, no. 2, pp. 290-295, March 1995.*

[11] Andrew Soh, "Parallel N-ary Speculative Computation of Simulated Annealing", *IEEE Transactions on Parallel and Distributed Systems, vol. 6, no. 10, pp. 997-1005, October 1995.*

[12] D. C. W. Pao, S. P. Lam and A. S. Fong, "Parallel implementation of simulated annealing using transaction processing", IEE Proc-Comput. Digit. Tech.. Vol. 146, No. 2, March 1999, pp. 107-113.

[13] Feng-Tse Lin, Cheng-Yan Kao, and Ching-Chi Hsu, "Applying the Genetic Approach to Simulated Annealing in Solving Some NP-Hard Problems", *IEEE Transactions on Systems, Man, and Cybernetics,* Vol. 23. No. 6, Nov./Dec. 1993.

[14] Dale R. Thompson and Griff L. Bilbro, "Sample-Sort Simulated Annealing", *IEEE Transactions on Systems, Man, and Cybernetics – PART B: Cybernetics,* Vol. 35, No. 3, pp. 625-632 Jun. 2005.

[15] Hao Chen, Nicholas S. Flann, and Daniel W. Watson, "Parallel Genetic Simulated Annealing: A Massively Parallel SIMD Algorithm", *IEEE Transactions on Parallel and Distributed Systems, vol. 9, no. 2, pp.126-136, February 1998.*

[16] K.L. Wong A.G.Constantinides, "Speculative parallel simulated annealing with acceptance prediction", *Electronics Letters, vol. 34, no. 3,* pp. 312-313, *5th February 1998.*

[17] L. Ingber and B. Rosen, "Genetic Algorithms and Very Fast Simulated Reannealing: A Comparison," *Mathematical Computer Modeling,* vol. 16, no. 11, pp. 87-100, 1992.

[18] Lipo Wang, Sa Li, Fuyu Tian, and Xiuju Fu, "A Noisy Chaotic Neural Network for Solving Combinatorial Optimization Problems: Stochastic Chaotic Simulated Annealing", *Transactions on Systems, Man, and Cybernetics – PART B: Cybernetics,* Vol. 34, No. 5 pp. 2119-2125, Oct. 2004.

[19] Yuyao He, "Chaotic Simulated Annealing With Decaying Chaotic Noise", IEEE Transactions on Neural Networks, vol. 13, no. 6, pp. 1526-1531, November 2002.

[20] Sitao Wu and Tommy W. S. Chow, "Self-Organizing and Self-Evolving Neurons: A New Neural Network for Optimization", *IEEE Transactions on Neural Networks, vol. 18, no. 2,* pp. 385-396, *March 2007.*

[21] J. Jang, C. Sun, E. Mizutani, "Neuro-Fuzzy and Soft Computing", Proc. of the Prentice Hall 1997.

[22] G. Dueck and T. Scheuer, "Threshold accepting: A general purpose optimization algorithm appearing superior to simulated annealing," *J. Computer. Phys.*, vol. 90, 1990, pp. 161–175.

[23] *G. Reinelt. Tsplib95, 1995. Available at: http://www.iwr.uni-heidelberg.de/groups/comopt/software/TSPLIB95.*

[24] M. Saadatmand-Tarzjan, M. Khademi, M. R. Akbarzadeh-T., and H. Abrishami Moghaddam, "A Novel Constructive-Optimizer Neural Network for the Traveling Salesman Problem" *IEEE Transactions on Systems, Man, and Cybernetics – PART B: Cybernetics,* Vol. 37, No. 4, Aug. 2007.

[25] Necati Aras, I. Kuban Altınel, and John Oommen, "A KOHONEN-LIKE DECOMPOSITION METHOD FOR THE EUCLIDEAN TRAVELING SALESMAN PROBLEM KNIES_DECOMPOSE", *IEEE Transactions on Neural Networks, vol. 14, no. 4, July 2003.*

[26] Chun-Hung Cheng, Wing-Kin Lee, and Kam-Fai Wong, "A Genetic Algorithm-Based Clustering Approach for Database Partitioning", *IEEE Transactions on Systems, Man, and Cybernetics – PART C: Applications and Reviews,* Vol. 32, No. 3, Aug. 2002.

[27] Kwong-Sak Leung, Hui-Dong Jin, and Zong-Ben Xu, "An expanding Self-Organizing neural network for the traveling salesman problem", *Neurocomputing,* Vol. 62, pp. 267-292, Dec. 2004.

[28] Hui-Dong Jin, Kwong-Sak Leung, Man-Leung Wong and Zong-Ben Xu, "An Efficient Self-Organizing Map Designed by Genetic Algorithms for the Traveling Salesman Problem", *IEEE Transactions on Systems, Man, and Cybernetics – PART B: Cybernetics,* Vol. 33, No. 6, pp. 877-888, Dec. 2003.

[29] J. C. Creput, A. Koukam, "A memetic neural network for the Euclidean traveling salesman problem", *Neurocomputing Accepted 22, January 2008.*

13

Multilevel Large-Scale Modules Floorplanning/Placement with Improved Neighborhood Exchange in Simulated Annealing

Kuan-Chung Wang[1] and Hung-Ming Chen[2]
[1]*SpringSoft, Inc., Hsinchu Science-Based Industrial Park*
[2]*Department of Electronics Engineering, National Chiao Tung University*
Hsinchu, Taiwan

1. Introduction

Modern system designs become more and more complex due to the progress of VLSI manufacturing technologies. In nanometer IC technologies and SoC (System on Chip) design flow, existing placement approaches face many serious challenges, including large size(billions of transistors), mix-size cell placement, wire congestion, and more complex design constraints (delay, noise, manufacturability, etc). Since the IC design market is more and more competitive, it is necessary to have faster time to market, smaller silicon area utilization, and less wire length for layout. Efficient and effective design methodologies of large scale design placement are essential for modern SoC designs.

Many placement methods have been presented in the literature (Chang et al., 2000; Guo et al., 1999; Lin & Chang, 2001; 2002a; Lin et al., 2003; Murata et al., 1995; Nakatake et al., 1996; Otten, 1982; Wong & Liu, 1986). Because of inflexibility in representing non-slicing placement and non-hierarchical data structures, the performance of traditional placement algorithms were not very good. Until recently, the B*-tree representation (Chang et al., 2000) provided an efficient, effective, and flexible data structure for non-slicing placement. Furthermore, MB*-tree algorithm (Lee et al., 2003) has presented multilevel framework which is more facilitating to solve large-scale floorplanning/placement problem. However applying simulated annealing approach in declustering stage spent much more time to search for better solutions.

On the other hand, the ϵ-neighborhood and λ-exchange algorithm, first presented in (Goto, 1981) and further applied in (Chan et al., 2000), was used for standard cell based placement. This method, for permuting cells with wire length driven approach, gave better performance compared with randomly interchanges of cells in simulated annealing paradigm. This limited trial permutation enable us to find a good local optimum solution more efficiently. The challenge lies in the modification of this approach to large-scale modules placement.

In this work, we transform the ϵ-neighborhood and λ-exchange to fit in the large-scale modules placement and use it in the refinement stage of MB*-tree algorithm. This method searches the solutions in the whole permutation of the selected modules. Although our ϵ-neighborhood and λ-exchange approach takes much time for one perturbation, its efficiency will compensate for the computation time by comparing with randomly interchanges, and more efficient in general compared with original MB*-tree. The results are encouraging. We have obtained

comparable or better results in area and wirelength metrics in less time spent (up to 30% improvement).
The remainder of this work is organized as follows. Section 2 gives a brief review on the B*-tree representation and MB*-tree, and describes previous ϵ-neighborhood and λ-exchange method. Section 3 presents our two-stage algorithm, clustering followed by declustering, mainly showing our effective refined approach to obtaining good candidates more efficiently. Section 4 shows the experimental results and Section 5 draws the conclusion.

2. Large-Scale Modules Placement with Neighborhood Exchange

In this section, we briefly review B*-tree representation and MB*-tree multilevel framework. We then introduce previous ϵ-neighborhood and λ-exchange method originally for standard cell placement.

2.1 Review of B*-tree and MB*-tree

Given a compacted placement that can neither move down nor move left called an *admissible placement*, we can represent it by a unique B*- tree (Chang et al., 2000) (See Figure 1 for the B*-tree representing the placement). A B*-tree is an ordered binary tree whose root corresponds to the module on the bottom-left corner. Using the depth-first search (DFS) procedure, the B*-tree for an admissible placement can be constructed in a recursive fashion. Starting from the root, we first recursively construct the left subtree and then the right subtree. Let R_i denote the set of modules located on the right-hand side and adjacent to m_i. The left child of the node n_i corresponds to the lowest module in R_i that is unvisited. The right child of n_i represents the lowest module located above m_i, with its x-coordinate equal to that of m_i. The B*-tree keeps the geometric relationship between two modules as follows. If node n_j is the left child of node n_i, module m_j must be located on the right-hand side of m_i, with $x_j = x_i + w_i$. Besides, if node n_j is the right child of n_i, module m_j must be located above module m_i, with the x-coordinate of m_j equal to that of m_i; i.e., $x_j = x_i$. Also, since the root of T represents the bottom-left module, the coordinate of the module is $(x_{root}, y_{root}) = (0, 0)$.
Inheriting from nice properties of ordered binary trees, the B*-tree is simple, efficient, effective, and flexible for handling non-slicing floorplans. It is particularly suitable for representing a non-slicing floorplan with various types of modules and for creating or incrementally updating a floorplan. What is more important, its binary-tree based structure directly corresponds to the framework of a hierarchical scheme, which makes it a superior data structure for multilevel large-scale building module floorplanning/placement. In (Lee et al., 2003), a multilevel floorplanning/placement framework based on the B*-tree representation, called MB*-tree, is presented to handle the floorplanning and packing for large-scale building modules. There were already many works that manipulated multilevel or hierarchical approach to disentangle the large scale issue in VLSI years ago: in graph/circuit partitioning such as Chaco (Hendrickson & Leland, 1995), hMetis (Karypis & Kumar, 1999), and ML (Alpert et al., 1998); in placement such as MPL (Chan et al., 2000); in routing such as MRS (Cong et al., 2001), MR (Lin & Chang, 2002b), and MARS (Cong et al., 2002).
The MB*-tree adopts a two-stage technique, clustering followed by declustering. The clustering stage iteratively groups a set of modules based on a cost metric guided by area utilization and module connectivity, and at the same time establishes the geometric relations for the newly clustered modules by constructing a corresponding B*-tree for them. The declustering stage iteratively ungroups a set of the previously clustered modules (i.e., perform tree expansion) and then refines the floorplanning/placement solution by using a simulated annealing

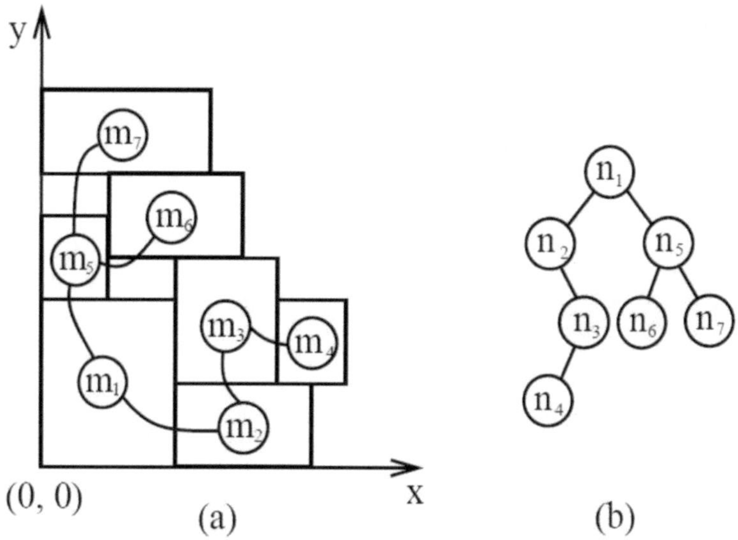

Fig. 1. An admissible placement and its corresponding B*-tree.

scheme. In particular, the MB*-tree preserves the geometric relations among modules during declustering, which makes the MB*-tree good for the multilevel floorplanning/placement framework.

2.2 Module Perturbation Based on Neighborhood Exchange

Those approaches were first brought forth in (Goto, 1981), and promoted in (Chan et al., 2000). But they are all about gate array/cell based placement. We first review those approaches in this subsection, then later show our improvement in our framework for efficient large-scale modules placement. Based on different definitions on ϵ-neighborhood and λ-exchange, we categorize them into two forms: unidirectional circulation form (UCF) and detoured circulation form (DCF).

2.2.1 Unidirectional Circulation Form

Consider a board on which every module is placed. Pick one module and move it while the other modules remain fixed. The wirelength of a signal net does not change as long as the signal net is not connected to this module. The median of module M is defined as a position where the routing length associated with module M is minimum. Then we sort all the wirelengths associated with module M with respect to the module M position in ascending order. Choose ϵ elements from the minimum one, the set of these ϵ positions is defined as the *ϵ-neighborhood for median of module M*.

Let S be the set of all feasible solutions of this placement and let x be a feasible solution, $x \in S$. Consider the neighborhood of x, denoted by $X(x)$, which is a subset of S. In the first step, x is set to a feasible solution and a search is made in $X(x)$ for a better solution x' to replace x. This process, which is referred to hereafter as a local transformation, is repeated until no such x' can be found. A solution x'' is said to be a local optimum if x'' is better than any other elements of $X(x)$. Many definitions may be considered for the neighborhood of a solution. The set of solutions transformable from x by exchanging not more than λ elements is regarded as the neighboorhood of x. A solution x is said to be λ-optimum if x is better than any other solutions in the neighborhood in this sense. Although the λ-optimum solution gets better as λ increases, the computation time can easily go beyond the acceptable limit when an exhaustive search is performed for large λ. Therefore (Goto, 1981) presented the following method which does not examine all the elements in the neighborhood. The illustrations of this approach are shown in Figure 2 and 3. Figure 2 shows the corresponding search tree for module interchange and Figure 3 shows the trial interchange of modules. In this example, we set ϵ=3 and λ = 4.

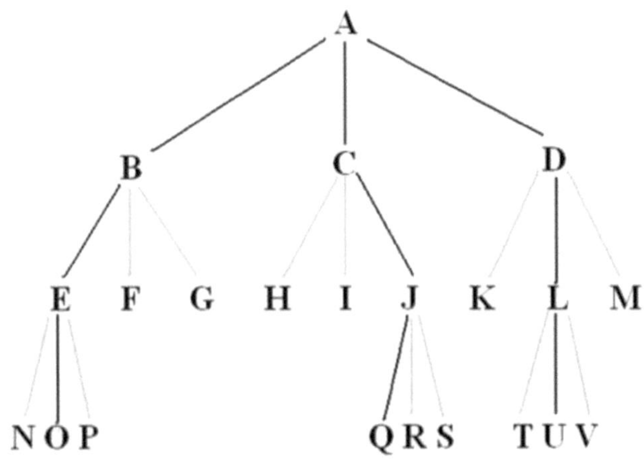

Fig. 2. The search tree of unidirectional circulation form, where ϵ=3 and λ = 4. Each node represents a module and each edge represents a trial transformation. A path connecting node *A* and one of the other nodes defines a possible interchange. The path $A \rightarrow B \rightarrow E \rightarrow O$ refers to the trial interchange of four modules, as shown in Figure 3. Module *A* is placed on the slot of *B*, then the median of *B* and its ϵ-neighborhood are generated. Here the ϵ-neighborhood module are *E*, *F*, and *G*. Thus interchanges $A \rightarrow B \rightarrow E$, $A \rightarrow B \rightarrow F$, and $A \rightarrow B \rightarrow G$ are tried.

2.2.2 Detoured Circulation Form

This form is presented in (Chan et al., 2000) and modified from previous form. Assuming all modules except module v are fixed in their current locations, we can compute v's optimal slot locations. Suppose v's optimal slot location is (r,c) where r is the row index and c is column index in our grid. Modules located in slots at (i,j), where $|i-r|+|j-c| \leqq \epsilon$, are called ϵ-neighbors of module v (Figure 4).

λ-exchange algorithm used in (Chan et al., 2000) is different from UCF as well. Since the search tree from previous form grows rapidly with slight increase in ϵ and λ, and module exchange sequence may not be the best possible, λ-exchange procedure has been modified. Suppose v_1 is the first module to be moved. We find its ϵ-neighbors and randomly pick one module, say v_2, among these modules. Then for v_2, we find its ϵ-neighbors, and randomly pick one module, and continue in this fashion until we have λ modules. For the λ modules, we try all of their placement permutations (the total number is λ!) and exchange modules according to the least cost permutation. Figure 5 illustrates this change. Experimental results in (Chan et al., 2000) show that UCF algorithm quickly gets stuck in local minimum. Later we

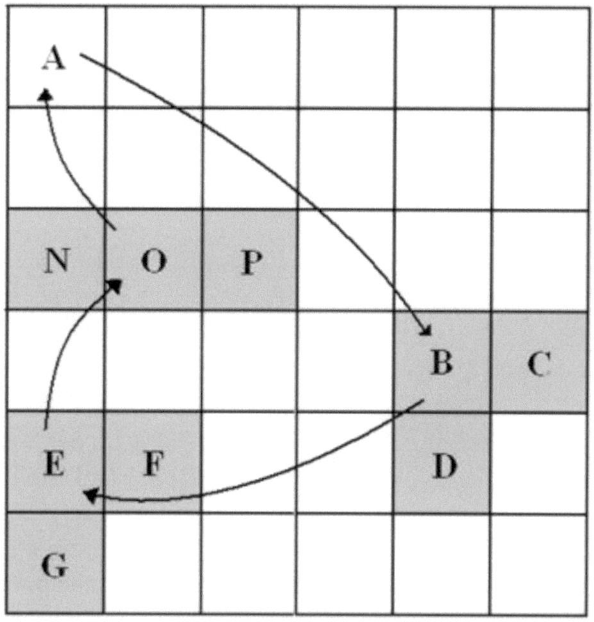

Fig. 3. Trial interchange of modules, $A \to B \to E \to O \to A$ in unidirectional circulation form. Module A is placed on the slot of B, B is placed on E, E on O, and O on A, in a round robin sequence. Although this transformation is a quadruple interchange, it includes a pairwise interchange as a special case, i.e., paths $A \to B$, $A \to C$, and $A \to D$.

show that we use detoured circulation form to develop our refined neighborhood exchange approach.

2.3 Problem Formulation

The problem we concerned about is described as follows, same as in MB*-tree. Let $M = \{m_1, m_2, \ldots, m_n\}$ be a set of n rectangular modules. Each module $m_i \in M$ is associated with a two tuple (h_i, w_i), where h_i and w_i denote the width and height of m_i, respectively. Let $N = \{n_1, n_2, \ldots, n_k\}$ be a set of k net. Each net $n_i \in N$ is a set of modules which are connected together. A placement $P = \{(x_i, y_i) \mid m_i \in M\}$ is an assignment of rectangular modules m_i's with the coordinates of their bottomleft corners being assigned to (x_i, y_i)'s so that no two modules overlap. The objective is to minimize a cost of combination of the area and half-perimeter wirelength.

3. The MBNE Algorithm

In this work, we decide to keep the multilevel hierarchy and the B*-tree representation of MB*-tree, but replace its simulated annealing refinement method by ϵ-neighborhood and λ-exchange algorithm for better performance. Since this algorithm combines the MB*-tree and ϵ-neighborhood and λ-exchange methods, we called it MBNE algorithm. We present our MBNE algorithm for multilevel large-scale building modules floorplanning/placement in this section. This algorithm adopts a two-stage approach, clustering followed by declustering, by using the B*-tree representation. Figure 6 shows the MBNE algorithm flow.

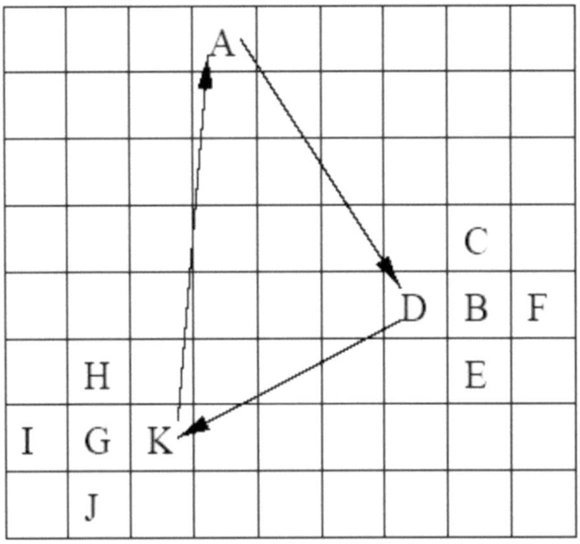

Fig. 4. The ϵ-neighbors in detoured circulation form. Suppose the optimal slot location of module A is occupied by module B. So A's 1-neighbors ($\epsilon = 1$) are $\{B, C, D, E, F\}$. Similarly, assuming that D's optimal slot is taken by G, we define module D's 1-neighbors are $\{G, H, I, J, K\}$.

The clustering operation results in two types of modules, namely primitive modules and cluster modules. A primitive module m is a module given as an input (i.e., $m \in M$) while a cluster one is created by grouping two or more primitive modules. Each cluster module is created by a clustering scheme $\{m_i, m_j\}$, where m_i (m_j) denotes a primitive or a cluster module.
In the following subsections, we give a detailed review on clustering and declustering algorithms in MB*-tree (Lee et al., 2003) and our refinement approaches in declustering phase to improve the packing results.

3.1 The Clustering Phase

In this stage, we iteratively group a set of (primitive or cluster) modules until a single cluster is formed (or until the number of cluster modules is smaller than a threshold) based on a cost metric of area and connectivity. The clustering metric is defined by the two criteria: area utilization (dead space) and the connectivity density among modules.
The area utilization for clustering two modules m_i and m_j can be measured by the resulting dead space s_{ij}, representing the unused area after clustering m_i and m_j. Let s_{tot} denote the dead space in the final floorplan P. We have $s_{tot} = A_{tot} - \sum_{m_i \in M} A_i$, where A_i denotes the area of module m_i and A_{tot} the area of the final enclosing rectangle of P. Since $\sum_{m_i \in M} A_i$ is a constant, minimizing A_{tot} is equivalent to minimizing the dead space s_{tot}.
Let the connectivity c_{ij} denote the number of nets between two modules m_i and m_j. The connectivity density d_{ij} between two (primitive or cluster) modules m_i and m_j is given by

$$d_{ij} = c_{ij}/(n_i + n_j) \tag{1}$$

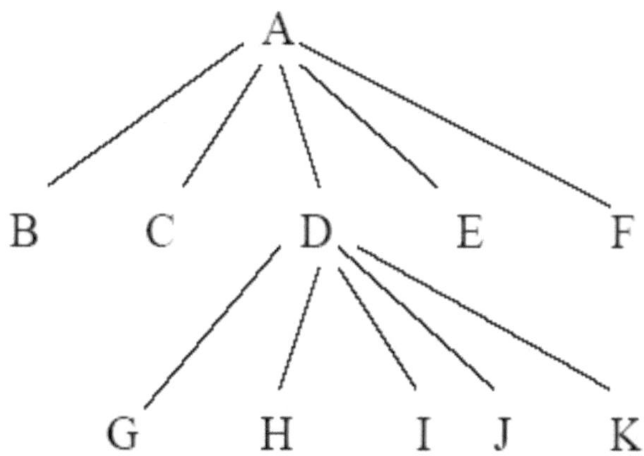

Fig. 5. Search tree from A in detoured circulation form. Suppose we pick modules A, D, and K. All six permutations will be tried: no exchange, $A \leftrightarrow D$, $A \leftrightarrow K$, $D \leftrightarrow K$, $A \rightarrow D \rightarrow K \rightarrow A$, $A \rightarrow K \rightarrow D \rightarrow A$.

where n_i (n_j) denotes the number of primitive modules in m_i (m_j). Often a bigger cluster implies a larger number of connections. The connectivity density considers not only the connectivity but also the sizes of clusters between two modules to avoid possible biases.
Obviously, the cost function of dead space is for area optimization while that of connectivity density is for timing and wiring area optimization. Therefore, the metric for clustering two (primitive or cluster) modules m_i and m_j, $\phi : \{m_i,m_j\} \rightarrow \Re^+ \bigcup \{0\}$, is then given by

$$\phi(\{m_i, m_j\}) = \alpha \hat{s}_{ij} + \frac{\beta}{\hat{d}_{ij}} \tag{2}$$

where $\hat{s}_{ij}$ and $\hat{d}_{ij}$ are respective normalized costs for s_{ij} and d_{ij}, α, β and K are user-specified parameters/constants.
Based on ϕ, we cluster a set of modules into one at each iteration by applying the aforementioned methods until a single cluster containing all primitive modules is formed or the number of modules is smaller than a given threshold. During clustering, we record how two modules m_i and m_j are clustered into a new cluster module m_k. If m_i is placed left to (below) m_j , then m_i is horizontally (vertically) related to m_j, n_j is the left (right) child of n_i in its corresponding B*-tree (see Figure 7). The relation for each pair of modules in a cluster is established and recorded in the corresponding B*-subtree during clustering. It will be used for determining how to expand a node into a corresponding B*-subtree during declustering.

3.2 The Declustering Phase

The declustering metric is defined by the two criteria: area utilization (dead space) and the wirelength among modules. Dead space is the same as that defined in previous subsection. The wirelength of a net is measured by half the bounding box of all the pins of the net, or by the length of the center-to-center interconnections between the modules if no pin positions are specified. The wirelength for clustering two modules m_i and m_j , w_{ij}, is measured by the total wirelength interconnecting the two modules. The total wirelength in the final floorplan P, w_{tot}, is the summation of the length of the wires interconnecting all modules.

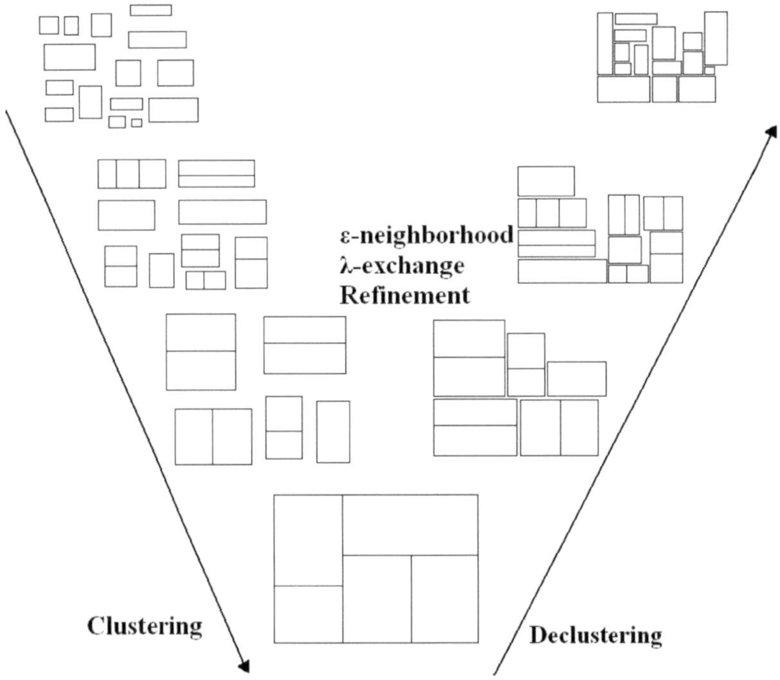

Fig. 6. The MBNE algorithm flow. First clustering, then followed by declustering, using our refined approaches to improve efficiency and the packing results.

Obviously, the cost function of dead space is for area optimization while that of wirelength is for timing and wiring area optimization. Therefore, the metric for refining a floorplan solution during declustering, $\psi_{ij}:\{m_i,m_j\}\rightarrow\Re^+\bigcup\{0\}$, is then given by

$$\psi_{ij} = \gamma\hat{s}_{ij} + \delta\hat{w}_{ij} \tag{3}$$

where $\hat{s}_{ij}$ and $\hat{w}_{ij}$ are respective normalized costs for s_{ij} and w_{ij}, and γ and δ are user-specified parameters.

In our approach, the declustering stage iteratively ungroups a set of previously clustered modules (i.e., expand a node into a subtree according to the B*-tree constructed at the clustering stage) and then refines the floorplan solution based on the ϵ-neighborhood and λ-exchange method. We apply the same declustering algorithm shown in (Lee et al., 2003) in our MBNE algorithm.

3.3 Our Refined Neighborhood Exchange Approach

At all levels of declustering, we apply the ϵ-neighborhood and λ-exchange method to refine the floorplan for gaining a better solution. We redefine the ϵ and λ in the B*-tree representation. The original definition of ϵ-neighborhood of module v in (Goto, 1981) is the modules located in slots at row i, column j where $|i-r|+|j-c| \leqq \epsilon$ and (r,c) is the optimal slot location of v. But in the non-slicing placement of large-scale circuit, the optimal slot location is hard to compute and it will shift when perturbing the modules. Hence we redefine the ϵ-neighborhood of module v as the modules away from v within ϵ branches in B*-tree. Figure 8 shows 1-neighborhood and 2-neighborhood of module n_2.

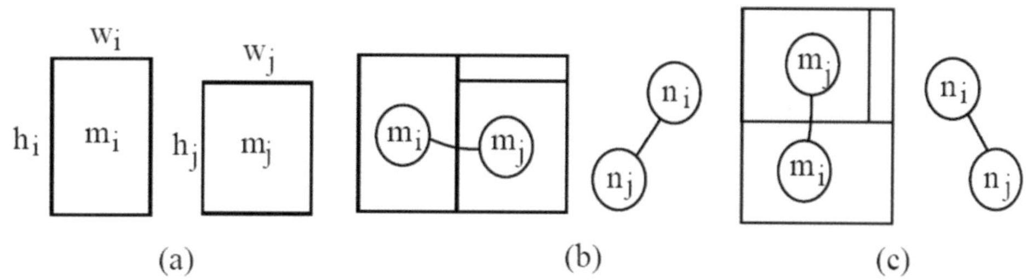

Fig. 7. The relation of two modules and their clustering (Lee et al., 2003) (a) Two candidate modules m_i and m_j. (b) The clustering and the corresponding B*-subtree for the case where m_i is horizontally related to m_j. (c) The clustering and the corresponding B*-subtree for the case where m_i is vertically related to m_j.

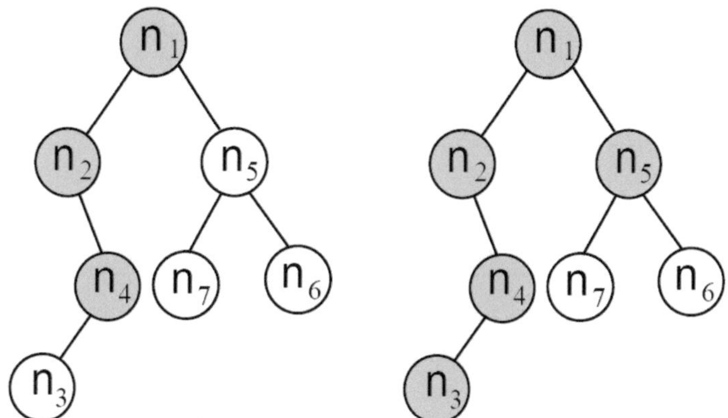

Fig. 8. The definition of ϵ-neighborhood in our refined neighborhood exchange approach. (a)c=1 and (b)c=2. The highlighted nodes besides node n_2 are the neighborhood modules.

In our refined neighborhood exchange algorithm, first we choose a starting module A, and select the module B which in the same net with module A. We then randomly pick the module B_λ in the ϵ-neighbors of module B, so we have A and B_λ for 2-exchange now. Furthermore, we can continue selecting the module C which in the same net with A and B, and randomly pick the module C_λ in ϵ-neighbors of module C for 3-exchange. Do this sequence until we have λ modules for λ-exchange (see Figure 9).

After we get all the λ modules, we try all of their placement permutations. Since this is a large-scale circuit placement, modules normally have different heights and widths. Therefore the rotation of modules will affect the placement's result. The total number of permutations is $\lambda! \times 2^\lambda$. Finally, we keep the permutation with the lowest cost and start the next turn of refinement.

3.4 Novel Move Based on Null Module Insertion

Our ϵ-neighborhood and λ-exchange approach can rotate and/or swap the modules to perturb the placement, but it can not move a module to another place. Thus, we replace one of the λ-exchange modules by null module for permutations. The null module does not connect to any module, and its height and width are equal to zero. When we decide to use null module

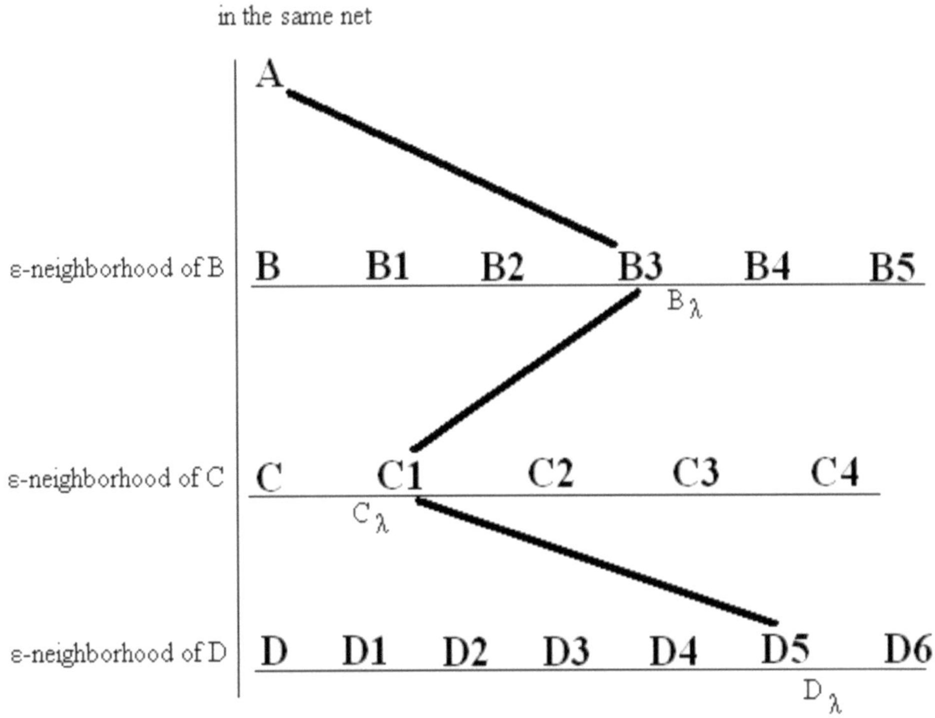

Fig. 9. An example of λ-exchange in our approach, where λ=4.

by some probability, we insert it to be the replaced λ-exchange module's child. When a module swap with the null module, it is equivalent with moving the module to be the replaced module's child. Figure 10 is an example of null module insertion for refinement.

We have applied the null module in the ϵ-neighborhood and λ-exchange refinement, so we can combine the original three operations (rotate, move, and swap) to perturb the placement, and get the lowest cost one.

3.5 Floorplanner Flow

The MBNE algorithm integrates the aforementioned three algorithms. We first perform clustering to reduce the problem size level by level and then enter the declustering stage. In the declustering stage, we perform floorplanning for the modules at each level using the ϵ-neighborhood and λ-exchange algorithm for refinement.

Figure 11 illustrates an execution of the MBNE algorithm (from (Lee et al., 2003)). For explanation, we cluster three modules each time. Figure 11(a) lists seven modules to be packed, m_i's, $1 \leq i \leq 7$. Figure 11(b)-(d) illustrates the execution of the clustering algorithm. Figure 11(b) shows the resulting configuration after clustering m_5, m_6, and m_7 into a new cluster module m_8 (i.e., the clustering scheme of m_8 is $\{\{m_5,m_6\},m_7\}$). Similarly, we cluster m_1,m_2, and m_4 into m_9 by using the clustering scheme $\{\{m_2, m_4\}, m_1\}$. Finally, we cluster m_3,m_8, and m_9 into m_{10} by using the clustering scheme $\{\{m_3, m_8\}, m_9\}$. The clustering stage is done, and the declustering stage begins, in which ϵ-neighborhood and λ-exchange method are applied to refine the coarse floorplan. In Figure 11(e), we first decluster m_{10} into m_3, m_8, and m_9 (i.e., expand the

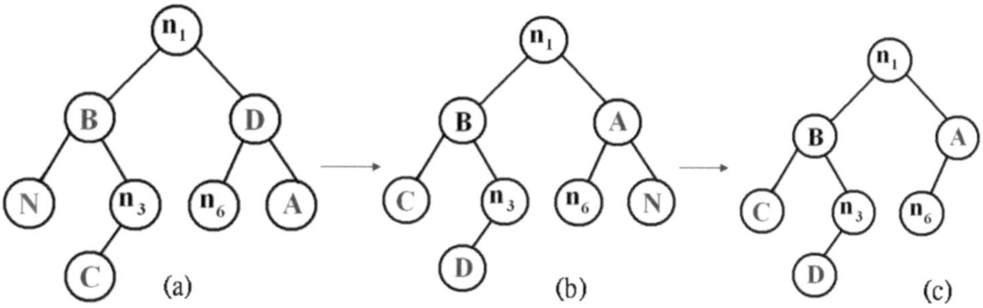

Fig. 10. An example of null module insertion in refined neighborhood exchange.(a)Insert modele *N* to replace modele *B* for swaping. (b)After swap $A \to D \to C \to N \to A$. (c)Delete module *N*.

node n_{10} into the B*-subtree illustrated in Figure 11(e)). We then move m_8 to the top of m_9 (perform Op2 for m_8) during ϵ-neighborhood and λ-exchange refinement (see Figure 11(f)). As shown in Figure 11(g), we further decluster m_9 into m_1, m_2, and m_4, and then rotate m_2 and move m_3 on top of m_2 (perform Op1 on m_2 and Op2 on m_3), resulting in the configuration shown in Figure 11(h). Finally, we decluster m_8 shown in Figure 11(i) to m_5, m_6, and m_7, and move m_4 to the right of m_3 (perform Op2 for m_4), which results in placement with good quality shown in Figure 11(j).

4. Experimental Results

We implement the MBNE algorithm in C++ programming language. The platform is Intel Pentium 4 2.4GHz CPU with 1.5GB memory. We have compared our approach with the MB*-tree algorithm on benchmarks including *industry* (Lee et al., 2003), MCNC and GSRC benchmarks for area, wirelength and simultaneous area and wirelength optimizations.
The circuit *industry* is a 0.18μm, 1GHz industrial design with 189 modules, 20 million gates and 9,777 center-to-center interconnections. It is a large chip design and consists of three modules with aspect ratios greater than 19 and as large as 36. Table 1 shows the results of MBNE compared with MB*-tree for this circuit. In each entry of the table, we list the best/average values obtained in ten runs of MBNE and MB*-tree. We have achieved less area and wirelength (WL) in averagely less time.
The *ami49* is the largest MCNC benchmark circuit, (Lee et al., 2003) has created seven synthetic circuits, named ami49_x, by duplicating the modules of ami49 by x times to test the capability of our algorithm. The largest circuit ami49_200 contains 9800 modules. Moreover, we use GSRC benchmarks which contains n100, n200, and n300 circuits as our experimental suites. Table 2 and Table 3 shows the results of MBNE compared with MB*-tree in these two sets of benchmarks. Again we have acheived less area and wirelength in less runtime. The reason is that we use our refined neighborhood exchange approach to effectively and efficiently search for solution cadidates, instead of near-random simulated annealing.
For demostrating the efficiency, we choose four circuits from the *industry*, MCNC, and GSRC benchmark to compare for efficiency between MBNE and MB*-tree algorithm. We spend 70% of runtime compared with MB*-tree algorithm for four circuits. Table 4 shows the results of area, dead space and runtime of MBNE and MB*-tree. MBNE obtains dead space of 2.34%, 2.11%, 2.89% and 2.32% while MB*-tree requires dead space of 2.32%, 2.62%, 3.18% and 3.84% in these four circuits.

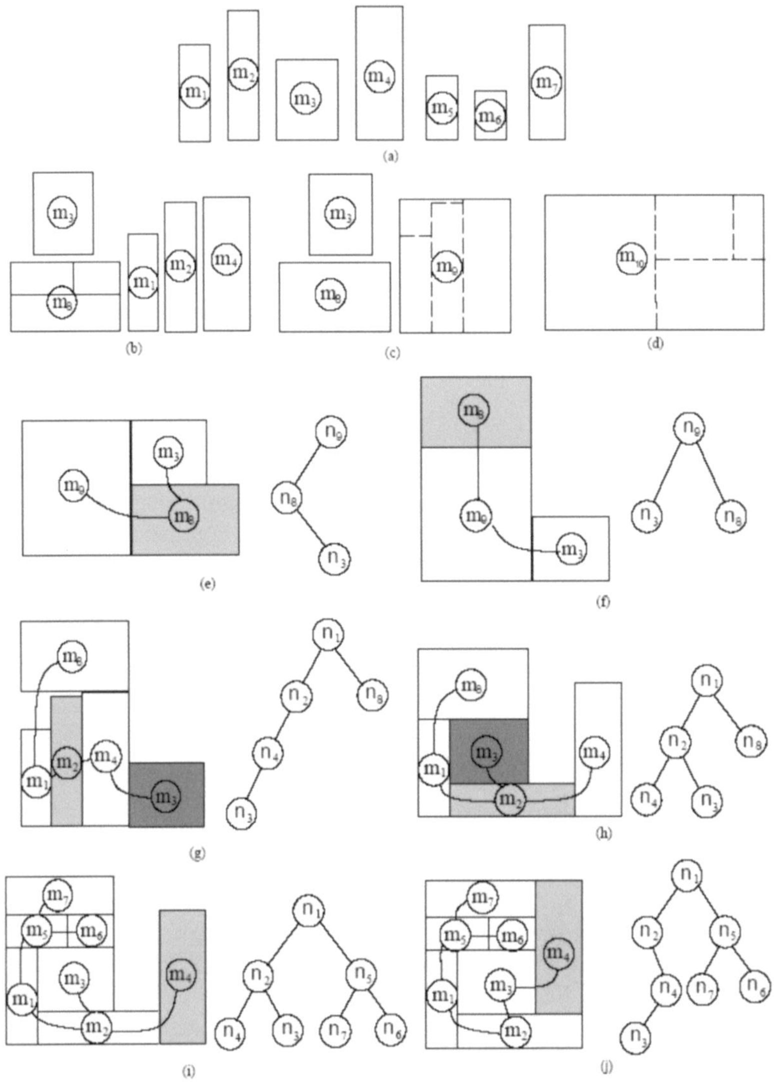

Fig. 11. An example of MBNE algorithm (Lee et al., 2003). In (f), we perform ϵ-neighborhood and λ-exchange refinement.

5. Conclusion

In this work, we have shown improved approaches on the multilevel hierarchical floorplan/placement for large-scale circuits. Our MBNE algorithm uses the improved format of ϵ-neighborhood and λ-exchange algorithm in simulated annealing based multilevel floorplanner. Experimental results have shown that the MBNE algorithm has better performance compared with the MB*-tree, state of the art floorplanner, in several benchmarks.

Package	Area optimization			WL optimization	
	Area(mm^2)	Dead space(%)	Time(min)	WL(mm)	Time(min)
MBNE	671.32/674.57	1.99/2.45	4.00/3.47	53723/58585	150.28/150.18
MB*-tree	673.60/679.41	2.32/3.15	3.95/3.84	55971/59759	180.45/184.54

Package	Simultaneous area and WL optimization			
	Area(mm^2)	Dead space(%)	WL(mm)	Time(min)
MBNE	730.70/742.07	9.95/11.30	63583/63956	150.12/150.10
MB*-tree	769.10/797.28	14.45/17.37	67179/66407	153.96/159.19

Table 1. Comparisons for area optimization alone, wirelength optimization alone, and simultaneous area and wirelength optimization between MBNE and MB*-tree based on the circuit *industry*.

Acknowledgement

We thank Mr. H.-C. Lee and Prof. Y.-W. Chang at National Taiwan University for their MB*-tree platform and benchmarks.

Circuit	# modules	Total area (mm^2)	MB*-tree			MBNE			Improvement in dead space (%)
			Area (mm^2)	Dead space (%)	Time (min)	Area (mm^2)	Dead space (%)	Time (min)	
ami49	49	35.445	36.46	2.79	1.19	36.22	2.14	1.00	0.65
ami49_4	196	141.780	146.86	3.46	6.29	144.86	2.12	5.00	1.34
ami49_20	980	708.908	732.19	3.18	10.21	727.81	2.60	10.08	0.58
ami49_60	2940	2126.724	2211.75	3.84	16.73	2195.76	3.14	15.17	0.70
ami49_100	4900	3544.540	3704.65	4.32	20.47	3681.56	3.72	20.18	0.60
ami49_150	7350	5316.750	5590.95	4.90	26.77	5560.33	4.38	25.58	0.52
ami49_200	9800	7089.808	7478.55	5.21	31.65	7454.86	4.91	30.13	0.30

Table 2. Comparisons for area and runtime between MBNE and MB*-tree in fabricated benchmarks from MCNC benchmark *ami*49.

n100	Area optimization			WL optimization	
	Area(0.001mm^2)	Dead space(%)	Time(min)	WL(mm)	Time(min)
MBNE	182.490	1.64	5.00	110.982	10.03
MB*-tree	184.338	2.62	5.17	111.819	10.89

n200	Area optimization			WL optimization	
	Area(0.001mm^2)	Dead space(%)	Time(min)	WL(mm)	Time(min)
MBNE	179.452	2.09	7.00	241.696	15.37
MB*-tree	180.000	2.39	7.78	244.233	15.94

n300	Area optimization			WL optimization	
	Area(0.001mm^2)	Dead space(%)	Time(min)	WL(mm)	Time(min)
MBNE	278.964	2.08	10.01	388.162	20.40
MB*-tree	279.310	2.20	10.17	391.651	21.45

Table 3. Comparisons for area and wirelength optimization between MBNE and MB*-tree with GSRC benchmarks.

Circuit	# modules	Total area ($0.001mm^2$)	MB*-tree			MBNE		
			Area ($0.001mm^2$)	Dead space (%)	Time (min)	Area ($0.001mm^2$)	Dead space (%)	Time (min)
industry	189	657,984	673,600	2.32	3.95	673,731	2.34	2.77
n100	100	179.500	184.338	2.62	5.17	183.365	2.11	3.61
ami49_20	980	708,908	732,190	3.18	10.21	729,982	2.89	7.57
ami49_60	2940	2,126,724	2,211,750	3.84	16.73	2,199,793	3.32	11.73

Table 4. Comparisons for efficiency between MBNE and MB*-tree with four benchmarks.

6. References

Alpert, C. J., Huang, J.-H. & Kahng, A. B. (1998). "Multilevel circuit partitioning", *IEEE Transactions on Computer-Aided Design of Integrated Circuits and Systems* **17**(8): 655–667.

Chan, T. F., Cong, J., Kong, T. & Shinnerl, J. R. (2000). "Multilevel optimization for large-scale circuit placement", *Proceedings IEEE/ACM International Conference on Computer-Aided Design*, pp. 171–176.

Chang, Y.-C., Chang, Y.-W., Wu, G.-M. & Wu, S.-W. (2000). "B*-trees: A new representation for non-slicing floorplans", *Proceedings IEEE/ACM Design Automation Conference*, pp. 458–463.

Cong, J., Fang, J. & Zhang, Y. (2001). "Multilevel approach to full-chip gridless routing", *Proceedings IEEE/ACM International Conference on Computer-Aided Design*, pp. 396–403.

Cong, J., Xie, M. & Zhang, Y. (2002). "An enhanced multilevel routing system", *Proceedings IEEE/ACM International Conference on Computer-Aided Design*, pp. 51–58.

Goto, S. (1981). "An efficient algorithm for the two-dimensional placement problem in electrical circuit layout", *IEEE Transactions on Circuits and Systems* **28**(1): 12–18.

Guo, P.-N., Cheng, C.-K. & Yoshimura, T. (1999). "An O-tree representation of non-slicing floorplan and its applications", *Proceedings IEEE/ACM Design Automation Conference*, pp. 268–273.

Hendrickson, B. & Leland, R. (1995). "A multilevel algorithm for partitioning graph", *Proceedings of Supercomputing*.

Karypis, G. & Kumar, V. (1999). "Multilevel k-way hypergraph partitioning", *Proceedings IEEE/ACM Design Automation Conference*, pp. 343–348.

Lee, H.-C., Chang, Y.-W., Hsu, J.-M. & Yang, H. H. (2003). "Multilevel floorplanning/placement for large-scale modules using B*-trees", *Proceedings IEEE/ACM Design Automation Conference*, pp. 812–817.

Lin, J.-M. & Chang, Y.-W. (2001). "TCG: A transitive closuer graph based representation for non-slicing floorplans", *Proceedings IEEE/ACM Design Automation Conference*, pp. 764–769.

Lin, J.-M. & Chang, Y.-W. (2002a). "TCG-S:Orthogonal coupling of P*-admissible representations for general floorplans", *Proceedings IEEE/ACM Design Automation Conference*, pp. 842–847.

Lin, J.-M., Chang, Y.-W. & Lin, S.-P. (2003). "Corner sequence: A P-admissible floorplan representation with a worst-case linear-time packing scheme", *IEEE Transactions on Very Large Scale Integration (VLSI) Systems* **11**(4): 679–686.

Lin, S.-P. & Chang, Y.-W. (2002b). "A novel framework for multilevel routing considering routability and performance", *Proceedings IEEE/ACM International Conference on Computer-Aided Design*, pp. 44–50.

Murata, H., Fujiyoshi, K., Nakatake, S. & Kajitani, Y. (1995). "Rectangle-packing based module placement", *Proceedings IEEE/ACM International Conference on Computer-Aided Design*, pp. 472–479.

Nakatake, S., Fujiyoshi, K., Murata, H. & Kajitani, Y. (1996). "Module placement on BSG-structure and IC layout applications", *Proceedings IEEE/ACM International Conference on Computer-Aided Design*, pp. 484–491.

Otten, R. H. J. M. (1982). "Automatic floorplan design", *Proceedings IEEE/ACM Design Automation Conference*, pp. 261–267.

Wong, D. F. & Liu, C. L. (1986). "A new algorithm for floorplan design", *Proceedings IEEE/ACM Design Automation Conference*, pp. 101–107.

14

Simulated Annealing and its Hybridisation on Noisy and Constrained Response Surface Optimisations

Pongchanun Luangpaiboon
Thammasat University
Thailand

1. Introduction

Optimisation of processes is an essential part of quality improvement in any industry. It will lead to the most efficient use of resources, with consequential environmental and financial benefits. Most manufacturing processes have some variables. Conventionally, a single response of our interest is influenced by these process variables. Care must be taken to operate industrial processes within safe limits, but optimal conditions are rarely attained and increased international competition means that deviations from the optimum can have serious financial consequences. In many cases the optimum changes with time and there is a need for a routine mode of operations to ensure that the process always operates at optimal or near-optimal conditions.

Response Surface Methodology (RSM) is a bundle of mathematical and statistical techniques that are helpful for modelling and analysing those problems. RSM describes how the yield of a process varies with changes in influential variables (Box and Draper, 1987). An objective of RSM is to determine the operating conditions or proper levels of these process variables to optimise the response. Estimation of such surfaces, and hence identification of near optimal settings for influential process variables is an important practical issue with interesting theoretical aspects. Many systematic methods for making an efficient empirical investigation of such surfaces have been proposed in the last fifty years. These are sometimes referred to as evolutionary operation (EVOP).

On the theory and practice of RSM, it is assumed that the mean response (η) is related to values of the process variables (x_1, x_2, ..., x_k) by an unknown function f. The functional relationship between the mean response and k process variables can be written as $\eta = f(X)$, if X denotes a column vector with elements x_1, x_2, ..., x_k. We usually represent a three dimensional response surface graphically as shown in Fig. 1, where η is plotted versus the levels of x_1 and x_2. To help visualise the shape of a response surface, we often plot the contours of the response surface. In the contour plot, lines of constant response are drawn in the x_1- x_2 plane. Each contour corresponds to a particular height of the response surface.

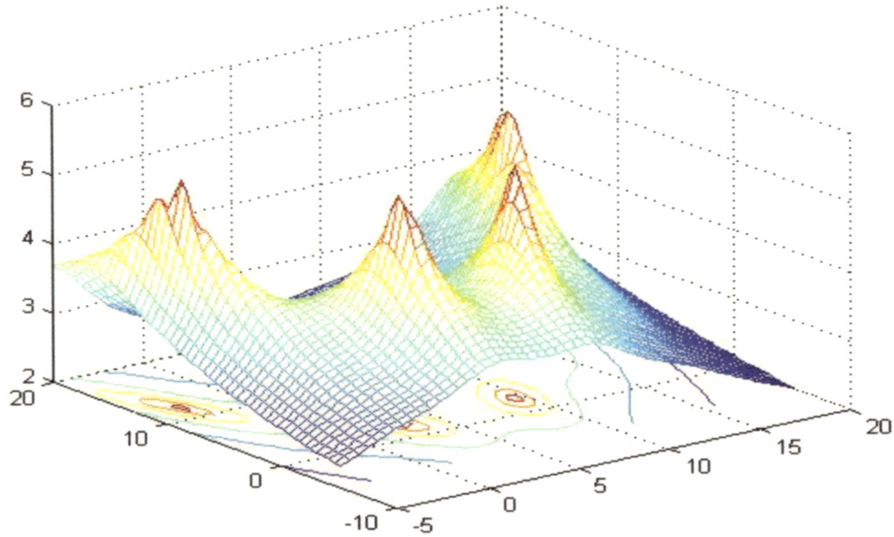

Fig. 1. A three dimensional response surface showing the expected yield with its contour plot

RSM uses statistical models, and therefore practitioners need to be aware that even the best statistical model is an approximation to reality. In practice, both the models and the parameter values are unknown, and subject to uncertainty on top of ignorance. Of course, an estimated optimal design point might not be the optimum in reality, because of the errors of the estimates and of the inadequacies of the model. Nonetheless, RSM has an effective track-record of helping researchers improve products and processes.

The optimisation of response surfaces is different from the conventional optimisation in various ways. Response surface optimisation is mainly an iterative procedure (Blum and Roli, 2003). Experiments, performed in one set, result in fitted models that indicate where to find improved levels of process variables in the next experiment. Thus, the coefficients in the fitted model may change during the response surface optimisation process. Moreover, the response surfaces are fitted from current experimental design points that usually contain random variability due to unknown or uncontrollable causes. If an experiment is repeated, the result will bring a different fitted response surface that may lead to different optimal levels of process variables. Therefore, sampling variability or noisy measurements should be concerned in this optimisation. It differs from the conventional optimisation in which the functions to be optimised are fixed and given.

Nowadays, many entrepreneurs face to extreme conditions for instances; costs, quality, sales and services. Technology has always been intertwined with our demands. Then almost manufacturers or assembling lines adopt it and come out with more complicated process inevitably. At this stage, product and process improvement need to be shifted from competitors with sustainability. Moreover, there are currently some problems associated with various process responses. If one can be assigned as the primary or the most important response and others return to be merely secondary responses or problem constraints. The constrained response surface optimisation is then proposed to find the new setting of optimal levels of process variables leading to the optimal level of the primary response and satisfying all other constraints of secondary responses. Moreover, lower and upper bounds of process variables can be included in order to avoid achieved solutions that extrapolate too far outside the feasible region of the experimental design points.

These difficulties associated with using response surface optimisations on complex, large-scale, noisy and constrained engineering problems have contributed researchers to seek the alternatives, based on simulations, learning, adaptation and evolution to solve these problems. Natural intelligence-inspired approximation optimisation techniques called meta-heuristics are then introduced. The common factor in meta-heuristics is that they combine rules and randomness to imitate natural phenomena. They widely grow and apply to solve many types of problems. The major reason is that meta-heuristic approaches can guide the stochastic search process to iteratively seek near optimal solutions in practical and desirable computational time. The meta-heuristic algorithms are then received more attention in the last few decades. They can be categorised into three classes: biologically-based inspiration, e.g. Genetic Algorithm or GA (Goldberg, 1989), Neural Network or NN (Haykin, 1999), Ant Colony Optimisation or ACO (Merz and Freisleben, 1999), Artificial Immune System (AIS) by Dasgupta (1998) and Hart and Timmis (2008), Particle Swarm Optimisation or PSO (Kennedy and Eberhart, 2001) and Shuffled Frog Leaping Algorithm or SFLA (Eusuff et al., 2006); socially-based inspiration, e.g. Taboo Search or TS (Glover, 1986); and physically-based inspiration such as Simulated Annealing or SA.

In this research we examine steepest ascent, simulated annealing and ant colony optimisation algorithms on various hypothetical unconstrained response surfaces with 2-5 process variables. Considering the solution space in a specified region, some surfaces contain global optimum and multiple local optimums and some are with the curved ridge. The comparisons are made for four different levels of measurement noise on the response. The noise is taken to be independently and normally distributed with mean of zero and standard deviations of 0, 1, 2 and 3. There are 100 realisations in each experimental level of measurement noise to check a consistency of numerical results. These algorithms have been developed through computer simulation programs. The effects of different choices of algorithms on different performance measures are investigated. The performance achievements consist of Taguchi's signal to noise ratio of the larger the better case, mean and standard deviation of responses. All the algorithms are run until they converge. The additional comparisons are made to constrained processes on turning machining and spring force problems (Khan et al., 1997). In order to improve the fine-tuning characteristic of the single algorithm, a hybridisation based on the most efficient algorithms are also introduced.

This paper is organised as follows. Sections 2, 3 and 4 describe the details of conventional steepest ascent, simulated annealing and ant colony optimisation algorithms, respectively. Section 5 provides experimental results on noisy unconstrained and constrained response surface optimisation problems. The conclusions and recommendations are also summarised in Section 6. It is followed by acknowledgments and references.

2. Steepest Ascent Algorithm (ST)

Box and Draper (1987) described a mechanistic model as a physically based mathematical formula, which represents the yield of a process in terms of those process variables, which are known to influence it. In contrast to this, a relatively simple function or typically some fitted polynomial which approximates the physical formula at least locally, is referred to as an empirical model. Often, the mechanistic model is a large-scale description of a process, which can be used to define some safe and economically viable region of operation. Empirical models can then be used to identify optimal conditions within this region.

Suppose the yield of a system depends on a number (k) of process variables, which are restricted to some region of safe operation. In geometric terms this equation can be represented by a surface in the k+1 dimension. The expected value of the yield is some unknown function of the k process variables, and the measured yields will vary about their expected values because of random errors. These errors are comprised of natural variation in the process and measurement errors, which occur when monitoring the yield, and are assumed to have a mean of zero and to be uncorrelated with the values taken by the k process variables. Errors in measuring the values of the k process variables are usually assumed to be negligible in comparison with the random errors associated with the yield. These random errors are also often assumed to be independently drawn from a normal distribution with constant variance, although this is not a requirement for the validity of the techniques presented here.

There are many response surface optimisation methods. One among those is called the steepest ascent algorithm (ST). It aims to seek a region around the global optimum via a first-order polynomial model from a factorial experimental design or its fraction. The ST procedure is that a hyperplane is fitted to the results from the initial design points. The direction of steepest ascent on the hyperplane is then determined by using a principle of regression analysis. The next run is carried out at a design point, which is some fixed distance in this direction, and further runs are carried out by continuing in this direction until no further increase in yield is noted. When the response first decreases another factorial design is carried out, centred on the preceding design point. A new direction of steepest ascent is estimated from this latest experiment. Provided at least one of the coefficients of the hyperplane is statistically significantly different from zero, the search continues in this manner (Myers and Montgomery, 1995). The pseudo code is used to briefly explain to all the procedures of the ST shown in Fig. 2.

Procedure of the ST Metaheuristic()
While *(termination criterion not satisfied) – (line 1)*
  Initialise ST parameters: the unit of the step length, limited moves and the significance level for tests of significance of slopes;
  Randomly select a starting point to be the centre of a factorial design;
  Calculate a fitness value in each design point at the centre and peripheral locations;
  Schedule activities
  Determine the significant first order model from the factorial design points;
    Schedule activities
    Move along the steepest ascent's path with a step length (Δ);
    Compute the fitness value;
    if *the new one is greater than the preceding* **then**
      Move ahead with another Δ;
    else
      Calculate two more fitness values to verify the descending trend;

if *one of which fitness values turn out to be greater than a preceding coordinate's fitness value* **then**
Use the biggest fitness value to continually move along the same path;
else
Use the closest preceding point as the centre for a new factorial design;
end if
end if
end schedule activities
end schedule activities
end while
end procedure

Fig. 2. Pseudo Code of the ST Metaheuristic.

3. Simulated Annealing Algorithm (SA)

Kirkpatrick and his colleagues (Kirkpatrick et al., 1983) first proposed a detailed analogy of an annealing in solids to the combinatorial optimisation called as Simulated Annealing (SA). The annealing processes are performed by first melting the system at a high temperature, then lowering the temperature slowly, finally spending a long time at freezing temperatures. During the annealing process, the time spent at each temperature level must be sufficiently long to allow the system to reach a thermal equilibrium or a steady state. If care is not taken in adhering to the annealing temperature schedule, undesirable random fluctuations may cause the shift of the ground state. The basic idea of statistical mechanics initiates a generalisation of the iterative improvement or the search for a better solution of the combinatorial optimisation.

The SA has been derived from an interesting analogy between problems in statistical mechanics and multivariate or combinatorial optimisation. This algorithm is a set of rules for searching large solution spaces in a manner that mimics the annealing process of metals. The algorithm simulates the behaviour of an ensemble of atoms in equilibrium at a given finite temperature (Bohachevsky et al., 1986) and its original framework can be traced to Metropolis et al. This algorithm has been regularly used in global function optimisation and statistical applications.

In case of maximisation, procedures of this algorithm start at a corresponding initial value of the objective function. The new objective value will be then determined. The new solution will be unconditionally accepted if its objective value is improved and the process regularly continues. Otherwise the difference or size of increment in objective values, δy, is calculated and with an auxiliary experiment the new solution would be accepted with probability $P(\delta y)$. This stochastic element is from Monte Carlo sampling. It occasionally allows the algorithm to accept the new solution to the problems, which deteriorate rather than improve the objective function value. The pseudo code is used to briefly explain to all the procedures of the SA shown in Fig. 3.

Procedure of the SA Metaheuristic()
Initialise SA parameters: number of iterations, a reducing rate, starting and freezing temperatures;
Find a starting temperature;
Find a random starting solution (s);

While not *the freezing temperature;*
    do while not *an equilibrium;*
      do *to get the neighbourhood solution* (s_n);
        Evaluate δy *of* $eval(s_n) - eval(s)$;
        if $\delta y \geq 0$ **then** $s \leftarrow s_n$
        else if *random(0,1)* $\leq$ *Boltzman()* ***then*** $s \leftarrow s_n$;
            end if
        end if
      $T \leftarrow cool(T)$;
      Report (s);
      loop
    loop
end while
end procedure

Fig. 3. Pseudo Code of the SA Metaheuristic.

4. Ant Colony Optimisation Algorithm (ACO)

Ant Colony Optimisation (ACO) was first proposed by Dorigo and his colleagues (Dorigo et al., 1996) as a multi-agent approach to optimisation problems, such as a travelling salesman problem (TSP) and a quadratic assignment problem (QAP). There is currently a lot of ongoing activity in the scientific community to extend or apply ant-based algorithms, especially in various discrete optimisation problems (Dorigo and Stutzle, 2004). Recent applications cover problems like a vehicle routing, a plant layout and so on. The ACO is inspired by observations of real ant colonies. Behaviour is direct more to the survival of the colony as a whole than to that of a single individual component of the colony. Social insects have captured the attention from many scientists because of a structure of their colonies, especially when compared with a relative simplicity of the colony's individual (Dorigo and Blum, 2005).

An important and interesting issue of ant colonies is their foraging behaviour and in particular how ants can find shortest paths between food sources and their nest. While walking from food sources to the nest and vice versa, ants deposit on the ground a substance called pheromone, forming in this way a pheromone trail. Ants can smell pheromone. When choosing their way, they tend to choose paths marked by strong pheromone concentrations. The pheromone trail allows the ant to find their way back to the food source or to the nest. Also, it can be used by other ants to find the location of the food sources found by their nest mates. The pseudo code is used to briefly explain to all the procedures of the ACO shown in Fig. 4.

Procedure of the ACO Metaheuristic()
While *(termination criterion not satisfied) – (line 1)*
    Initialise ACO parameter: number of iterations, ants and moves;
    Schedule activities
    Make the path or step for each ant;
    Evaluate the fitness values;

```
    Compare fitness values;
    if no improvement of the fitness value then
            Communicate with the best ant fitness value;
            Make the path or step from the local trap to best ant;
    else
            if ant found the better response function then
                Go to line 5;
            else
                Wait for the best ant communication;
            end if
    end if
    end schedule activities
end while
end procedure
```

Fig. 4. Pseudo Code of the ACO Metaheuristic.

5. Experimental Results

Response surface algorithms of the ST, SA and ACO with some modifications are applied to engineering optimisation problems with continuous process variables. Several examples taken from the standard benchmark engineering optimisation literature are used to show how the proposed approaches work. These examples have been previously solved using a variety of other techniques, which are useful to demonstrate the validity, effectiveness and robustness of the proposed algorithms. The performance measures of these algorithms consist of the sample mean and standard deviation (S) of yields including Taguchi signal to noise ratio in the cases of 'the larger the better', SN1, and 'the smaller the better', SN2 (Taguchi and Wu, 1980):

$$SN1 = -10*\log(\sum (1/y_i^2)/n)$$

$$SN2 = -10*\log(\sum (y_i^2)/n))$$

in which y_i represents the best yield at the end of trial i, and n is the number of trials. Some experiments include the design points used to achieve the final solution and the computational times as the additional performance measures.

5.1 Noisy and unconstrained response surface optimisation

In this subsection, eight non-linear continuous unconstrained functions (Fig. 5-12) in the context of response surface were used to test performance measures of the related algorithms whilst searching for the optimum. It is assumed that the current operating conditions correspond to process variables are randomly taken as the starting point for the algorithms. The comparisons are made for four different levels of measurement noise on the response. There are 100 realisations in each experimental level of measurement noise. The noise is taken to be independently and normally distributed with mean of zero and standard deviations of 0, 1, 2 and 3.

A. Branin Function

$$f(x) = 5 - \log_{10}[(x_2 - \frac{5.1}{4\pi^2}x_1^2 + \frac{5}{\pi}x_1 - 6)^2 + (10 - \frac{5}{4\pi}\cos(x_1)) + 10]$$

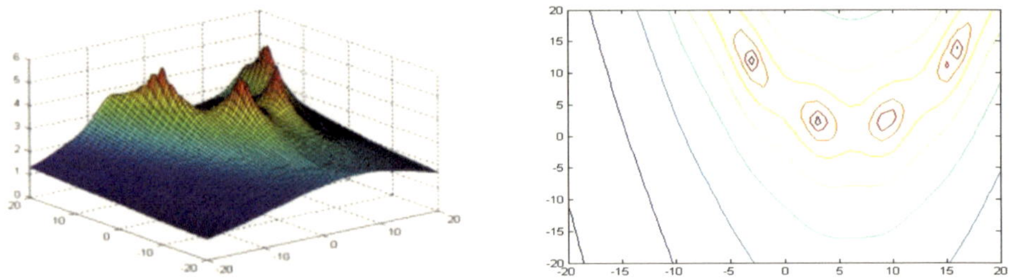

(a) (b)

Fig. 5. Branin surface (a) and its contour (b).

B. Camelback Function

$$f(x) = 10 - \log_{10}[x_1^2(4 - 2.1x_1^2 + \frac{1}{3}x_1^4) + x_1x_2 + 4x_2^2(x_2^2 + 1)]$$

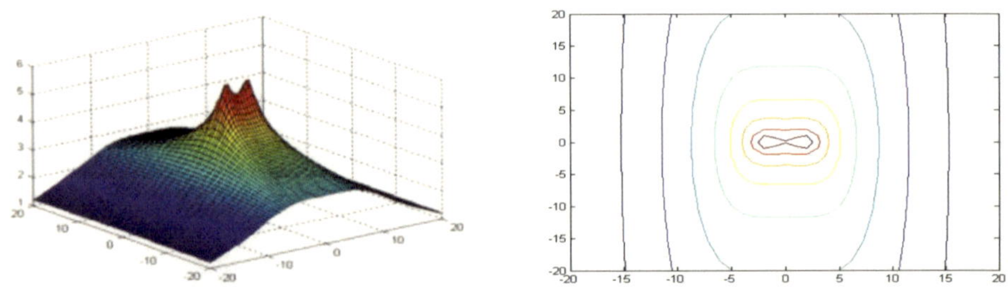

(a) (b)

Fig. 6. Camelback surface (a) and its contour (b).

C. Goldstein-Price Function

$$f(x) = 10 + \log_{10}[1 / \{1 + (1 + x_1 + x_2)^2(19 - 14x_1 + 3x_1^2 - 14x_2 + 6x_1x_2 + 3x_2^2)\} * \{30 + (2x_1 - 3x_2)^2(18 - 32x_1 + 12x_1^2 + 48x_2 - 36x_1x_2 + 27x_2^2)\}]$$

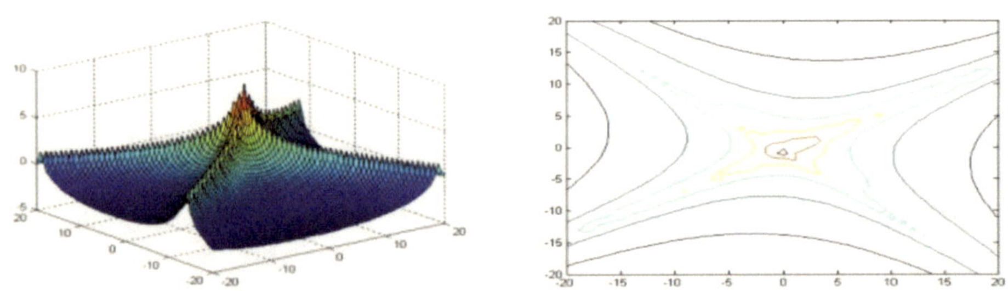

(a) (b)

Fig. 7. Goldstein-Price surface (a) and its contour (b).

D. Parabolic Function

$$f(x) = 12 - (\sum_{j=1}^{k} x_j^2 / 100)$$

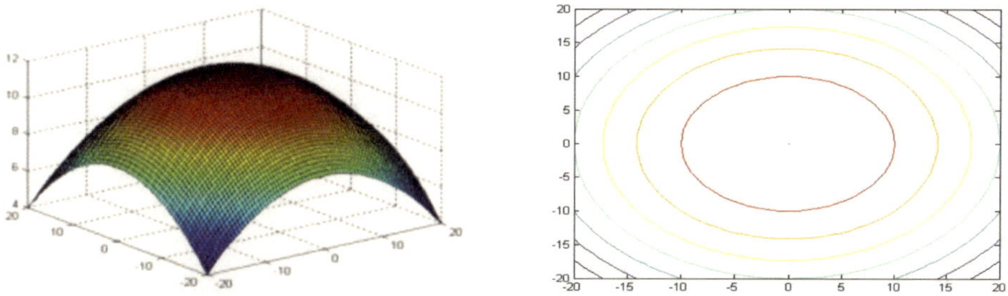

(a) (b)

Fig. 8. Parabolic surface (a) and its contour (b).

E. Rastrigin Function

$$f(x) = 80 - [20 + \sum_{j=1}^{k} x_j^2 - 10(\sum_{j=1}^{k} \cos 2\pi x_j)]$$

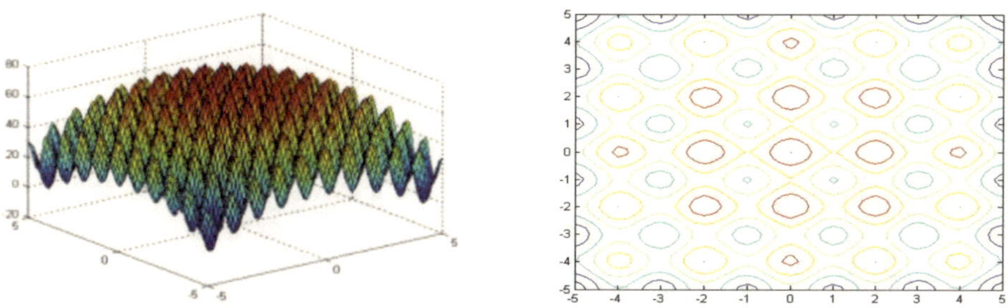

(a) (b)

Fig. 9. Rastrigin surface (a) and its contour (b).

F. Rosenbrock Function

$$f(x) = 70\,[(\{20 - ((-x_1 / a_1)^2 + \sum_{j=2}^{k}[(x_j / a_j) - (x_1 / a_1)^2]^2)\} + 150) / 170] + 10;$$

where a_1, a_2, a_3, a_4, and a_5 are set at 6, -7, -2, 4 and 5, respectively.

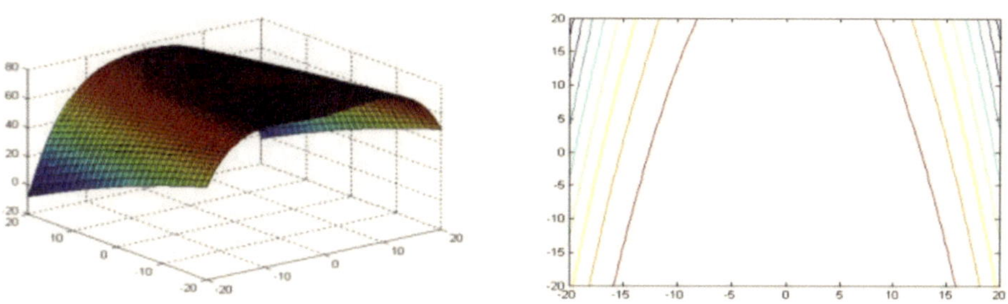

(a) (b)

Fig. 10. Rosenbrock surface (a) and its contour (b).

G. Shekel Function

$$f(x) = 100 \sum_{i=1}^{5} \frac{1}{c_i + \sum_{j=1}^{k} (x_j - a_{ij})^2};$$

where the parameters of local optimum locations (a_{ij}) and the local peak magnitude values (c_i) are shown on the table below.

i	a_{ij}					
	j					
	1	2	3	4	5	c_i
1	4	6	-2	2	4	9
2	0	0	-8	-5	6	20
3	-8	3	4	1	5	14
4	-8	-8	1	-7	-1	11
5	6	-7	-2	4	2	6

Table 1. Shekel function parameters

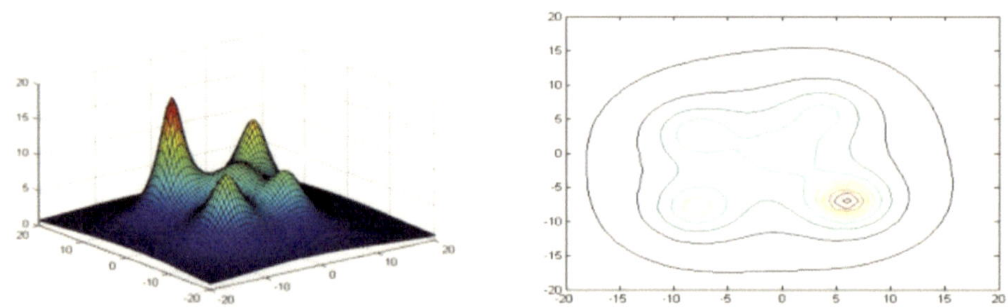

(a) (b)

Fig. 11. Shekel surface (a) and its contour (b).

H. Styblinski Function

$$f(x) = 275 - [(\frac{(x_1^4 - 16x_1^2 + 5x_1)}{2}) + (\frac{(x_2^4 - 16x_2^2 + 5x_2)}{2}) + \sum_{j=3}^{5}(x_j - 1)^2]$$

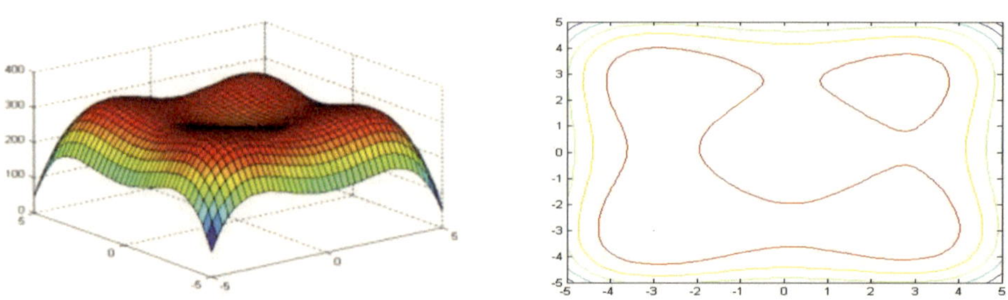

(a) (b)

Fig. 12. Styblinski surface (a) and its contour (b).

In this work, a computer simulation program was developed using Matlab 2006v.7.3B, and EVOPtimiser v.1.1.0. A Laptop computer with ASUS F83SE 2.20GHz Core Two T6600 processor and 4 GB RAM was used for all computational experiments. It is stated that some heuristic parameters have to be only positive integers. Consequently the process will confront with round-up error that would probably create a premature stop. The first phase of the designed experiments was aimed to investigate the appropriate parameter settings of the ST, SA and ACO algorithms. The ST contains three parameters namely, the number of iterations (α_{ST}), limited moves (β_{ST}) and the unit of the step length (γ_{ST}). The SA parameters are the number of iterations (α_{SA}), the starting temperature (β_{SA}) and the reducing rate (γ_{SA}). Finally the ACO contains three parameters of the number of iterations (α_{ACO}), ants (β_{ACO}) and moves (γ_{ACO}).

All parameters were considered at three levels and these values were based on the suggestions related to the algorithms available in the literatures. The experimental results were analysed via the Taguchi analyses as shown in Table 2 for the Branin function without noise and all main effects are given in Fig. 13. The results provided the most influential parameter of the number of limited moves via the largest magnitude (Delta) of the difference from all three levels or the first rank. The most proper level for the three parameters were 4000, 200 and 0.05 for the number of iterations, limited moves and step lengths, respectively. The overall parameter levels are summarised in Table 3.

Level	α_{ST}	β_{ST}	γ_{ST}
1	5.911	5.916	5.915
2	5.912	5.912	5.912
3	5.910	5.906	5.906
Delta	0.002	0.010	0.008
Rank	3	1	2

Table 2. Taguchi analyses of the ST parameters on the Branin function without noise

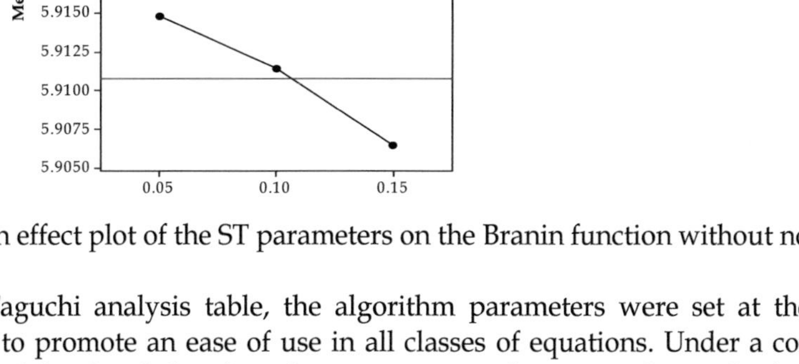

Fig. 13. Main effect plot of the ST parameters on the Branin function without noise

From the Taguchi analysis table, the algorithm parameters were set at the same levels throughout to promote an ease of use in all classes of equations. Under a consideration of recommended levels of the algorithm parameters, those may bring the benefit to solve industrial processes when the nature of the problems can be categorised as unimodal, multimodal or curve ridge including the mixed nature of multimodal and curve ridge response surfaces.

Surface	ST			SA			ACO		
	α_{ST}	β_{ST}	γ_{SA}	α_{SA}	β_{SA}	γ_{SA}	α_{ACO}	β_{ACO}	γ_{ACO}
Branin	4000	200	0.05	150	3	0.9	5	40	10
Parabolic	-	-	-	150	1	0.9	-	-	-
Rosenbrock	5000	400	0.10	120	2	0.9	-	-	-
Shekel	4000	200	0.05	150	1	0.9	5	40	10

Table 3. Taguchi analyses of the algorithm parameters on four functions without noise

For the ST algorithm, preferable levels of the number of iterations, limited moves and the unit of the step length are set at 4000, 200 and 0.05, respectively. While the SA parameters of the number of iterations, the starting temperature and the reducing rate are set at 120, 1 and 0.9, respectively. It is suggested that the setting of the ACO parameters on the number of iterations, ants and moves should be set at 5, 40 and 10, respectively.

The next phase of experiments was aimed to comparatively study the performance of the algorithms improving the process towards the optimum. The appropriate settings of all algorithm parameters determined in the previous experiment were applied. The proposed algorithms are designed to use three performance measures as improving trigger, rather than ordinary yields. The computational results obtained from 100 realisations were then analysed in terms of the sample mean and standard deviation including Taguchi signal to noise ratio.

The first scenario was to determine the effects of an increase in process variables on the performance measures of all three algorithms. It can be seen that the performances of the ACO based on the Parabolic surface were obviously insensitive to the increase of process variables according to the mean, the standard deviation and the signal to noise ratio. However, the SA provided the more preferable when compared with the standard deviation. The sensitivity results to an increase of process variables on the Parabolic surface were shown in Fig. 14. In general, the ACO seemed to be the insensitive strategy that only worked well on all surfaces in terms of the sample means and signal to noise ratios for all levels of process variables. The SA was rather sensitive to the number of process variables, but this may not be a serious drawback in the context of automatic process control.

The second scenario was to determine the effects of an increase in the noise standard deviation on the performance measures of all three algorithms. On all surfaces, the algorithms provided the same level of performance measures of the sample mean, standard deviation and signal to noise ratio when the standard deviation of the errors was low. However, when the standard deviation of the errors increased, the ACO can be the only strategy to rely upon to locate the optimum on all performance measures, especially the signal to noise ratio on the Camelback multi peak surface (Fig. 15).

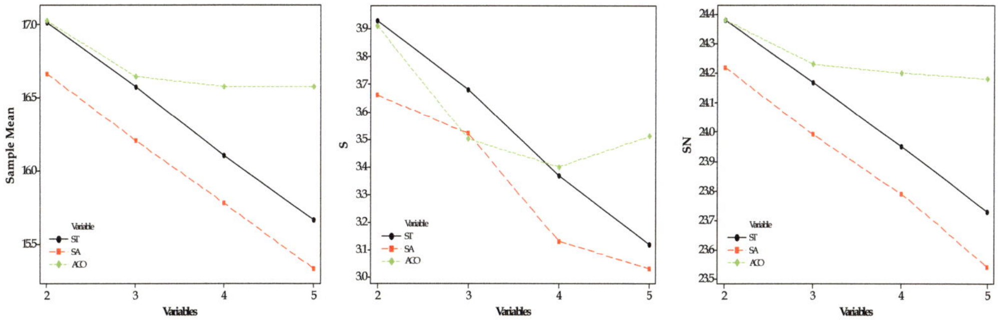

Fig. 14. Sensitivity analysis on all algorithms to an increase of process variables for the Parabolic function.

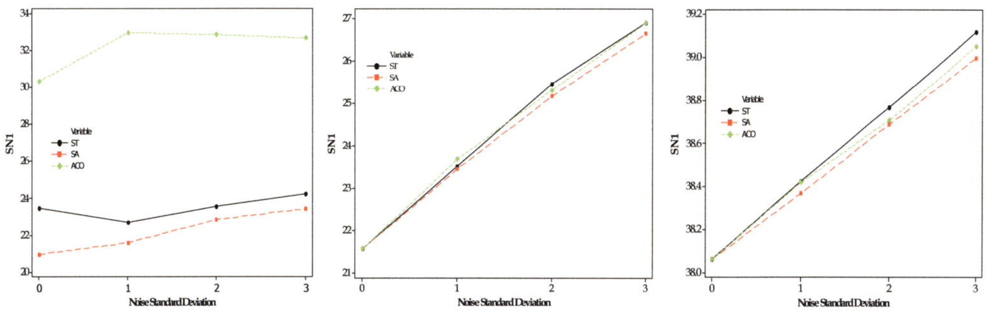

Fig. 15. Sensitivity analyses on the SN1 to an increase of the noise standard deviation for the Camelback, Parabolic and Rosenbrock functions.

From Table 4, it can be seen that the ACO found the better solutions in terms of the sample mean of the yields on all response surfaces with two process variables. The number of design points and computational time for all tested functions for the SA were dramatically better than those results obtained from the ACO. On average the computational time taken by the SA was on average 25 times quicker than the computational time required by the ACO. The average of the process yields on the Parabolic and Rosenbrock functions were not statistically significant at 95% confidence interval or there was no difference among these algorithms.

The additional experimental results on surfaces with three, four and five similarly suggested that only the ACO can provide an acceptable solution or even an optimal solution. The average computational time required by the ST and the SA was dramatically faster than the ACO. However, the SA significantly gave the fewer design points when compared as shown in Table 5. In summary, when the surface is more complicated especially with three, four and five process variables or higher levels of noise, the ACO seems more suitable to exploit a solution space as a local search without a consideration of the computational time and design points. Although the SA is quick to converge to the optimum on the design points, some of these runs lead to relatively low yields.

From experimental results above we can conclude the performance measures of the best so far response, Insensitivity to Noise, design points and computational time each algorithm in

Table 6. Most of the best so far responses from the ACO are quite close to the optimum and insensitive to various conditions, but the SA can quickly converge to the optimum when compared. A hybridisation of the ACO and the SA are then selected to determine the performances of various industrial problems.

Model	Response	P-Value	ST	SA	ACO
Branin	Yield	0.007			✓
	Design Point	0.000		✓	
	Computational Time	0.000	✓	✓	
Camelback	Yield	0.000			✓
	Design Point	0.000		✓	
	Computational Time	0.000	✓	✓	
Goldstein Price	Yield	0.000			✓
	Design Point	0.000		✓	
	Computational Time	0.000	✓	✓	
Parabolic	Yield	0.843			
	Design Point	0.000		✓	
	Computational Time	0.000	✓	✓	
Rastrigin	Yield	0.000			✓
	Design Point	0.000		✓	
	Computational Time	0.000	✓	✓	
Rosenbrock	Yield	0.625			
	Design Point	0.000		✓	
	Computational Time	0.000		✓	
Shekel	Yield	0.000			✓
	Design Point	0.000		✓	
	Computational Time	0.000	✓	✓	
Styblinski	Yield	0.000	✓		✓
	Design Point	0.000		✓	
	Computational Time	0.000		✓	

Table 4. Performance measures on all tested problems with two process variables

Model	Response	Variable			ST	SA	ACO
		3	4	5			
		P-Value	P-Value	P-Value			
Parabolic	Yield	0.774	0.413	0.095			
	Design Point	0.000	0.000	0.000		✓	
	Computational Time	0.000	0.000	0.000		✓	
Rastrigin	Yield	0.000	0.000	0.000			✓
	Design Point	0.000	0.000	0.000		✓	
	Computational Time	0.000	0.000	0.000		✓	
Rosenbrock	Yield	0.153	0.009	0.000			✓
	Design Point	0.000	0.000	0.000		✓	
	Computational Time	0.000	0.000	0.000		✓	

Shekel	Yield	0.000	0.000	0.000			✓
	Design Point	0.000	0.006	0.000		✓	
	Computational Time	0.000	0.000	0.000		✓	
Styblinski	Yield	0.000	0.000	0.000	✓		✓
	Design Point	0.000	0.000	0.000		✓	
	Computational Time	0.000	0.000	0.000		✓	

Table 5. Performance measures on all tested problems with three, four and fives process variables

Performance Measure	Good		Poor
Best So Far Response	ACO	ST	SA
Insensitivity to Noise	ACO	ST	SA
Design Point	SA	ACO	ST
Computational Time	SA	ST	ACO

Table 6. Advantage and disadvantage of all response surface algorithms on noisy unconstrained response surface optimisation problems

5.2 Constrained response surface optimisation

Industrial problems of turning machining and spring force models were also use to determine the performances of the algorithms. Hati and Rao (HR) model is the mathematical functions for a multi-pass turning optimisation of the mild steel work-piece using a carbide tool. An objective function is to minimise a production cost in dollars/piece. Ermer (E) and Ermer and Kromodihardjo (EK) models minimise a production cost in dollars/piece for single pass turning. Iwata, Oba and Murotsu (IOM) model has been proposed for multi-pass turning operation of medium carbon steel using carbide tool where an objective is to minimise the production cost in yens/piece (Khan et al., 1997). A spring force (SP) model is finally applied to study the performance of the algorithms. The mathematical model is defined to maximise a spring force which reacts to spring conditions or parameters.

A. HR-model

$$\text{MIN COST} = n\left(3141.59V^{-1}f^{-1}d^{-4} + 2.879\times10^{-8}V^{4}f^{0.75}d^{-0.025} + 10\right)$$

Subject to the following constraints:

(1) Minimal and maximal cutting speeds (m/min): $50 \le V \le 400$

(2) Minimal and maximal feed rates (mm/rev): $0.30 \le f \le 0.75$

(3) Allowable range of depths of cut (mm): $1.20 \le d \le 2.75$

(4) Cutting force (kg): $Fc \le 85$

; where

$$F_C = \left(28.10V^{0.07} - 0.525V^{0.5}\right)d\times f\left(1.59 + 0.946\frac{(1+x)}{\sqrt{(1-x)^2 + x}}\right)$$

and

$$x = \left(\frac{V}{142}\exp(2.21f)\right)^2$$

(5) Cutting power (kW): $Pc \le 2.25$

; where

$$P_C = \frac{0.746 F_C V}{4500}$$

(6) Tool life (min): $25 \le TL \le 45$

; where

$$TL = 60\left(\frac{10^{10}}{V^5 f^{1.75} d^{0.75}}\right)$$

(7) Temperature (°C) $T \le 1000$

; where

$$T = 132 V^{0.4} f^{0.2} d^{0.105}$$

(8) Limitations on the value of the depth of cut in removing 'A' in 'n' passes: (A = 5 mm. d = 2.5 mm.)

$$\frac{A}{d} = n$$

B. E-model

$$\text{MIN COST} = 1.25 V^{-1} f^{-1} + 1.8 \times 10^{-8} V^3 f^{0.16} + 0.2$$

Subject to the following constraints:

(1) Surface finish (µin): $SF \le 100$

; where $SF = 1.36 \times 10^8 V^{-1.52} f^{1.004}$

(2) Feed rate (in/rev): $F \le 0.01$

(3) Cutting force (hp): $HP \le 2.0$

; where $HP = 3.58 V^{0.91} f^{0.78}$

C. EK-model

$$\text{MIN COST} = 1.2566 V^{-1} f^{-1} + 1.77 \times 10^{-8} V^3 f^{0.16} + 0.2$$

Subject to the following constraints:

(1) Feed rate (in/rev): $f \le 0.1$

(2) Horse power (hp): $HP \le 4$

; where $HP = 2.39 V^{0.91} f^{0.78} d^{0.75}$

(3) Surface finish (µin): $SF \le 50$

; where $SF = 204.62 \times 10^6 V^{-1.52} f^{1.004} D^{0.25}$

D. IOM-model

$$\text{MIN COST} = \sum_{i=1}^{n} 3927 V_i^{-1} f_i^{-1} + 1.95 \times 10^{-8} V_i^{2.88} f_i^{-1} \exp(5.884 f_i) d_i^{-1.117} + 60$$

Subject to the following constraints:

(1) Minimal and maximal feed rates (mm/rev): $0.001 \le f \le 5.6$

(2) Minimal and maximal cutting speeds (m/min): $14.13 \le V \le 1005.3$

(3) Minimal and maximal depth of cut (mm): $0 \le d \le A$

; where 'A' is the depth of material to be cut.

(4) Maximal cutting force (kg): $FC \le 170$

; where $F_C = 290.73 V^{-0.1013} f^{0.725} d$

(5) Stable cutting region related to the cutting surface: $fV^2 \ge 2230.5$

(6) Maximal allowed surface roughness: $0.356f^2 \le H_{max}$
; where H_{max} ranges from 0.01 to 0.06 mm.

(7) Maximal power consumption (kW): $P_c = 7.5$
; where $P_C = \frac{F_C V}{4896}$

(8) The sum of depths of cut of the 'n' passes used to remove the total depth 'A' of the material

$$\sum_{i=1}^{n} d_i = A$$

E. SP-model

$$\text{MAX } f(X) = (300 + 16x_5)\left(\frac{140}{x_1} - 1\right) + x_3\left(x_2 + (x_5 - 20)\left(\frac{280}{x_1} - 1\right) - x_4\right)\left(\frac{280}{x_1} - 1\right)$$

Subject to the following constraints:

(1) Minimal and maximal edge of paper which faces to shaft: $100 \le x_1 \le 180$

(2) Minimal and maximal joint of spring: $35 \le x_2 \le 75$

(3) Minimal and maximal strength of spring: $5 \le x_3 \le 15$

(4) Minimal and maximal compression distance of spring: $20 \le x_4 \le 50$

(5) Minimal and maximal paper thickness: $0 \le x_5 \le 50$

This section presents the performance study of the algorithms on industrial problems. Cost minimisation from a turning machine is determined at different conditions i.e. a cutting speed, a feed rate, a depth and a cutting force illustrated from the previous section. In addition, a spring test is also studied in different conditions of independent factors such as a joint, strength and a compression distance to maximise the spring force. The ACO and an integrated algorithm of the SA and ACO, HYBRID, are proposed to eliminate a disadvantage of the computational time. The results are summarised in Tables 7-9 below.

Performance Measure	Turning Machine Models							
	HR		E		EK		IOM	
	Design point	Yield	Design point	Yield	Design point	Yield	Design point	Yield
Mean	14532	79.28	7200	6.29	7200	1.55	14954	122.6
S	13	0.153	0	0.034	0	0.000	26.8	0.050
Max	14555	79.60	7200	6.39	7200	1.55	15005	122.6
Min	14508	79.14	7200	6.26	7200	1.55	14923	122.5
SN2	-	37.98	-	15.97	-	3.82	-	41.8

Table 7. Detailed results of turning machining problems through the ACO

From the ANOVA table for the HR-model (Table 10), it can be seen that both proposed heuristics were statistically significant in this case with a 95% confidence interval since having the P-value less than or equal to 0.05. The ACO significantly contributed the best solution for all industrial problems. Almost responses from the ACO were better than the HYBRID as described in Table 11 and the box-plots (Fig. 16). However, the HYBRID which was developed from the SA and ACO enabled to search the optimal response of constrained problems faster. That is the strong point of the simulated annealing algorithm. However, it has to trade off searching ability for the optimal response with the computational time. The selection of the suitable method based on the types of problems should be carefully considered as shown in Table 12.

Performance Measure	Turning Machine Model							
	HR		E		EK		IOM	
	Design point	Yield	Design point	Yield	Design point	Yield	Design point	Yield
Mean	6000	79.44	6000	6.31	6000	1.56	6000	124.01
S	0	0.12	0	0.02	0	0.002	0	0.75
Max	6000	79.61	6000	6.33	6000	1.56	6000	125.64
Min	6000	79.22	6000	6.27	6000	1.55	6000	122.73
SN2	-	38.00	-	16.00	-	3.84	-	41.87

Table 8. Detailed results of turning machining problems through the HYBRID

Performance Measures	ACO		HYBRID	
	Design point	Yield	Design point	Yield
Mean	1968640	3166.56	7393	2604.85
S	927	125.03	470	162.50
Max	1970073	3368.71	8165	2926.80
Min	1967196	2869.09	6750	2372.61
SN1	-	69.992	-	68.281

Table 9. Detailed results of a spring force problem through the ACO and the HYBRID

Source	DF	SS	MS	F	P-Value
Heuristics	1	0.2016	0.2016	10.76	0.003
Error	28	0.5247	0.0187		
Total	29	0.7263			

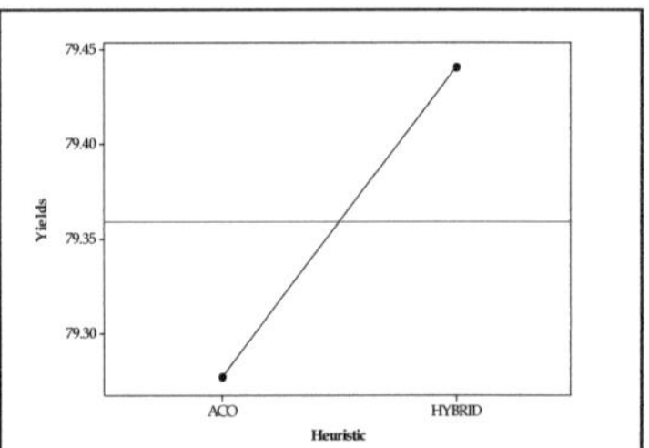

Table 10. ANOVA table and the main effect plot of the process yields on the HR-model

Model	Response	P-Value	ACO	HYBRID
HR	Mean of Yield	0.003	✓	
	Stdev of Yield	0.403		
	SN2	0.027	✓	
	Design Point	0.000		✓
	Computational Time	0.000	✓	
E	Mean of Yield	0.121		
	Stdev of Yield	0.379		
	SN2	0.245		

	Design Point	0.000		✓
	Computational Time	0.000	✓	
EK	Mean of Yield	0.000	✓	
	Stdev of Yield	0.009	✓	
	SN2	0.001	✓	
	Design Point	0.000		✓
	Computational Time	0.000	✓	
IOM	Mean of Yield	0.000	✓	
	Stdev of Yield	0.001	✓	
	SN2	0.006	✓	
	Design Point	0.000		✓
	Computational Time	0.000	✓	
SP	Mean of Yield	0.000	✓	
	Stdev of Yield	0.908		
	SN1	0.044		✓
	Design Point	0.000		✓
	Computational Time	0.000		✓

Table 11. Performance measures on all constrained problems

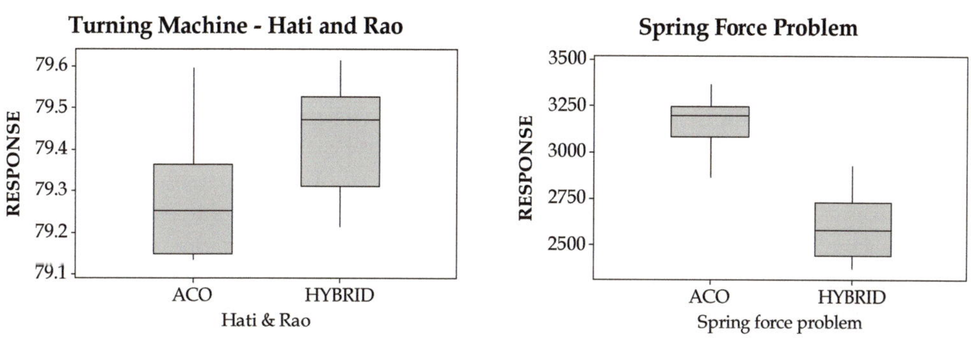

Fig. 16. Box plot of the minimal operating cost for the turning machine and the maximal force for the spring problems

Performance Measure	**Good**	**Poor**
Best So Far Response	ACO	HYBRID
Design Point	HYBRID	ACO
Computational Time	HYBRID	ACO

Table 12. Advantage and disadvantage of the algorithms on constrained response surface optimisation problems

6. Conclusions and recommendations

For two process variable cases without noise, three performance achievements on all proposed algorithms were not different for all shapes of response surfaces. The computational time for all algorithms was merely the same in each surface. When lower

levels of noise have been indicated in the surfaces, the computational time was increased as expected but not statistically significant. The ST seems to be more efficient, in terms of speed of convergence, but there was no difference on all performance achievements when compared. When the higher levels of noise applied, SA gave the better performance achievements. Based on overall surfaces and process variables, the preferable operating conditions were obtained by the ACO, especially on response surfaces with more than four process variables. However, the weakest point of the ACO is the higher levels of computational time for searching the best response. The effects of the number of process variables on the computational time were also increased significantly for all proposed algorithms except the SA. The SA was then more efficient than others, in terms of numbers of runs for finding the maximum, but some of these runs did lead to relatively lower yields.
Hence, we tried to combine the ACO with the SA to eliminate that weakness whilst searching for the optimum. A hybridisation of the SA and the ACO is then developed for the refinement of constrained response surfaces of turning process and spring force problems. Results in the last experiments indicated that the hybridisation method worked faster but the better solution can be still achieved by the ACO. There is only a success in reducing the computational time for constrained response surface problems that is the strong point of the SA. However, it has to trade off searching ability for the optimal response with the computational time. Further applications on other processes could be determined to confirm the performance.
In summary, the ACO seems to work more properly on unconstrained response surface problems at the lower levels of noise whereas the SA is preferable when higher noise levels applied. On constrained response surface optimisation problems, the hybridisation of the ACO and the SA seems to be better than the ACO in terms of speed of convergence. However, the ACO can search for the better yield. As stated earlier, the response surfaces on this research were restricted to some proposed number of process variables and systems. Consequently, comparisons and conclusions between the algorithms may not be valid for other families of functions. Other stochastic approaches such as harmony search, bees or variable neighbourhood search algorithms could be extended to the steepest ascent algorithm based on conventional factorial designs to increase its performance.
It should be remembered that these algorithms are being considered for automatic process control (APC) in which case there will not usually be any operator interaction. Many repetitions of the same design are quite feasible in this context. In particular, not applying EVOP corresponds to repetitions at the current operating conditions. The algorithms can be used as the basis for a feedback control, for which stability is guaranteed. In a practical application the yield would be measured on the process and actuators would set the process variables to the new design positions.

7. Acknowledgments

This work was supported by the Thailand Research Fund (TRF), the National Research Council of Thailand (NRCT), the Commission on Higher Education of Thailand and the Industrial Statistics and Operational Research Unit (ISO-RU), the Department of Industrial Engineering, Faculty of Engineering, Thammasat University, THAILAND.

8. References

Blum, C. & Roli, A. (2003). Metaheuristics in Combinatorial Optimisation: Overview and Conceptual Comparison. *ACM Computing Surveys*, Vol. 35, No. 3, pp. 268-308

Bohachevsky, I.O.; Johnson M.E. & Stein, M.L. (1986) Generalised Simulated Annealing for Function Optimisation. *Technometrics*, Vol. 28, No. 3, pp. 209-217

Box, G.E.P. & Draper, N.R. (1987). *Empirical Model-Building and Response Surfaces*. John Wiley & Sons, Inc., New York

Dasgupta, D. (1998). *Artificial Immune Systems and their Applications*. Springer-Verlag

Dorigo, M. & Blum, C. (2005). Ant Colony Optimisation Theory: A survey. *Theoretical Computer Science*, Vol. 344, No.2-3, pp. 243-278

Dorigo, M.; Maniezzo V. & Colorni, A. (1996). Ant System: Optimisation by a Colony of Cooperating Agents. *IEEE Transactions on Systems, Man, and Cybernetics Part B*, Vol. 26, numéro 1, pp. 29-41

Dorigo, M. & Stutzle, T. (2004). *Ant Colony Optimisation*. Bradford Book, Massachusetts

Eusuff, M.; Lansey, K. & Pasha, F. (2006). Shuffled Frog-Leaping Algorithm: A Memetic Metaheuristic for Discrete Optimisation. *Engineering Optimisation*, Vol. 38, No. 2, pp. 129-154

Glover, F. (1986). Tabu Search - Part i". *ORSA Journal on Computing*, Vol. 1, No. 3, pp. 190-206

Goldberg, D.E. (1989). *Genetic Algorithms in Search, Optimisation and Machine Learning*. Addison-Wesley, Massachusetts

Hart, E.A. & Timmis, J. (2008). Application Areas of AIS: The Past, the Present and the Future. *Applied Soft Computing*, Vol. 8, No. 1, pp. 191-201

Haykin, S. (1999). *Neural Networks: A Comprehensive Foundation*. Prentice Hall, New Jercy

Kennedy, J. & Eberhart, R.C. (2001). *Swarm Intelligence*. Morgan Kaufmann Publishers, San Francisco, CA

Khan, Z.; Prasad, B., & Singh, T. (1997). Machining Condition Optimisation by Genetic Algorithms and Simulated Annealing, *Computers Ops Res.*, Vol. 24, pp. 647-657

Kirkpatrick, S.; Gelatt, C.D. Jr., & Vecchi, M.P. (1983) Optimisation by Simulated Annealing. *Science*, Vol. 220, pp. 671-680

Merz, P. & Freisleben, B. (1999). A Comparison of Memetic Algorithms, Tabu Search, and Ant Colonies for the Quadratic Assignment Problem", *Proceedings of Evolutionary Computation*, pp. 2063-2070, IEEE Press

Myers, R.H. & Montgomery, D.C. (1995). *Response Surface Methodology: Process and Product Optimisation Using Designed Experiments*, John Wiley, New York

Taguchi, G. & Wu, Y. (1980). *Introduction to Off-Line Quality Control.* Central Japan Quality Control Association, Nagoya

15

Simulated Annealing for Control of Adaptive Optics System

Huizhen Yang[1] and Xinyang Li[2]
[1]*Huaihai Institute of Technology,*
[2]*Institute of Optics and Electronics, Chinese Academy of Science*
China

1. Introduction to adaptive optics system

Many optical systems, such as imaging systems or laser communication systems, suffer performance degradation due to distortions in the optical wave-front. An optical wave propagates through an optically inhomogeneous medium such as the atmosphere, differences in the index of refraction along the propagation path cause variations in the speed of light propagation, which lead to phase distortions. Adaptive Optics (AO) techniques are often used to compensate these static or dynamic aberrations of a light beam after propagation through a distorting medium (Hardy, 1998). Although originally proposed for astronomical telescopes in 1953 (Babcock, 1953), adaptive optics did not become a reality until the 1970s, when it was developed for national defence applications, specifically laser beam compensation and satellite imaging. It consists of using an active optical element such as a deformable mirror to correct the instantaneous wavefront distortions. These are measured by a device called a wavefront sensor which delivers the signals necessary to drive the correcting element. The first adaptive optics system able to sharpen two-dimensional images was built at Itek by Hardy and his co-workers (Hardy et al, 1977).

AO provides a means to perform real-time correction of aberrations imposed on light waves as they travel from the source to the imaging system. While AO has its roots the field of astronomy it is currently used in a wide variety of medical, military and industrial applications. The papers by Milonniand (Milonni, 1999) and Parenti (Parenti, 1992) provide an excellent introduction to the use of AO in Astronomy. A comprehensive review of the medical and industrial applications of AO can be found in the technology tracking report by Greenaway and Burnett (Greenaway, & Burnett, 2004).

The most common conventional adaptive optics systems (Fig. 1) is implemented with a wave-front corrector to correct the distorted wave-front, a wave-front sensor to measure the aberrations present in the incoming beam, and a feedback control algorithm to link these two elements in real time. Although the technique based on rapid wave-front measurement has been found useful in astronomical applications, this approach to the control problem is much difficult to be used in situations where wave-front distortions can not be measured directly, for example in atmospheric laser communications or anisoplanatic imaging conditions.

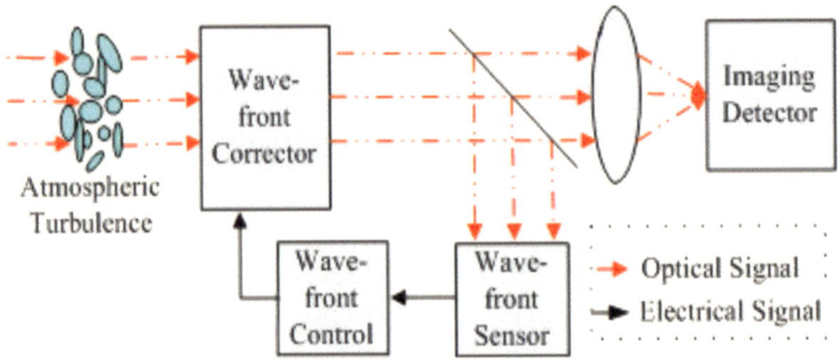

Fig. 1. Block diagram of conventional adaptive optics systems.

When a performance metric can be defined, stochastic optimization methods provide an alternative approach to the control problem that does not require the use of any a prior knowledge of a system model(Muller & Buffington, 1974). A common strategy used by model-free optimization techniques in adaptive optics systems (Fig.2) is to consider the performance metric as a function of the control parameters and then use certain optimization algorithm to improve the performance metric, which means that a wave-front sensor is no longer necessary. More and more researchers on adaptive optics system control are attaching importance to this kind of control technique because of its simpleness in system architecture and adaptability to the complicated conditions.

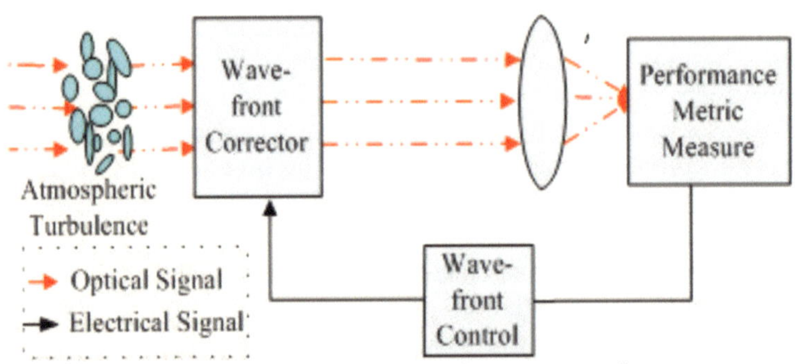

Fig. 2. Block diagram of adaptive optics systems without a wave-front sensor.

An appropriate optimization control algorithm is the key to correcting distorted wave-fronts successfully for this kind of adaptive optics system. Because most systems are multi-channel and real time systems, the control algorithm must meet the following requirements: rapid convergence so that the adaptive optics systems can keep up with changes of distorted wave-fronts, high correction capability for wave-front aberrations, and being carried out easily. The optical problem can be mapped onto a model for crystal roughening that served as a motivation to implement the Simulated Annealing algorithm (SA). In other words, SA is an optimization algorithm designed to find the extremum of a certain cost function, which can be regarded as the energy of the system and will be called hence forth the energy function. The energy function is also called as the system performance metric in application of adaptive optics.

2. Simulated Annealing

Simulated annealing (Kirkpatrick et al 1983) is based on the physical annealing process by which a solid is heated to a temperature close to its melting point, after which it is allowed to cool slowly so as to relieve internal stresses and non-uniformites. The aim is to achieve a structure with long-range order that is as close as possible to the ground-state configuration. Presenting an optimization technique, SA can: (a) process cost functions possessing quite arbitrary degrees of nonlinearities , discontinuities, and stochasticity; (b) process quite arbitrary boundary conditions and constraints imposed on these cost functions; (c) be implemented quite easily with the degree of coding quite minimal relative to other nonlinear optimization algorithms; (d) statistically guarantee finding an optimal solution.

Generally, SA algorithm consists of three functional relationships per iteration: probability density of state-space of control parameters to create perturbation vector $\Delta u^{(k)} = \{\Delta u_l\}^{(k)}$; acceptance probability $p^{(k)} = \exp(\Delta J^{(k)} / T^{(k)})$ to adjudge whether the new solution is accepted, which is also called as the Metropolis criterion (Metropolis etal 1953); and schedule of "annealing" in annealing-time steps $T^{(k)}$. In this text, we use the standard simulated annealing.

In order to investigate correction ability of the simulated annealing for adaptive optics system, we compare it with some other stochastic parallel optimization algorithms, such as Stochastic Parallel Gradient Descent (SPGD)(Vorontsov & Carhart, 1997), Genetic Algorithm (GA)(Goldberg, 1989), and Algorithm Of Pattern Extraction (Alopex)(Harth & Tzanakou, 1974). These algorithms optimize control parameters in a parallel way, which can accelerate the convergence of algorithms, and have some stochastic specialty, which can help the algorithm escape away from local extremums to some extent. The main advantage of these stochastic parallel optimization algorithms over traditional adaptive optics correction algorithms is that wavefront sensing is no longer required. The reduction in complexity, cost, and size is extremely beneficial. Even though the absence of a wavefront sensor makes the algorithm less efficient, advantages from increased speed, parallelism, and simplicity make it attractive in certain applications. These algorithms are both model-free as well as independent of the deformable mirror characteristics. This independence, as well as being a simple straightforward algorithm to implementation, allows a great deal of latitude in system design. The reason why we compare these algorithms with the simulated annealing is that these algorithms has ever been used to control the adaptive optics system and obtained some valuable research results, such as GA (Yang et al 2007), Alopex (Zakynthinaki & Saridakis, 2003), SA(Zommer et al 2006), SPGD (Vorontsov & Carhart, 2000).

3. The model of AO system with the simulated annealing

3.1 AO System Model

The AO system model is shown in Fig. 3, where $\varphi(r)$ is the distorted wavefront, $u(r)$ is the compensation phase, $\phi(r) = \varphi(r) + u(r)$ is the residual phase, J is the performance metric and $u = \{u_1, u_2, ...u_{61}\}$ is the control signal of actuators of 61-element deformable mirror.

$\varphi(r)$ and $u(r)$ are continuous functions ($r = \{x, y\}$ is a vector in the plane orthogonal to the optical axes). The AO system mainly includes a 61-element deformable mirror to correct the wave-front aberrations $\varphi(r)$, an imaging system to record the focal spot, a performance metric analyzer to calculate the system performance metric J from the data of focal spot, the simulated annealing algorithm to produce control signals $u = \{u_1, u_2, ...u_{61}\}$ for the 61-element deformable mirror according to changes of the performance metric J.

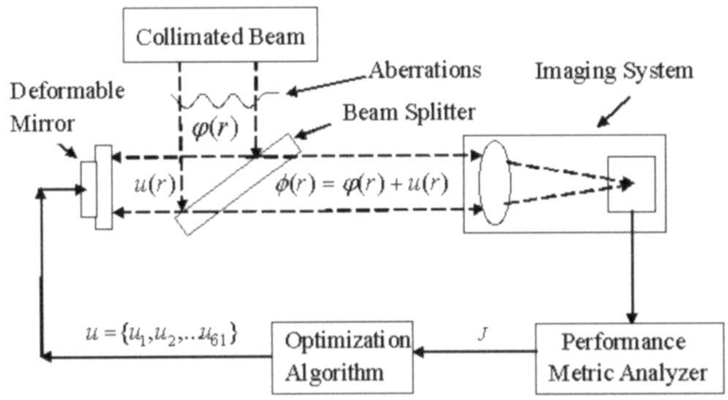

Fig. 3. Block diagram of simulation.

3.2 Specifications of 61-element deformable mirror

The phase compensation $u(r)$, introduced by the deformable mirror, can be combined linearly with response functions of actuators:

$$u(r) = \sum_{j=1}^{61} u_j S_j(r) \tag{1}$$

Where u_j is the control signal and $S_j(r)$ is the response function of the $j'th$ actuator. On the basis of real measurements, we know the response function of 61-element deformable mirror actuators is Gaussian distribution approximately (Jiang & etal 1991):

$$S_j(r) = S_j(x, y) = \exp\{\ln \omega[\sqrt{(x - x_j)^2 + (y - y_j)^2} / d]^\alpha\} \tag{2}$$

Where (x_j, y_j) is the location of the $j'th$ actuator, ω is the coupling value between actuators and is set to 0.08, d is the distance between actuators, and α is the Gaussian index and is set to 2. Fig. 4 gives the location distribution of 61-element deformable mirror actuators. The circled line in the figure denotes the effective aperture and the layout of all actuators is triangular.

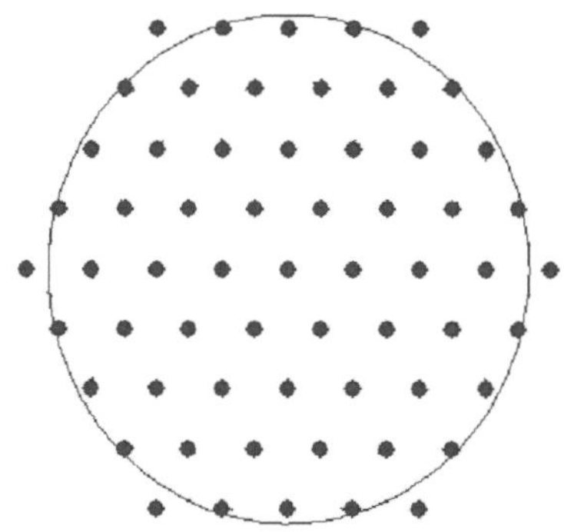

Fig. 4. Distribution of actuators location of 61-element deformable mirror.

3.3 Atmospheric turbulence conditions

We use the method proposed by N. Roddier, which makes use of a Zernike expansion of randomly weighted Karhunen-Loeve functions, to simulate atmospherically distorted wavefronts (Roddier, 1990). Considering that the low-order aberrations (tilts, defocus, astigmatism, etc) have the most significant impact on image quality, we use the first 104 Zernike polynomial orders. Different phase screens generated according to this method are not correlated to each other and represent the Kolmogorov spectrum. The phase screens are defined over 128×128 pixels which is also the grid of the wave-front corrector and don't include the tip/tilt aberrations. The tip/tilt aberrations are usually controlled by another control loop and are considered as being removed completely in our simulation.

Atmospheric turbulence strength for a receiver system with aperture size D can be characterized by the following two parameters: the ratio D/r_0 and the averaged Strehl Ratio (SR) of phase fluctuations, where r_0 is the turbulence coherence length and SR is defined as the ratio of the maximum intensities of the aberrated point spread function and the diffraction-limited point spread function. Phase screens of different atmospheric turbulence strength can be obtained through changing r_0 in the simulation program. The correction capability of the AO system based on simulated annealing is analyzed when D/r_0 is 10 and corresponding averaged SR is about 0.1.

3.4 Considerations for the performance metric J

Possible measures of energy spread in the focal plane that can be used as the energy function of simulated annealing J are:

(1). The Strehl ratio(SR):

$$SR = \max(I(r))/\max(I^{dl}(r)), \tag{3}$$

where $I(r)$ is the intensity distribution of focal plane with the turbulence and $I^{dl}(r)$ is the diffraction-limited laser intensity distribution achievable in the absence of the turbulence. This quantity is not difficult to measure on the focal plane. It does not seem to be very informative because it does not account for the whole intensity distribution. We use the SR as the reference of correction capability in the text.

(2). The encircled energy (EE):

$$EE = \int_{\Re} I(r)dr \tag{4}$$

where $\Re$ is a region with a laser hot spot where maximum energy is to be collected. This metric also does not necessarily take into account the whole intensity distribution. In addition, it depends on the choice of area $\Re$.

(3). Image sharpness (IS_{mn}) used in various active imaging applications:

$$IS_{mn} = \int \left| \frac{\partial^{m+n} I(r)}{\partial^m x \partial^n y} \right|^2 dr, \qquad (m+n) = 0, 1, \ldots.. \tag{5}$$

This quantity is relatively simple to measure, and is intuitively appealing since smaller tighter intensity distributions have wider spatial frequency spectrum and, therefore, larger sharpness.

(4). The mean radius (MR):

$$MR = \frac{\int |r - \overline{r}| I(r) d^2 r}{\int I(r) d^2 r}, \qquad \overline{r} = \frac{\int r I(r) d^2 r}{\int I(r) d^2 r} \tag{6}$$

where $\overline{r}$ is the intensity distribution centroid. MR can be easily measured either by a single photodetector with a special mask attached to it or by postprocessing a matrix detector output. This measure appears to be the most attractive one for it gives straightforward mathematical meaning to the idea of energy spread, it is nonparametric, and it accounts for the whole intensity distribution.

For imaging applications metrics 1-3 are proven (Muller & Buffington, 1974) to attain their global maxima for the diffraction-limited image. It is clear that the global minimum of the MR metric corresponds to the smallest energy spread. It is also possible to invent other functions, including vector functions, as well as to create compound cost functions with additional penalty terms. All these possibilities deserve thorough investigation. However, only the MR metric is used in our simulations.

The relationship between the performance metric J and control parameters $\{u_j\}$ is

$$J \propto J[\phi(r)] = J[\varphi(r) + u(r)] \tag{7}$$

$J = J(u_1, u_2, \ldots u_{61})$ can be considered as the non-linear function of 61 control signals because the $\varphi(r)$ keeps unchanged during a relatively short time. In real applications, we can get the performance metric data from the photoelectric detector, for example from a CCD or a pinhole, and then define different performance metrics based on different applications.

3.5 Descriptions of other stochastic parallel optimization algorithms

(1). SPGD (Vorontsov & Carhart, 2000) control is a "hill-climbing" technique implemented by the direct optimization of a system performance metric applied through an active optical component. Control is based on the maximization (or, with equal complexity minimization) of a system performance metric by small adjustments in actuator displacement in the mirror array. SPGD requires small random perturbations $\Delta u = \{\Delta u_1, \Delta u_2, ...\Delta u_{61}\}$ with fixed amplitude $|\Delta u_j = \sigma|$ and random signs with equal probabilities for $\Pr(\Delta u_j = \pm\sigma) = 0.5$ (Spall, 1992), to be applied to all 61 deformable mirror control channels simultaneously. Then for a given single random Δu, the control signals are updated with the rule:

$$u^{(k+1)} = u^{(k)} + \gamma \Delta u^{(k)} \Delta J^{(k)} \tag{8}$$

where γ is a gain coefficient which scales the size of the control parameters. Note that non-Bernoulli perturbations are also allowed in the algorithm, but one must be careful that the mathematical conditions (Spall, 1992) are satisfied.
SPGD follows the rule during the iteration of algorithm:

$$\Delta J^{(k)} = J_+^{(k)} - J_-^{(k)} \tag{9}$$

where

$$J_+^{(k)} = J(u^{(k)} + \Delta u^{(k)}) \tag{10.a}$$

$$J_-^{(k)} = J(u^{(k)} - \Delta u^{(k)}) \tag{10.b}$$

From the introduction to SPGD, we know there are only two parameters to be adjusted in algorithm: one is perturbation amplitude σ and the other is gain coefficient γ.

(2). GA is a kind of evolutionary computation, which represents a class of stochastic search and optimization algorithms that use a Darwinian evolutionary model, adopts the concept of survival of the fittest in evolution to find the best solution to some multivariable problem, and includes mainly three kinds of operation in every generation: selection, crossover and mutation. GA works with a population of candidate solutions and randomly alters the solutions over a sequence of generations according to evolutionary operations of competitive selection, mutation and crossover. The fitness of each population element to survive into the next generation is determined by a selection scheme based on evaluating the performance metric function for each element of the population. The selection scheme is such that the most favourable elements of the population tend to survive into the next generation while the unfavourable elements tend to perish.
The control vector $\{u_j\}$ was considered as the individual to be evolved and the performance metric is called as fitness function. After the initial population is made according to the roulette selection principle, excellent individuals are selected from the population with a ratio r_s. Then new individuals are obtained by randomly crossing the chromosomes of the old individuals with a probability of P_c. Finally, some chromosome positions of individuals are mutated randomly with a mutation rate of P_m for introducing a new individual. By going

through above process, GA will gradually find the optimum mirror shape that can yield the best fitness. Parameter r_s , P_c and P_m are set at 0.2, 0.65 and 0.65 accord to the corresponding reference value (Chen, etal 1996). The population size N and the number of evolving generation L are needed to adjust.

(3). Alopex is a stochastic correlative learning algorithm which updates the control parameters by making use of correlation between the variations of control parameters and the variations of performance metric without needing (or explicitly estimating) any derivative information. Since its introduction for mapping visual receptive fields (Harth & Tzanakou, 1974), it has subsequently been modified and used in many applications such as models of visual perception, pattern recognition, and adaptive control, learning in neural networks, and learning decision trees. Empirically, the Alopex algorithm has been shown to be robust and effective in many applications.

We used a two timescale version Alopex, called as 2t-Alopex (Roland, etal 2002). The control signals are updated according to the rules:

$$u^{(k+1)} = u^{(k)} + \eta \Delta u^{(k)} \tag{11}$$

$$\Delta u^{(k)} = \begin{cases} 1 & \text{probability } \mathrm{p}^{(k)} \\ -1 & \text{probability } 1\text{-}\mathrm{p}^{(k)} \end{cases} \tag{12}$$

$$p^{(k)} = p^{(k-1)} + \theta(\beta^{(k)} - p^{(k-1)}) \tag{13}$$

$$\beta^{(k)} = 1/(1 + \exp(\Delta u^{(k)} \Delta J^{(k)} / \eta T^{(k)})) \tag{14}$$

$T^{(k)}$ in equation (12) is a "temperature" parameter updated every M iterations(for a suitably chosen M) using the following annealing schedule:

$$T^{(k)} = \begin{cases} T^{(k-1)} & \text{if k is not a multiple of M} \\ \dfrac{\eta}{\mathrm{M}} \sum\limits_{k'=k-M}^{k} |\Delta J^{(k')}| & \textit{otherwise} \end{cases} \tag{15}$$

Where η and θ are step-size parameters such that $\eta = o(\theta)$. There are at least two parameters to be adjusted: η and θ.

4. Results and Analysis

We perform the adaptation process over 100 phase realizations. The averaged evolution curves, the standard deviation evolution curves of the metric and corresponding SR evolution curves are the recorded simulation results.

4.1 Selection of different algorithm parameters

Every algorithm has its rational limit of parameters for a given application. We select the most optimal parameters of every algorithm through large numbers of simulation tests when D/r_0 is 10.

In SA, the adjustment coefficient δ and the cooling rate λ are main factors for convergence rate and correction effect and we set δ was 0.15 and λ was 0.98. The key parameters of Alopex are step-size parameters η and θ, and we set η was 0.03 and θ was 0.55.

The amplitude σ and the gain coefficient γ are two main factors which affect convergence rate and correction capability of SPGD. For a fixed σ, there exists an optimal range for γ. Too small γ will cause too slow convergence rate, while too big γ will make the algorithm trap into local extrumums and the evolution curve of performance metric appears dither. We find the effective range of σ is within 0.01-1.5 for SPGD. We fixed the same σ at 0.2 for SPGD, r is set at 5

After probability parameters r_s, P_c and P_m in GA are established on the basis of experience, the convergence rate is affected by the population size N and the number of evolution generation L. For the same correction effect, L will be fewer if N is bigger, while the algorithm will need more times of evolution when N is smaller. If GA not only converge rapidly but also has good correction effect, it's necessary to balance N and L. We set N at 100 and L at 500 in simulation.

4.2 Adaptation process

In order to converge completely, we set the iteration number of algorithms respectively. SA is set at 4000 times, GA 500 generations, Alopex 4000 times and SPGD 1500 times. The averaged evolution curves, the standard deviation (SD) evolution curves of the metric MR over 100 phase realizations and corresponding averaged SR evolution curves are given in Fig. 5, Fig. 6, Fig. 7 and Fig. 8, in which the value of MR is normalize by that of diffraction-limited focal plane and the standard deviation(SD) is calculated as follows:

$$SD = \frac{< (J - < J >)^2 >^{1/2}}{< J >} \tag{16}$$

Fig. 5 to Fig. 8 show simulation results when SA, GA, SPGD and Alopex are use to control the AO system respectively. Averaged curves of MR are given in Fig. 5(a) to Fig. 8(a), in which averaged evolution curves are normalized to be 1 in the optimal case. Corresponding standard deviation curves over 100 different phase realizations and averaged SR curves are presented in Fig. 5(b) to Fig. 8(b) and Fig. 5(c) to Fig. 8(c). All MR curves have converged after complete iterations in Fig. 5(a) to Fig. 8(a). From Fig. 5(b) to Fig. 8(b), we can see that SA, GA and Alopex have relatively smaller standard deviations than SPGD, which shows that SA, GA and Alopex have stronger adaptability to different turbulence realizations than SPGD. The averaged SR's of these four different control algorithms are very close to each other in Fig. 5(c) to Fig. 8(c), which indicates SA, GA, SPGD and Alopex have almost equal correction ability under $D / r_0 = 10$.

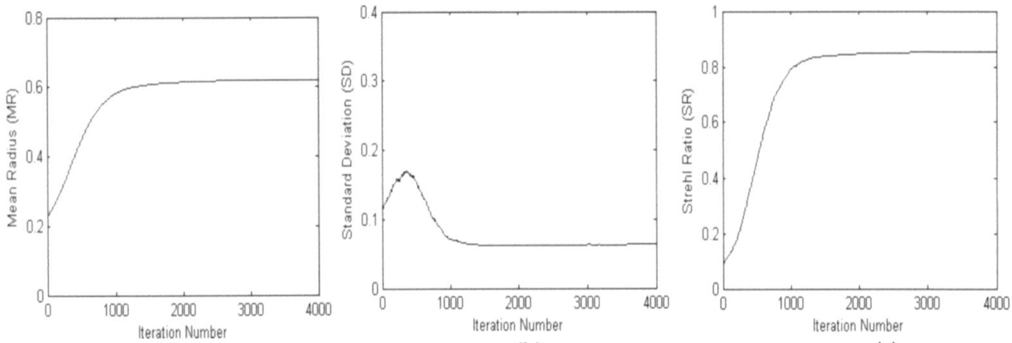

(a) (b) (c)

Fig. 5. Adaptation process of adaptive optics system when SA is used as the control algorithm. (a): averaged curves of MR, (b): the standard deviation curve of MR over 100 different phase realizations and (c): averaged SR curves during 4000 iterations.

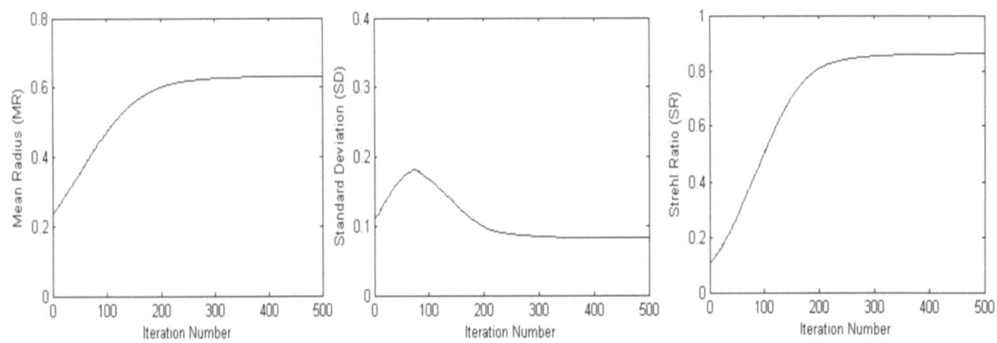

(a) (b) (c)

Fig. 6. Adaptation process of adaptive optics system when GA is used as the control algorithm. (a): averaged curves of MR, (b): the standard deviation curve of MR over 100 different phase realizations and (c): averaged SR curves during 500 generations.

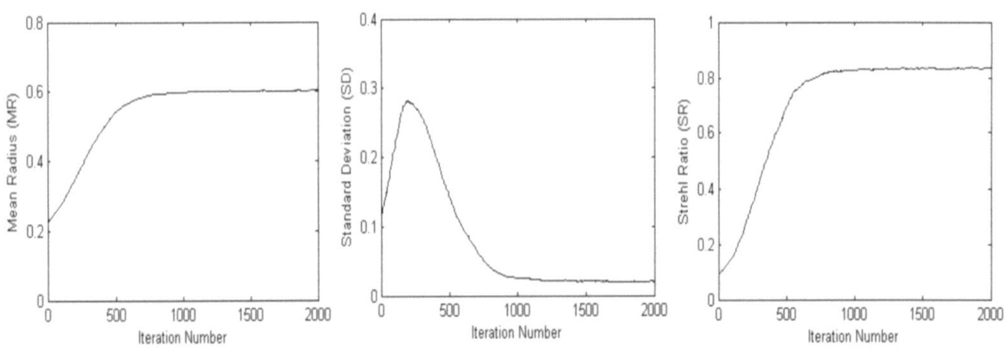

(a) (b) (c)

Fig. 7. Adaptation process of adaptive optics system when SPGD is used as the control algorithm. (a): averaged curves of MR, (b): the standard deviation curve of MR over 100 different phase realizations and (c): averaged SR curves(c) during 2000 iterations.

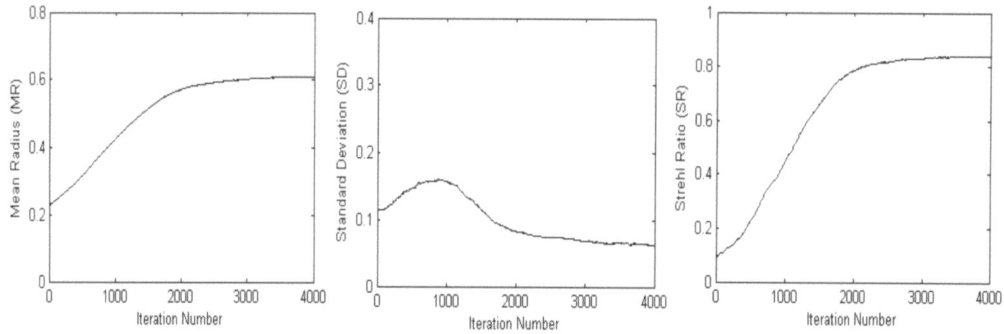

(a) (b) (c)

Fig. 8. Adaptation process of adaptive optics system when Alopex is used as the control algorithm. (a): averaged curves of MR, (b): the standard deviation curve of MR over 100 different phase realizations and (c): averaged SR curves during 4000 iterations.

Fig. 9 gives the averaged focal spot when SA, GA, SPGD and Alopex are use as the control algorithm of the AO system respectively. For purposes of comparison, we also fit the 61-element deformable mirror figure to the phase screens using least squares to obtain the best correction achievable with the given 61-element DM.

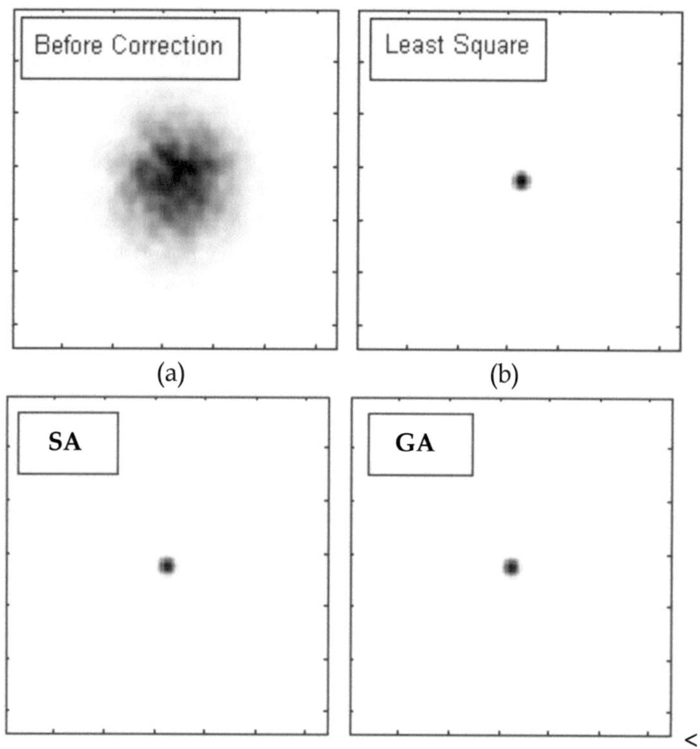

(a) (b)

(c) (d)

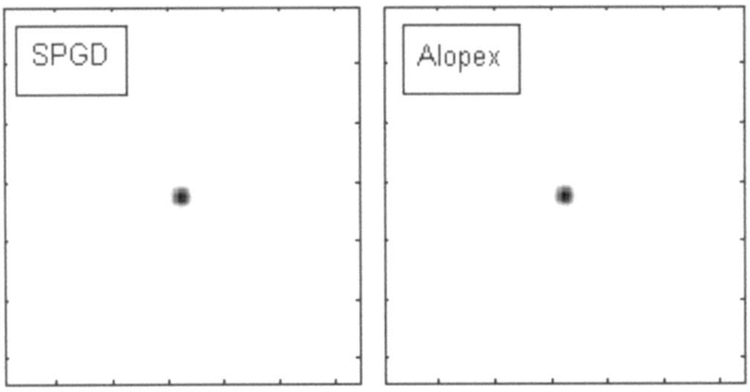

(e) (f)

Fig. 9. Comparison of focal spots before correction (a) and after correction with SA (c), with GA (d), with SPGD (e) and with Alopex (f) ; (b) is the averaged focal spot of the residual wave-front with the least squares fitting.

From Fig. 9, we can get these four different algorithms have strong ability to atmospheric turbulence when D/r_0 is 10. Compared with the least squares fitting, they almost obtain the best correction achievable for the 61-element DM.

4.3 Analysis of averaged convergence speed

The convergence speed is an important criterion on which the algorithm can be applied to real-time adaptive optics system. Fig. 5 (a) to Fig. 8(a) give the averaged curves of MR over 100 different phase realizations. The abscissa in Fig. 5(a) to Fig. 8(a) is the iteration number of algorithm for SA, SPGD and Alopex and the number of evolution generation for GA. It seems that GA has the rapidest speed from the averaged curves of MR because of its fewer evolution generation. This result is not true because the number of small perturbations sent to the system per iteration is different for different algorithms. From the introduction to the basic idea of several algorithms in section 3.5, we know that SA and Alopex need one perturbation per iteration; SPGD needs two perturbations per iteration and GA needs 100 perturbations per generation. Note that the number of perturbation in GA bears on the number of the population size. To reduce the number of perturbation, one can choose a relative small population size but the convergence of system will need more generations. The related analysis can refer to section 4.1. We use the number of small perturbations not the number of iteration or generation to estimate the averaged convergence speed of different algorithms.

Consulting results in Fig. 5(a) to Fig. 8(a) and above analysis, we make use of the number of small perturbations needed by achieving the 80% of the range of MR during the adaptation process under control of different algorithms. Corresponding data are in Table 1.

	Value of 80% MR Range	Iterations or Generations	Perturbations
SA	0.54	767	767
GA	0.548	143	143*100=14300
SPGD	0.524	464	464*2=928
Alopex	0.532	1609	1609

Table 1. Comparison of the number of small perturbations sent to the system when the adaptive optics system achieves the 80% of the range of MR during the adaptation process under control of different algorithms.

The value of MR is 0.54 for SA, 0.548 for GA, 0.524 for SPGD and 0.532 for Alopex respectively in Table 1. These data show the range of MR of different algorithms are close to each other because their start value of MR is the same. The number of iterations or generations is 767 for SA, 143 for GA, 464 for SPGD and 1609 for Alopex but the number of small perturbation is 767 for SA, 14300 for GA, 928 for SPGD and 1609 for Alopex respectively. These data show GA is the slowest algorithm and the number of pertubations is almost as 20 times as that of SA, 15 times as SPGD and 9 times as Alopex, while SA is the fastest algorithm becauese of its the fewest perturbations. The advantage of GA is that it is far more likely that the global extremum will be found, as the data shown in second column in Table 1; the disadvantage is that if often takes a long time to converge. Above simulation results express relative differences of these algorithms in convergence rate, which can offer us some references in choosing stochastic parallel optimization algorithm for real applications.

4.4 Zernike order and wavefront of the same single frame phase screen

Fig. 10 gives Zernike coefficients 3-104 decomposed from the same phase screen when SA, GA, SPGD and Alopex are used as control algorithm of adaptive optics system respectively. Corresponding wavefronts are shown in Fig. 11.

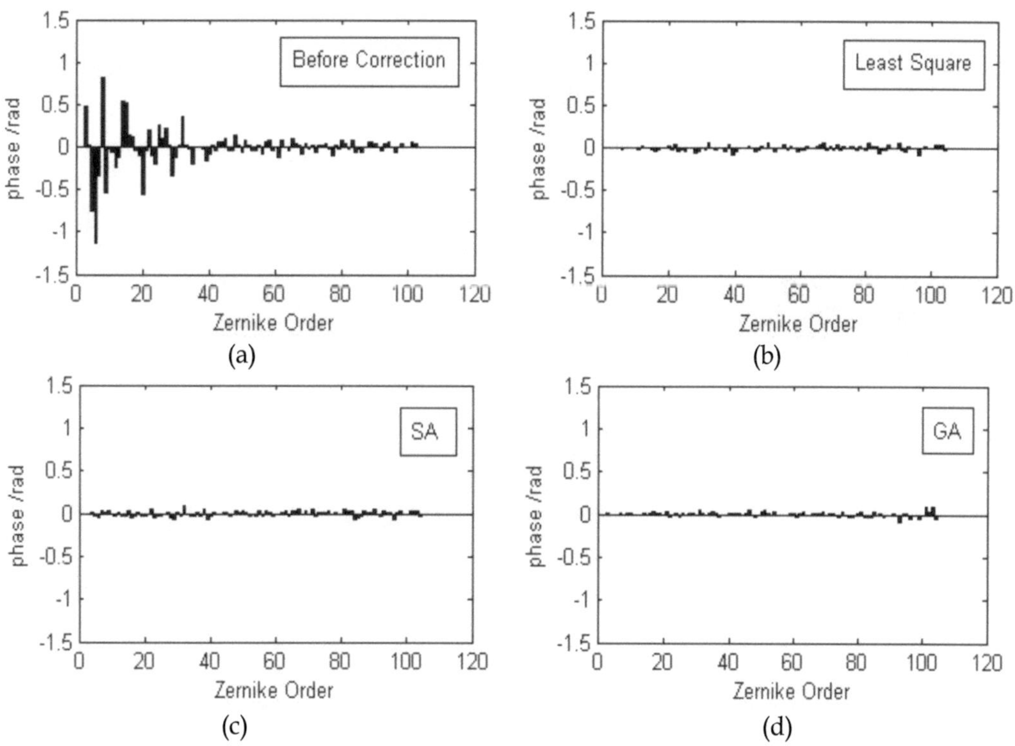

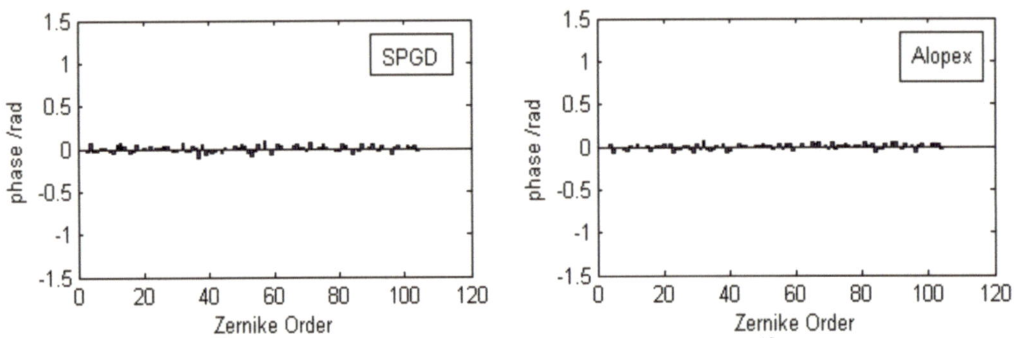

(e) (f)

Fig. 10. Comparison of Zernike coefficients 3-104 before correction (a) and after correction with SA (c), GA (d), SPGD (e) and Alopex (f) ; (b) is the Zernike coefficients of the residual wave-front with the least squares fitting.

We also fit the DM figure to the phase screen using least squares to obtain the best correction achievable with the given 61-element DM. The fitting results are also shown in Fig. 10 and Fig. 11. The unit in Fig. 10 is rad and wavelength λ in colour bar of Fig. 11.

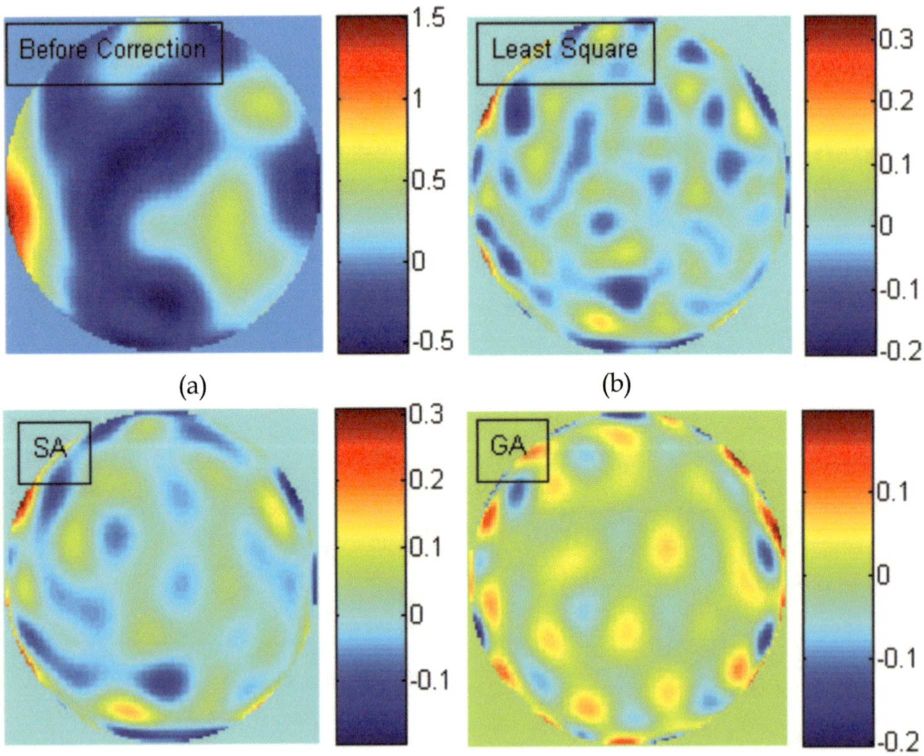

(a) (b)

(c) (d)

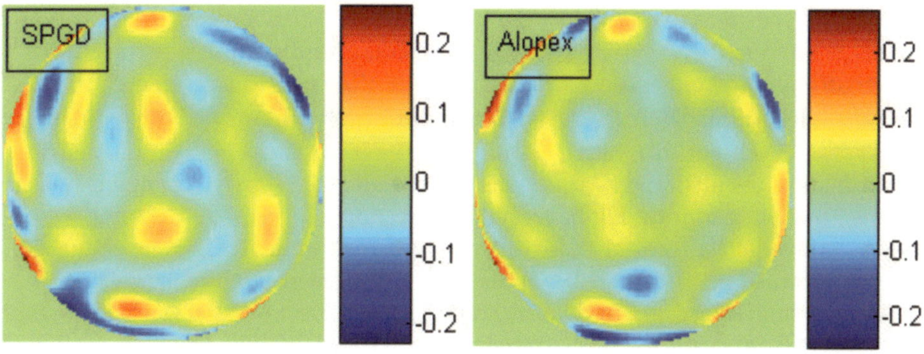

(e) (f)

Fig. 11. Comparison of wavefronts before correction (a) and after correction with SA (c), GA (d), SPGD (e) and Alopex (f); (b) is the residual wave-front with the least squares fitting. The unit of colour bar is wavelength λ.

From Fig. 10 and Fig. 11, we can obtain that these four different algorithms have strong ability to atmospheric turbulence when D/r_0 is 10. Compared with the least squares fitting, they almost obtain the best correction achievable for the 61-element DM.

5. Conclusion

We presented basic principles of Simulated Annealing, Genetic Algorithm, Stochastic Parallel Gradient Descent, and Algorithm of pattern extraction in control application of adaptive optics system. Based on above stochastic parallel optimization algorithms, we simulated an adaptive optics system with a 61-element deformable mirror and compared these algorithms in convergence speed, correction capability.

From section 4.2 and 4.4, we can get these four different algorithms have strong ability to atmospheric turbulence when D/r_0 is 10. Compared with the least squares fitting, they almost obtain the best correction achievable for the 61-element DM. The correction effect of GA is litter better than other algorithms and SA is the secondly better algorithm. But SA, GA and Alopex have stronger adaptability to different turbulence realizations than SPGD because of its relatively big standard deviation.

From section 4.3, we can conclude SA is the fastest and GA is the slowest in these algorithms. The number of perturbation by GA is almost as 20 times as that of SA, 15 times as SPGD and 9 times as Alopex. GA begins with a population of candidate solutions (individuals) and evolves towards better solutions through techniques inspired by evolutionary biology (such as natural selection or mutation). Perhaps the main problem of GA is the time cost of it. The algorithm may converge, and it may be a guaranteed global extremum, however, if this requires excessive a mounts of computer equipment or if it takes an unreasonable length of time to provide the solution, then it will not be suitable. But if the real-time is not required by adaptive optics system in some special application fields, GA is the best choice.

In real applications, after the deformable mirror is established, the correction time of AO system is mainly affected by the read-out and computation time of performance metric, which occupies the most part time of control algorithm. This point is the same in both simulation test and real AO systems. Above simulation results express relative differences of these algorithms in convergence rate, which can offer us some references in choosing stochastic parallel optimization algorithm for specific applications.

In conclusion, we can get that each algorithm has its advantages and disadvantages from above simulation results and discussions. For static or slowly changing wavefront aberrations, these algorithms all have high correction ability. For dynamic wavefront aberrations, convergence rates of these algorithms are slow relative to the change rate of atmosphere turbulence. They can be applied to real-time wavefront correction if being combined with high speed photo-detector, high speed data processing and high response frequency wave-front corrector. More research is necessary to this problem. Such as, how about these algorithms applied to much stronger turbulence conditions and much more elements deformable mirror or other kinds of wavefront corrector?

6. References

J, W. Hardy (1998). *Adaptive optics for astronomical telescopes,* Oxford University Press, New York

H. W. Babcock (1953). The possibility of compensating astronomical seeing, *Pub. Astr. Soc. Pac.* Vol. 65, pp. 229-236

J. W. Hardy, J. E. Lefebvre, &C. L. Koliopoulos (1977). Real-time atmospheric compensation, *J. Opt. Soc. Am.* Vol. 67, pp. 360-369

P. W. Milonni (1999). Adaptive optics for astronomy, *American Journal of Physics,* Vol. 67, No. 6, pp. 476-485

P. R. Parenti (1992). Adaptive optics for astronomy, *The Lincoln Laboratory Journal,* vol. 54, No. 1, pp. 93-113

A. Greenaway, & J. Burnett (2004). *Technology tracking : Industrial and medical applications of adaptive optics,* Institute of Physics Publishing Ltd, London

R. A. Muller, & A. Buffington (1974). Real-time correction of atmospherically degraded telesope images through image sharpening, *J. Opt. Soc. Am. A.* Vol. 64, No. 9, pp. 1200-1210

S. Kirkpatrick, C. D. Gelatt, & M. P. Vecchi (1983). Optimization by simulated annealing, *Science,* Vol. 220, pp. 671-680

N. Metropolis, A. W. Rosenbluth, & M. N. Rosenbluth (1953). Equation of state calculations by fast computing machines, *J. Chem. Phys.* Vol. 21, pp. 1087-1092

M. A. Vorontsov, & G. W. Carhart (1997). Adaptive phase-distortion correction based on parallel gradient-descent optimizatin, *Opt. Lett.* Vol. 22, No. 12, pp. 907-909

D. E. Goldberg (1989). *Genetic algorithms in search, optimization and machine learning,* 1st Edition, Addison-Wesley Publishing Company, Boston

E. Harth, & E. Tzanakou (1974). Alopex: a stochastic method for determining visual receptive fields. *Vis. Res.* , Vol. 14, pp. 1475-1482

P. Yang, Y. Liu, W. Yang, & et al (2007). An adaptive laser beam shaping technique based on a genetic algorithm. Chinese *Optics Letters,* Vol. 5, No. 9, pp. 497-500

M. S. Zakynthinaki, & Y. G. Saridakis (2003). Stochastic optimization for adaptive real-time wave-front correction, *Numerical Algorithms,* Vol. 33, pp. 509-520

S. Zommer, E. N. Ribak, S. G. Lipson, & et al (2006). Simulated annealing in ocular adaptive optics, Vol. 31, No. 7, pp. 1-3

M. A. Vorontsov, & G. W. Carhart (2000). Adaptive optics bassed on analog parallel stochastic optimizatin: analysis and experimental demonstration, *J. Opt. Soc. Am. A.* Vol. 17, No. 8, pp. 1440-1453

W. H. Jiang, N. Ling, X. J. Rao, & et al (1991). Fitting capability of deformable mirror, Proceedings of SPIE, Vol. 1542, pp. 130-137, ISBN :9780819406705

N. Roddier (1990). Atmosphseric wavefront simulation using Zernike polynomials, *Optical Engineering,* Vol. 9, No. 10, pp. 1174-1180

J. C. Spall(1992). Multivariate stochastic approximation using a simulataneous perturbation gardient approximation, *IEEE Trans. On Automatic Control, Vol.* 37, pp. 332-341

G. L. Chen, F. X. Wang, & Z. Zhuang (1996). *Genetic algorithm and its application (in Chinese),* Post & Telecom Press, Beijing

P. S. Sastry, M. Magesh, & K. P. Ummikrishnan (2002). Two timescale analysis of the alopex algorithm for optimization, *Neural Computation,* Vol. 14, pp. 2729-2750